GAMERZ HEAVEN

Volume 1

MAKI MURAKAMI PRESENTS

CONTENTS MENU

SAVE FILE

1 2 3 4 5 6 7 8 9 0

File 01   3

File 02   47

File 03   91

File 04   133

MAKI MURAKAMI
PRESENTS
GAMERZ HEAVEN
VOLUME1

GAMERZ HEAVEN

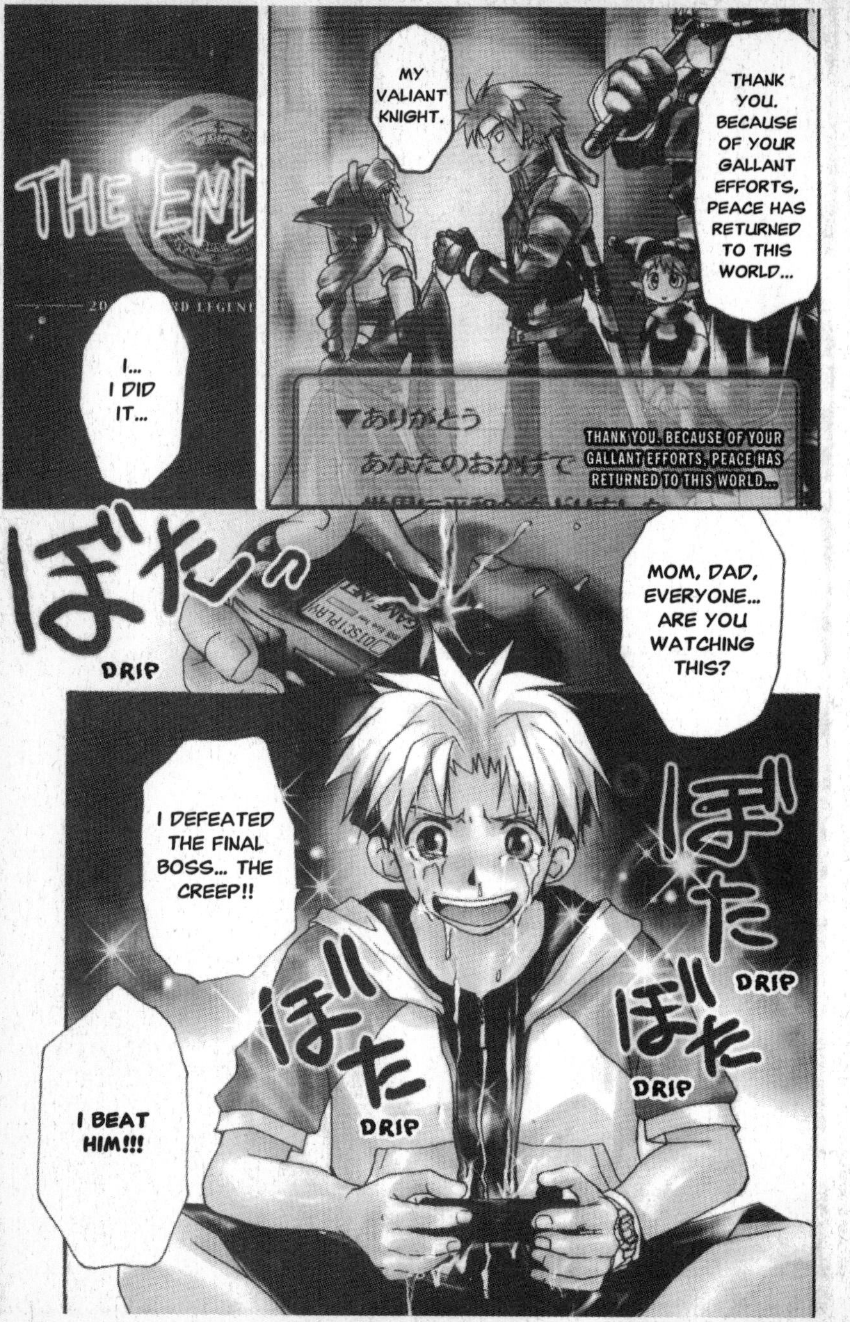

THANK YOU. BECAUSE OF YOUR GALLANT EFFORTS, PEACE HAS RETURNED TO THIS WORLD...
MY VALIANT KNIGHT.
▼ありがとう
あなたのおかげで
THANK YOU. BECAUSE OF YOUR GALLANT EFFORTS, PEACE HAS RETURNED TO THIS WORLD...
THE END
I... I DID IT...
MOM, DAD, EVERYONE... ARE YOU WATCHING THIS?
ぼた
DRIP
I DEFEATED THE FINAL BOSS... THE CREEP!!
ぼた
DRIP
ぼた
DRIP
ぼた
DRIP
I BEAT HIM!!!

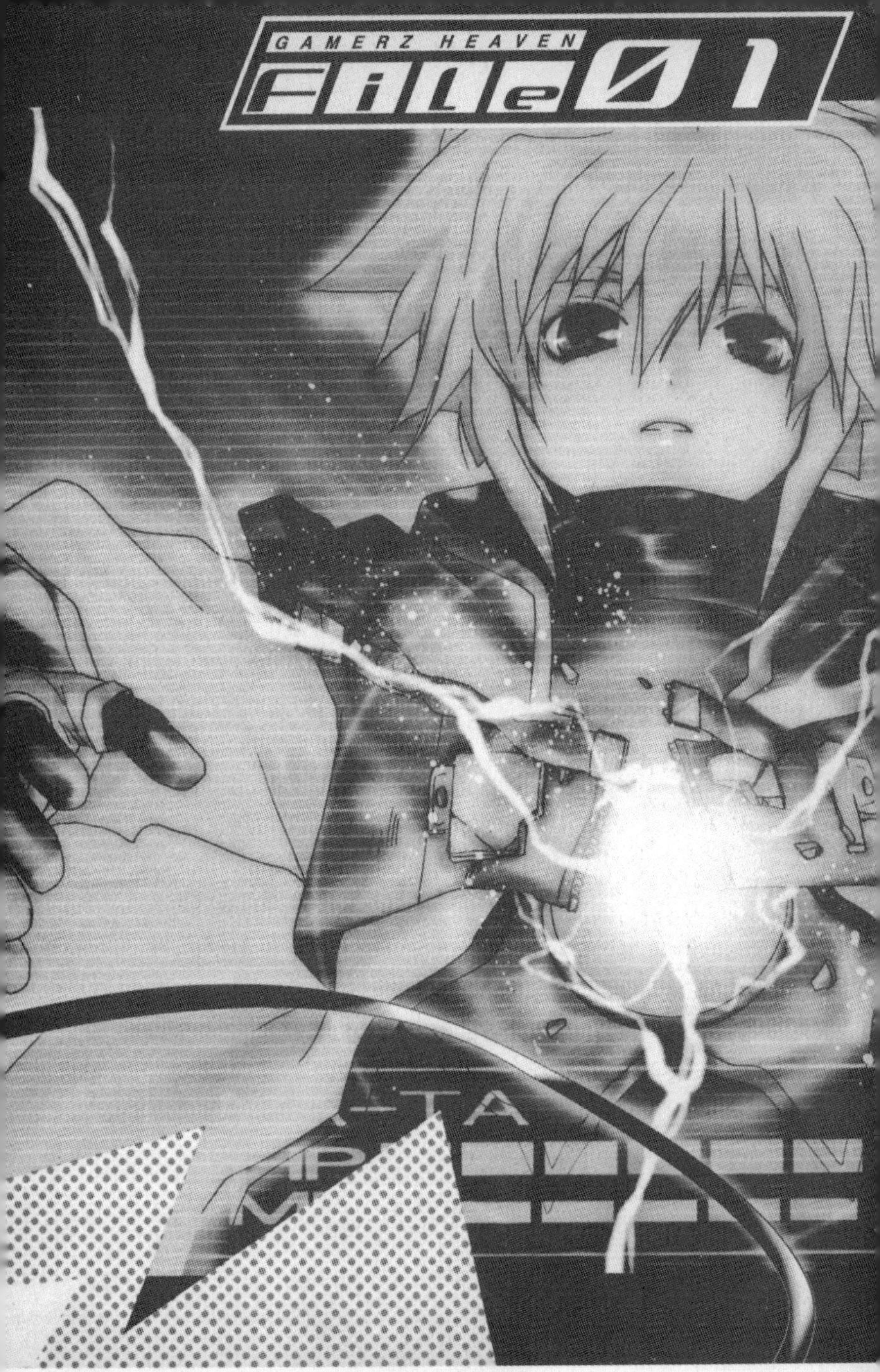
GAMERZ HEAVEN
FiLe 01

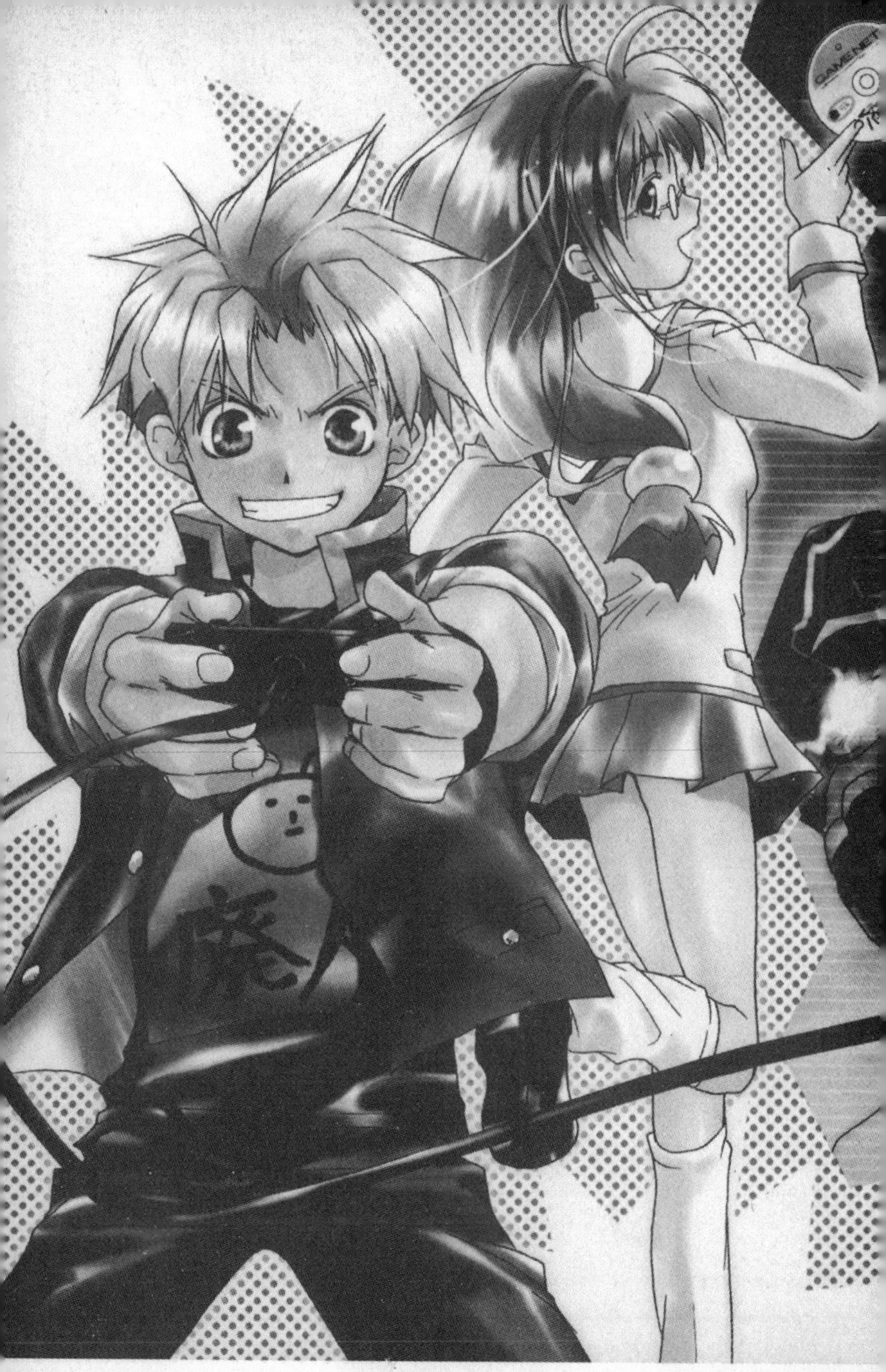
GAME NET

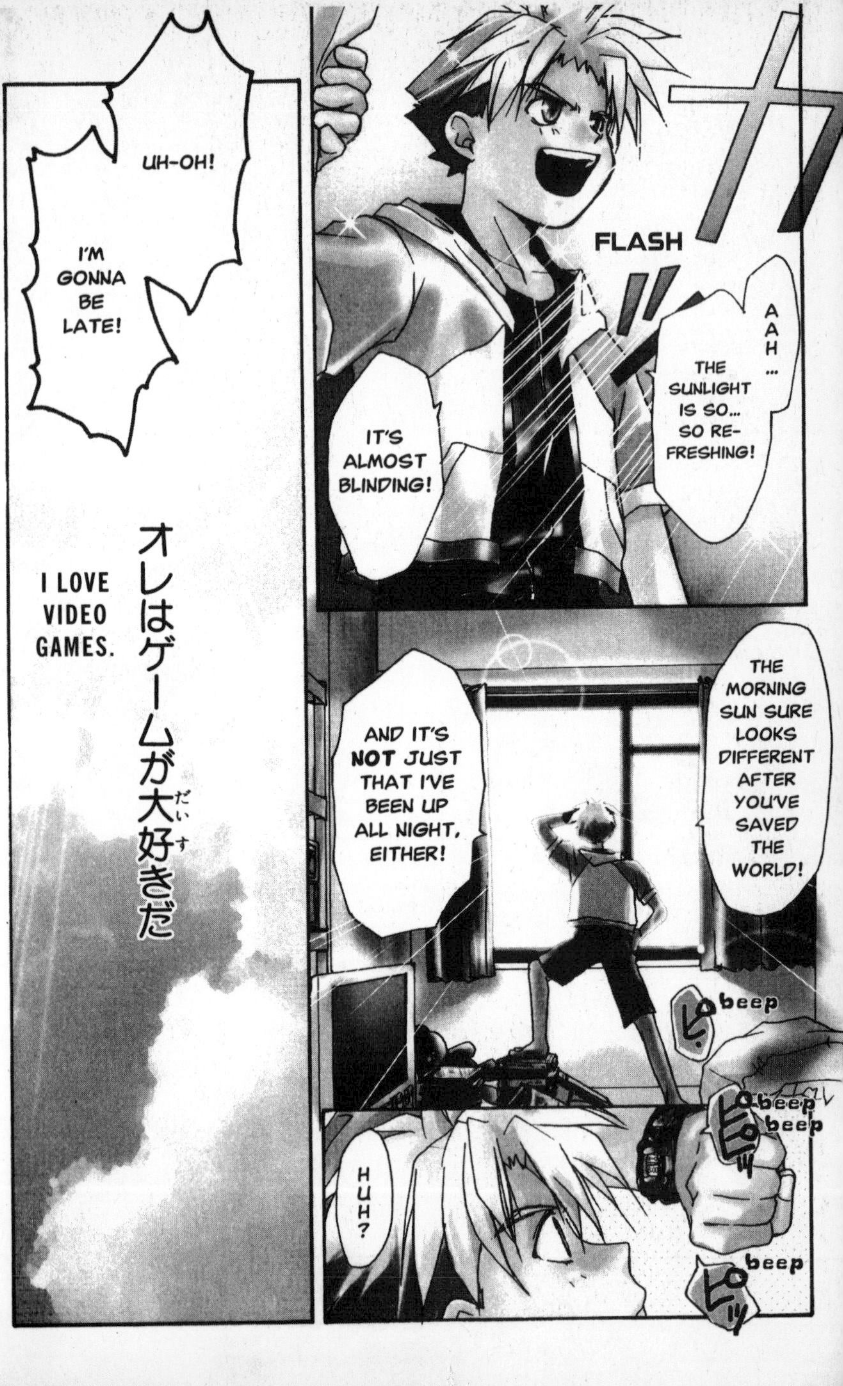
FLASH
AAH... THE SUNLIGHT IS SO... SO RE-FRESHING!
IT'S ALMOST BLINDING!
THE MORNING SUN SURE LOOKS DIFFERENT AFTER YOU'VE SAVED THE WORLD!
AND IT'S NOT JUST THAT I'VE BEEN UP ALL NIGHT, EITHER!
beep
beep beep
HUH?
beep
UH-OH!
I'M GONNA BE LATE!
I LOVE VIDEO GAMES.
オレはゲームが大好きだ

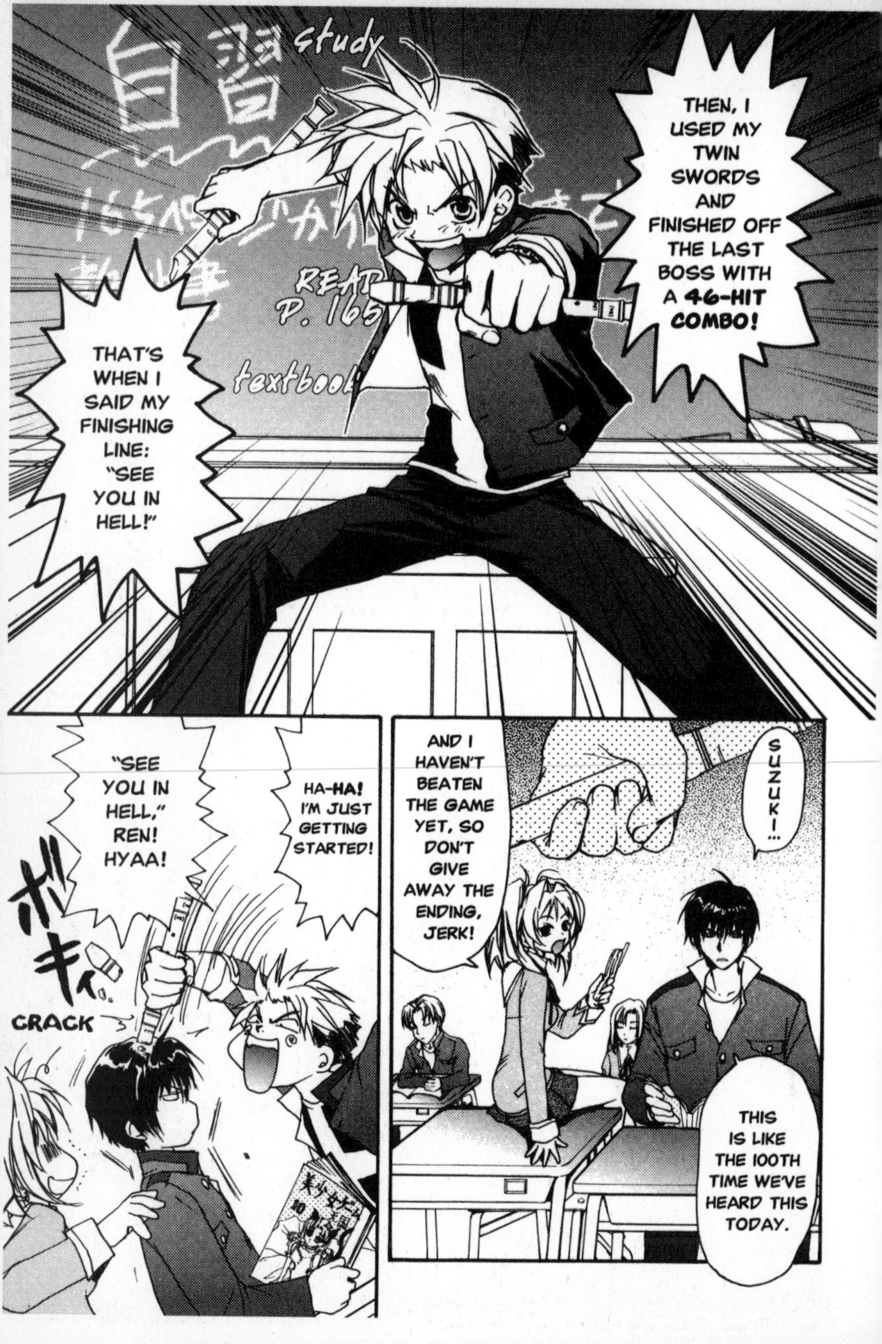
study
READ P. 165
textbook
THEN, I USED MY TWIN SWORDS AND FINISHED OFF THE LAST BOSS WITH A **46-HIT COMBO!**
THAT'S WHEN I SAID MY FINISHING LINE: "SEE YOU IN HELL!"
SUZUKI!...
AND I HAVEN'T BEATEN THE GAME YET, SO DON'T GIVE AWAY THE ENDING, JERK!
THIS IS LIKE THE 100TH TIME WE'VE HEARD THIS TODAY.
HA-HA! I'M JUST GETTING STARTED!
"SEE YOU IN HELL," REN! HYAA!
CRACK

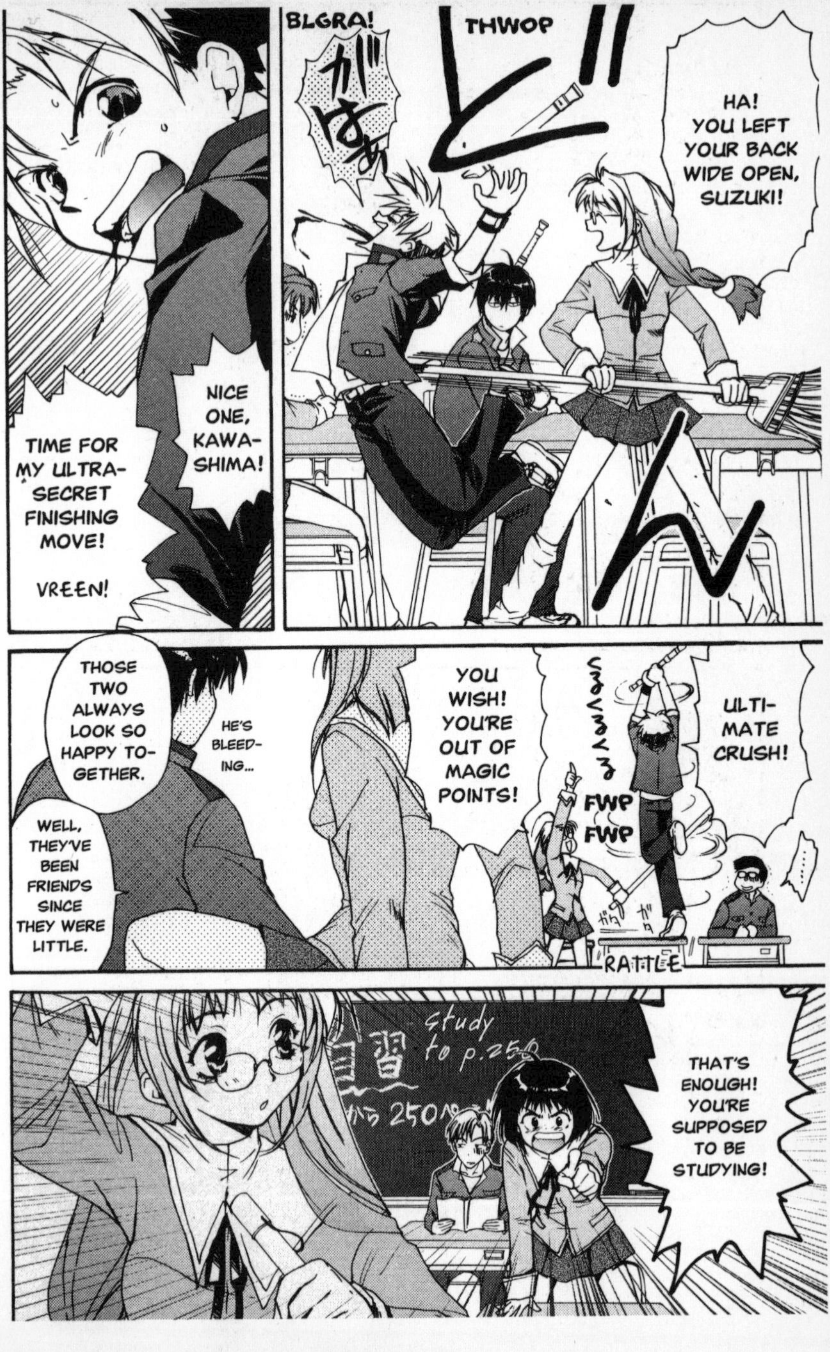
BLGRA!
がはぁ
THWOP
ど
HA! YOU LEFT YOUR BACK WIDE OPEN, SUZUKI!
NICE ONE, KAWA-SHIMA!
TIME FOR MY ULTRA-SECRET FINISHING MOVE!
VREEN!
ULTI-MATE CRUSH!
FWP FWP
YOU WISH! YOU'RE OUT OF MAGIC POINTS!
THOSE TWO ALWAYS LOOK SO HAPPY TO-GETHER.
HE'S BLEED-ING...
WELL, THEY'VE BEEN FRIENDS SINCE THEY WERE LITTLE.
RATTLE
...
Study to p.250
自習
から250ペ
THAT'S ENOUGH! YOU'RE SUPPOSED TO BE STUDYING!

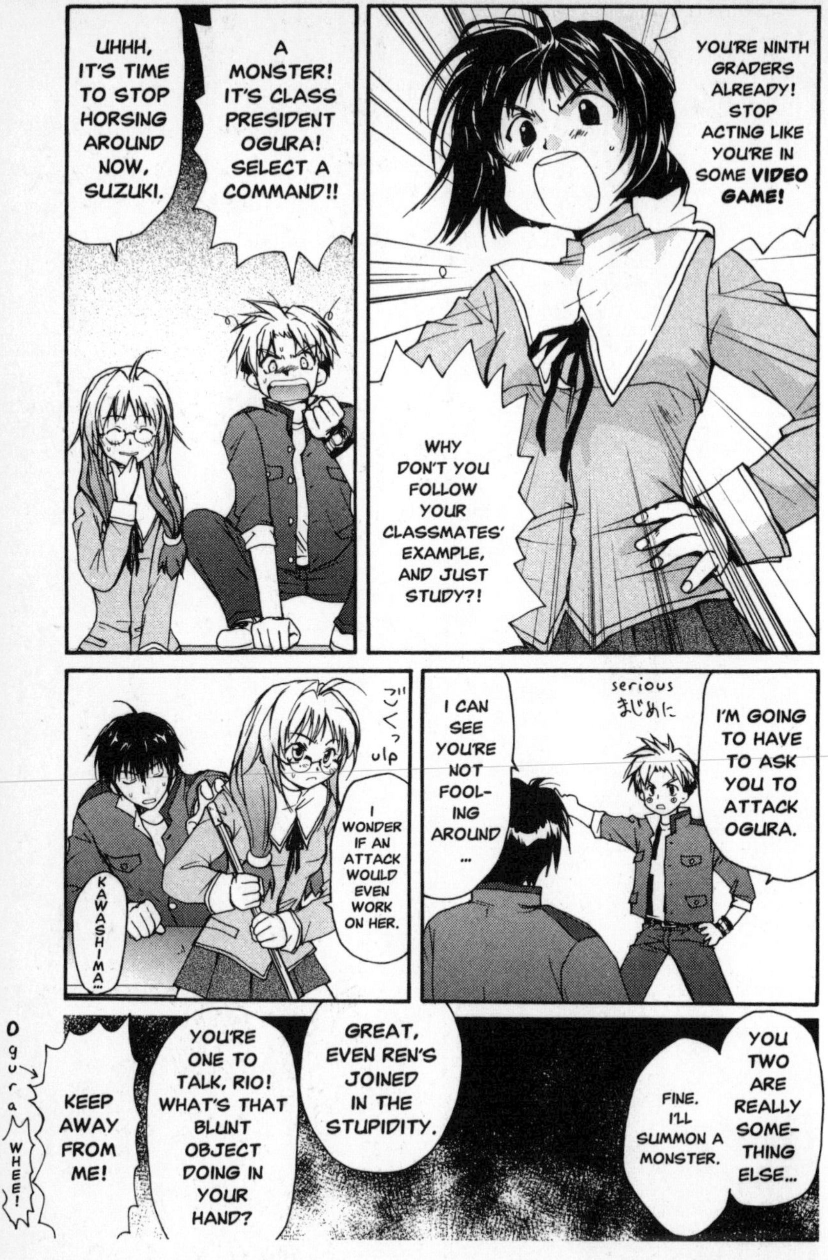
YOU'RE NINTH GRADERS ALREADY! STOP ACTING LIKE YOU'RE IN SOME VIDEO GAME!
WHY DON'T YOU FOLLOW YOUR CLASSMATES' EXAMPLE, AND JUST STUDY?!
A MONSTER! IT'S CLASS PRESIDENT OGURA! SELECT A COMMAND!!
UHHH, IT'S TIME TO STOP HORSING AROUND NOW, SUZUKI.
まじめに
serious
I'M GOING TO HAVE TO ASK YOU TO ATTACK OGURA.
I CAN SEE YOU'RE NOT FOOLING AROUND...
ごくっ
ulp
I WONDER IF AN ATTACK WOULD EVEN WORK ON HER.
KAWASHIMA...
YOU TWO ARE REALLY SOMETHING ELSE...
FINE. I'LL SUMMON A MONSTER.
GREAT, EVEN REN'S JOINED IN THE STUPIDITY.
YOU'RE ONE TO TALK, RIO! WHAT'S THAT BLUNT OBJECT DOING IN YOUR HAND?
KEEP AWAY FROM ME!
Ogura
WHEE!

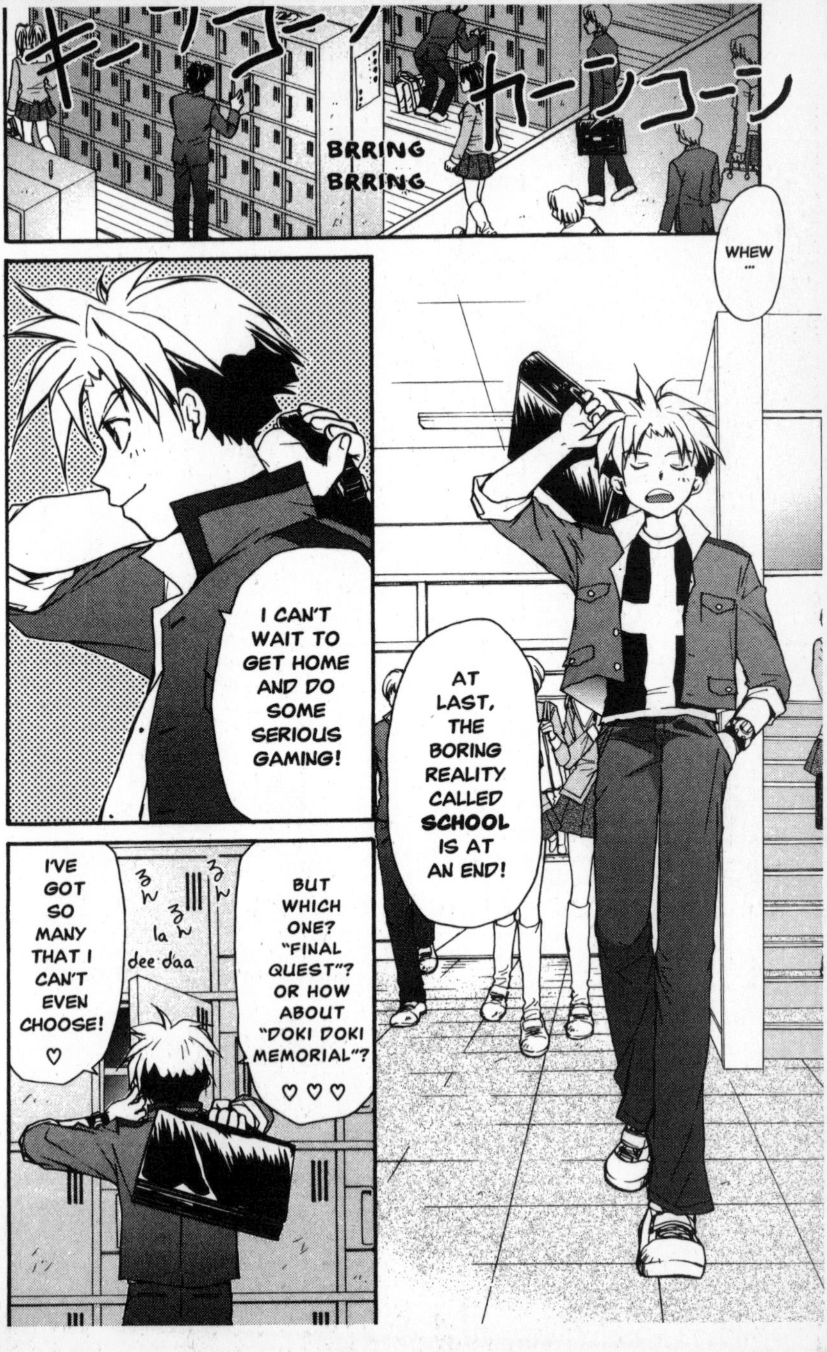
BRRING
BRRING
WHEW...
AT LAST, THE BORING REALITY CALLED SCHOOL IS AT AN END!
I CAN'T WAIT TO GET HOME AND DO SOME SERIOUS GAMING!
BUT WHICH ONE? "FINAL QUEST"? OR HOW ABOUT "DOKI DOKI MEMORIAL"? ♡ ♡ ♡
la dee daa
I'VE GOT SO MANY THAT I CAN'T EVEN CHOOSE! ♡

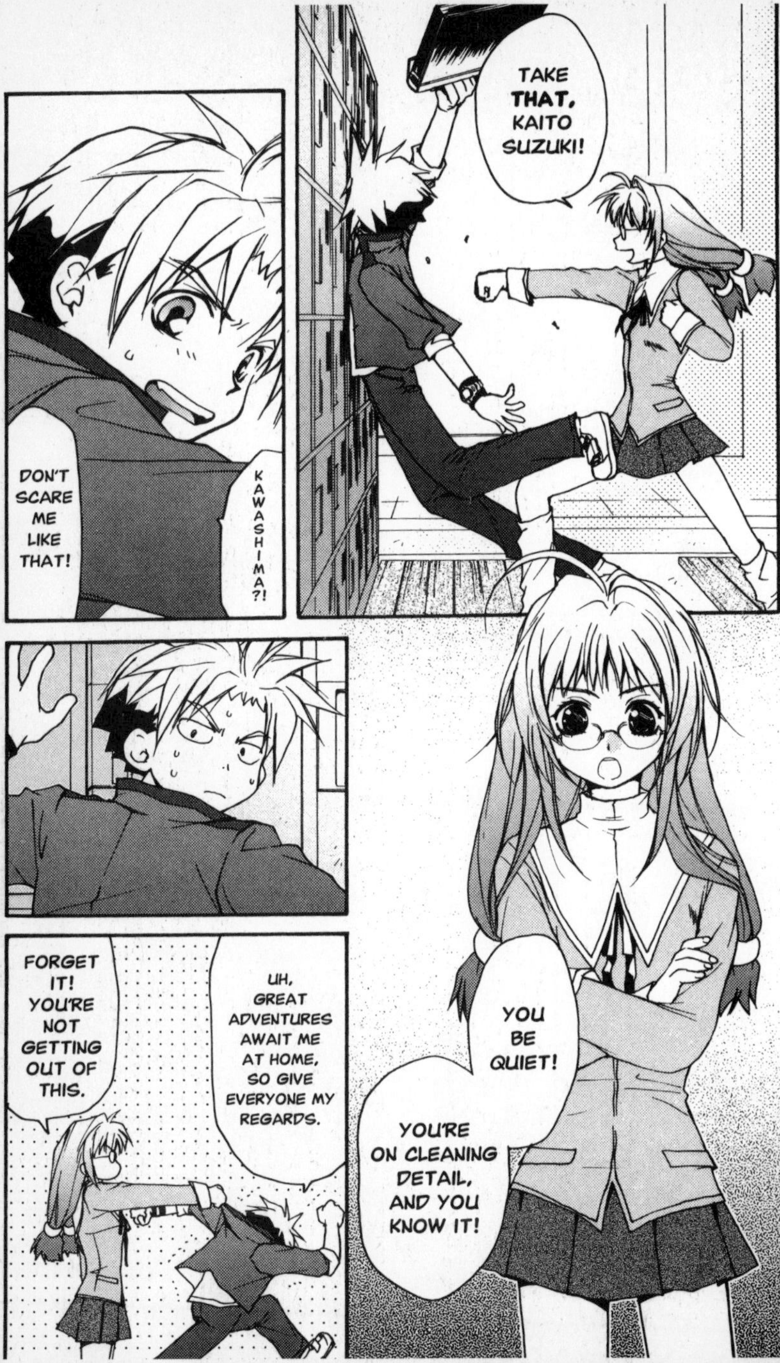
TAKE THAT, KAITO SUZUKI!
KAWASHIMA?!
DON'T SCARE ME LIKE THAT!
YOU BE QUIET!
YOU'RE ON CLEANING DETAIL, AND YOU KNOW IT!
UH, GREAT ADVENTURES AWAIT ME AT HOME, SO GIVE EVERYONE MY REGARDS.
FORGET IT! YOU'RE NOT GETTING OUT OF THIS.

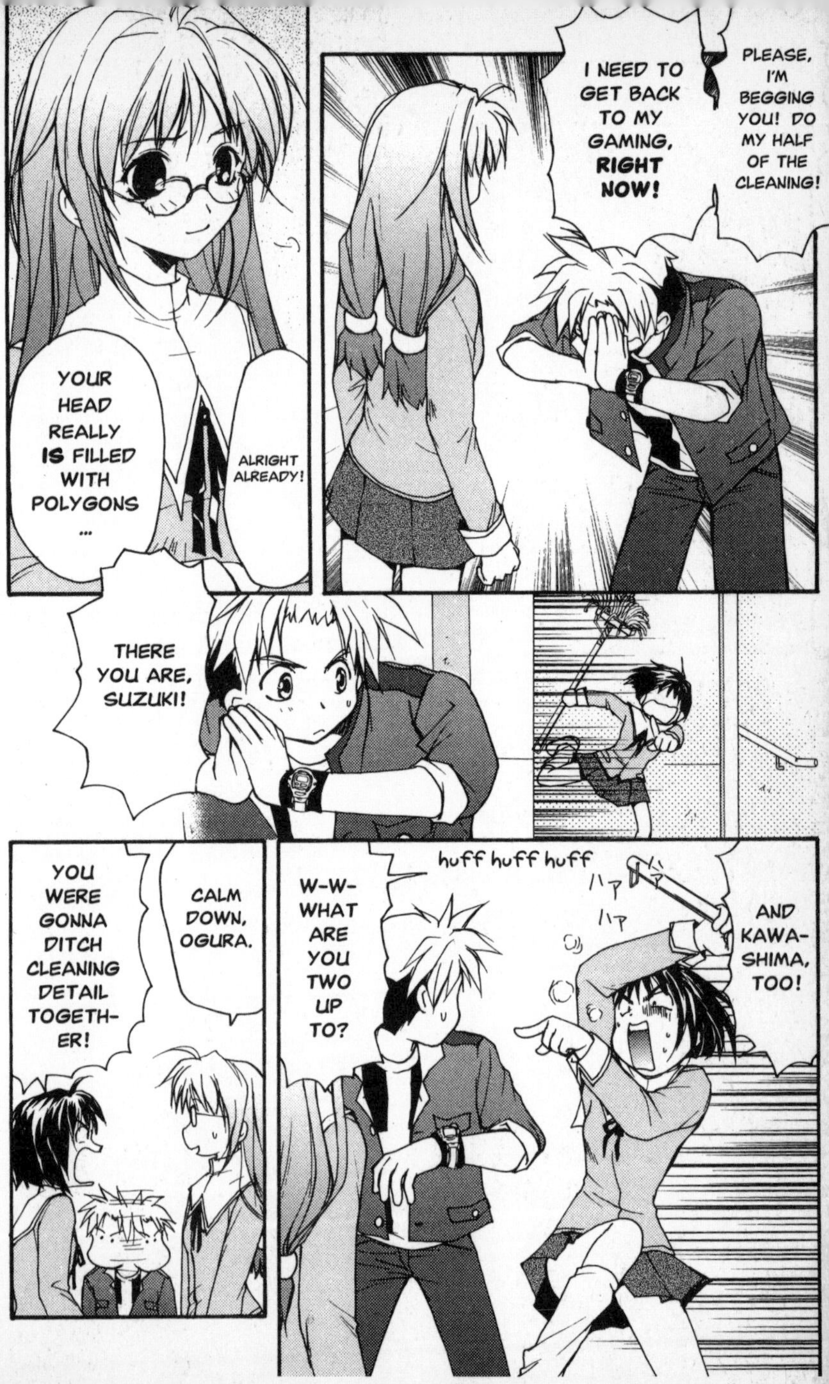
PLEASE, I'M BEGGING YOU! DO MY HALF OF THE CLEANING!
I NEED TO GET BACK TO MY GAMING, RIGHT NOW!
ALRIGHT ALREADY!
YOUR HEAD REALLY IS FILLED WITH POLYGONS ...
THERE YOU ARE, SUZUKI!
AND KAWA-SHIMA, TOO!
huff huff huff
ハァ ハァ
W-W-WHAT ARE YOU TWO UP TO?
CALM DOWN, OGURA.
YOU WERE GONNA DITCH CLEANING DETAIL TOGETH-ER!

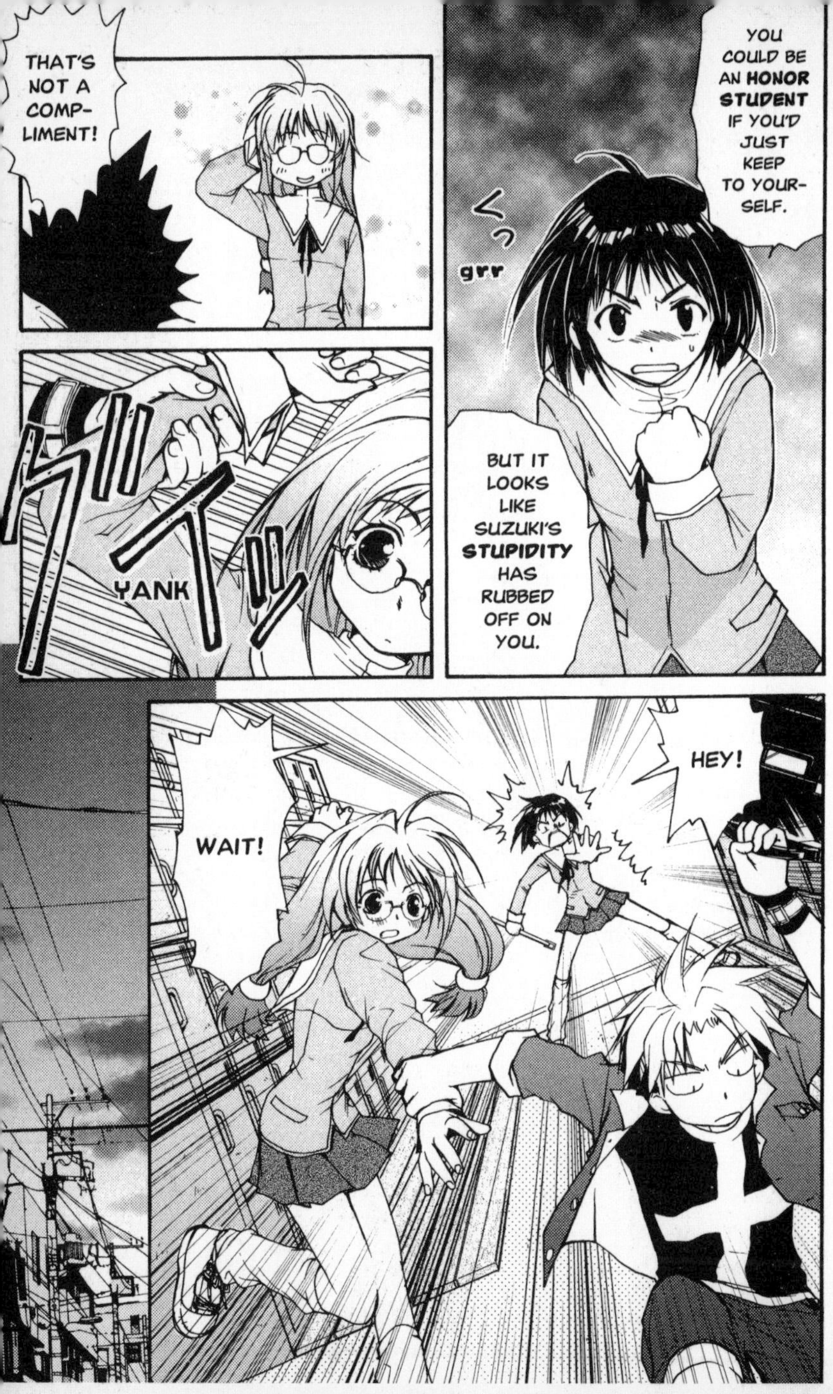
YOU COULD BE AN **HONOR STUDENT** IF YOU'D JUST KEEP TO YOURSELF.
くっ
grr
BUT IT LOOKS LIKE SUZUKI'S **STUPIDITY** HAS RUBBED OFF ON YOU.
THAT'S NOT A COMPLIMENT!
YANK
HEY!
WAIT!

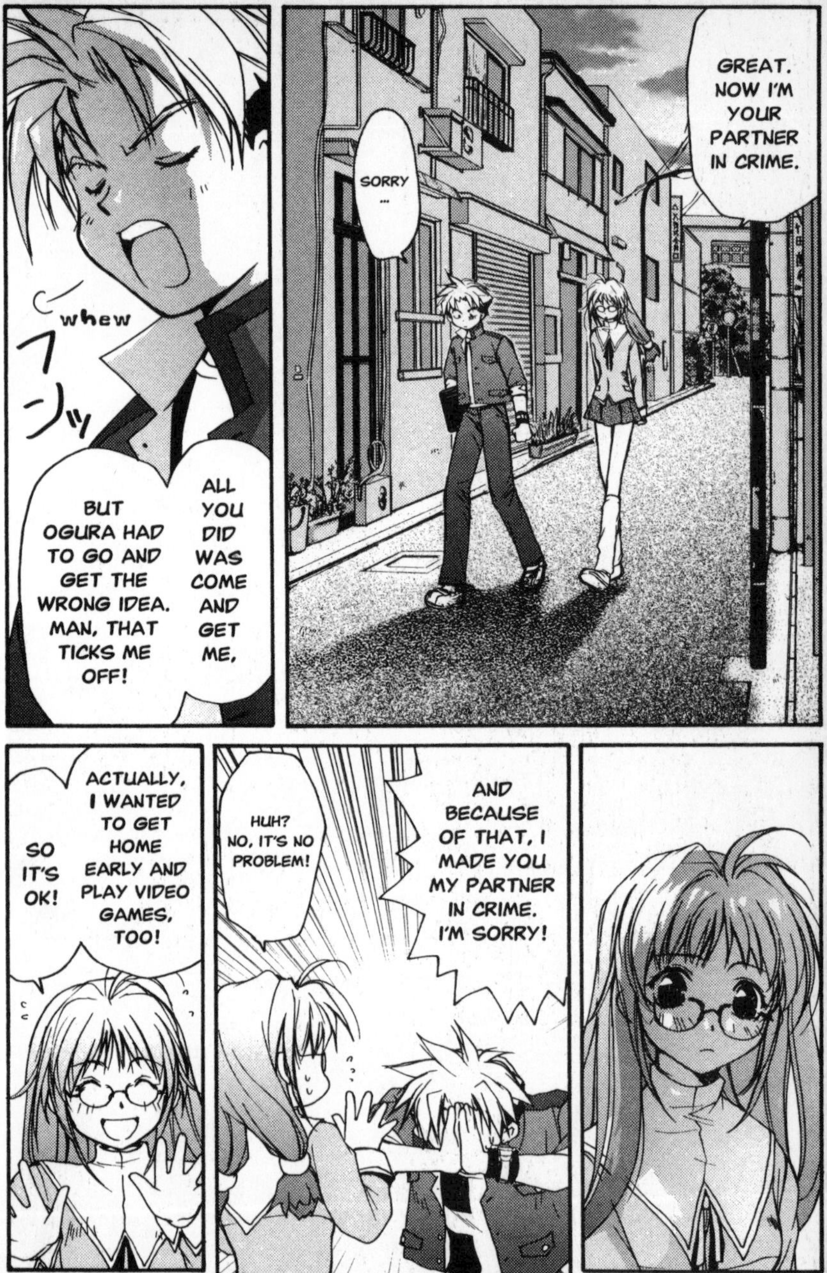
GREAT. NOW I'M YOUR PARTNER IN CRIME.
SORRY ...
ALL YOU DID WAS COME AND GET ME,
BUT OGURA HAD TO GO AND GET THE WRONG IDEA. MAN, THAT TICKS ME OFF!
whew
フンッ
AND BECAUSE OF THAT, I MADE YOU MY PARTNER IN CRIME. I'M SORRY!
HUH? NO, IT'S NO PROBLEM!
ACTUALLY, I WANTED TO GET HOME EARLY AND PLAY VIDEO GAMES, TOO!
SO IT'S OK!

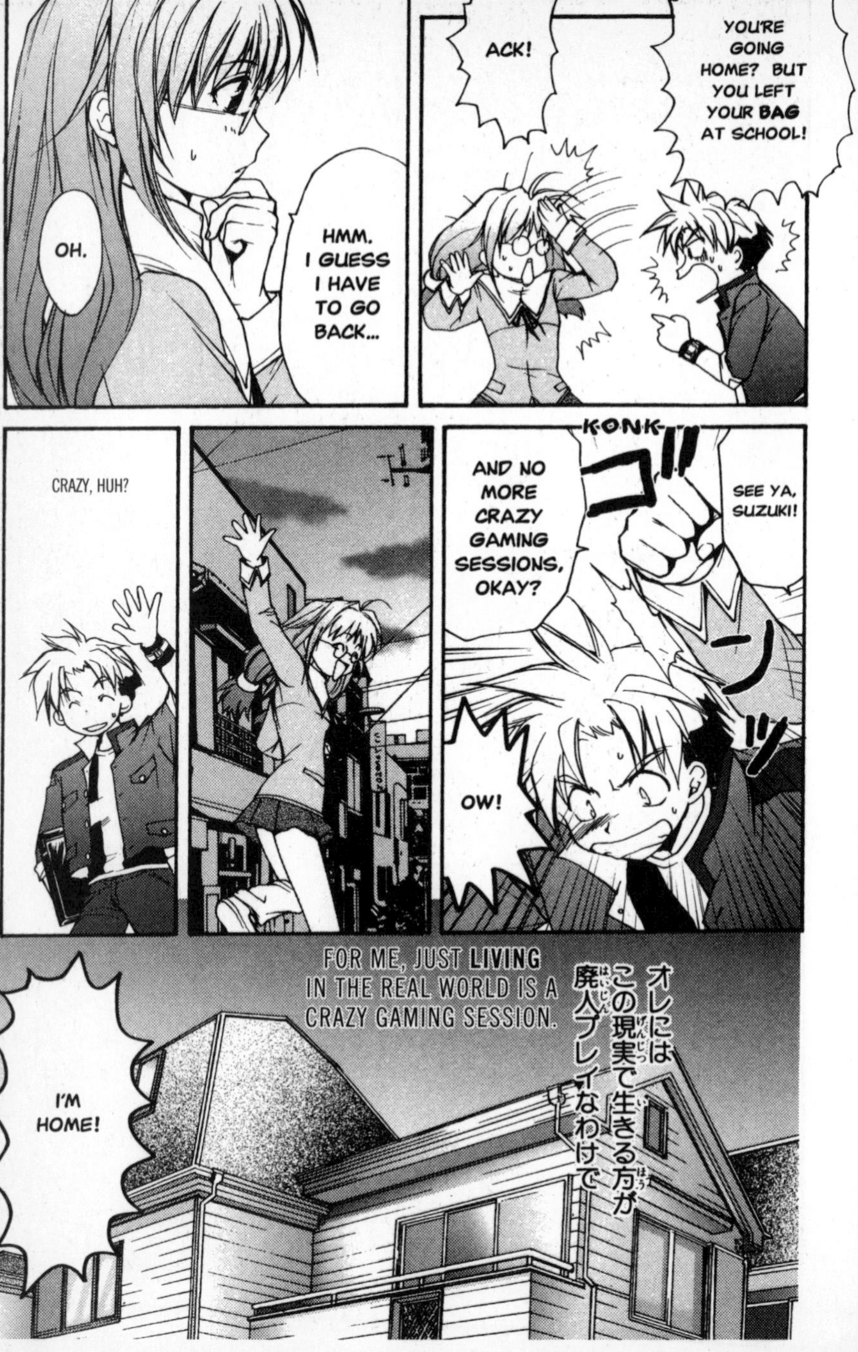
YOU'RE GOING HOME? BUT YOU LEFT YOUR BAG AT SCHOOL!
ACK!
HMM. I GUESS I HAVE TO GO BACK...
OH.
KONK
SEE YA, SUZUKI!
AND NO MORE CRAZY GAMING SESSIONS, OKAY?
OW!
CRAZY, HUH?
オレには
この現実で生きる方が
廃人プレイなわけで
FOR ME, JUST LIVING IN THE REAL WORLD IS A CRAZY GAMING SESSION.
I'M HOME!

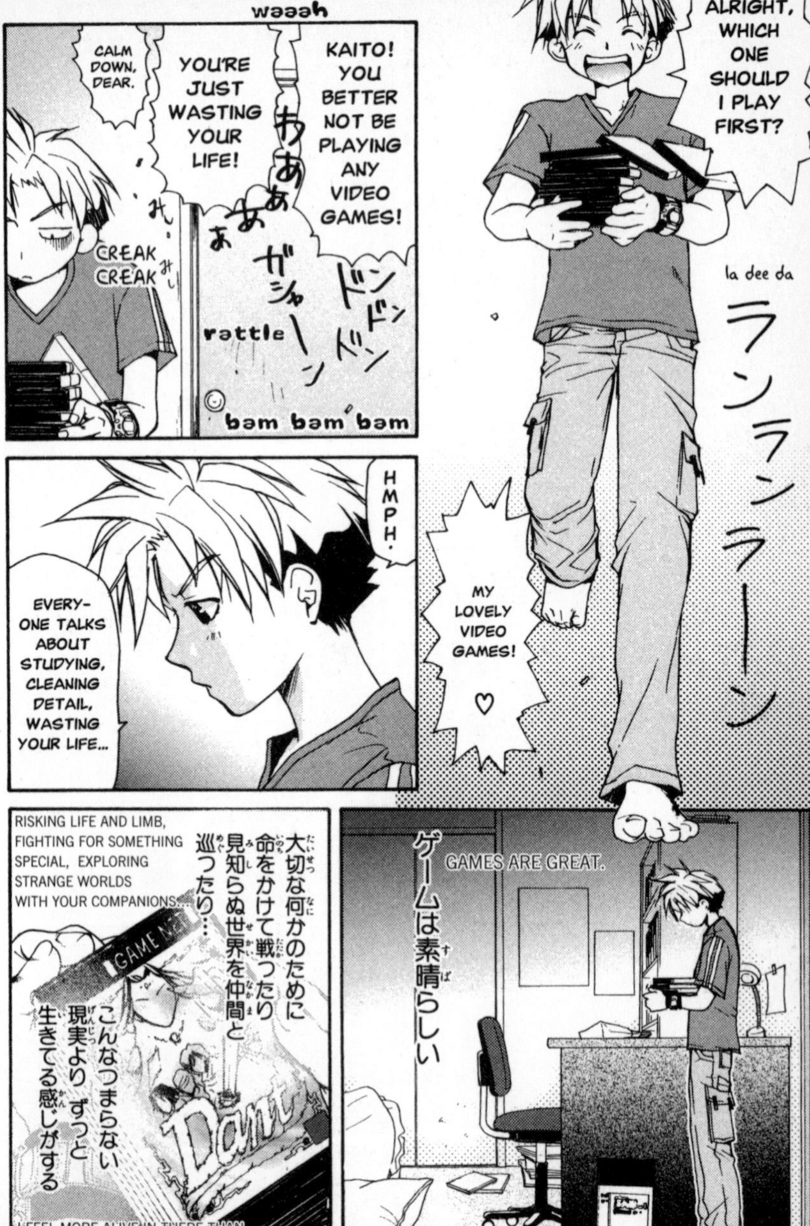
ALRIGHT, WHICH ONE SHOULD I PLAY FIRST?
la dee da
ランランラーン
MY LOVELY VIDEO GAMES! ♡
KAITO! YOU BETTER NOT BE PLAYING ANY VIDEO GAMES!
waaah
おあぁぁ
YOU'RE JUST WASTING YOUR LIFE!
CALM DOWN, DEAR.
ドンドンドン
bam bam bam
ガシャーン
rattle
みしみし
CREAK CREAK
HMPH.
EVERYONE TALKS ABOUT STUDYING, CLEANING DETAIL, WASTING YOUR LIFE...
ゲームは素晴らしい
GAMES ARE GREAT.
大切な何かのために命をかけて戦ったり見知らぬ世界を仲間と巡ったり……
RISKING LIFE AND LIMB, FIGHTING FOR SOMETHING SPECIAL, EXPLORING STRANGE WORLDS WITH YOUR COMPANIONS...
こんなつまらない現実よりずっと生きてる感じがする
I FEEL MORE ALIVE IN THERE THAN IN THIS HUMDRUM REAL WORLD.

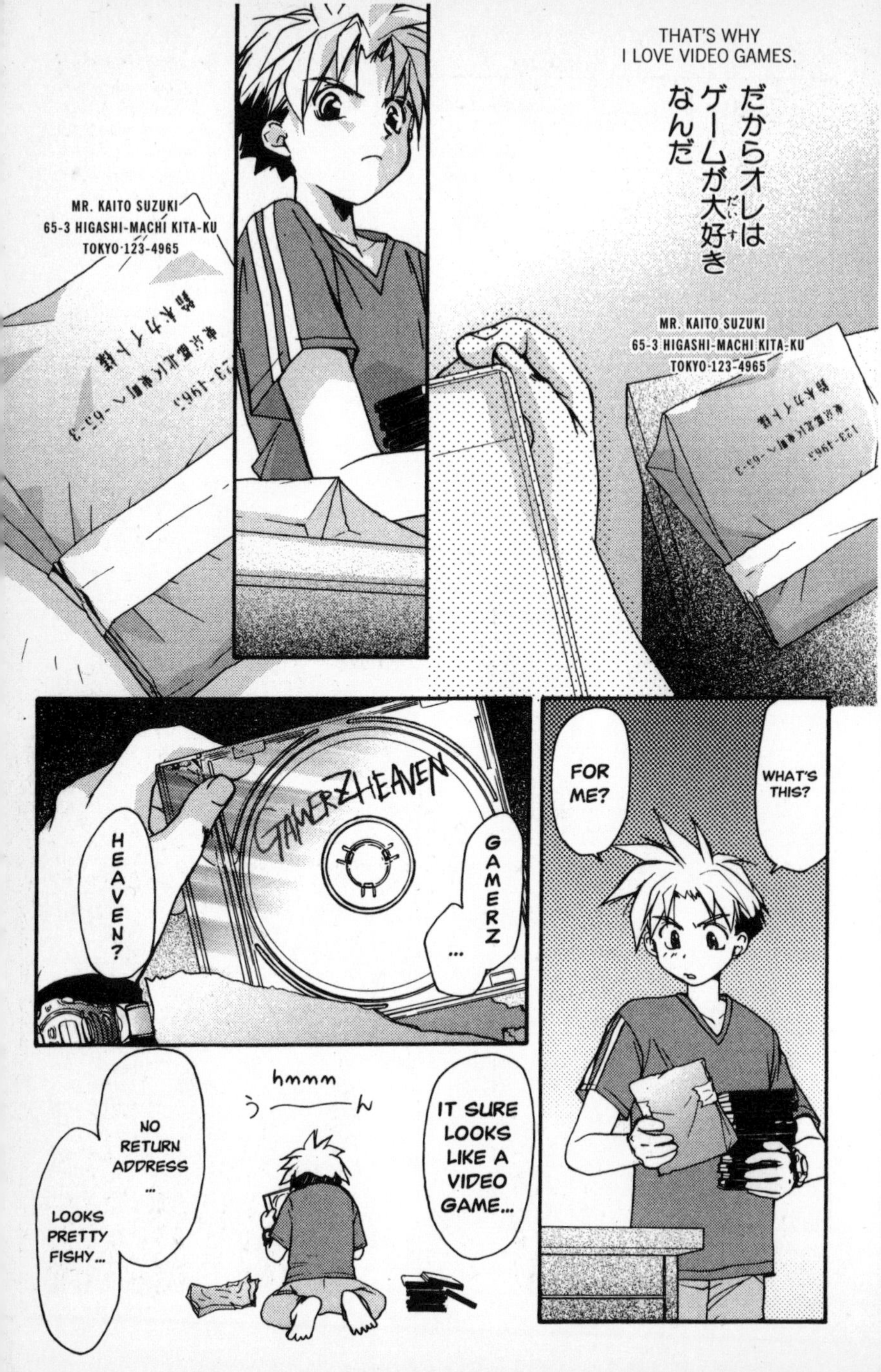
THAT'S WHY I LOVE VIDEO GAMES.
だからオレはゲームが大好きなんだ
MR. KAITO SUZUKI
65-3 HIGASHI-MACHI KITA-KU
TOKYO 123-4965
MR. KAITO SUZUKI
65-3 HIGASHI-MACHI KITA-KU
TOKYO 123-4965
WHAT'S THIS?
FOR ME?
GAMERZ HEAVEN
GAMERZ ...
HEAVEN?
IT SURE LOOKS LIKE A VIDEO GAME...
hmmm
うーーん
NO RETURN ADDRESS ...
LOOKS PRETTY FISHY...

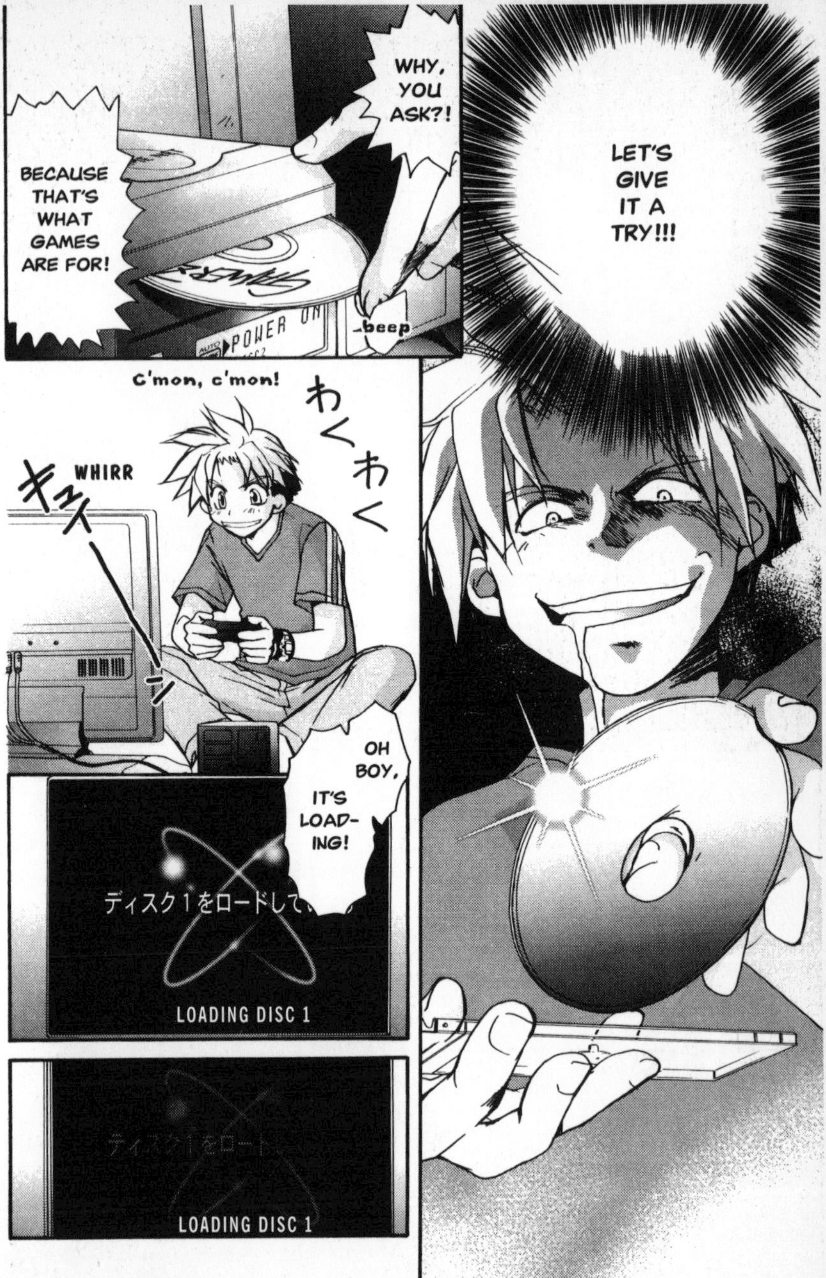
LET'S GIVE IT A TRY!!!
WHY, YOU ASK?!
BECAUSE THAT'S WHAT GAMES ARE FOR!
POWER ON
beep
C'mon, c'mon!
わくわく
WHIRR
キュイーーン
OH BOY, IT'S LOADING!
LOADING DISC 1
ディスク1をロード
LOADING DISC 1

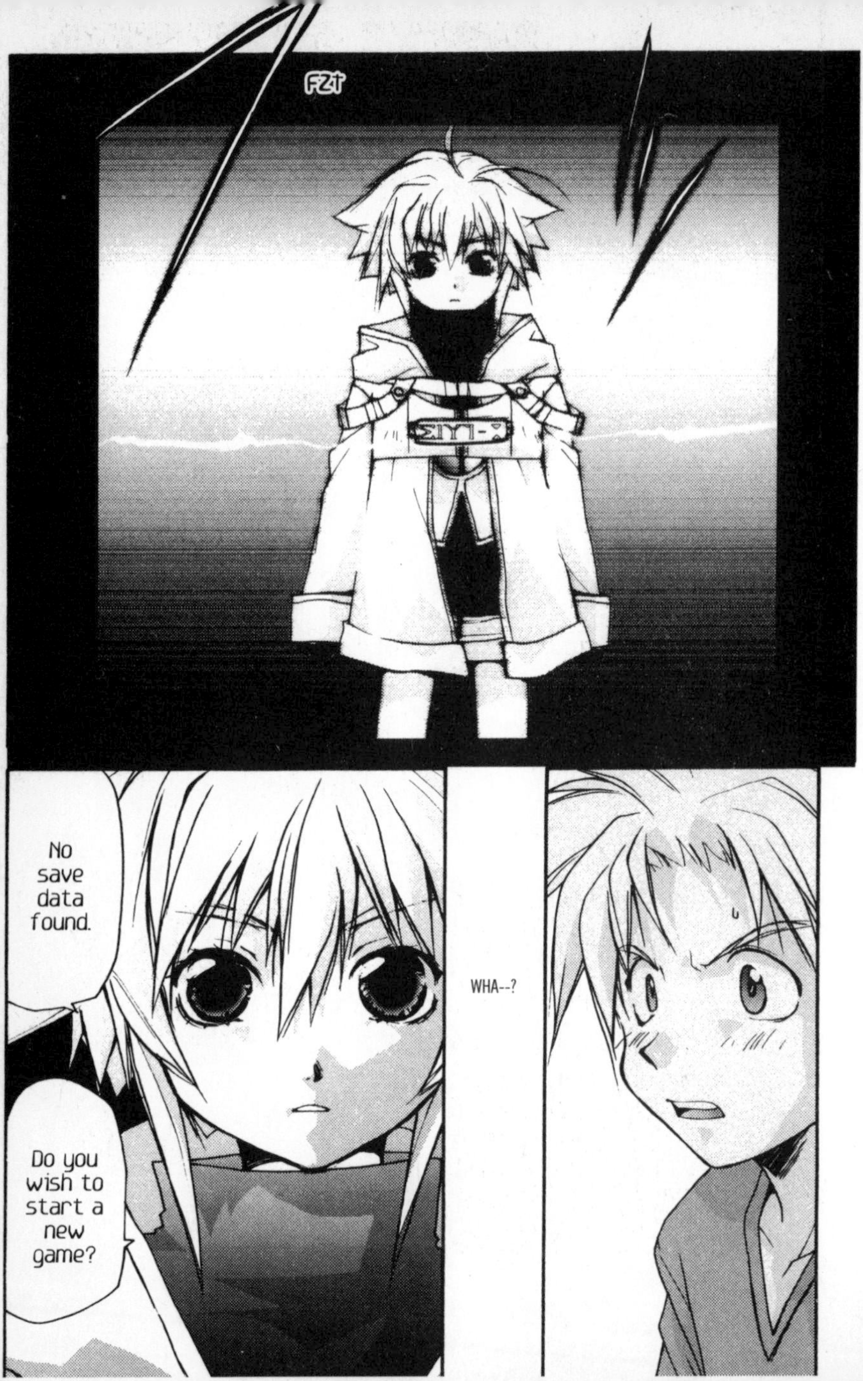
FZT
No save data found.
Do you wish to start a new game?
WHA--?

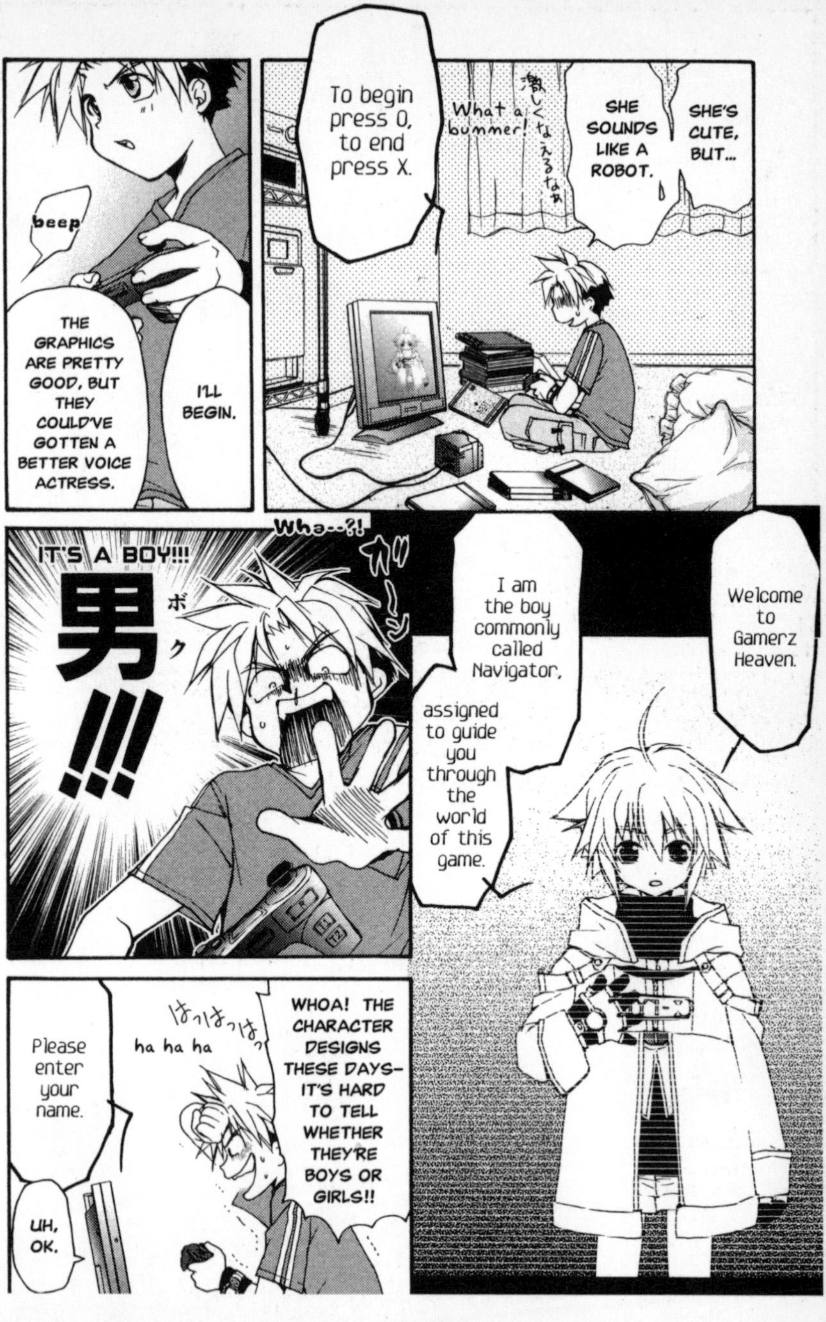
SHE'S CUTE, BUT...
SHE SOUNDS LIKE A ROBOT.
What a bummer!
激しくなえるなぁ
To begin press O, to end press X.
beep
I'LL BEGIN.
THE GRAPHICS ARE PRETTY GOOD, BUT THEY COULD'VE GOTTEN A BETTER VOICE ACTRESS.
Welcome to Gamerz Heaven.
I am the boy commonly called Navigator,
assigned to guide you through the world of this game.
Wha--?!
ガーン
IT'S A BOY!!!
男!!!
ボク
WHOA! THE CHARACTER DESIGNS THESE DAYS– IT'S HARD TO TELL WHETHER THEY'RE BOYS OR GIRLS!!
はっはっはっ
ha ha ha
Please enter your name.
UH, OK.

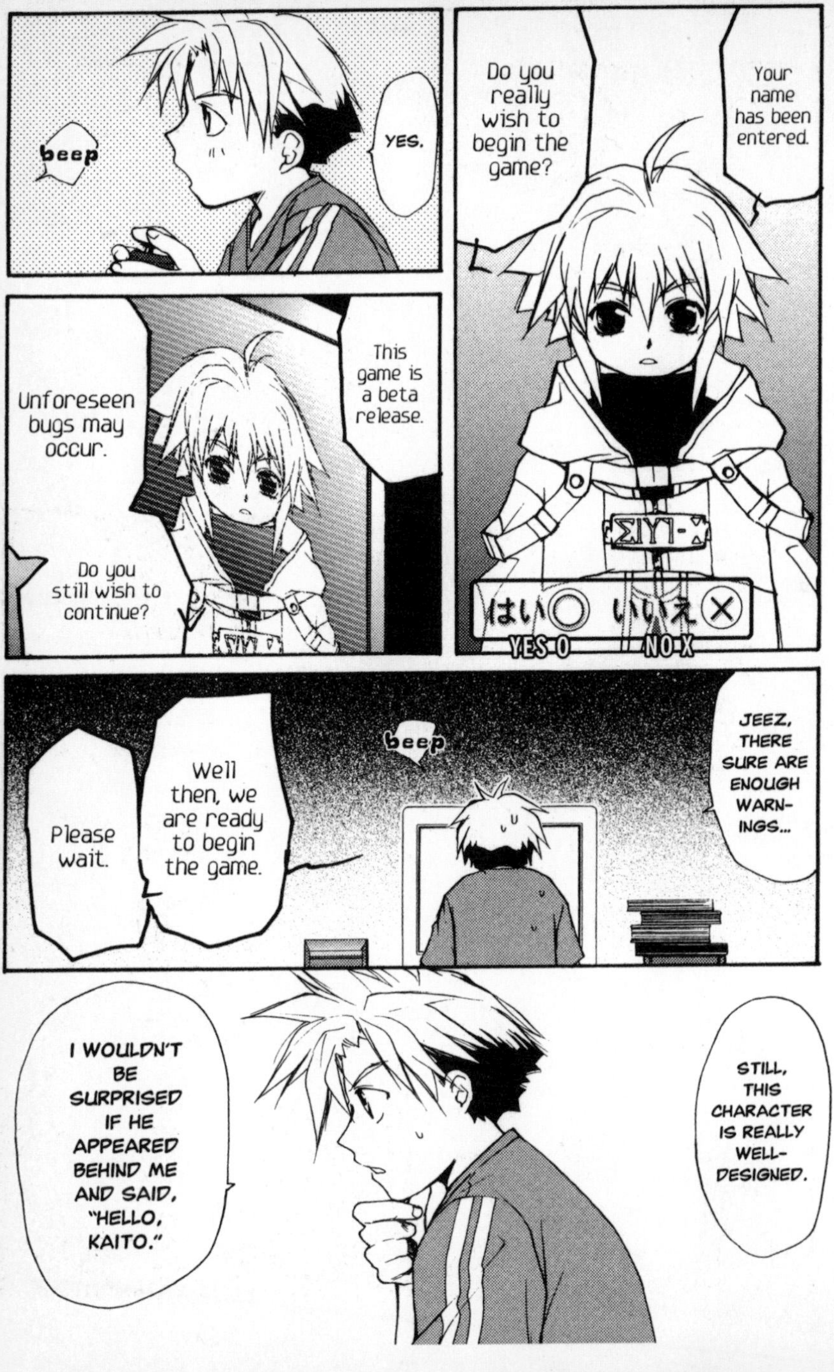
Your name has been entered.
Do you really wish to begin the game?
はい○ いいえ×
YES O NO X
YES.
beep
This game is a beta release.
Unforeseen bugs may occur.
Do you still wish to continue?
JEEZ, THERE SURE ARE ENOUGH WARN-INGS...
beep
Well then, we are ready to begin the game.
Please wait.
STILL, THIS CHARACTER IS REALLY WELL-DESIGNED.
I WOULDN'T BE SURPRISED IF HE APPEARED BEHIND ME AND SAID, "HELLO, KAITO."

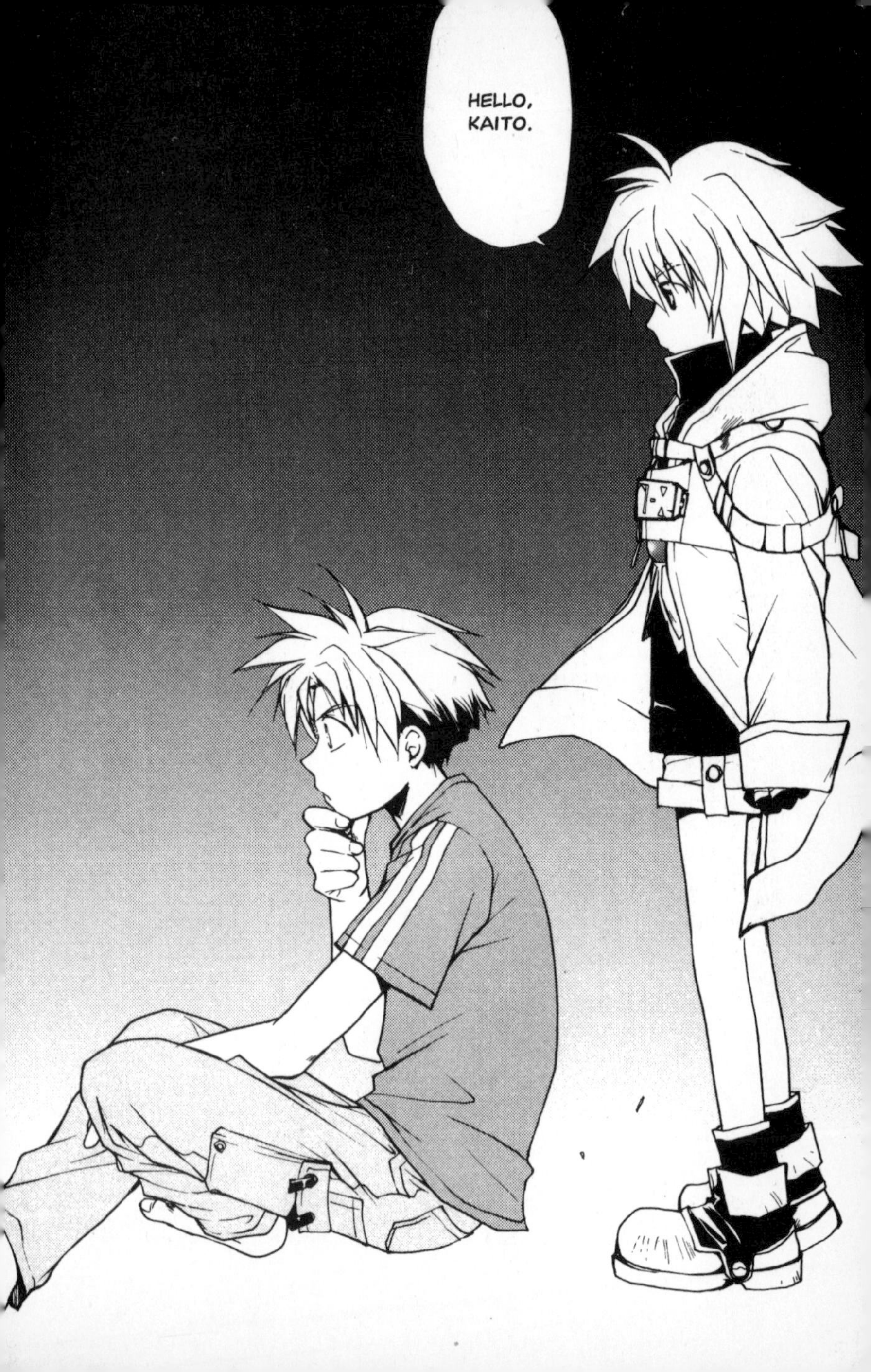
HELLO, KAITO.

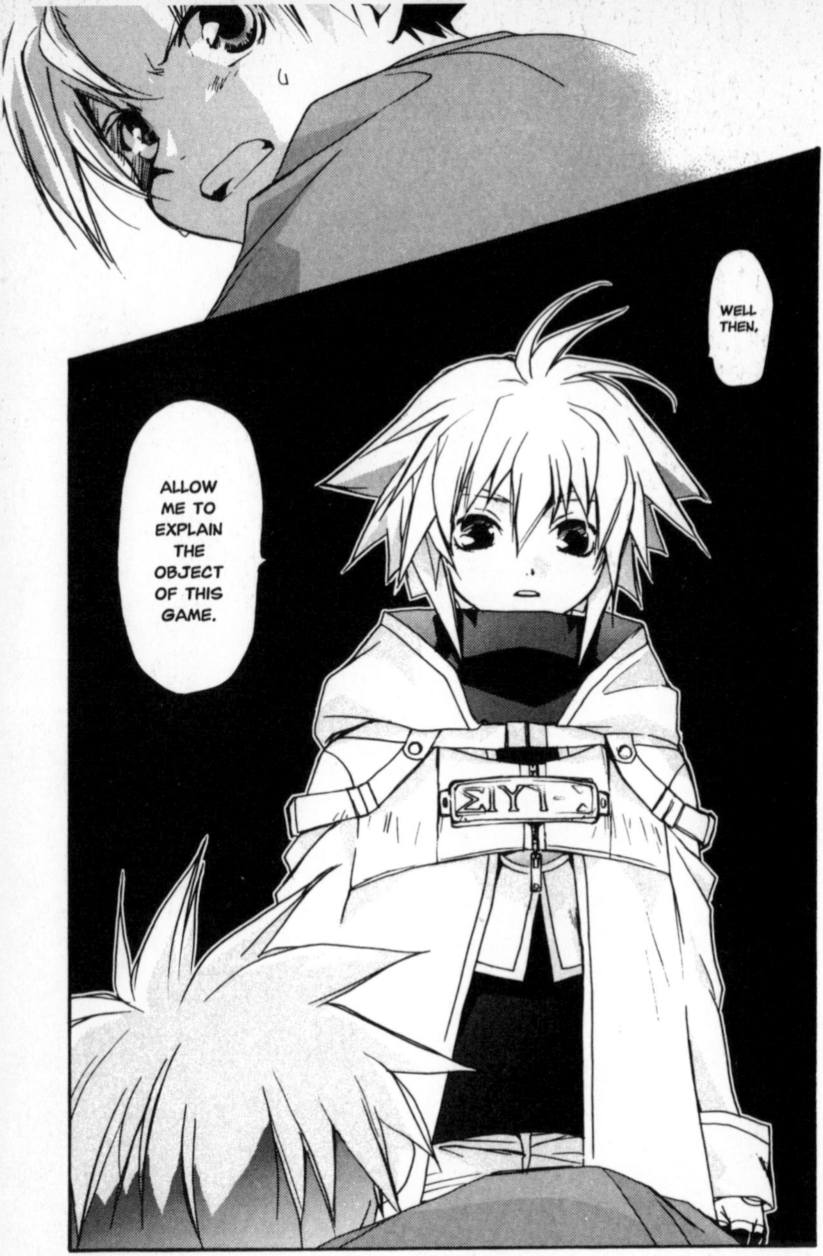
WELL THEN,
ALLOW ME TO EXPLAIN THE OBJECT OF THIS GAME.

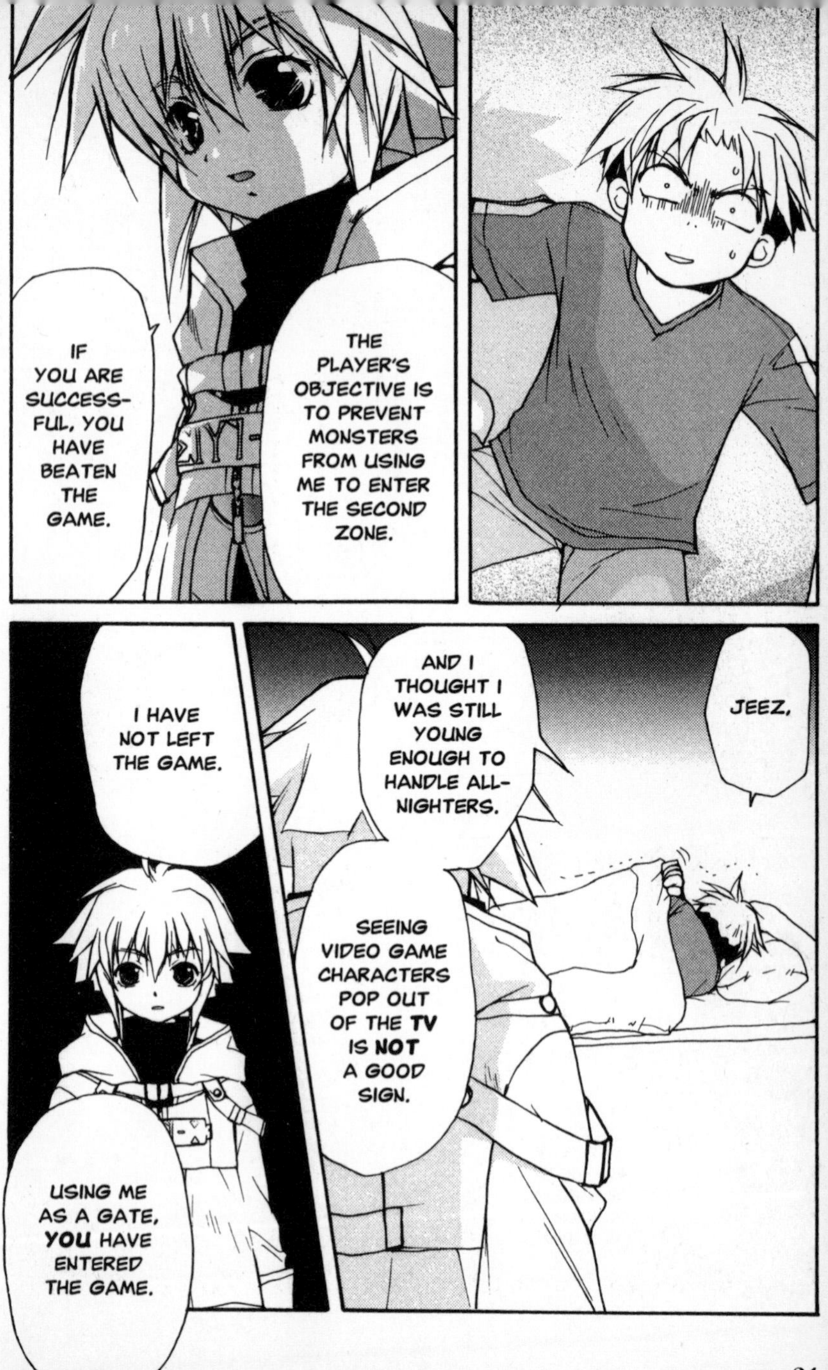
THE PLAYER'S OBJECTIVE IS TO PREVENT MONSTERS FROM USING ME TO ENTER THE SECOND ZONE.
IF YOU ARE SUCCESS-FUL, YOU HAVE BEATEN THE GAME.
JEEZ,
AND I THOUGHT I WAS STILL YOUNG ENOUGH TO HANDLE ALL-NIGHTERS.
SEEING VIDEO GAME CHARACTERS POP OUT OF THE **TV** IS **NOT** A GOOD SIGN.
I HAVE NOT LEFT THE GAME.
USING ME AS A GATE, **YOU** HAVE ENTERED THE GAME.

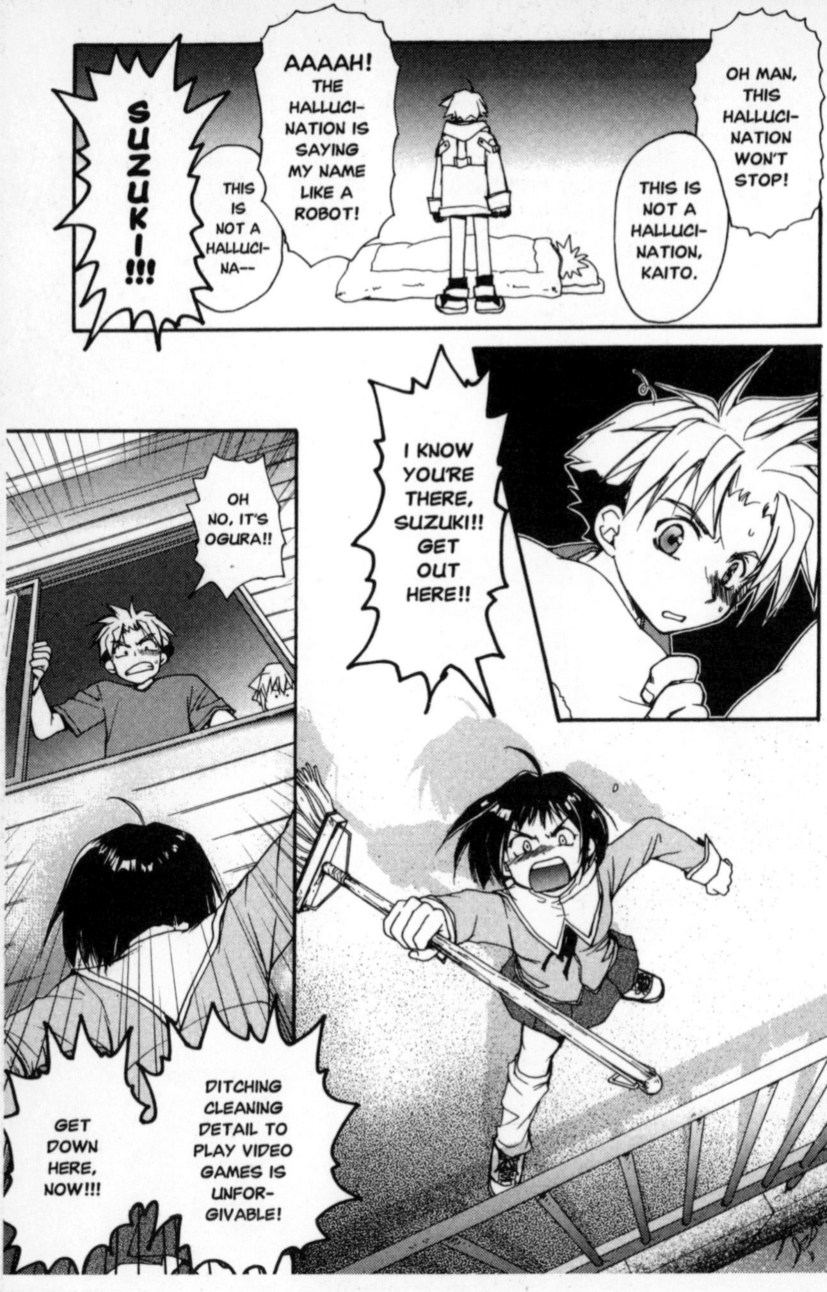

OH MAN, THIS HALLUCI-NATION WON'T STOP!
THIS IS NOT A HALLUCI-NATION, KAITO.
AAAAH! THE HALLUCI-NATION IS SAYING MY NAME LIKE A ROBOT!
THIS IS NOT A HALLUCI-NA--
SUZUKI!!!
I KNOW YOU'RE THERE, SUZUKI!! GET OUT HERE!!
OH NO, IT'S OGURA!!
DITCHING CLEANING DETAIL TO PLAY VIDEO GAMES IS UNFOR-GIVABLE!
GET DOWN HERE, NOW!!!

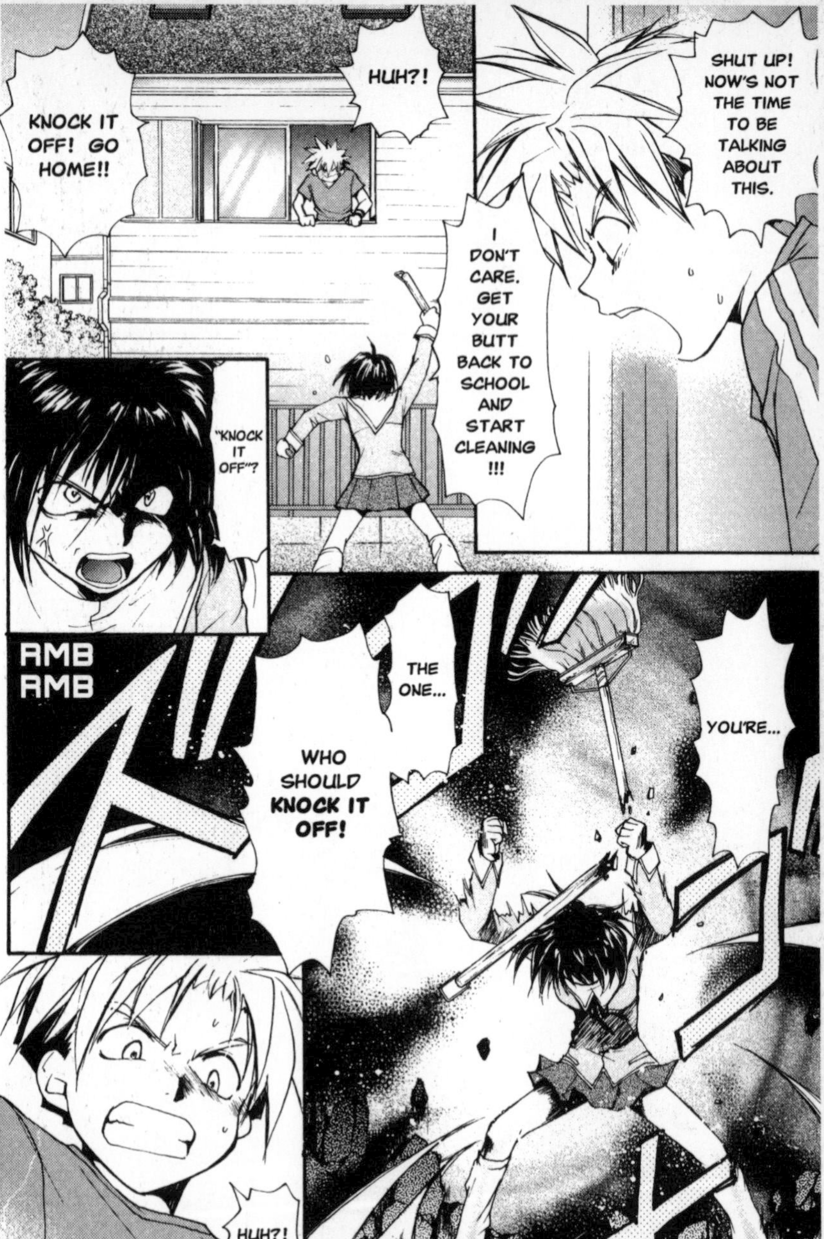
SHUT UP! NOW'S NOT THE TIME TO BE TALKING ABOUT THIS.
I DON'T CARE. GET YOUR BUTT BACK TO SCHOOL AND START CLEANING!!!
HUH?!
KNOCK IT OFF! GO HOME!!
"KNOCK IT OFF"?
YOU'RE...
THE ONE...
WHO SHOULD **KNOCK IT OFF!**
RMB RMB
HUH?!

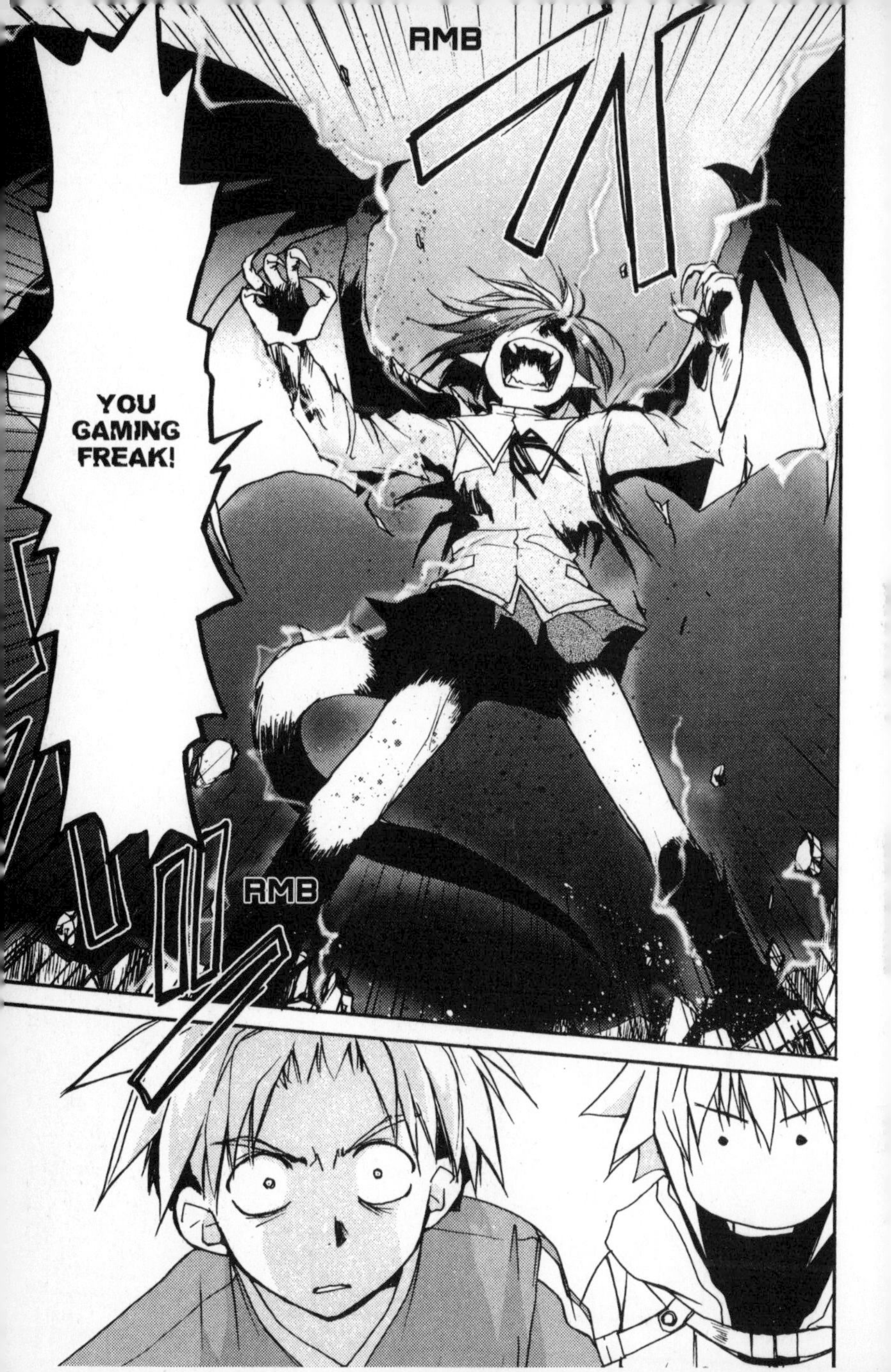
RMB
YOU GAMING FREAK!
RMB

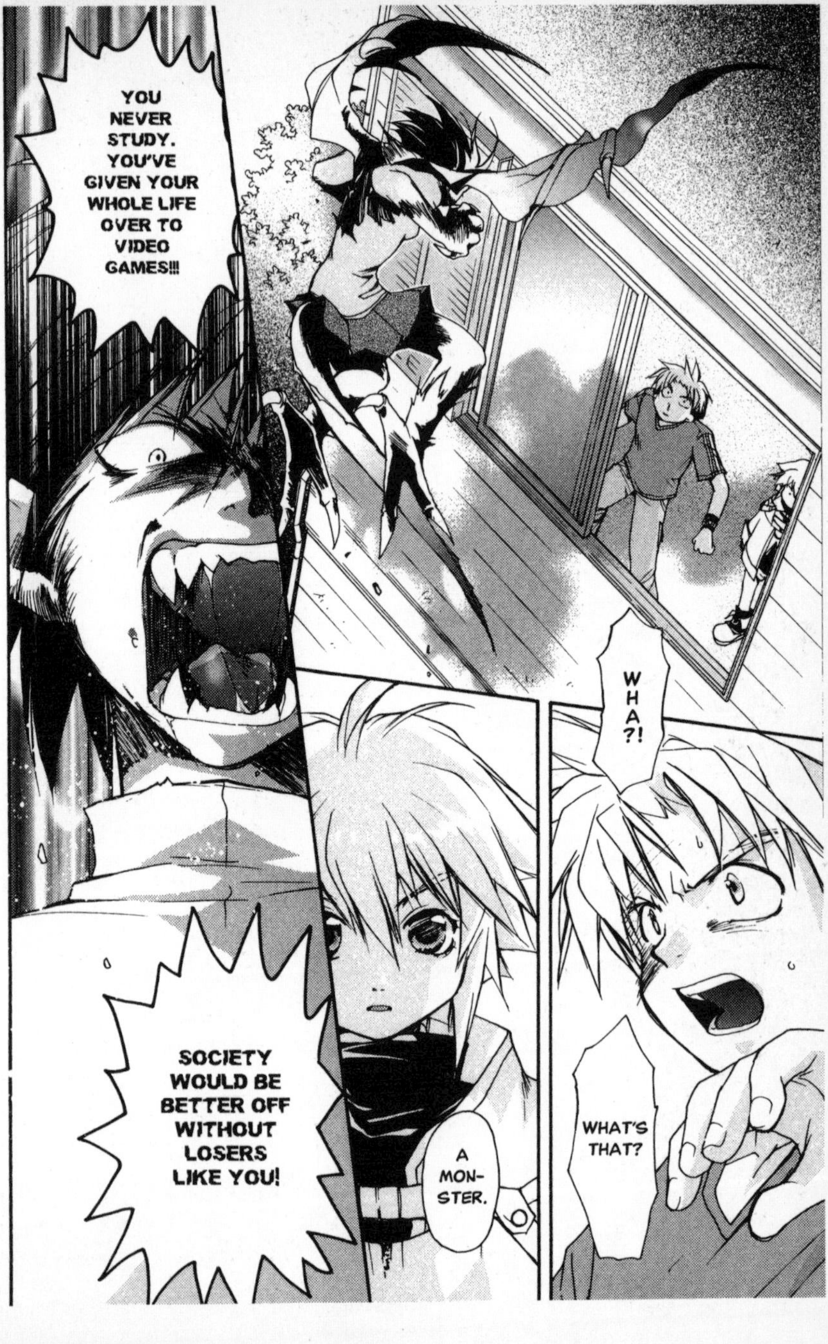
YOU NEVER STUDY. YOU'VE GIVEN YOUR WHOLE LIFE OVER TO VIDEO GAMES!!!
WHA?!
SOCIETY WOULD BE BETTER OFF WITHOUT LOSERS LIKE YOU!
WHAT'S THAT?
A MON-STER.

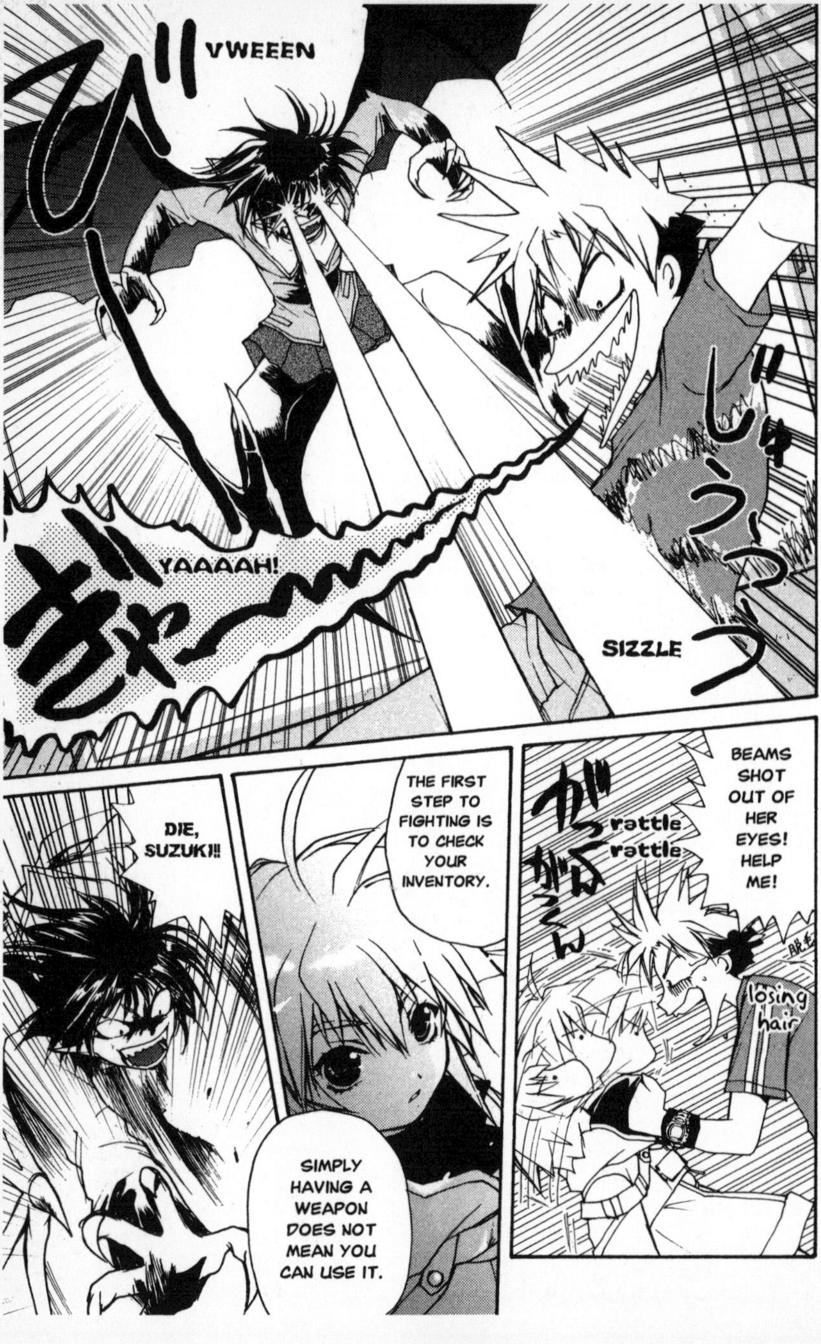
VWEEEN
YAAAAH!
SIZZLE
BEAMS SHOT OUT OF HER EYES! HELP ME!
rattle rattle
losing hair
THE FIRST STEP TO FIGHTING IS TO CHECK YOUR INVENTORY.
SIMPLY HAVING A WEAPON DOES NOT MEAN YOU CAN USE IT.
DIE, SUZUKI!!

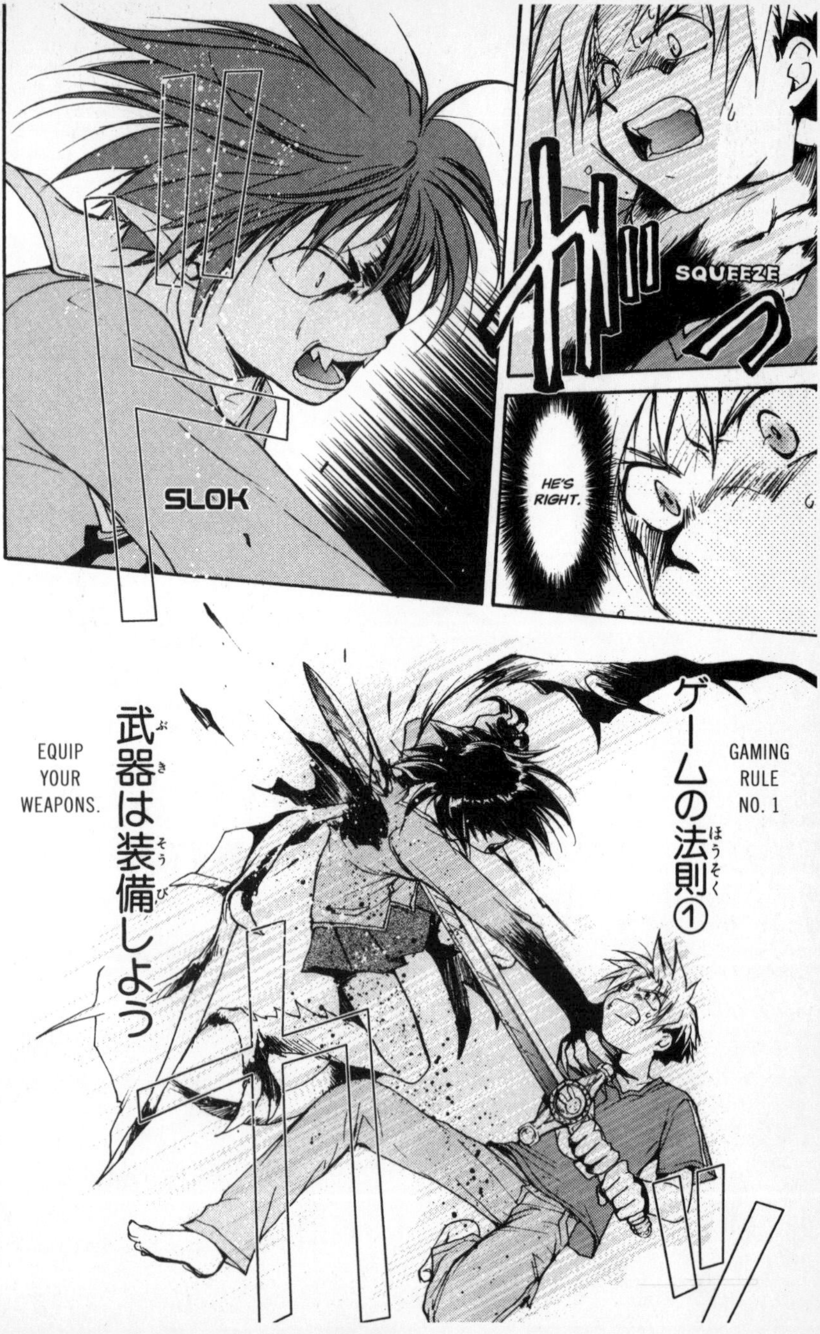
SQUEEZE
SLOK
HE'S RIGHT.
ゲームの法則①
GAMING RULE NO. 1
武器は装備しよう
EQUIP YOUR WEAPONS.

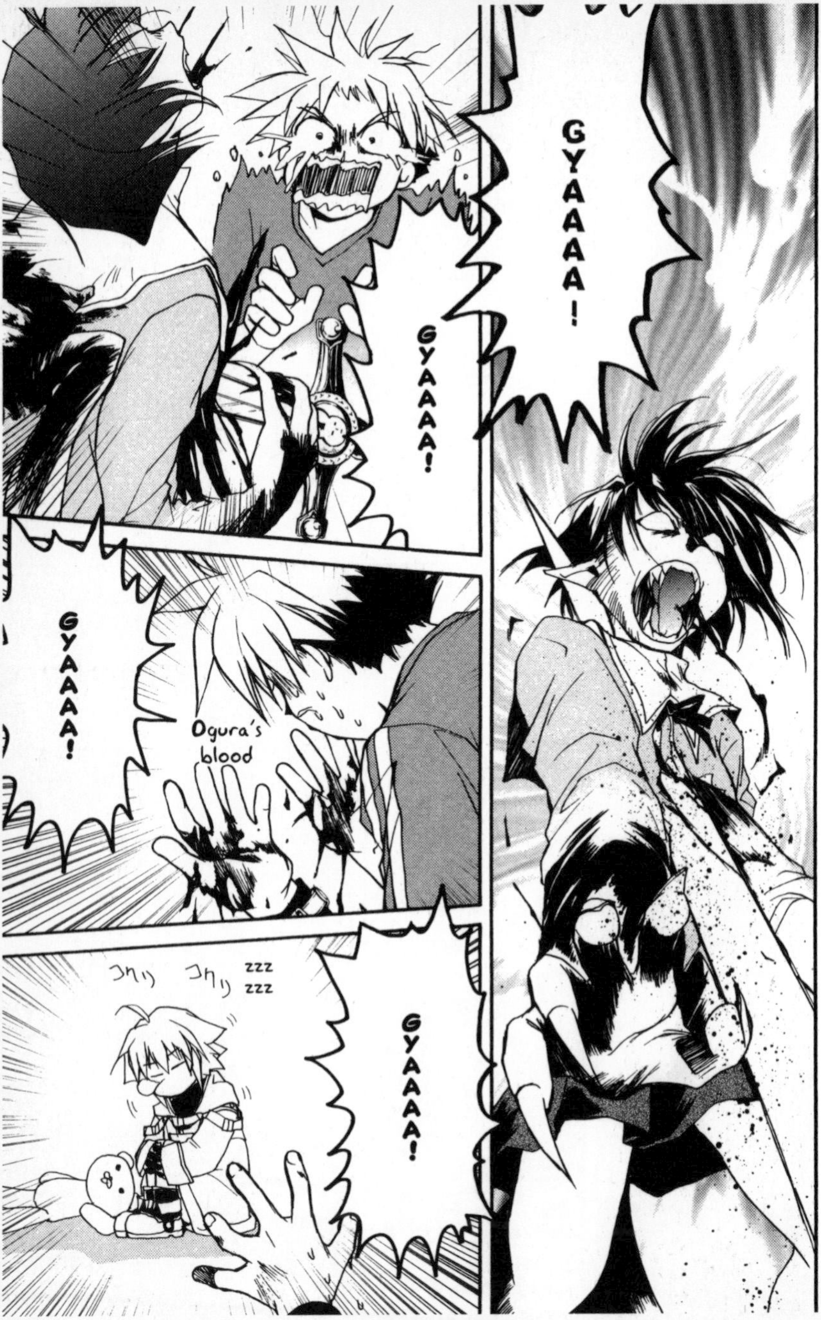
GYAAAAA!
GYAAAA!
GYAAAAA!
Ogura's blood
GYAAAAA!
zzz
zzz

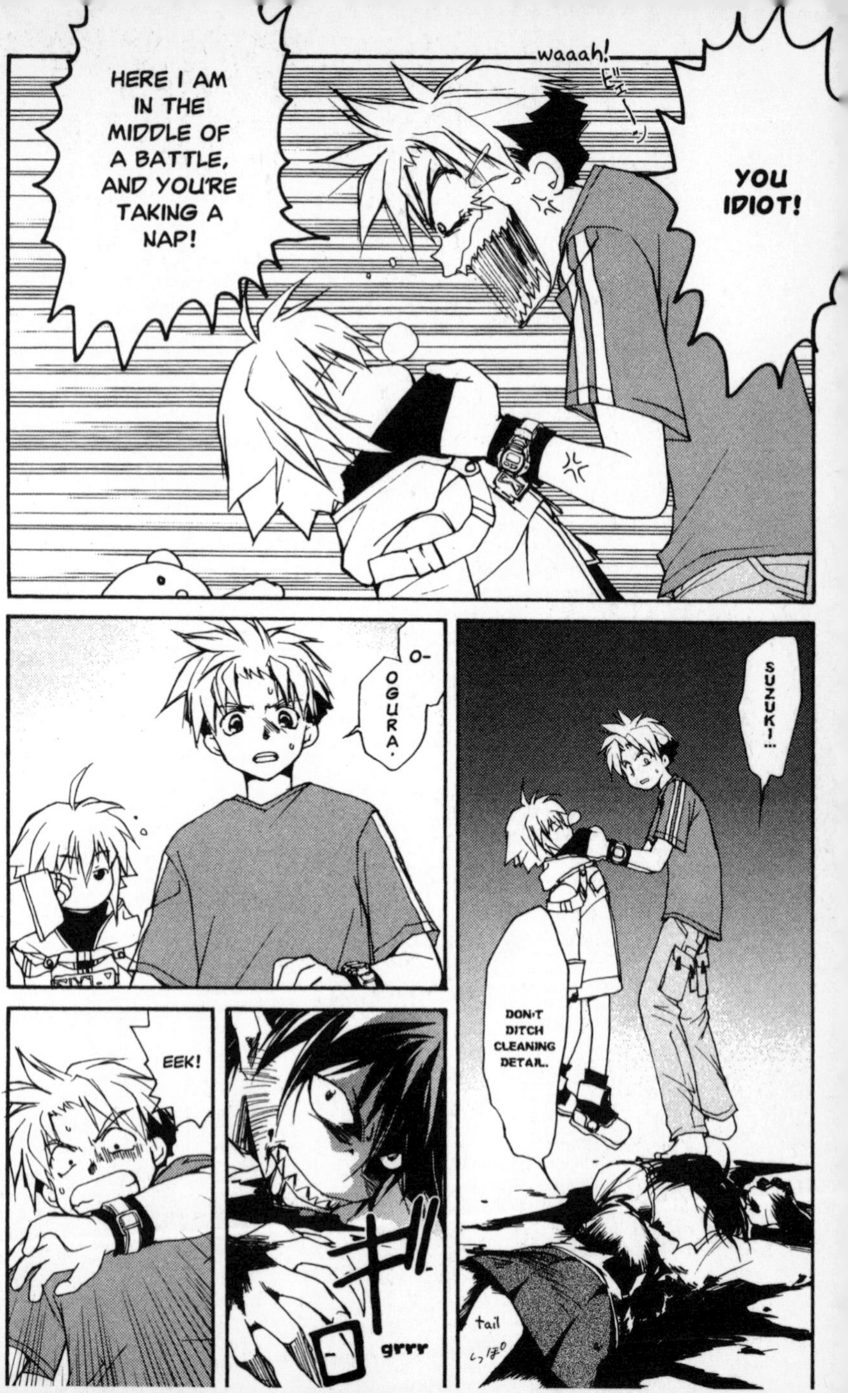
waaah!
YOU IDIOT!
HERE I AM IN THE MIDDLE OF A BATTLE, AND YOU'RE TAKING A NAP!
SUZUKI!!
DON'T DITCH CLEANING DETAIL.
tail
O-OGURA.
grrr
EEK!

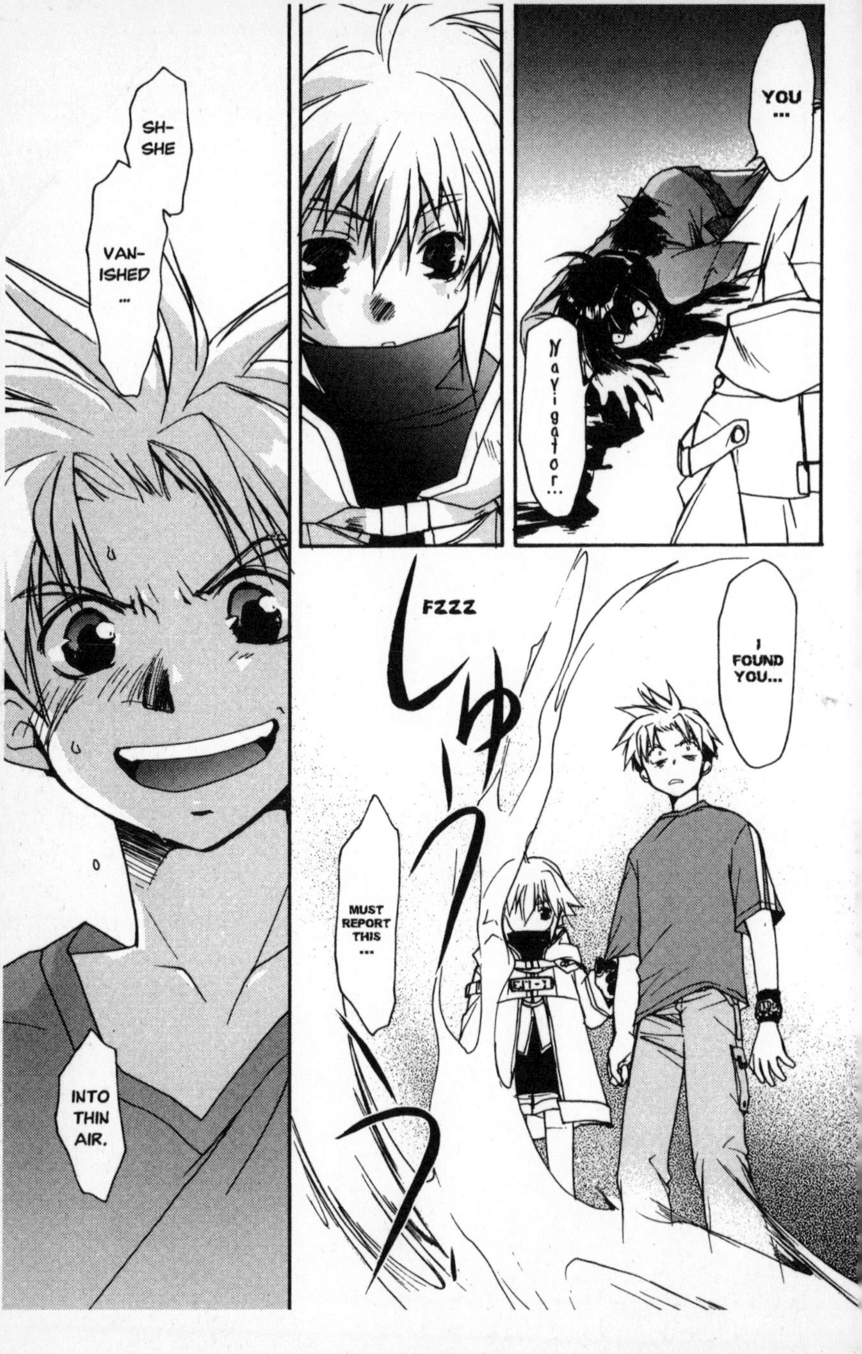
YOU ...
Navigator...
FZZZ
I FOUND YOU...
MUST REPORT THIS ...
SH- SHE VAN- ISHED ...
INTO THIN AIR.

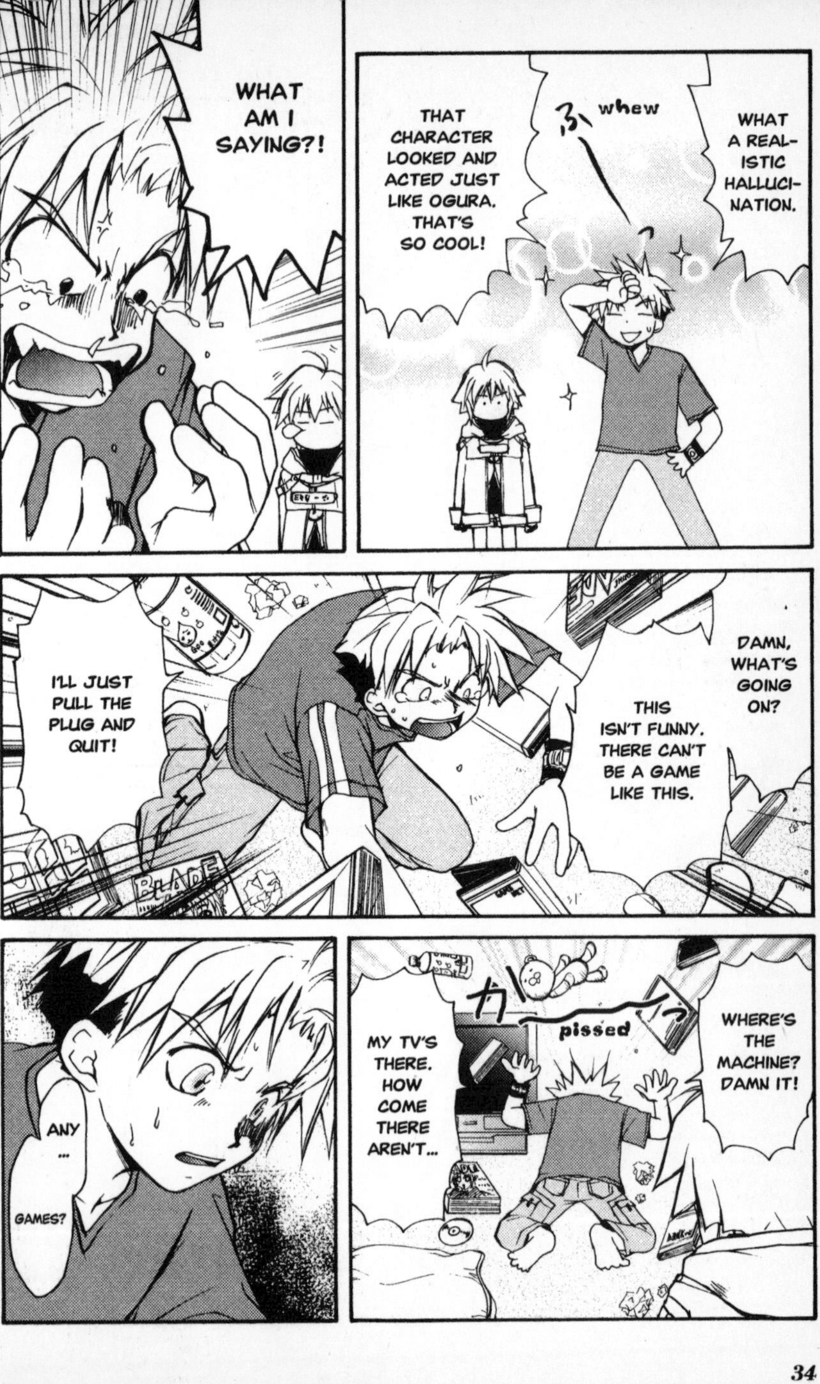
WHAT A REAL-ISTIC HALLUCI-NATION.
whew
THAT CHARACTER LOOKED AND ACTED JUST LIKE OGURA. THAT'S SO COOL!
WHAT AM I SAYING?!
DAMN, WHAT'S GOING ON?
THIS ISN'T FUNNY. THERE CAN'T BE A GAME LIKE THIS.
I'LL JUST PULL THE PLUG AND QUIT!
WHERE'S THE MACHINE? DAMN IT!
pissed
MY TV'S THERE. HOW COME THERE AREN'T...
ANY ...
GAMES?

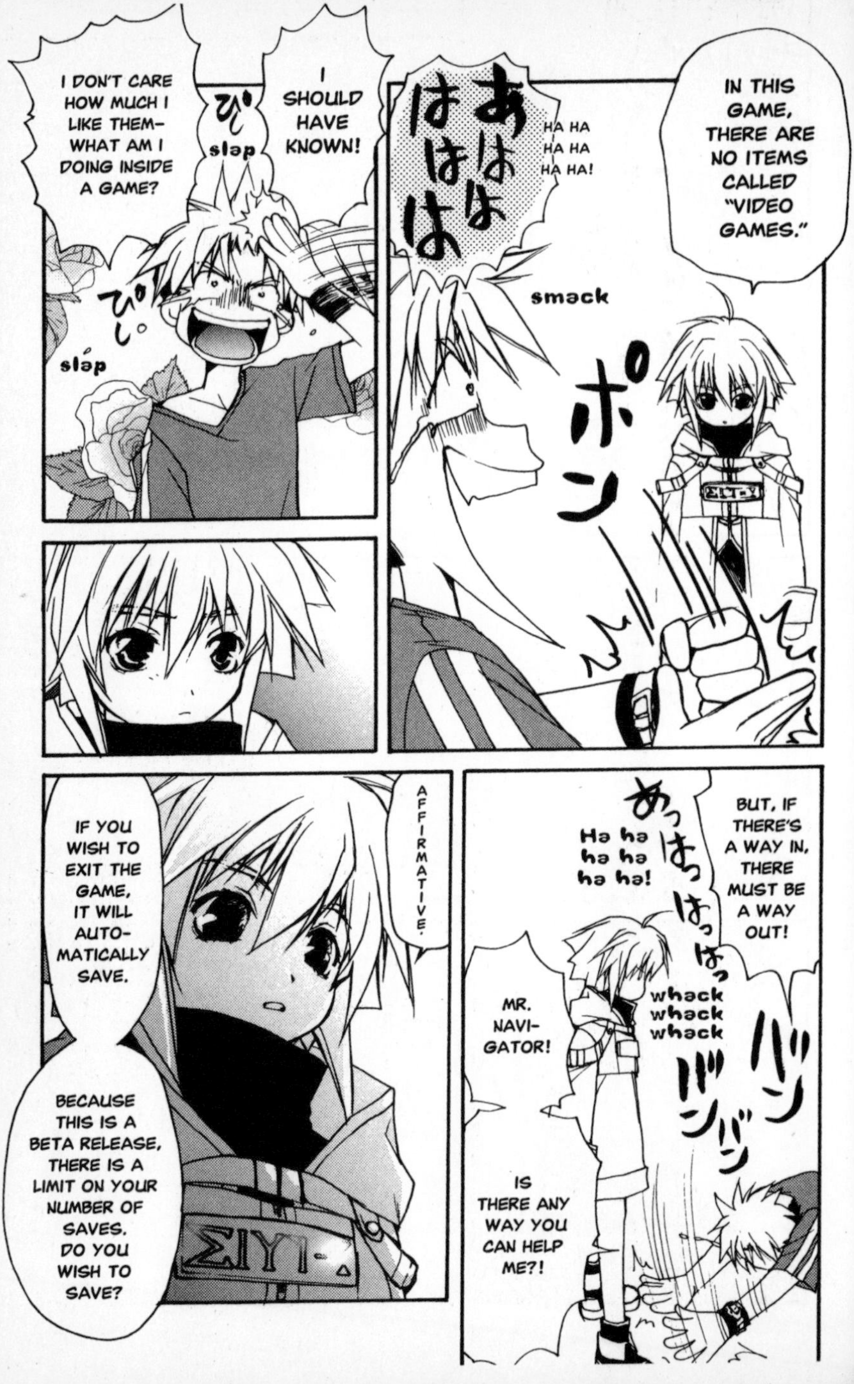
IN THIS GAME, THERE ARE NO ITEMS CALLED "VIDEO GAMES."
あははははは
HA HA HA HA HA HA!
smack
ポン
I SHOULD HAVE KNOWN!
ぴし
slap
I DON'T CARE HOW MUCH I LIKE THEM- WHAT AM I DOING INSIDE A GAME?
ぴし
slap
BUT, IF THERE'S A WAY IN, THERE MUST BE A WAY OUT!
あっはっはっはっ
Ha ha ha ha ha ha!
whack whack whack
MR. NAVI-GATOR!
IS THERE ANY WAY YOU CAN HELP ME?!
AFFIRMATIVE.
IF YOU WISH TO EXIT THE GAME, IT WILL AUTO-MATICALLY SAVE.
BECAUSE THIS IS A BETA RELEASE, THERE IS A LIMIT ON YOUR NUMBER OF SAVES. DO YOU WISH TO SAVE?

I JUST WANNA GO HOME!
waah
エーン
waah
エーン
waah
エーン
WHAT AM I SAYING? THIS IS MY HOME.
......
I WILL SAVE THE GAME AND TRANSFER YOU TO THE SECOND ZONE.
PLEASE WAIT.
HUH?
"SECOND ZONE"?
beep
rmb

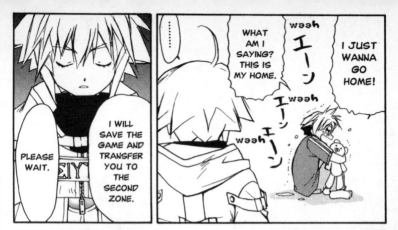

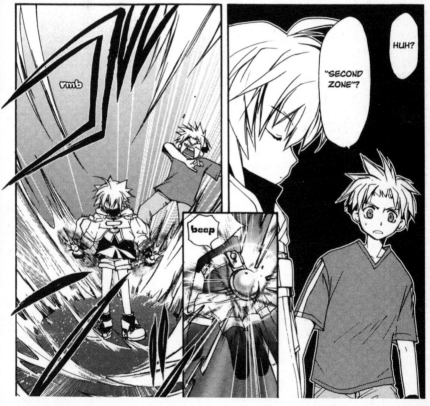

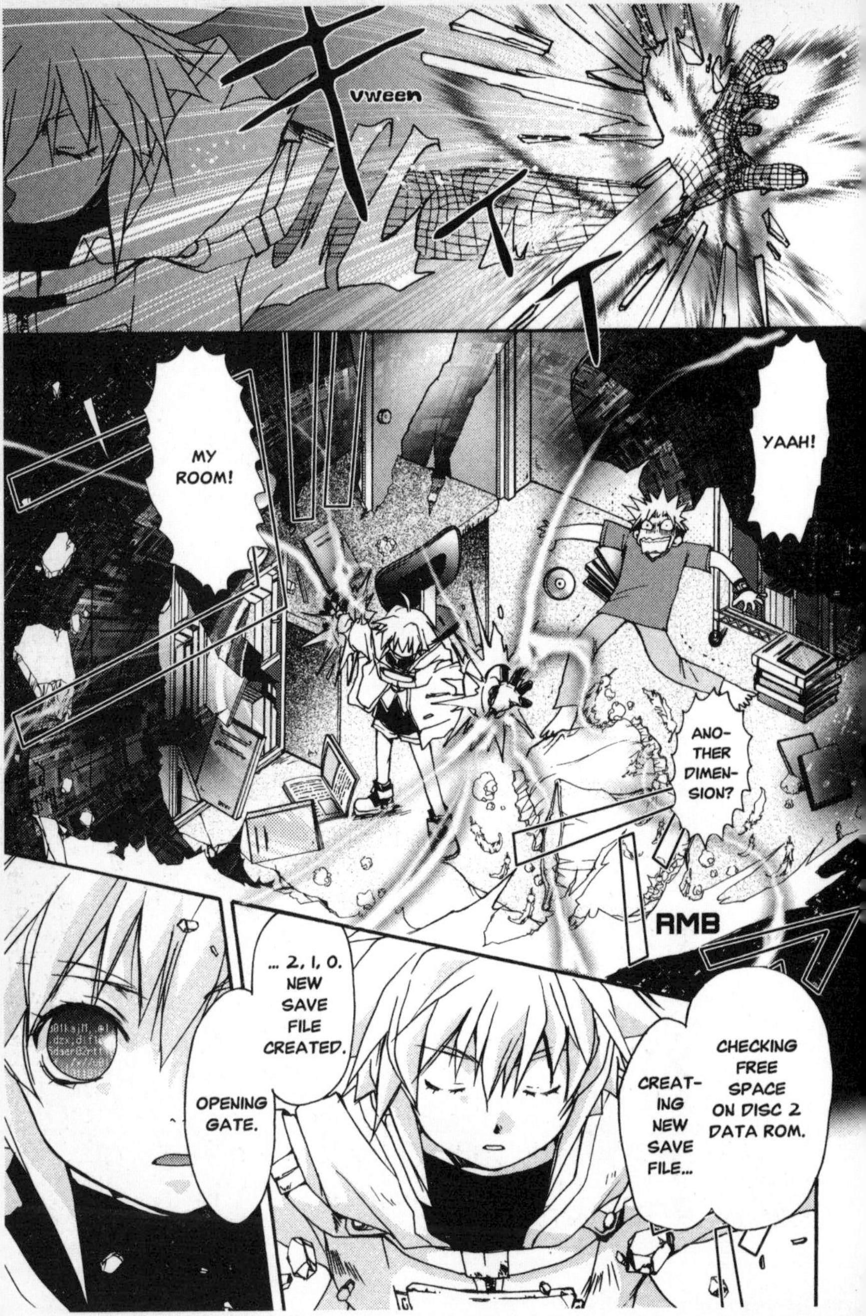
vween
YAAH!
MY ROOM!
ANOTHER DIMENSION?
RMB
CHECKING FREE SPACE ON DISC 2 DATA ROM.
CREATING NEW SAVE FILE...
... 2, 1, 0. NEW SAVE FILE CREATED.
OPENING GATE.

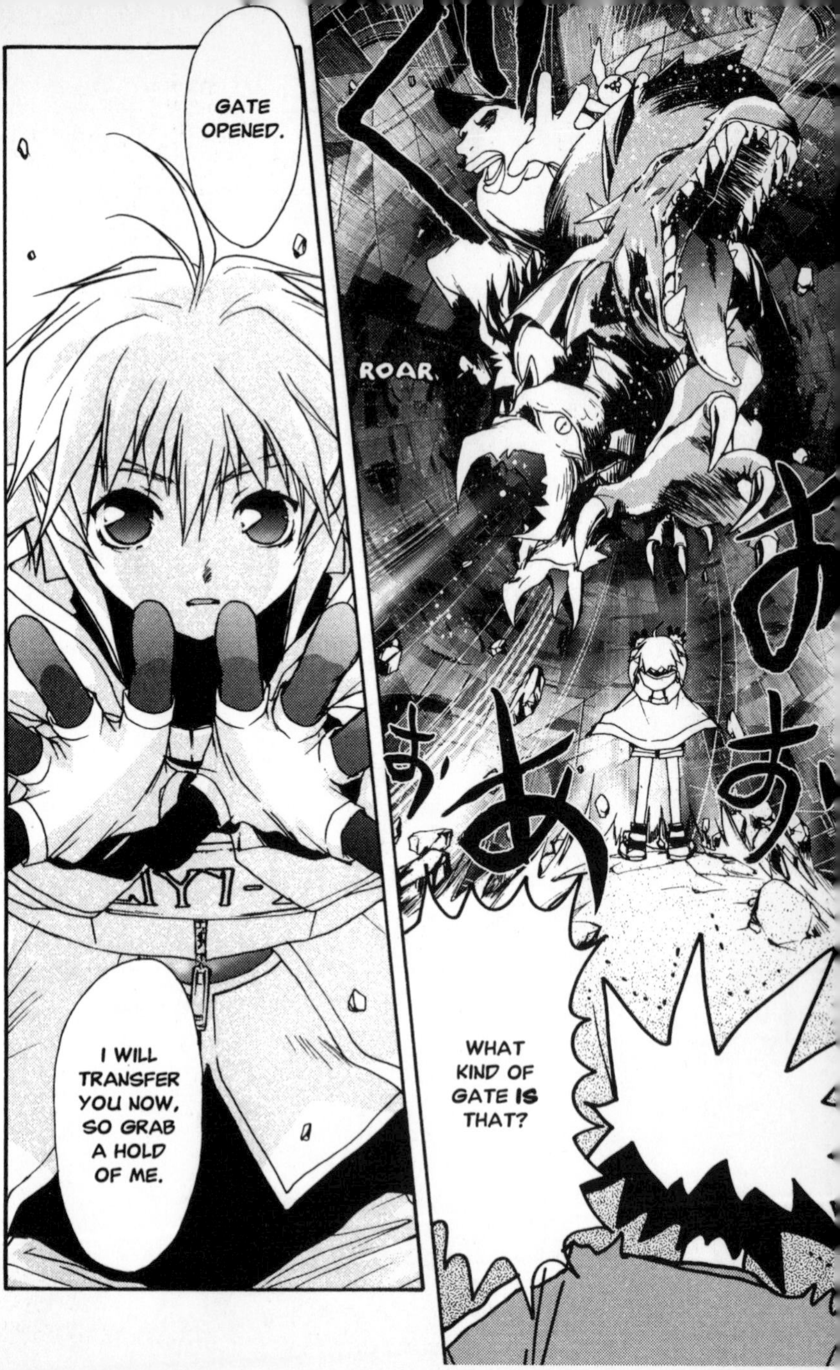
ROAR.
WHAT KIND OF GATE IS THAT?
GATE OPENED.
I WILL TRANSFER YOU NOW, SO GRAB A HOLD OF ME.

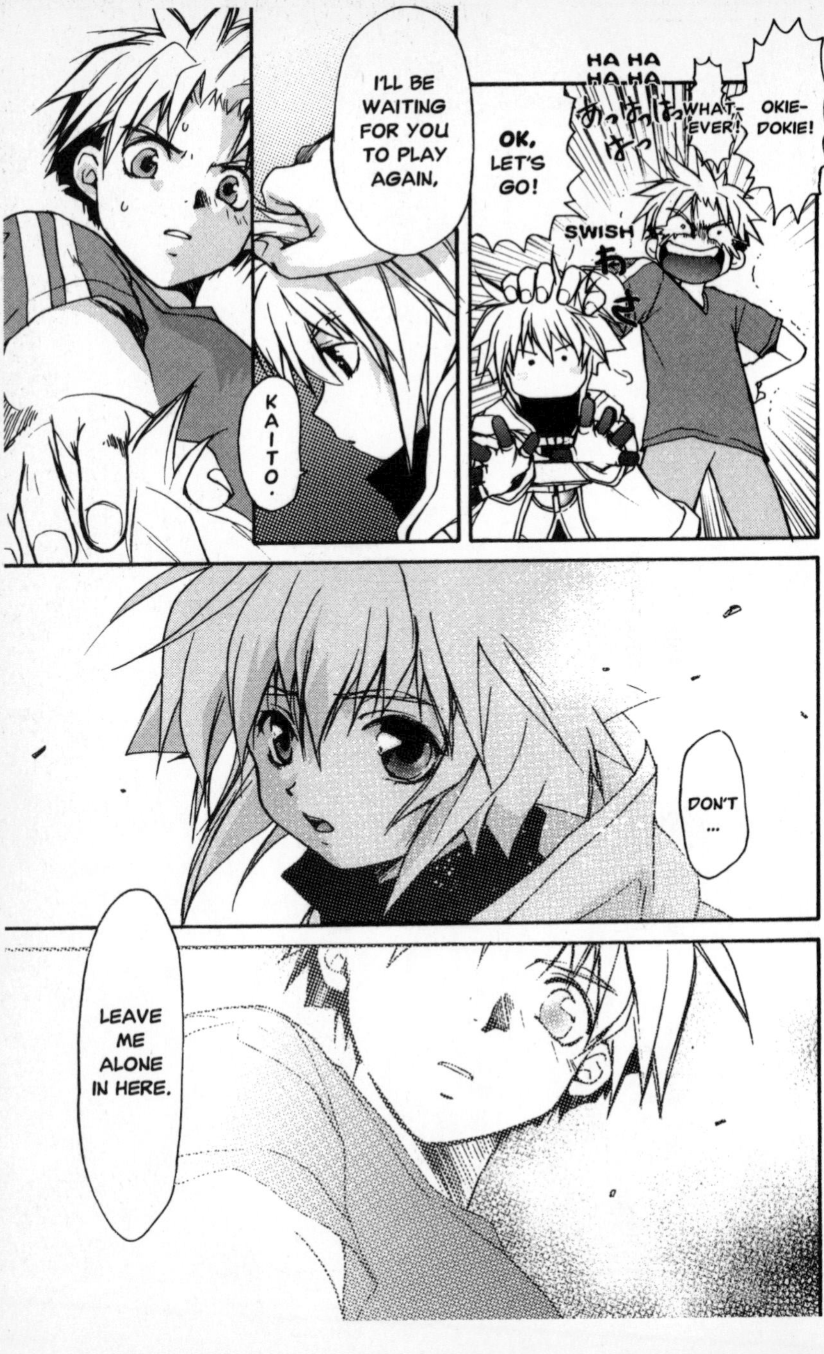
OKIE-DOKIE!
WHAT-EVER!
HA HA HA HA
あっはっはっはっ
SWISH
わさ
OK, LET'S GO!
I'LL BE WAITING FOR YOU TO PLAY AGAIN,
KAITO.
DON'T ...
LEAVE ME ALONE IN HERE.

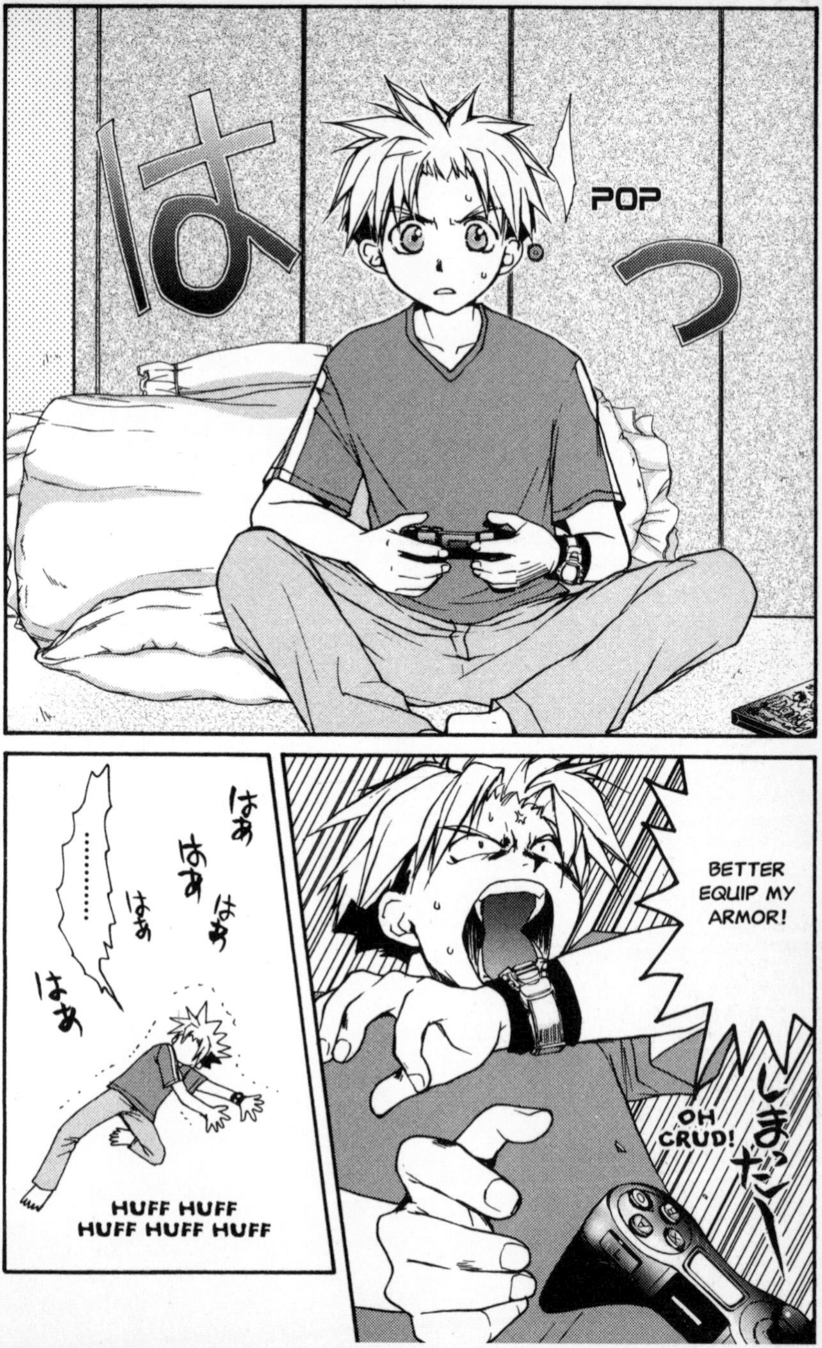
はっ
POP
BETTER EQUIP MY ARMOR!
OH CRUD!
はあ
はあ
はあ
はあ
はあ
HUFF HUFF HUFF HUFF HUFF

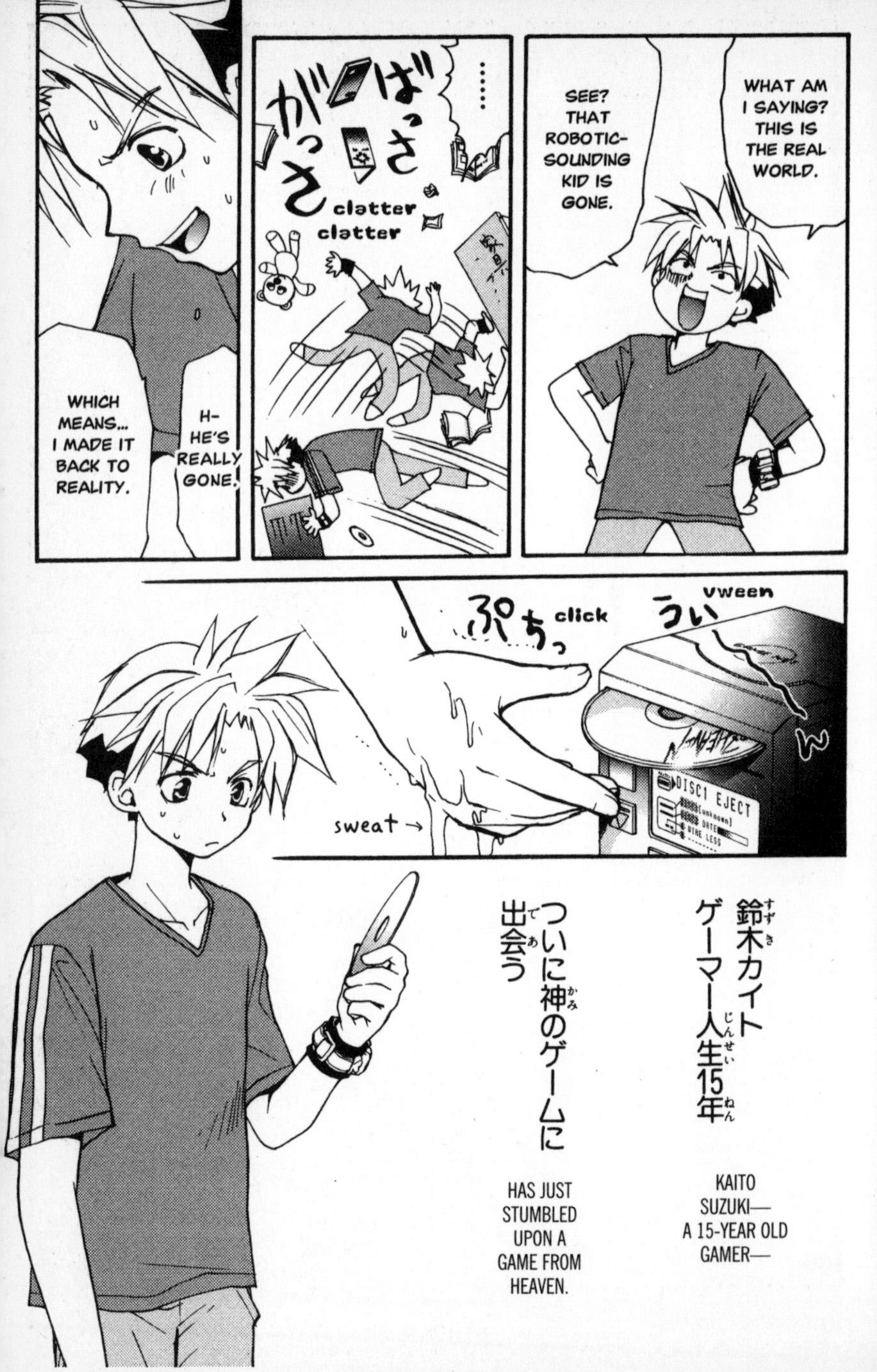
WHAT AM I SAYING? THIS IS THE REAL WORLD.
SEE? THAT ROBOTIC-SOUNDING KID IS GONE.
……
がっさ ばっさ
clatter clatter
H-HE'S REALLY GONE.
WHICH MEANS... I MADE IT BACK TO REALITY.
ういーん
vween
ぷちっ
click
DISC1 EJECT
sweat →
鈴木カイト ゲーマー人生15年
ついに神のゲームに出会う
KAITO SUZUKI— A 15-YEAR OLD GAMER—
HAS JUST STUMBLED UPON A GAME FROM HEAVEN.

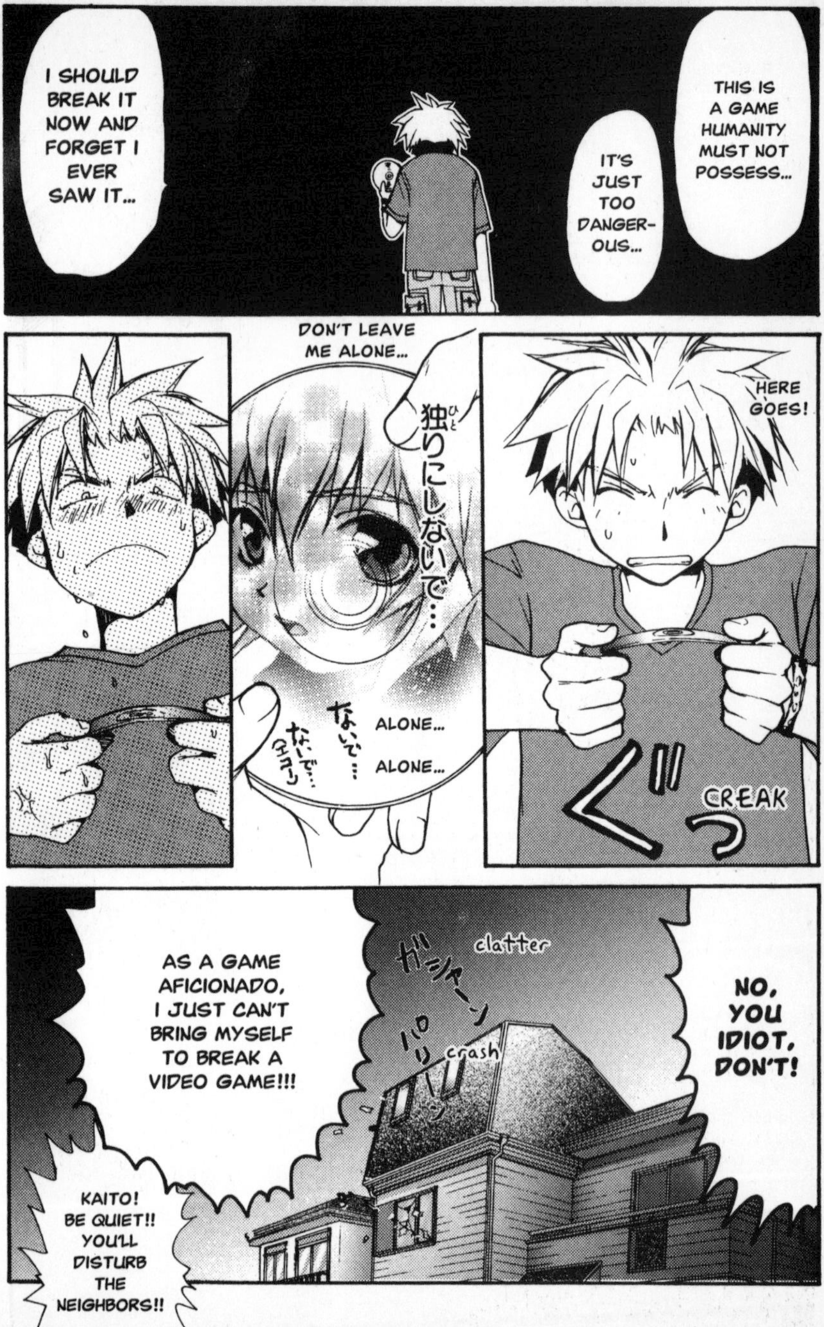
THIS IS A GAME HUMANITY MUST NOT POSSESS...
IT'S JUST TOO DANGER-OUS...
I SHOULD BREAK IT NOW AND FORGET I EVER SAW IT...
HERE GOES!
CREAK
DON'T LEAVE ME ALONE...
独りにしないで…
ないで…
ALONE...
ALONE...
NO, YOU IDIOT, DON'T!
clatter
crash
AS A GAME AFICIONADO, I JUST CAN'T BRING MYSELF TO BREAK A VIDEO GAME!!!
KAITO! BE QUIET!! YOU'LL DISTURB THE NEIGHBORS!!

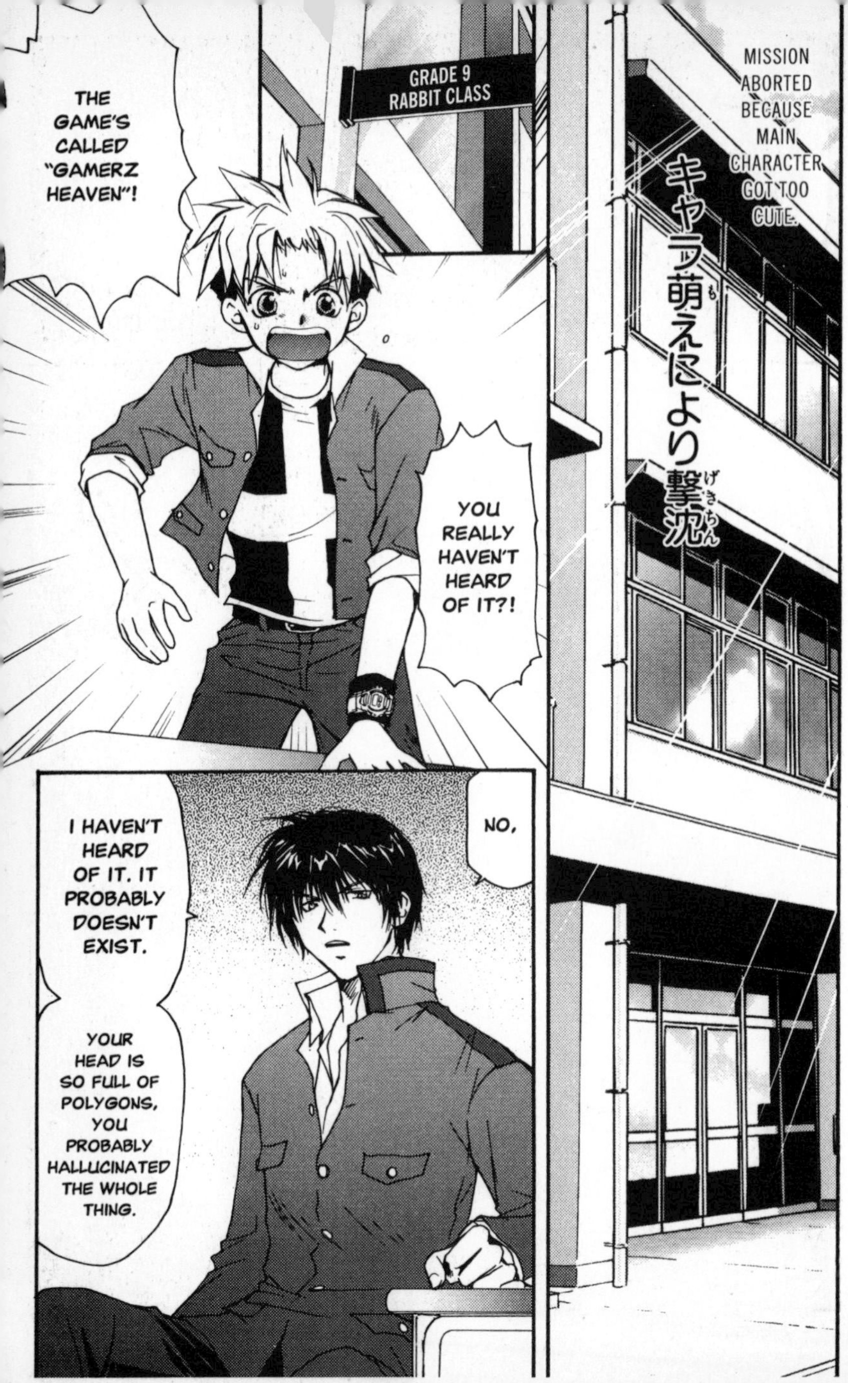

キャラ萌えにより撃沈
MISSION ABORTED BECAUSE MAIN CHARACTER GOT TOO CUTE.
GRADE 9 RABBIT CLASS
THE GAME'S CALLED "GAMERZ HEAVEN"!
YOU REALLY HAVEN'T HEARD OF IT?!
NO,
I HAVEN'T HEARD OF IT. IT PROBABLY DOESN'T EXIST.
YOUR HEAD IS SO FULL OF POLYGONS, YOU PROBABLY HALLUCINATED THE WHOLE THING.

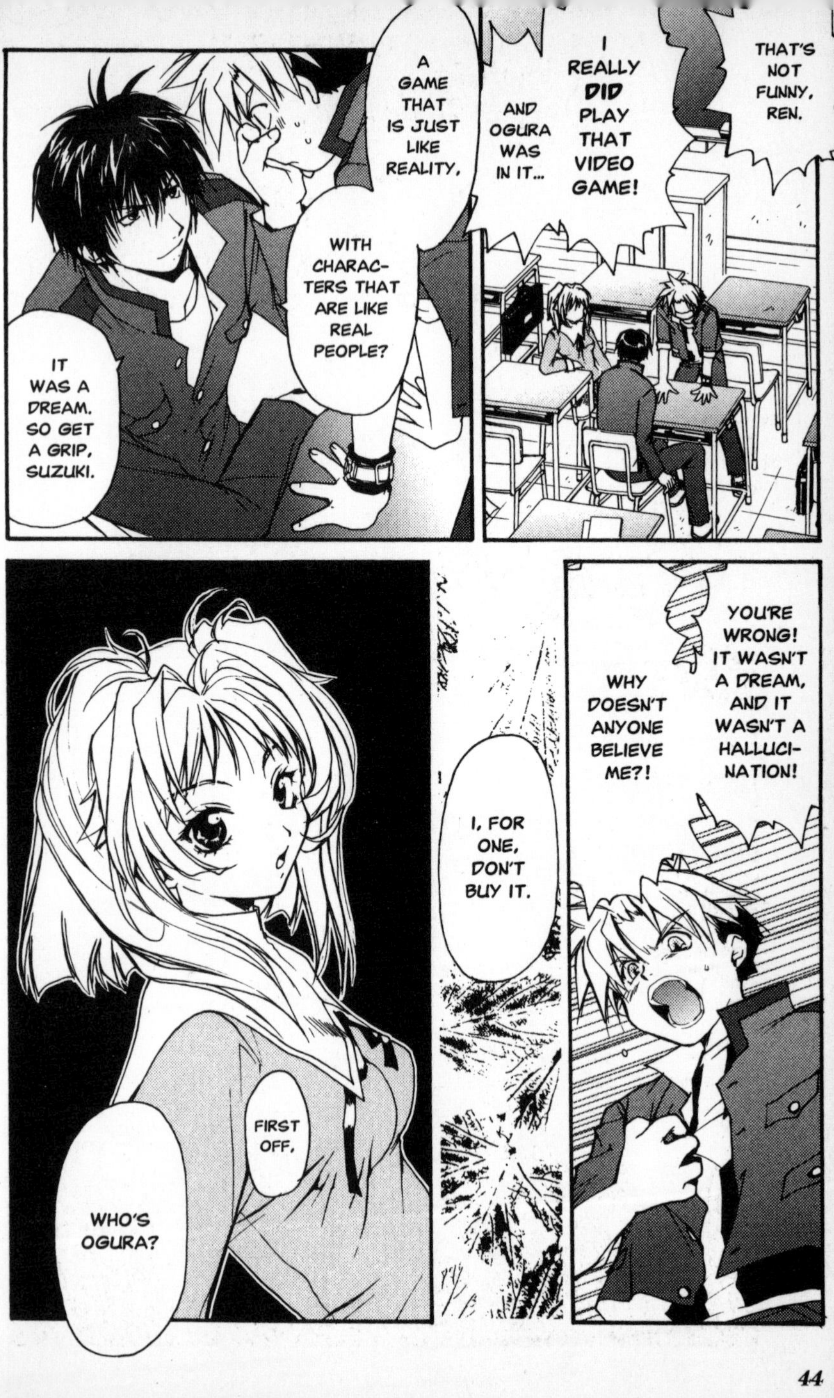
THAT'S NOT FUNNY, REN.
I REALLY DID PLAY THAT VIDEO GAME!
AND OGURA WAS IN IT...
A GAME THAT IS JUST LIKE REALITY,
WITH CHARACTERS THAT ARE LIKE REAL PEOPLE?
IT WAS A DREAM. SO GET A GRIP, SUZUKI.
YOU'RE WRONG! IT WASN'T A DREAM, AND IT WASN'T A HALLUCINATION!
WHY DOESN'T ANYONE BELIEVE ME?!
I, FOR ONE, DON'T BUY IT.
FIRST OFF,
WHO'S OGURA?

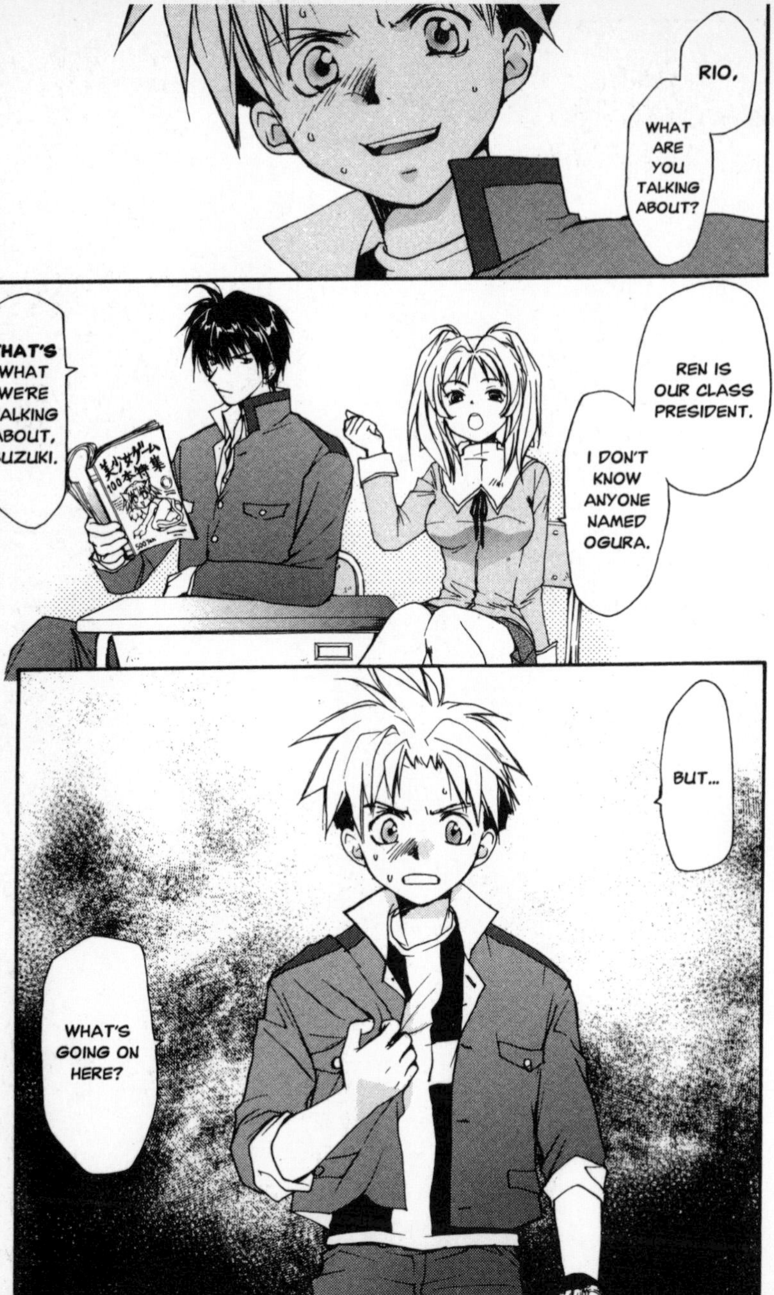
RIO,
WHAT ARE YOU TALKING ABOUT?
REN IS OUR CLASS PRESIDENT.
I DON'T KNOW ANYONE NAMED OGURA.
THAT'S WHAT WE'RE TALKING ABOUT, SUZUKI.
BUT...
WHAT'S GOING ON HERE?

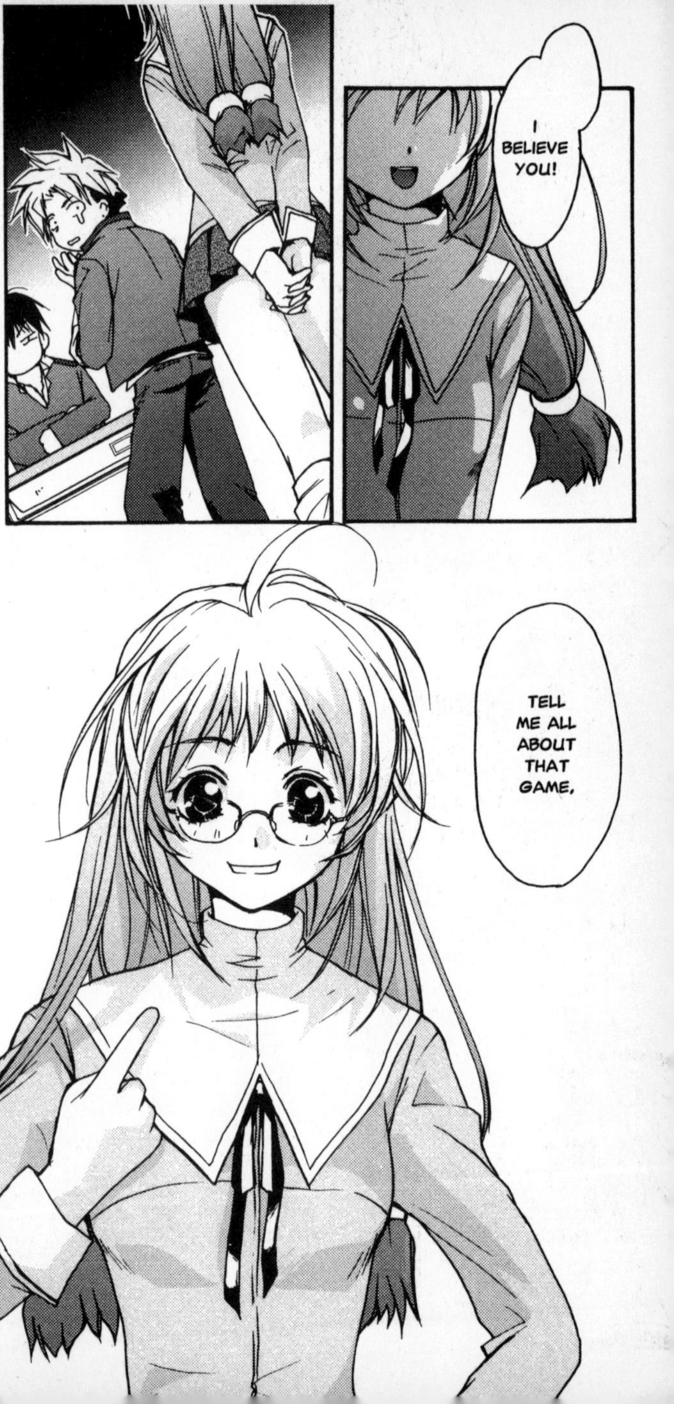
I BELIEVE YOU!
TELL ME ALL ABOUT THAT GAME,
SUZUKI!

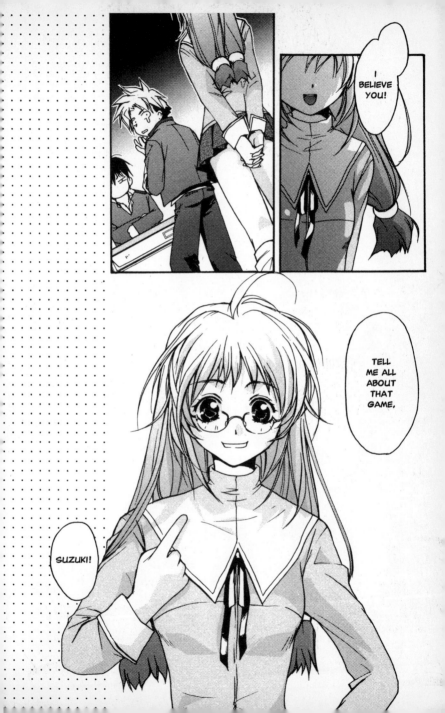

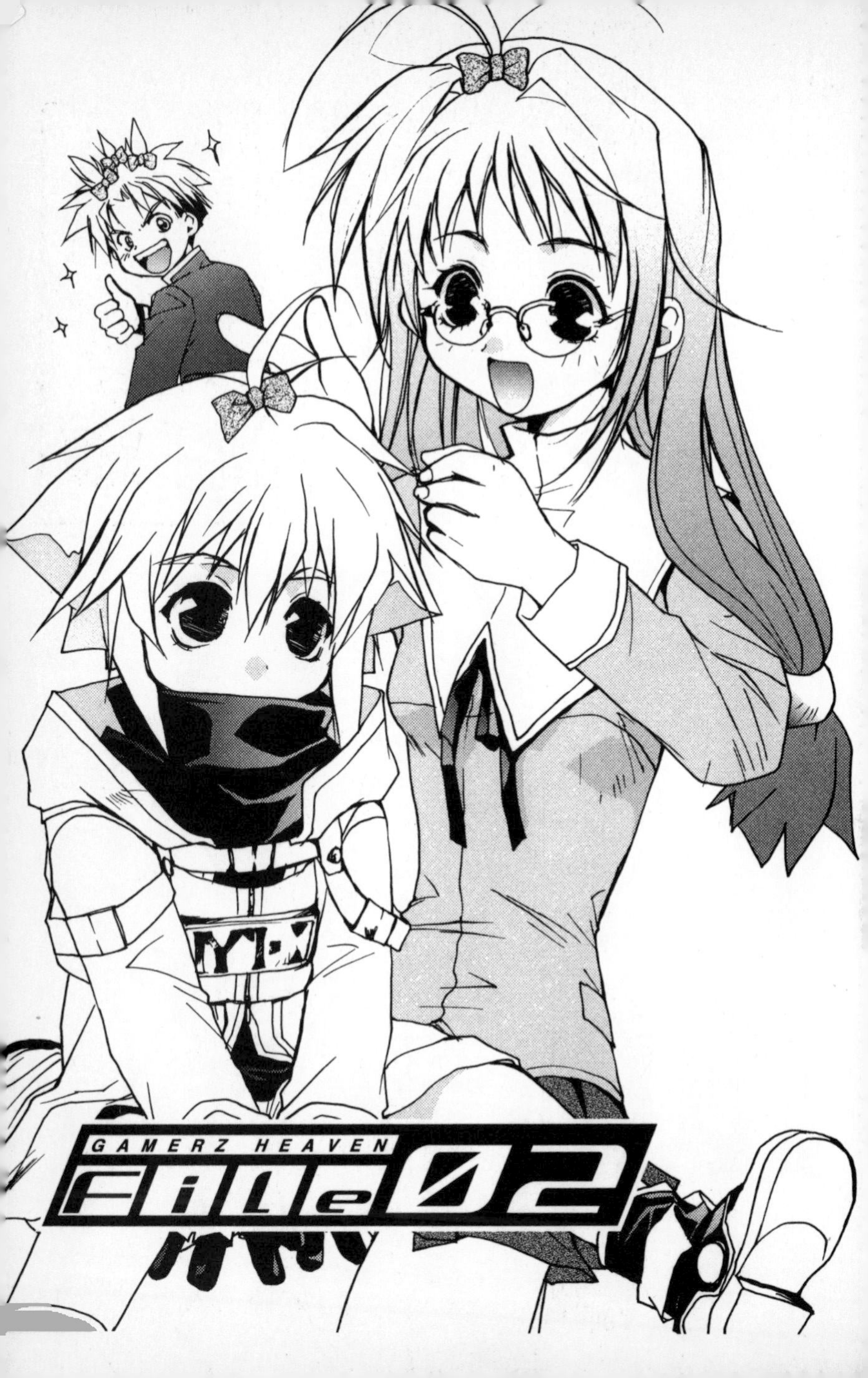
GAMERZ HEAVEN
FiLe 02
Y-X

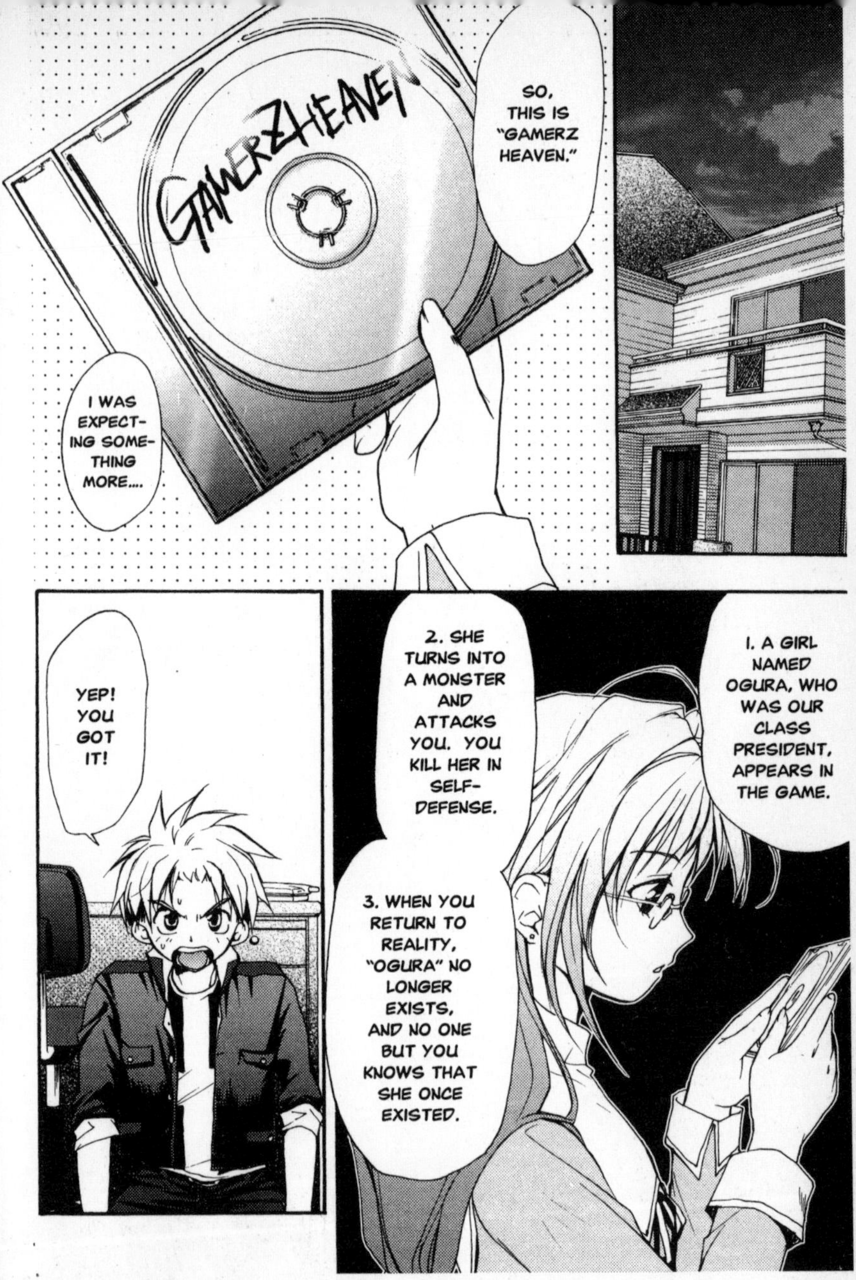
GAMERZ HEAVEN
SO, THIS IS "GAMERZ HEAVEN."
I WAS EXPECTING SOMETHING MORE....
1. A GIRL NAMED OGURA, WHO WAS OUR CLASS PRESIDENT, APPEARS IN THE GAME.
2. SHE TURNS INTO A MONSTER AND ATTACKS YOU. YOU KILL HER IN SELF-DEFENSE.
3. WHEN YOU RETURN TO REALITY, "OGURA" NO LONGER EXISTS, AND NO ONE BUT YOU KNOWS THAT SHE ONCE EXISTED.
YEP! YOU GOT IT!

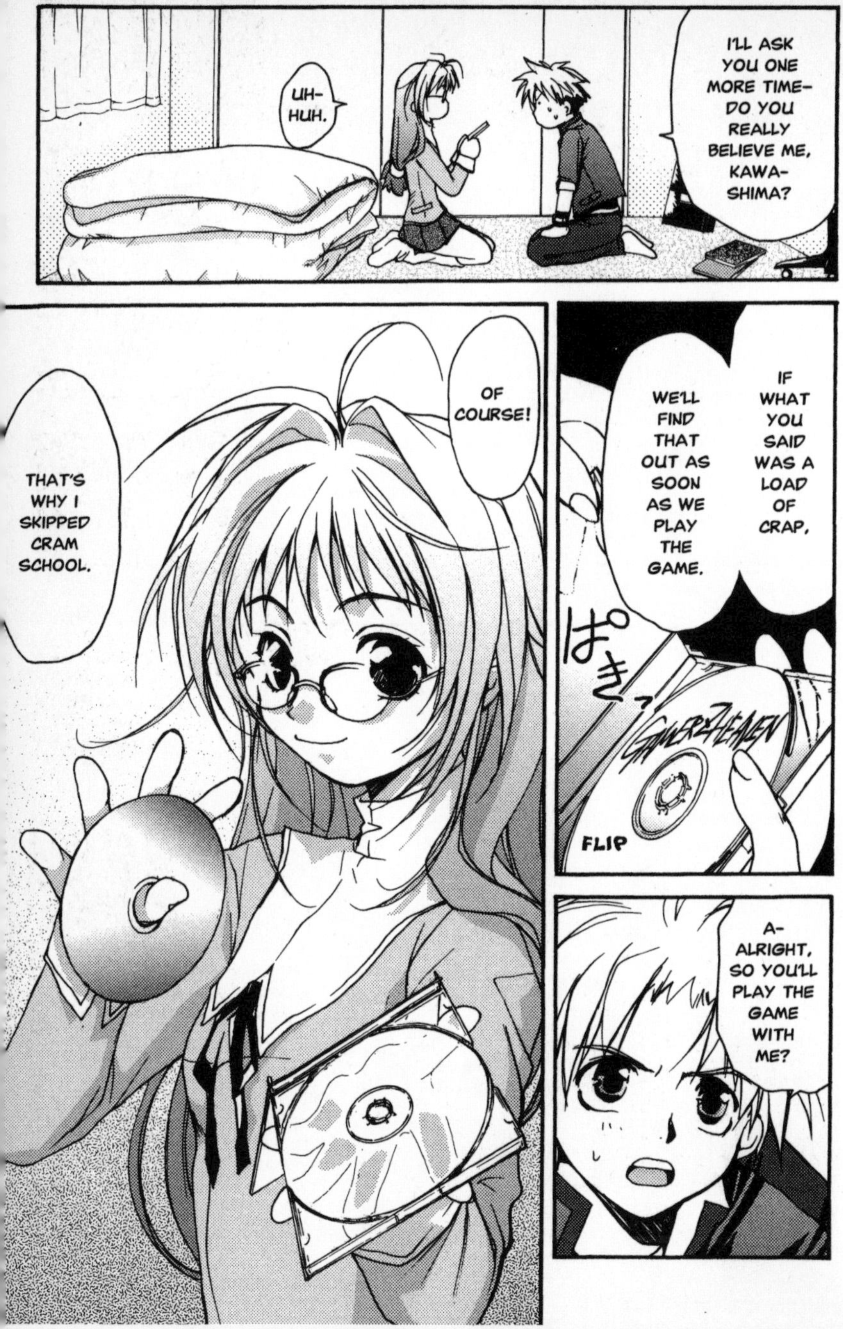
I'LL ASK YOU ONE MORE TIME— DO YOU REALLY BELIEVE ME, KAWA-SHIMA?
UH-HUH.
IF WHAT YOU SAID WAS A LOAD OF CRAP,
WE'LL FIND THAT OUT AS SOON AS WE PLAY THE GAME.
ぱきっ
FLIP
A-ALRIGHT, SO YOU'LL PLAY THE GAME WITH ME?
OF COURSE!
THAT'S WHY I SKIPPED CRAM SCHOOL.

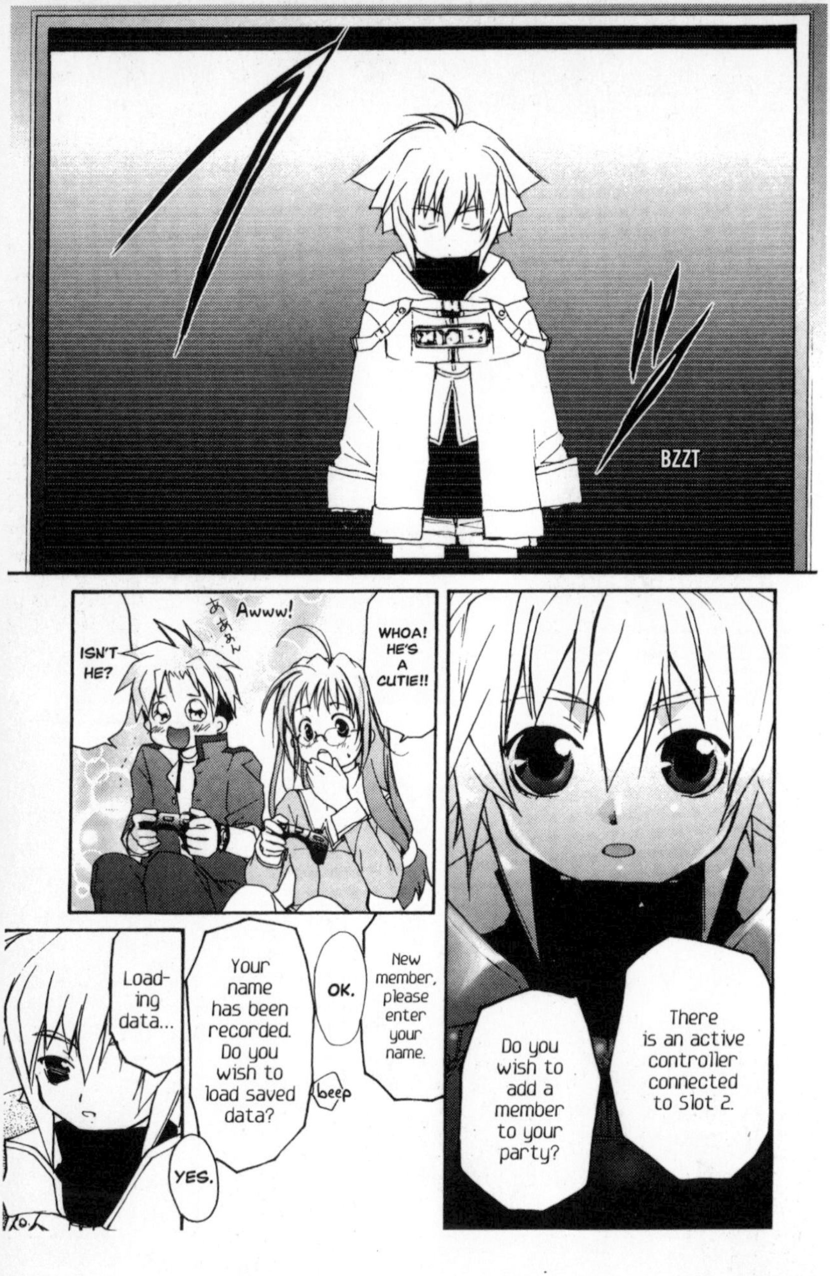
BZZT
There is an active controller connected to Slot 2.
Do you wish to add a member to your party?
WHOA! HE'S A CUTIE!!
Awww!
ISN'T HE?
New member, please enter your name.
OK.
beep
Your name has been recorded. Do you wish to load saved data?
YES.
Loading data...

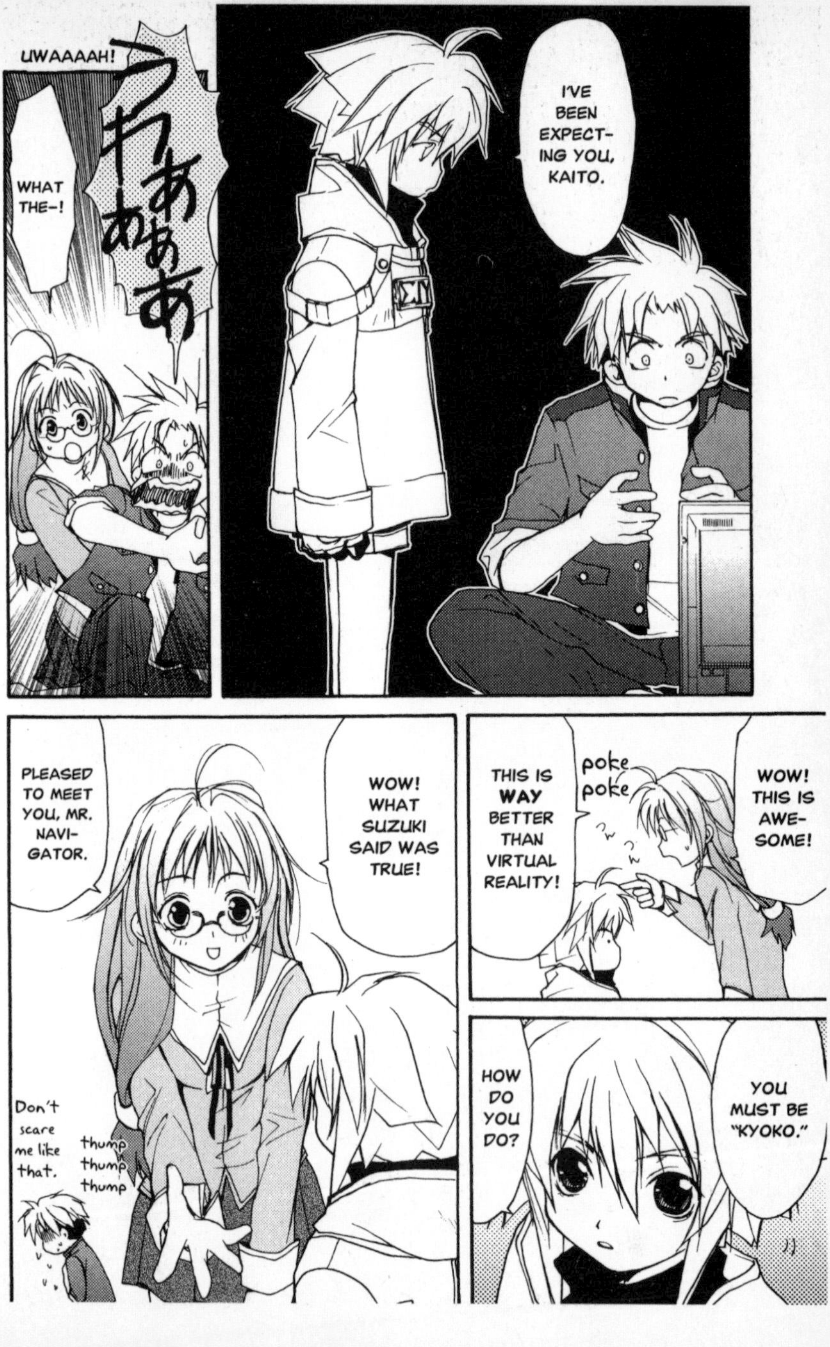
I'VE BEEN EXPECTING YOU, KAITO.
UWAAAAH!
うわああああ
WHAT THE-!
WOW! THIS IS AWE-SOME!
poke poke
THIS IS WAY BETTER THAN VIRTUAL REALITY!
YOU MUST BE "KYOKO."
HOW DO YOU DO?
WOW! WHAT SUZUKI SAID WAS TRUE!
PLEASED TO MEET YOU, MR. NAVI-GATOR.
thump thump thump
Don't scare me like that.

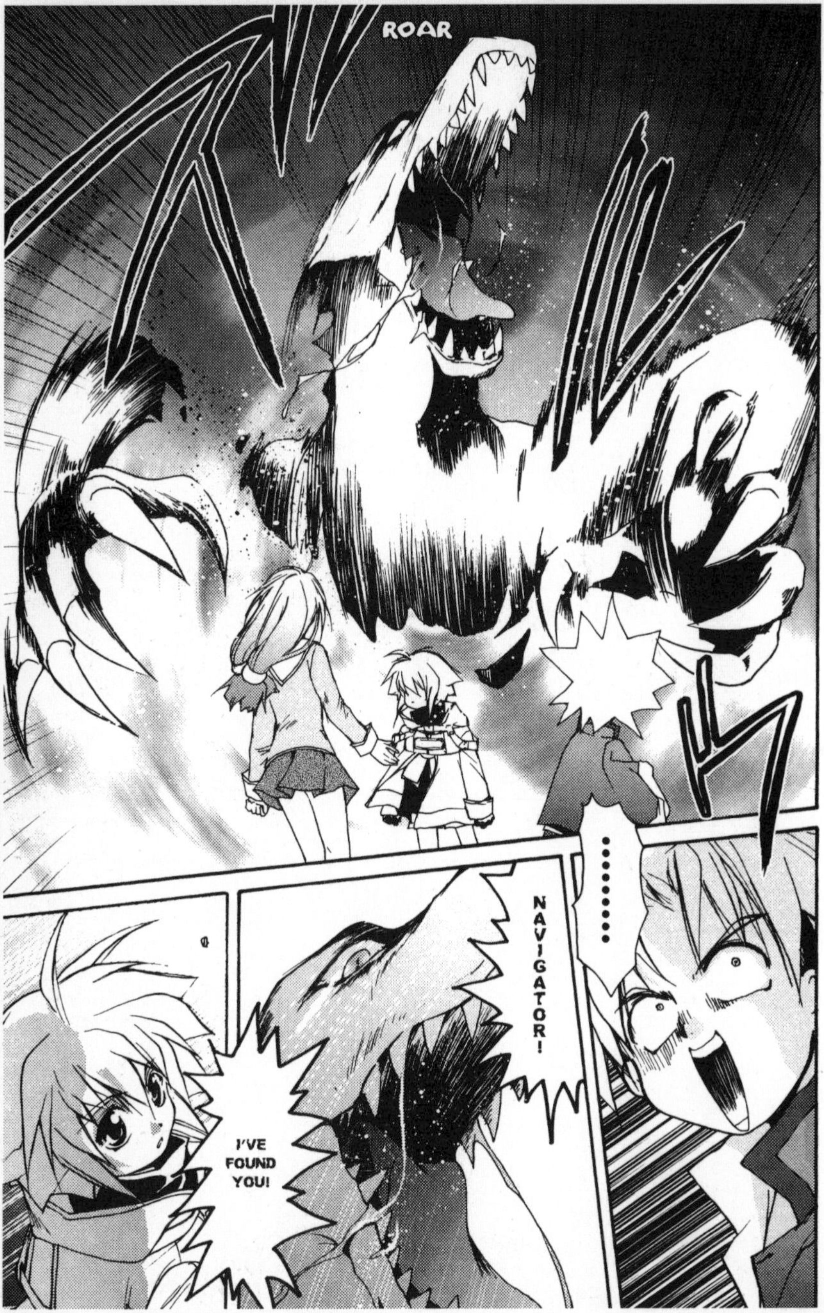
ROAR
....
NAVIGATOR!
I'VE FOUND YOU!

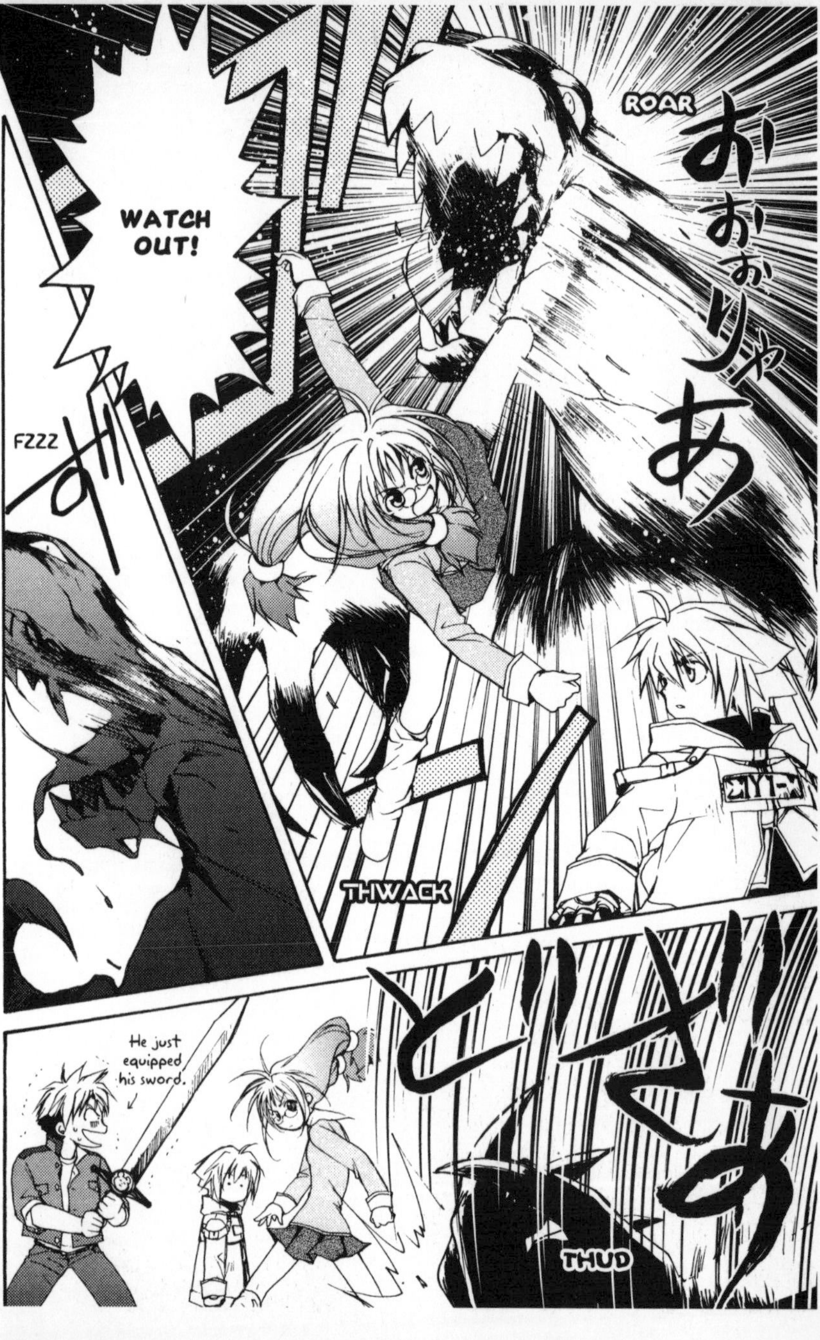
ROAR
WATCH OUT!
FZZZ
THWACK
THUD
He just equipped his sword.

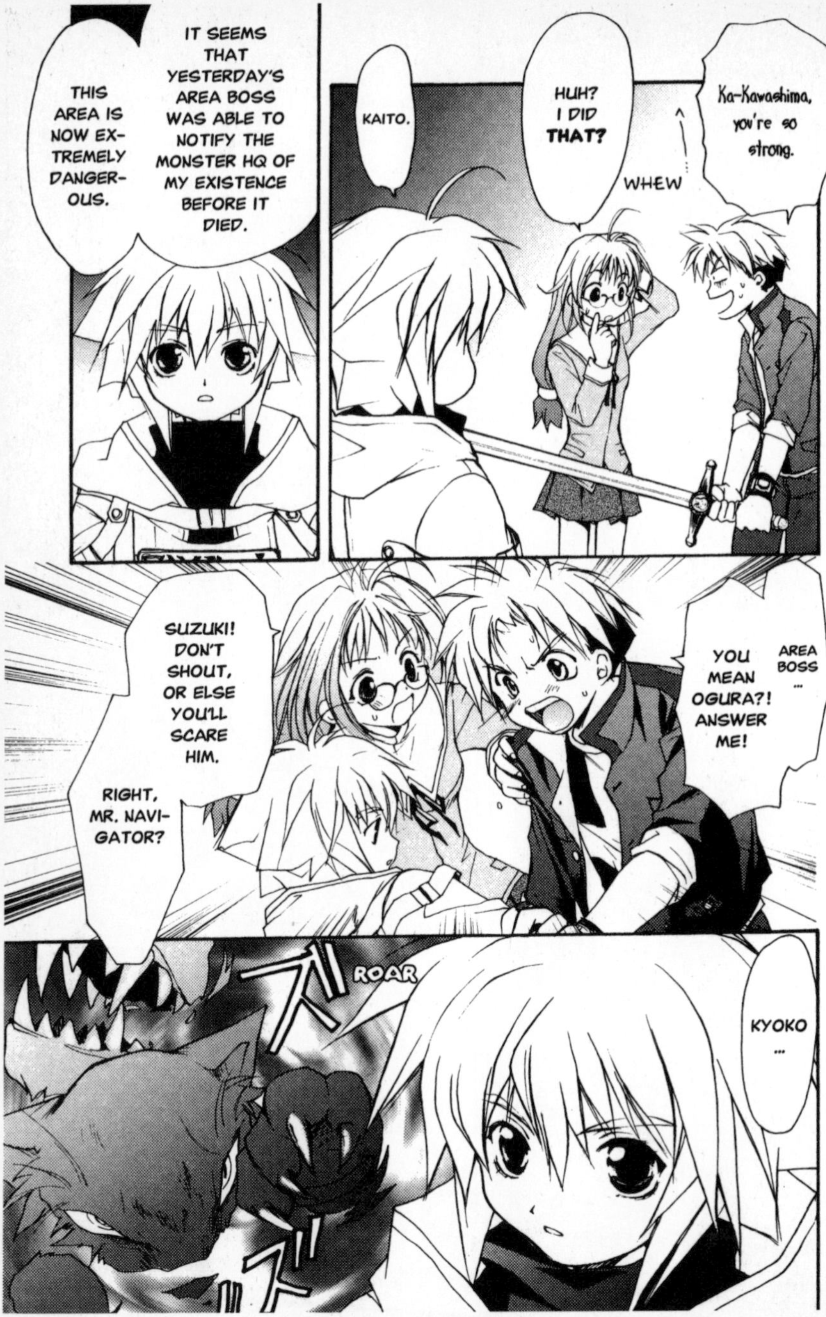
Ka-Kawashima, you're so strong.
WHEW
HUH? I DID THAT?
KAITO.
IT SEEMS THAT YESTERDAY'S AREA BOSS WAS ABLE TO NOTIFY THE MONSTER HQ OF MY EXISTENCE BEFORE IT DIED.
THIS AREA IS NOW EXTREMELY DANGEROUS.
AREA BOSS ...
YOU MEAN OGURA?! ANSWER ME!
SUZUKI! DON'T SHOUT, OR ELSE YOU'LL SCARE HIM.
RIGHT, MR. NAVIGATOR?
KYOKO ...
ROAR

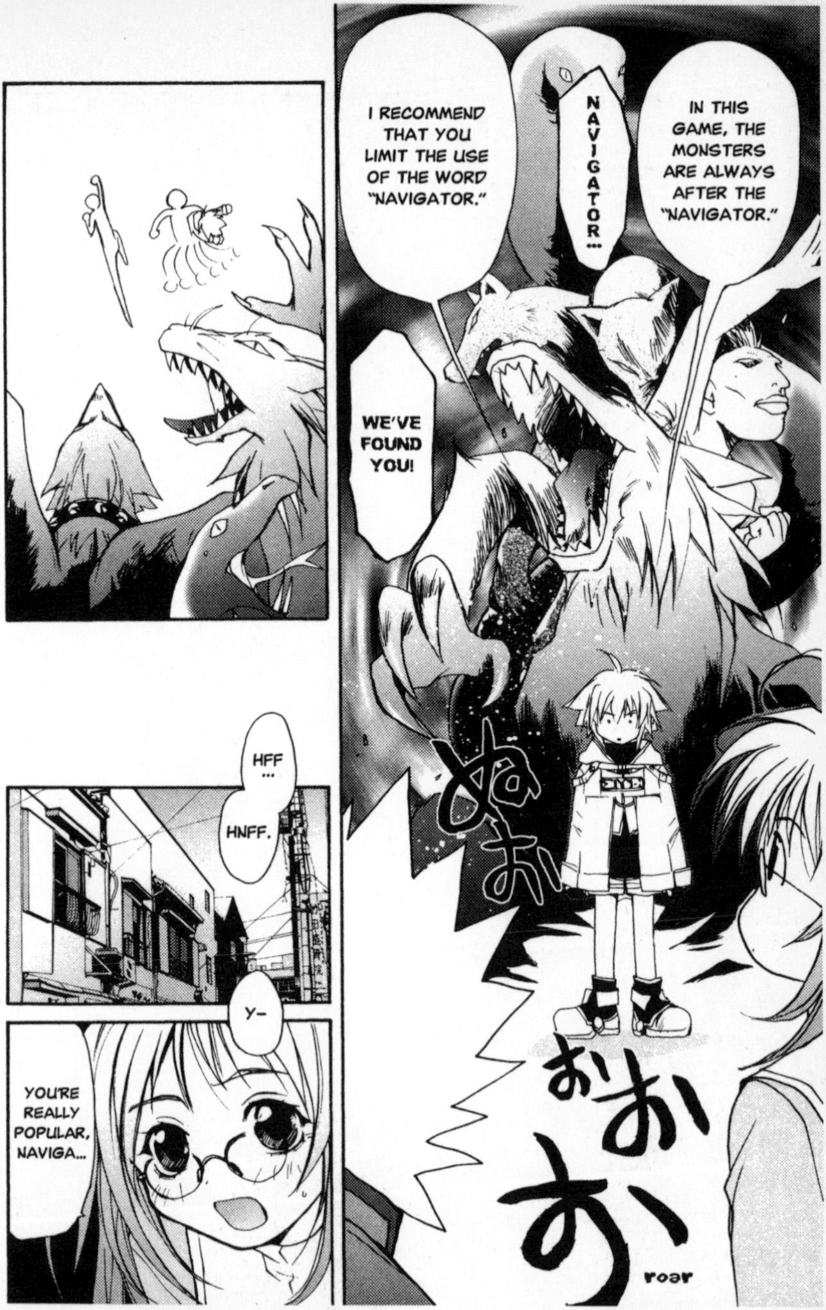
IN THIS GAME, THE MONSTERS ARE ALWAYS AFTER THE "NAVIGATOR."
NAVIGATOR...
I RECOMMEND THAT YOU LIMIT THE USE OF THE WORD "NAVIGATOR."
WE'VE FOUND YOU!
ぬおおおお
roar
HFF...
HNFF.
Y-
YOU'RE REALLY POPULAR, NAVIGA...

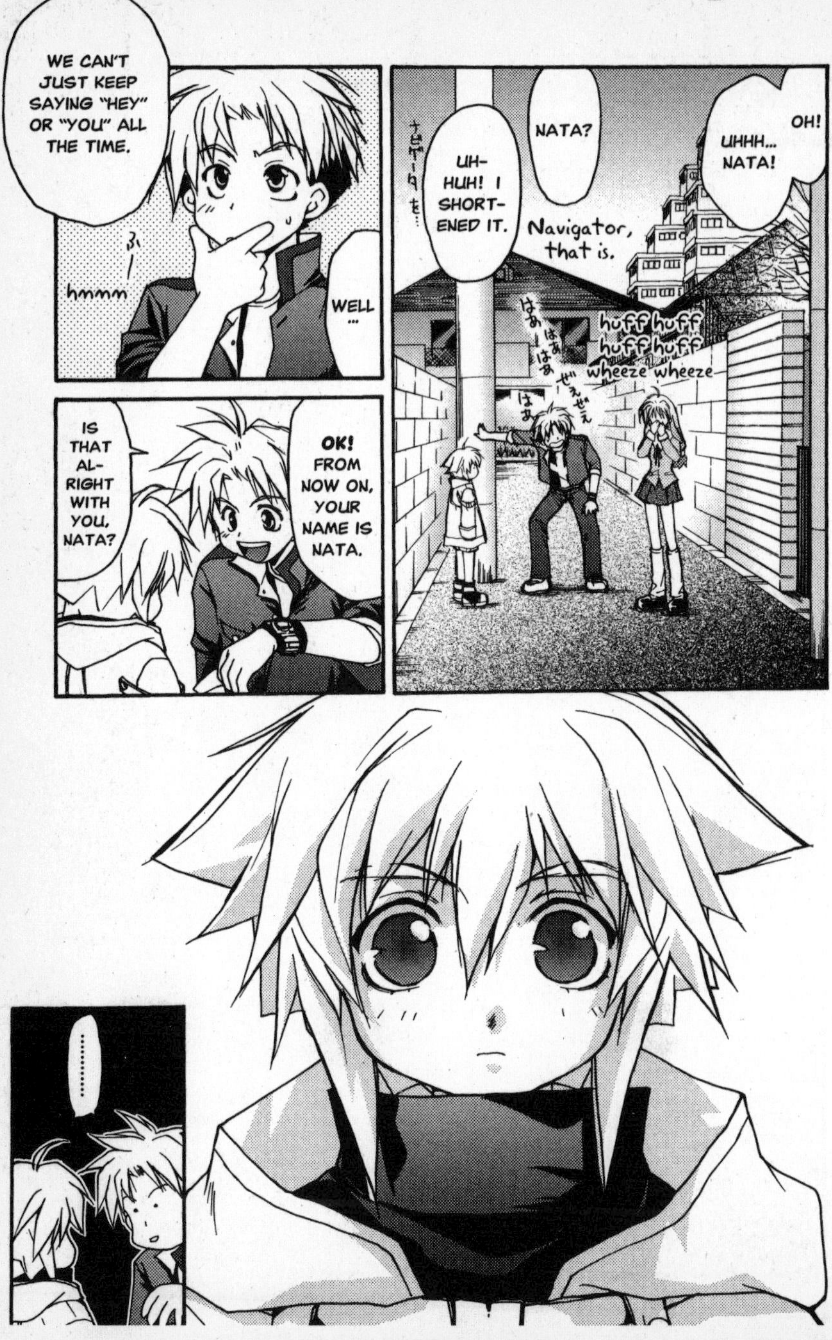

OH! UHHH... NATA!
NATA?
UH-HUH! I SHORTENED IT.
ナビゲータを…
Navigator, that is.
はぁはぁはぁはぁ
huff huff huff huff
ぜぇぜぇ
wheeze wheeze
WE CAN'T JUST KEEP SAYING "HEY" OR "YOU" ALL THE TIME.
ふー
hmmm
WELL ...
OK! FROM NOW ON, YOUR NAME IS NATA.
IS THAT ALRIGHT WITH YOU, NATA?
!.........

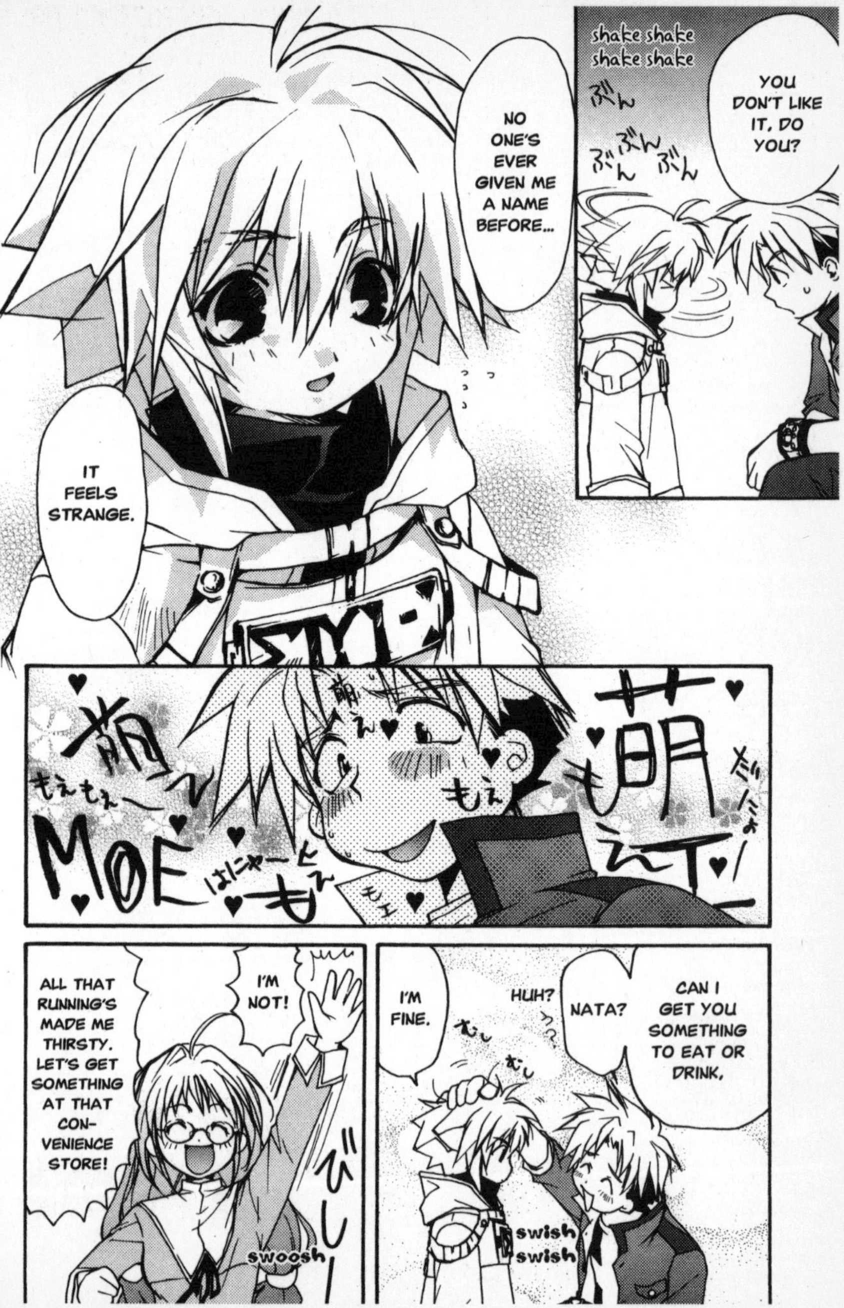

shake shake
shake shake
YOU DON'T LIKE IT, DO YOU?
NO ONE'S EVER GIVEN ME A NAME BEFORE...
IT FEELS STRANGE.
MOE
CAN I GET YOU SOMETHING TO EAT OR DRINK,
NATA?
HUH?
I'M FINE.
swish
swish
ALL THAT RUNNING'S MADE ME THIRSTY. LET'S GET SOMETHING AT THAT CON-VENIENCE STORE!
I'M NOT!
swoosh

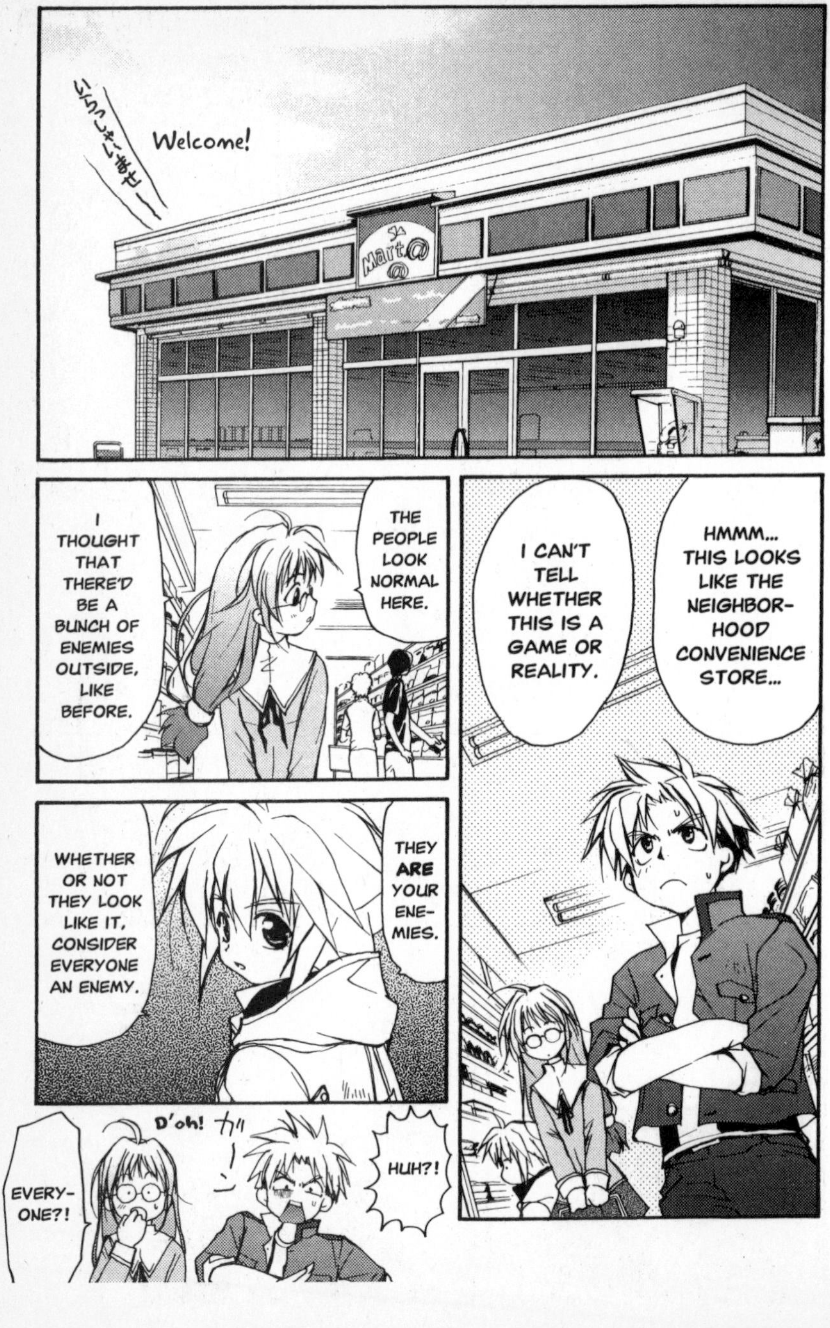
いらっしゃいませー
Welcome!
HMMM... THIS LOOKS LIKE THE NEIGHBOR-HOOD CONVENIENCE STORE...
I CAN'T TELL WHETHER THIS IS A GAME OR REALITY.
THE PEOPLE LOOK NORMAL HERE.
I THOUGHT THAT THERE'D BE A BUNCH OF ENEMIES OUTSIDE, LIKE BEFORE.
THEY **ARE** YOUR ENE-MIES.
WHETHER OR NOT THEY LOOK LIKE IT, CONSIDER EVERYONE AN ENEMY.
HUH?!
D'oh!
ガ
EVERY-ONE?!

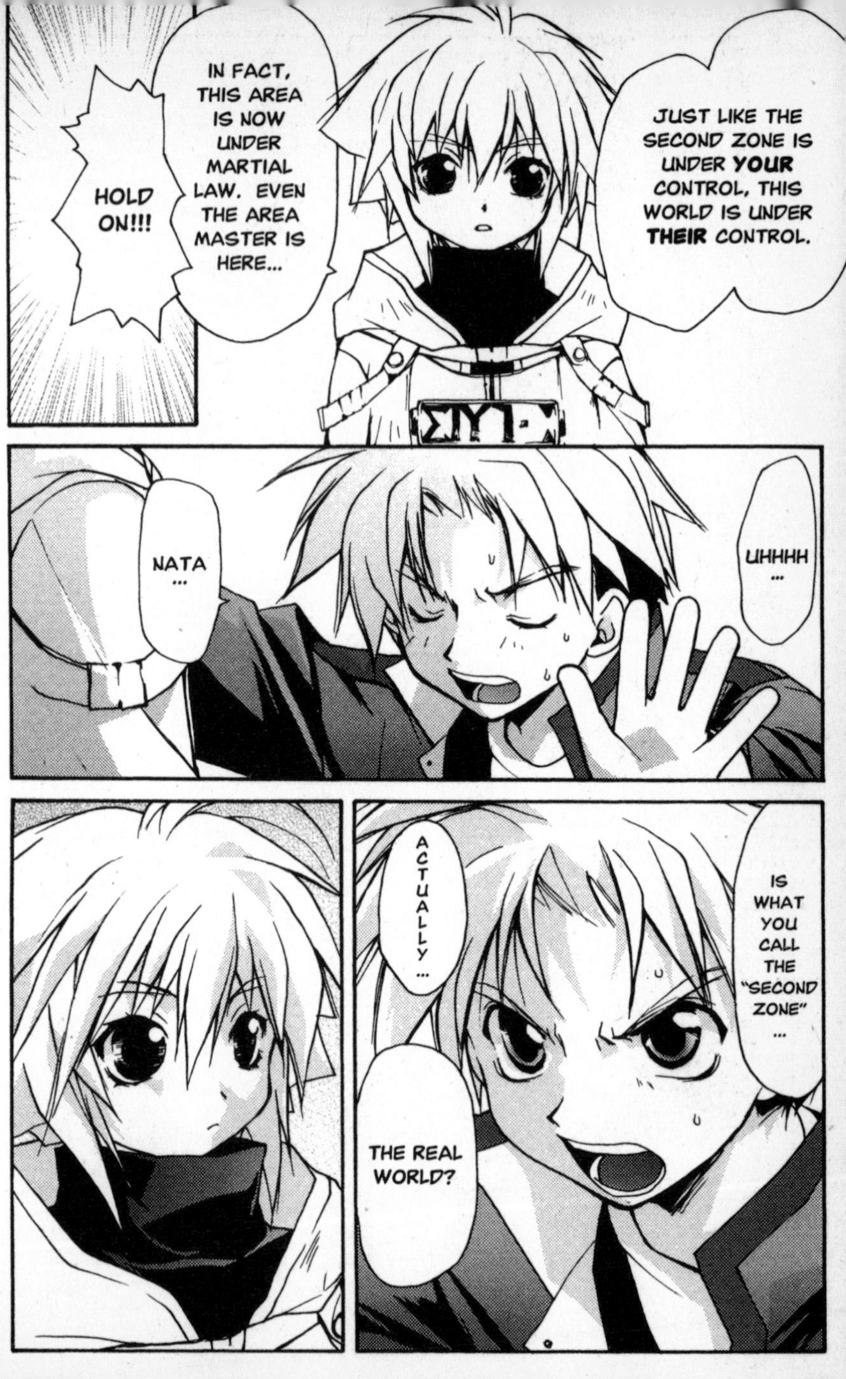
JUST LIKE THE SECOND ZONE IS UNDER **YOUR** CONTROL, THIS WORLD IS UNDER **THEIR** CONTROL.
IN FACT, THIS AREA IS NOW UNDER MARTIAL LAW. EVEN THE AREA MASTER IS HERE...
HOLD ON!!!
UHHHH...
NATA...
IS WHAT YOU CALL THE "SECOND ZONE"...
ACTUALLY...
THE REAL WORLD?

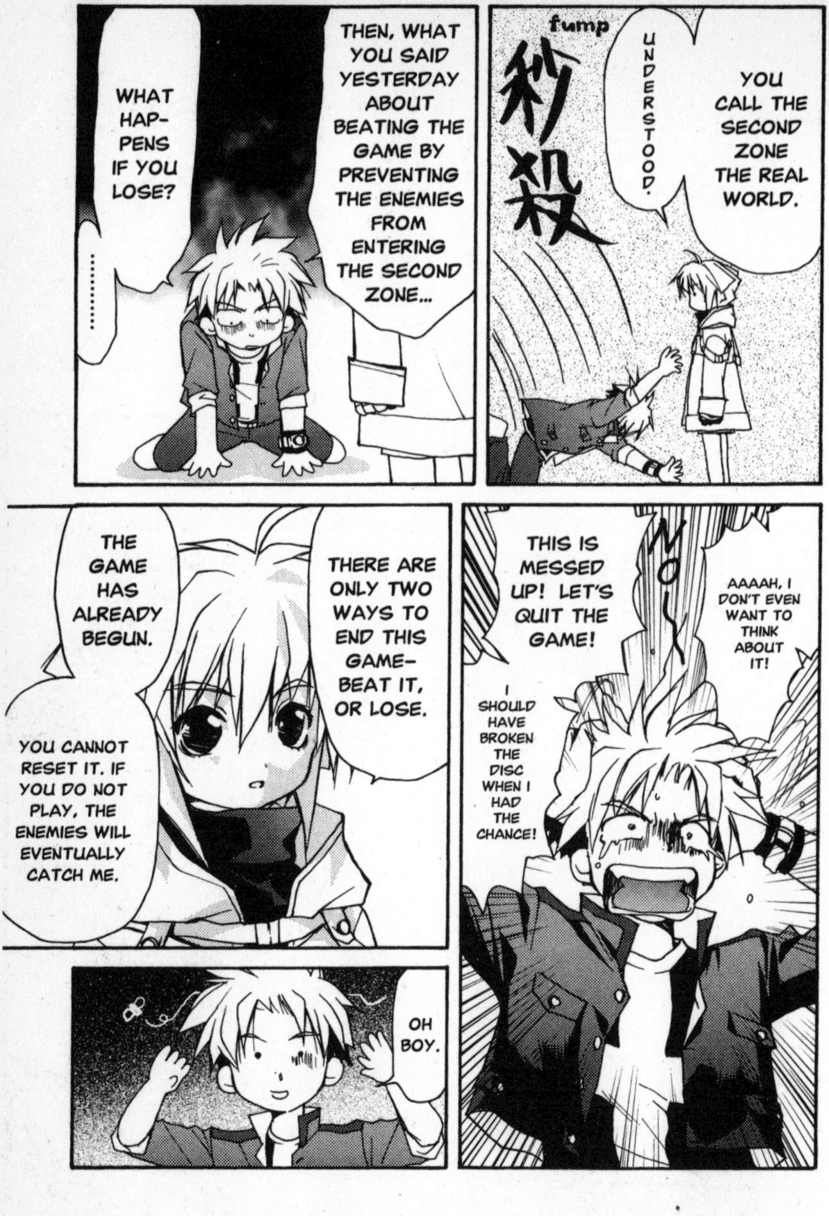
YOU CALL THE SECOND ZONE THE REAL WORLD.
UNDERSTOOD.
fump
秒殺
THEN, WHAT YOU SAID YESTERDAY ABOUT BEATING THE GAME BY PREVENTING THE ENEMIES FROM ENTERING THE SECOND ZONE...
WHAT HAP-PENS IF YOU LOSE?
....
AAAAH, I DON'T EVEN WANT TO THINK ABOUT IT!
THIS IS MESSED UP! LET'S QUIT THE GAME!
NO!
I SHOULD HAVE BROKEN THE DISC WHEN I HAD THE CHANCE!
THERE ARE ONLY TWO WAYS TO END THIS GAME- BEAT IT, OR LOSE.
THE GAME HAS ALREADY BEGUN.
YOU CANNOT RESET IT. IF YOU DO NOT PLAY, THE ENEMIES WILL EVENTUALLY CATCH ME.
OH BOY.

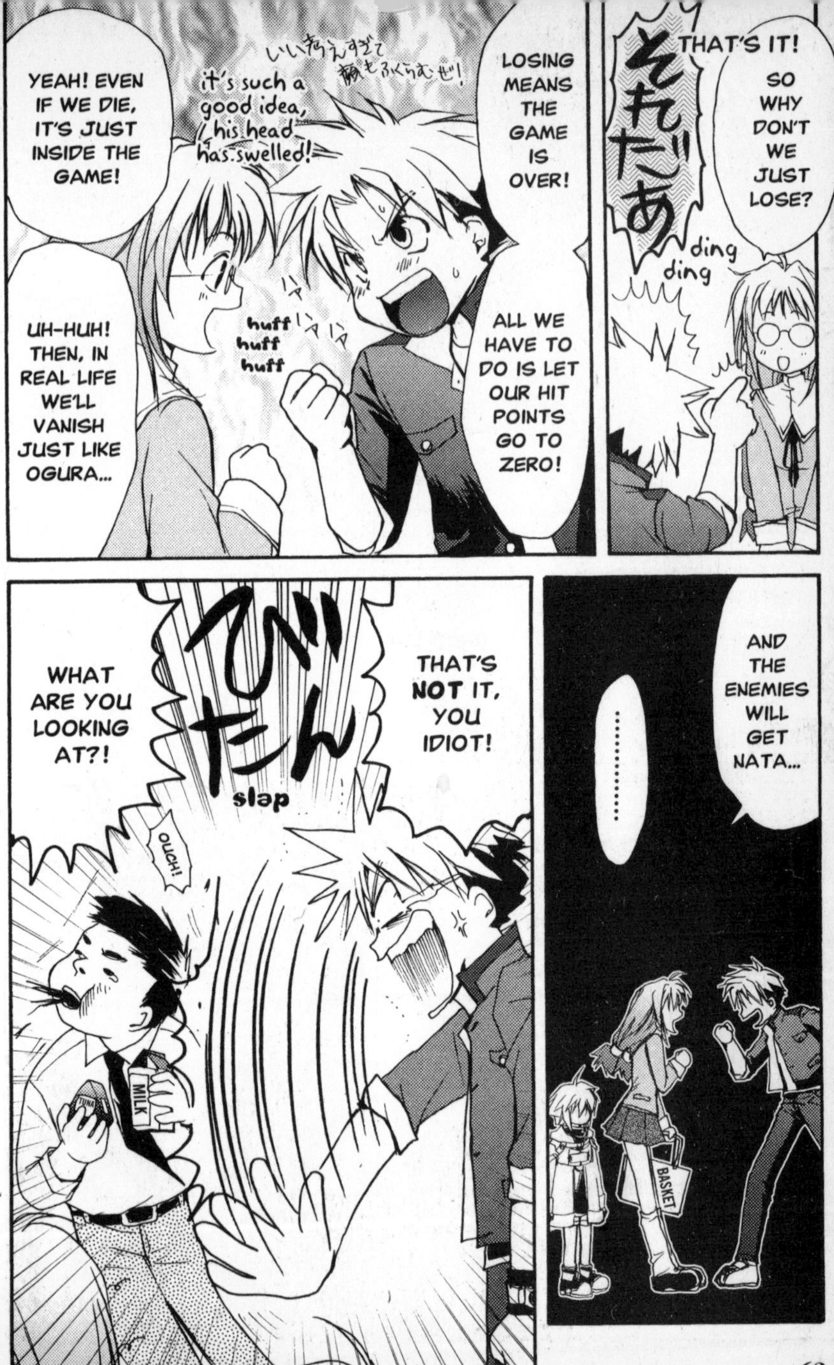
THAT'S IT!
SO WHY DON'T WE JUST LOSE?
それだあ
ding ding
LOSING MEANS THE GAME IS OVER!
ALL WE HAVE TO DO IS LET OUR HIT POINTS GO TO ZERO!
it's such a good idea, his head has swelled!
huff huff huff
YEAH! EVEN IF WE DIE, IT'S JUST INSIDE THE GAME!
UH-HUH! THEN, IN REAL LIFE WE'LL VANISH JUST LIKE OGURA...
AND THE ENEMIES WILL GET NATA...
....
BASKET
THAT'S **NOT** IT, YOU IDIOT!
びたん
slap
WHAT ARE YOU LOOKING AT?!
OUCH!
MILK
TUNA

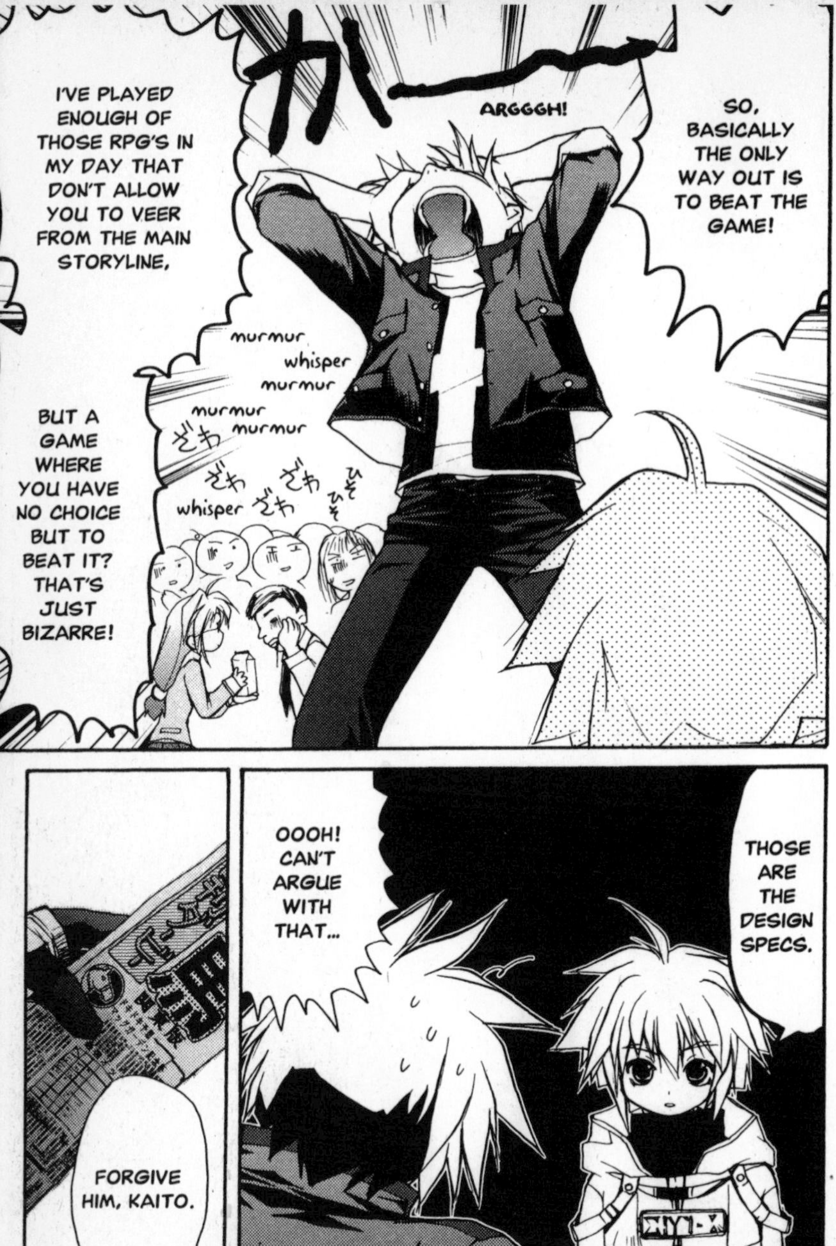
カー
ARGGGH!
SO, BASICALLY THE ONLY WAY OUT IS TO BEAT THE GAME!
I'VE PLAYED ENOUGH OF THOSE RPG'S IN MY DAY THAT DON'T ALLOW YOU TO VEER FROM THE MAIN STORYLINE,
murmur whisper murmur murmur murmur
ざわ ざわ ざわ ざわ
ひそ ひそ
whisper
BUT A GAME WHERE YOU HAVE NO CHOICE BUT TO BEAT IT? THAT'S JUST BIZARRE!
THOSE ARE THE DESIGN SPECS.
OOOH! CAN'T ARGUE WITH THAT...
FORGIVE HIM, KAITO.

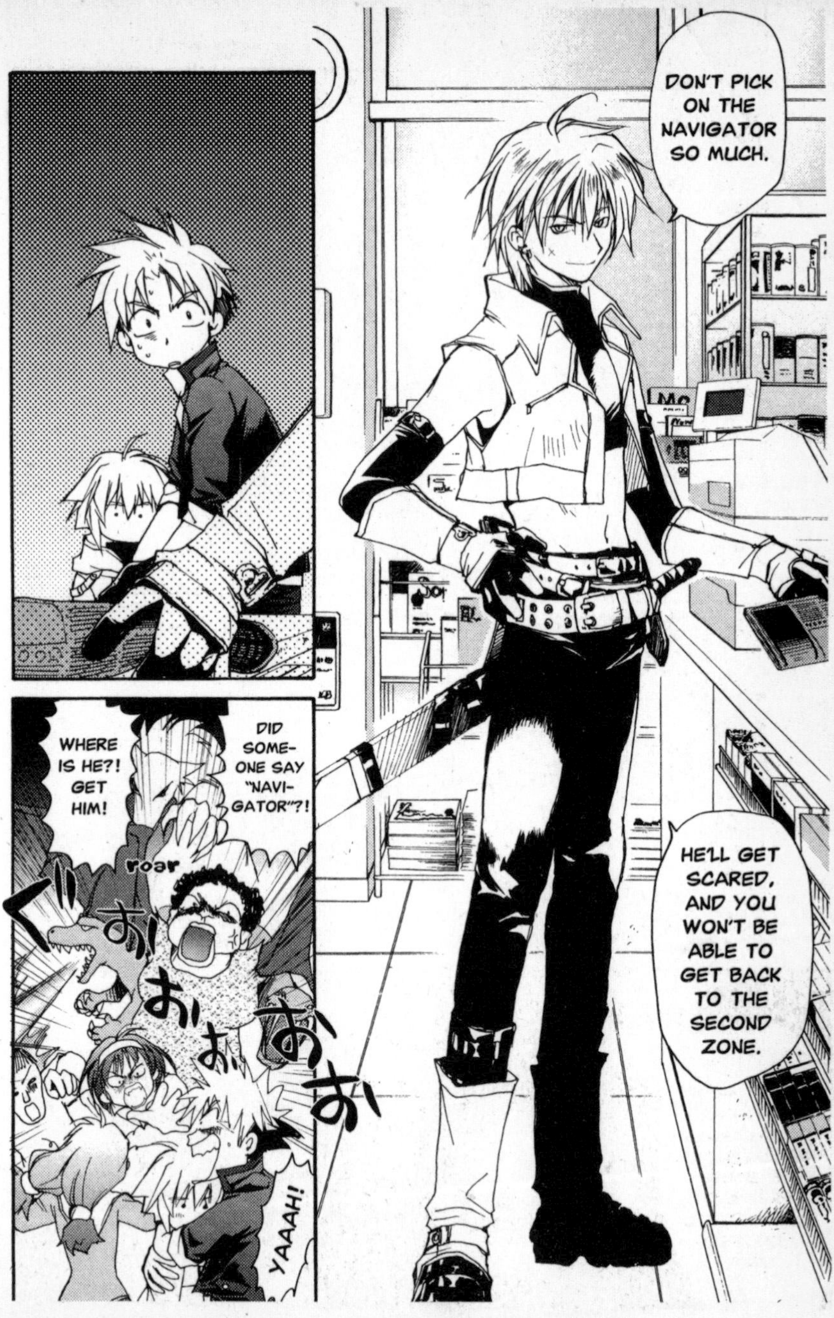
DON'T PICK ON THE NAVIGATOR SO MUCH.
HE'LL GET SCARED, AND YOU WON'T BE ABLE TO GET BACK TO THE SECOND ZONE.
DID SOME-ONE SAY "NAVI-GATOR"?!
WHERE IS HE?! GET HIM!
roar
ぐぉぉぉぉぉ
YAAAH!

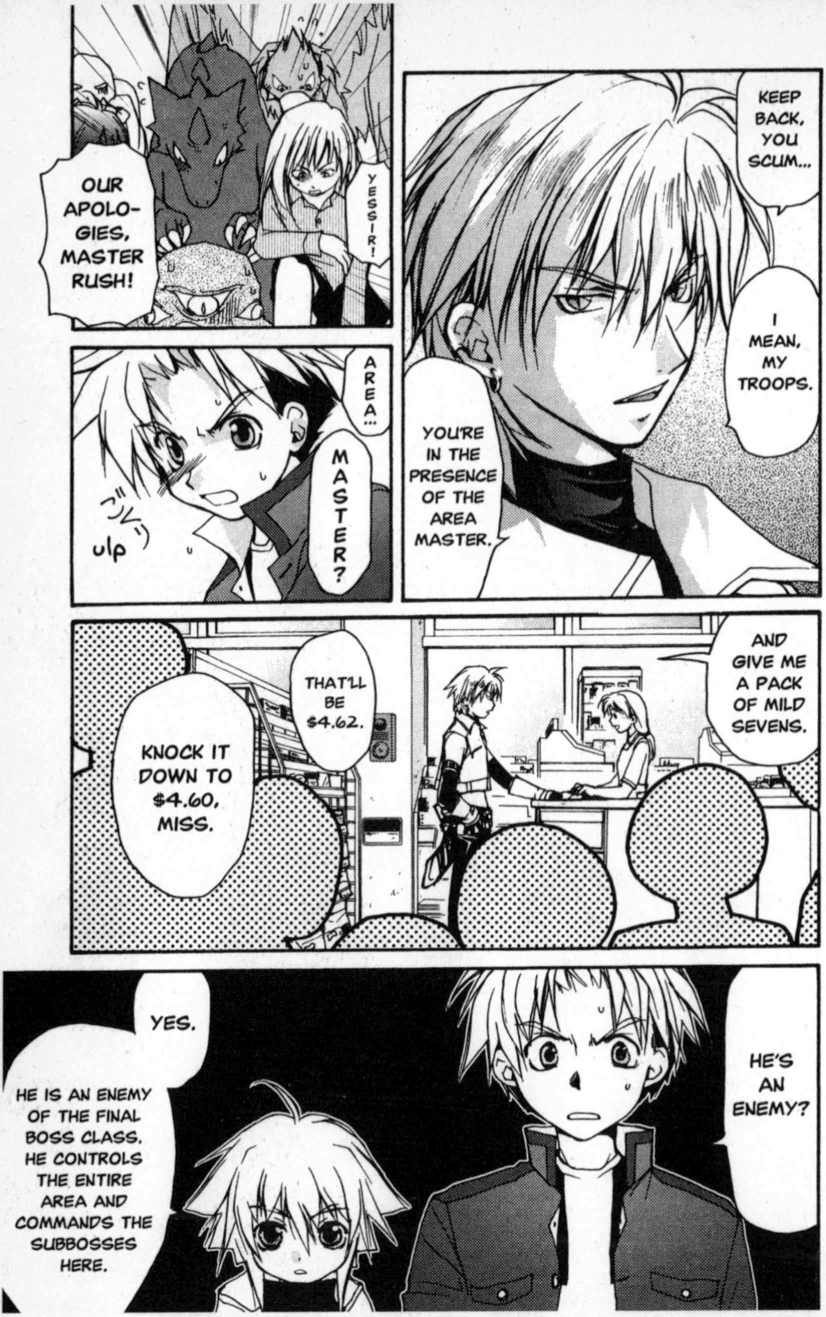
KEEP BACK, YOU SCUM...
I MEAN, MY TROOPS.
YOU'RE IN THE PRESENCE OF THE AREA MASTER.
YESSIR!
OUR APOLOGIES, MASTER RUSH!
AREA...
MASTER?
ゴクリ
ulp
AND GIVE ME A PACK OF MILD SEVENS.
THAT'LL BE $4.62.
KNOCK IT DOWN TO $4.60, MISS.
HE'S AN ENEMY?
YES.
HE IS AN ENEMY OF THE FINAL BOSS CLASS. HE CONTROLS THE ENTIRE AREA AND COMMANDS THE SUBBOSSES HERE.

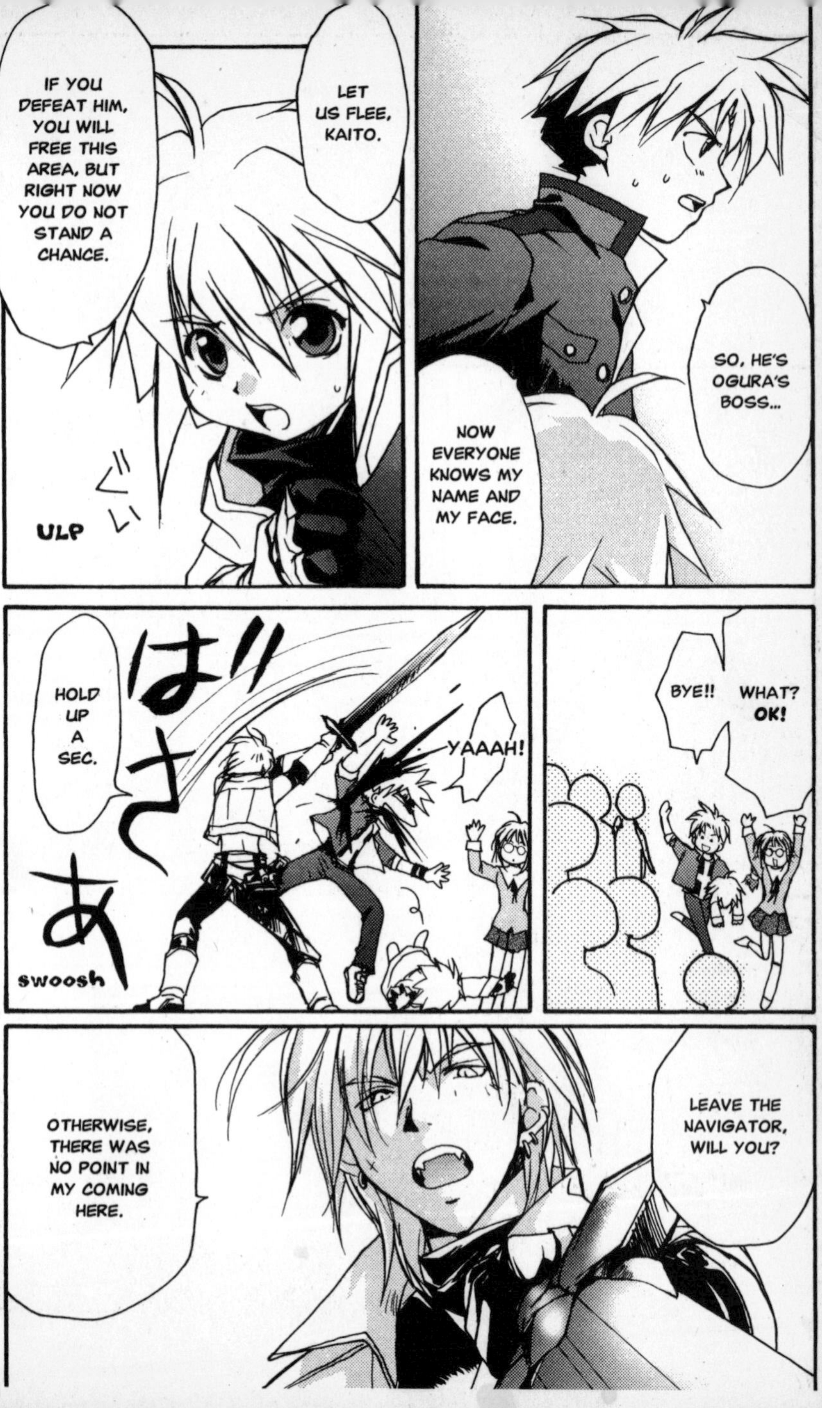
SO, HE'S OGURA'S BOSS...
NOW EVERYONE KNOWS MY NAME AND MY FACE.
LET US FLEE, KAITO.
IF YOU DEFEAT HIM, YOU WILL FREE THIS AREA, BUT RIGHT NOW YOU DO NOT STAND A CHANCE.
ぐい
ULP
WHAT? OK!
BYE!!
YAAAH!
HOLD UP A SEC.
あ
swoosh
LEAVE THE NAVIGATOR, WILL YOU?
OTHERWISE, THERE WAS NO POINT IN MY COMING HERE.

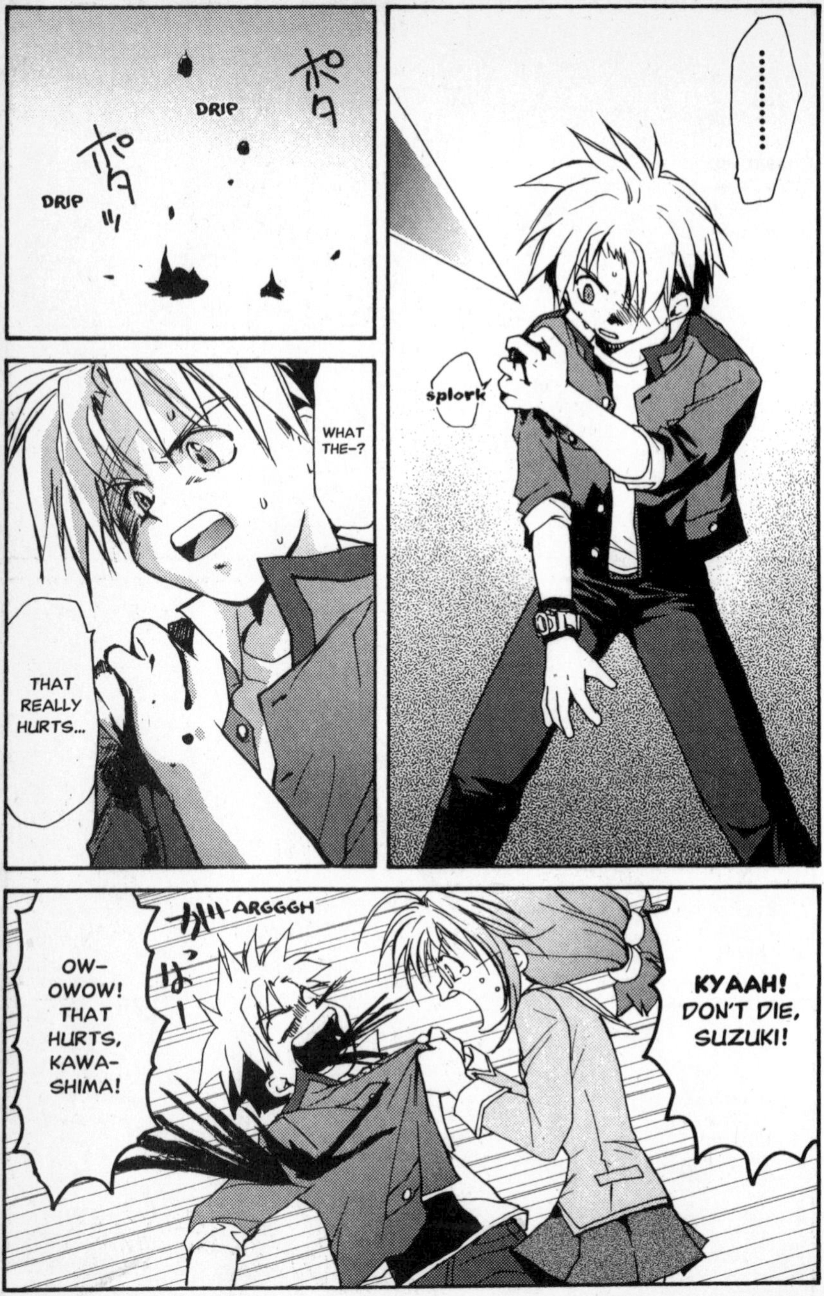

......
splork
ポタ
DRIP
ポタッ
DRIP
WHAT THE-?
THAT REALLY HURTS...
KYAAH! DON'T DIE, SUZUKI!
ARGGGH
OW-OWOW! THAT HURTS, KAWASHIMA!

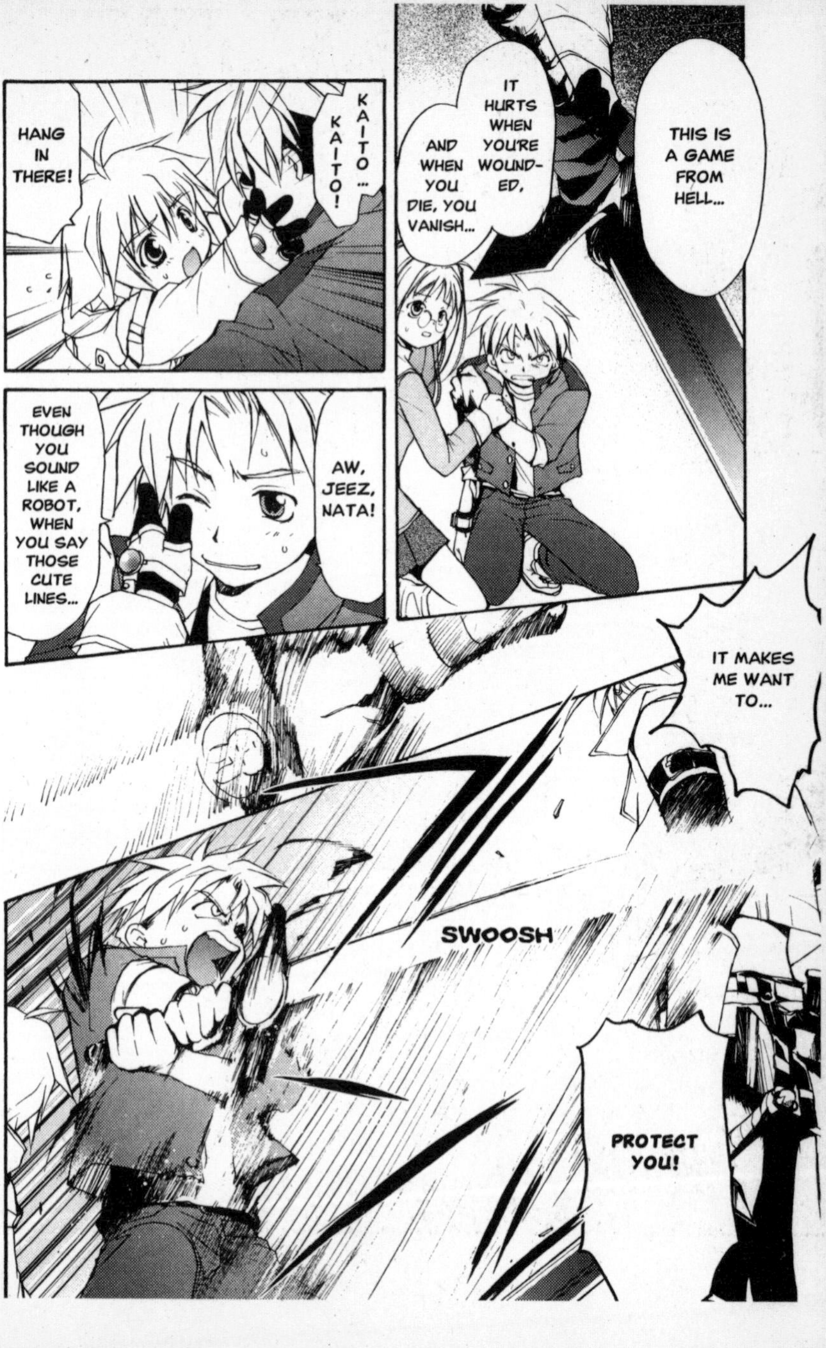
THIS IS A GAME FROM HELL...
IT HURTS WHEN YOU'RE WOUNDED,
AND WHEN YOU DIE, YOU VANISH...
KAITO... KAITO!
HANG IN THERE!
AW, JEEZ, NATA!
EVEN THOUGH YOU SOUND LIKE A ROBOT, WHEN YOU SAY THOSE CUTE LINES...
IT MAKES ME WANT TO...
SWOOSH
PROTECT YOU!

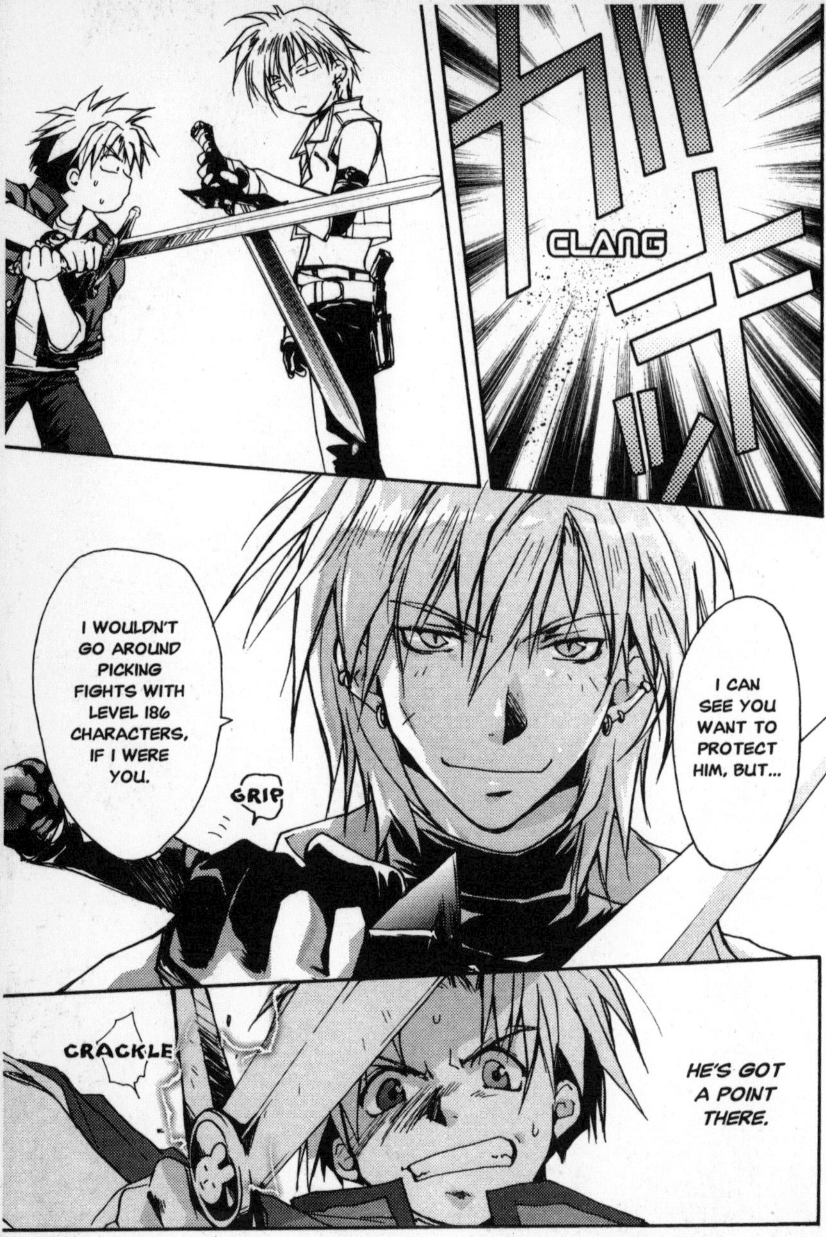
CLANG
I CAN SEE YOU WANT TO PROTECT HIM, BUT...
I WOULDN'T GO AROUND PICKING FIGHTS WITH LEVEL 186 CHARACTERS, IF I WERE YOU.
GRIP
HE'S GOT A POINT THERE.
CRACKLE

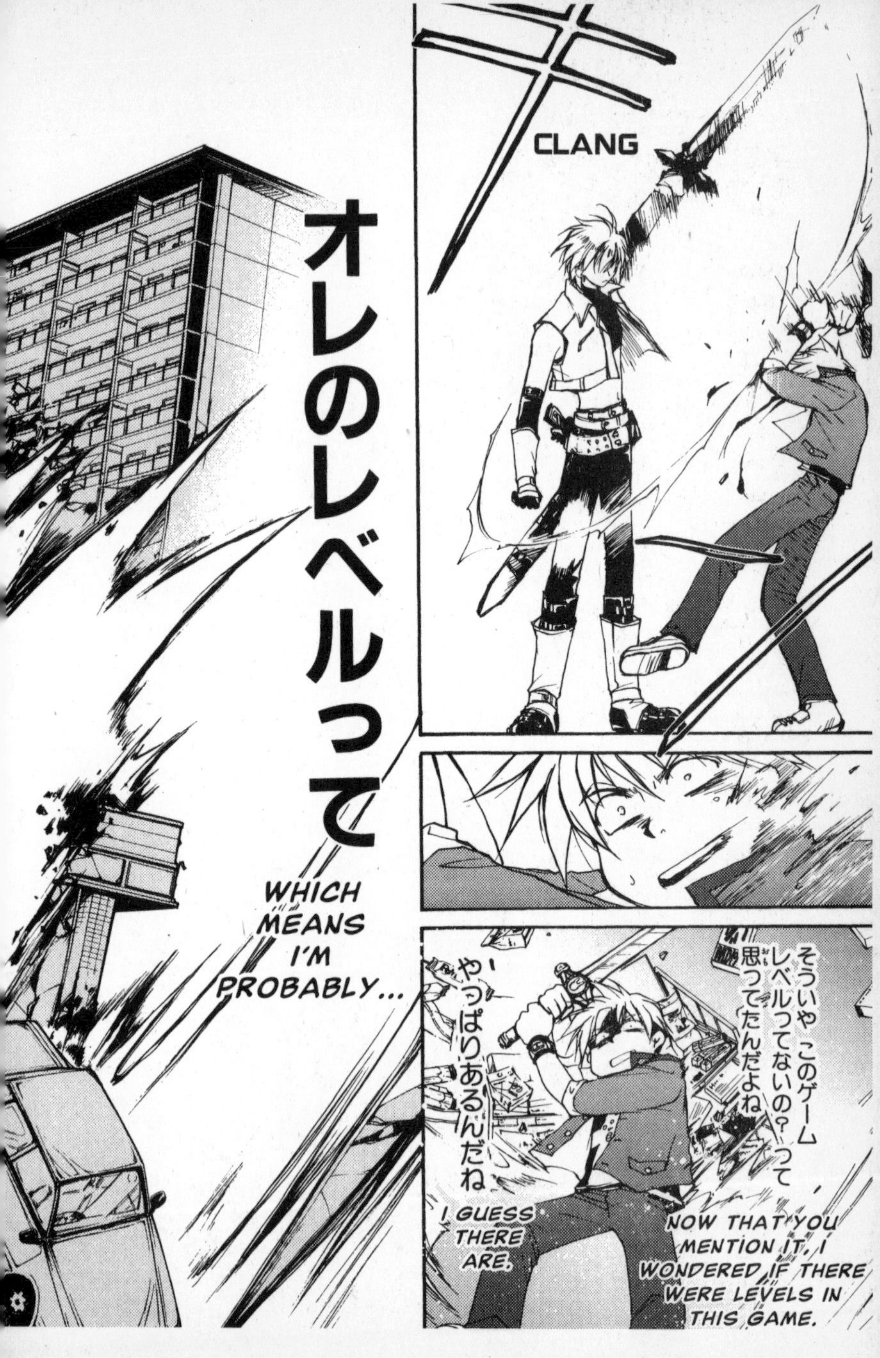
CLANG
そういや このゲーム レベルってないの?って 思ってたんだよね
NOW THAT YOU MENTION IT, I WONDERED IF THERE WERE LEVELS IN THIS GAME.
やっぱりあるんだね
I GUESS THERE ARE.
オレのレベルって
WHICH MEANS I'M PROBABLY...

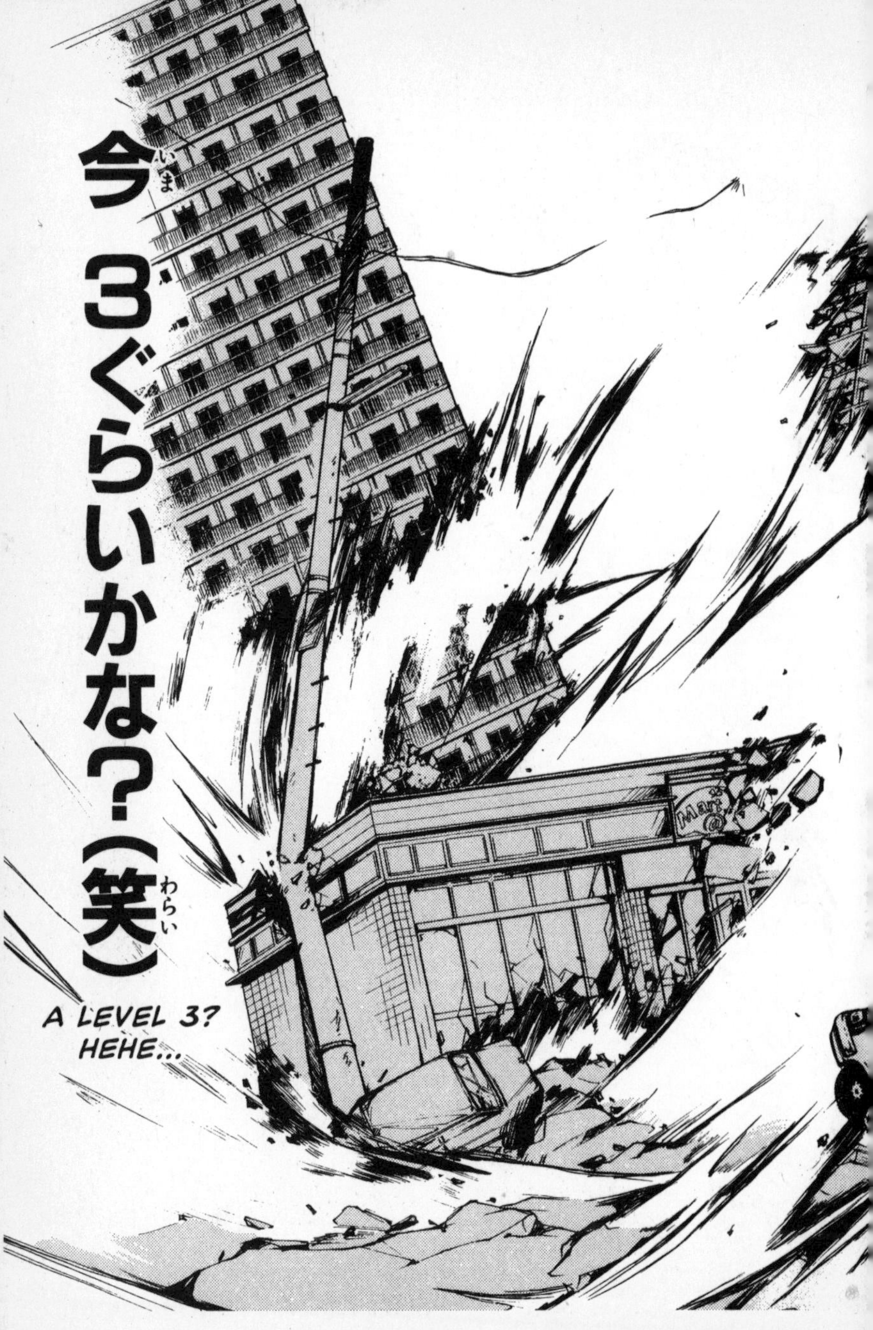

今3ぐらいかな?(笑)
A LEVEL 3? HEHE...

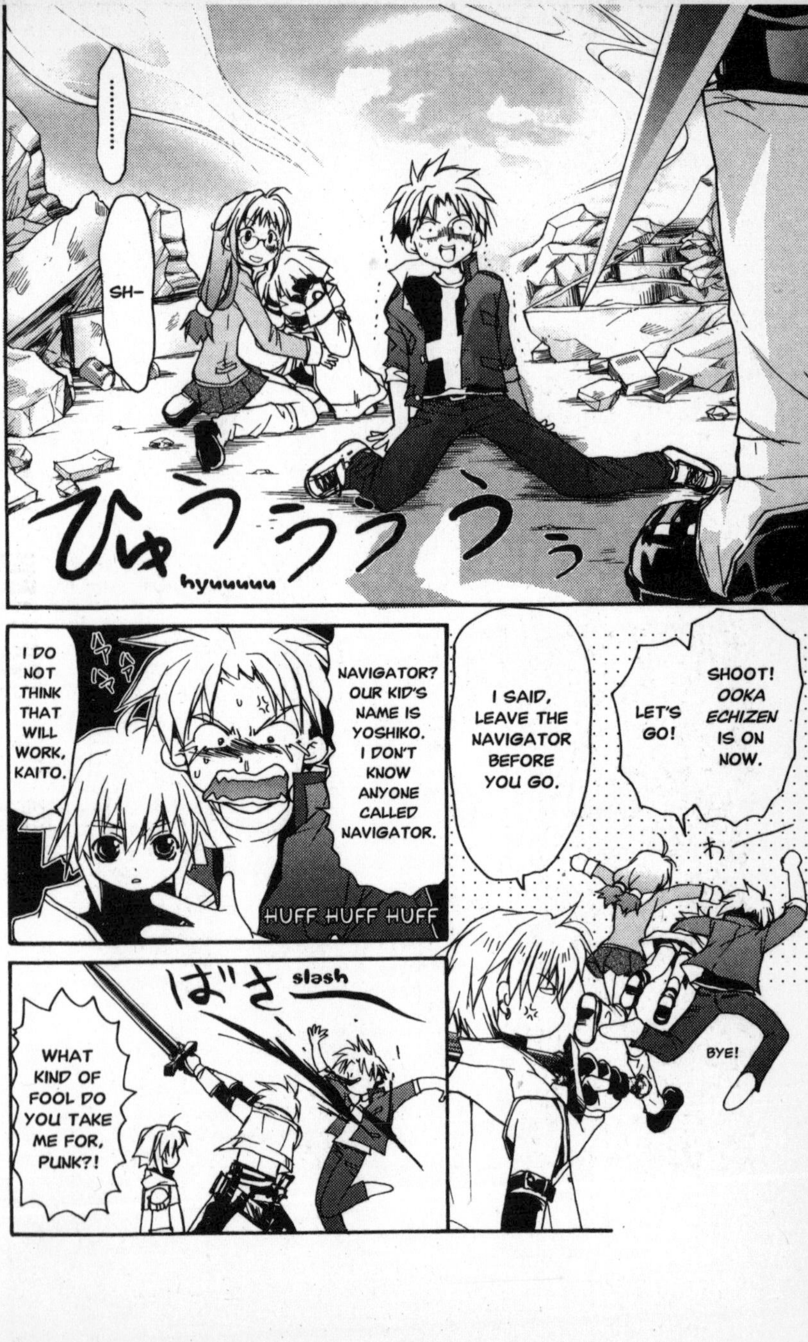
......
SH-
ひゅうううう
hyuuuuu
SHOOT! OOKA ECHIZEN IS ON NOW.
LET'S GO!
I SAID, LEAVE THE NAVIGATOR BEFORE YOU GO.
NAVIGATOR? OUR KID'S NAME IS YOSHIKO. I DON'T KNOW ANYONE CALLED NAVIGATOR.
I DO NOT THINK THAT WILL WORK, KAITO.
HUFF HUFF HUFF
BYE!
ばき——
slash
WHAT KIND OF FOOL DO YOU TAKE ME FOR, PUNK?!

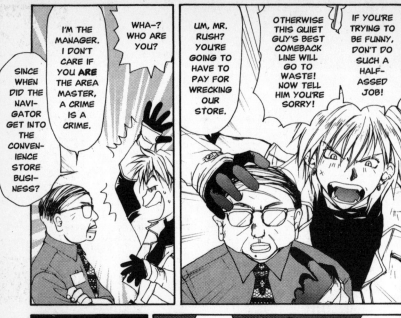

IF YOU'RE TRYING TO BE FUNNY, DON'T DO SUCH A HALF-ASSED JOB!
OTHERWISE THIS QUIET GUY'S BEST COMEBACK LINE WILL GO TO WASTE! NOW TELL HIM YOU'RE SORRY!
UM, MR. RUSH? YOU'RE GOING TO HAVE TO PAY FOR WRECKING OUR STORE.
WHA-? WHO ARE YOU?
I'M THE MANAGER. I DON'T CARE IF YOU **ARE** THE AREA MASTER, A CRIME IS A CRIME.
SINCE WHEN DID THE NAVIGATOR GET INTO THE CONVENIENCE STORE BUSINESS?
WELL, ANYWAY ...
RUMI, CALL THE POLICE.
YES, SIR.

(室温 2度) TEMPERATURE 36°F

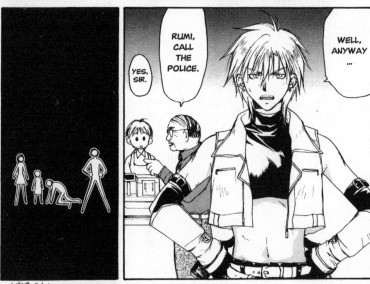

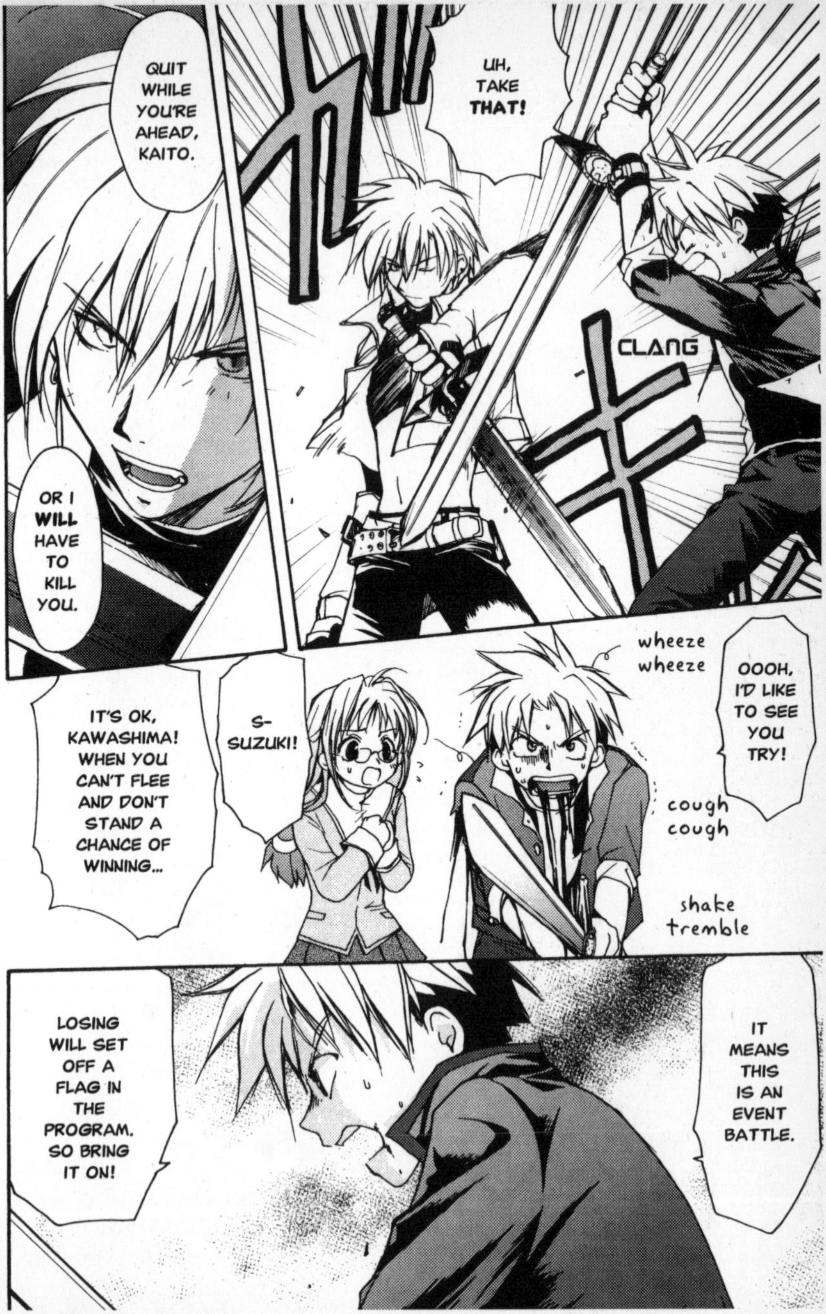
UH, TAKE THAT!
CLANG
QUIT WHILE YOU'RE AHEAD, KAITO.
OR I WILL HAVE TO KILL YOU.
OOOH, I'D LIKE TO SEE YOU TRY!
wheeze wheeze
cough cough
shake tremble
S-SUZUKI!
IT'S OK, KAWASHIMA! WHEN YOU CAN'T FLEE AND DON'T STAND A CHANCE OF WINNING...
IT MEANS THIS IS AN EVENT BATTLE.
LOSING WILL SET OFF A FLAG IN THE PROGRAM. SO BRING IT ON!

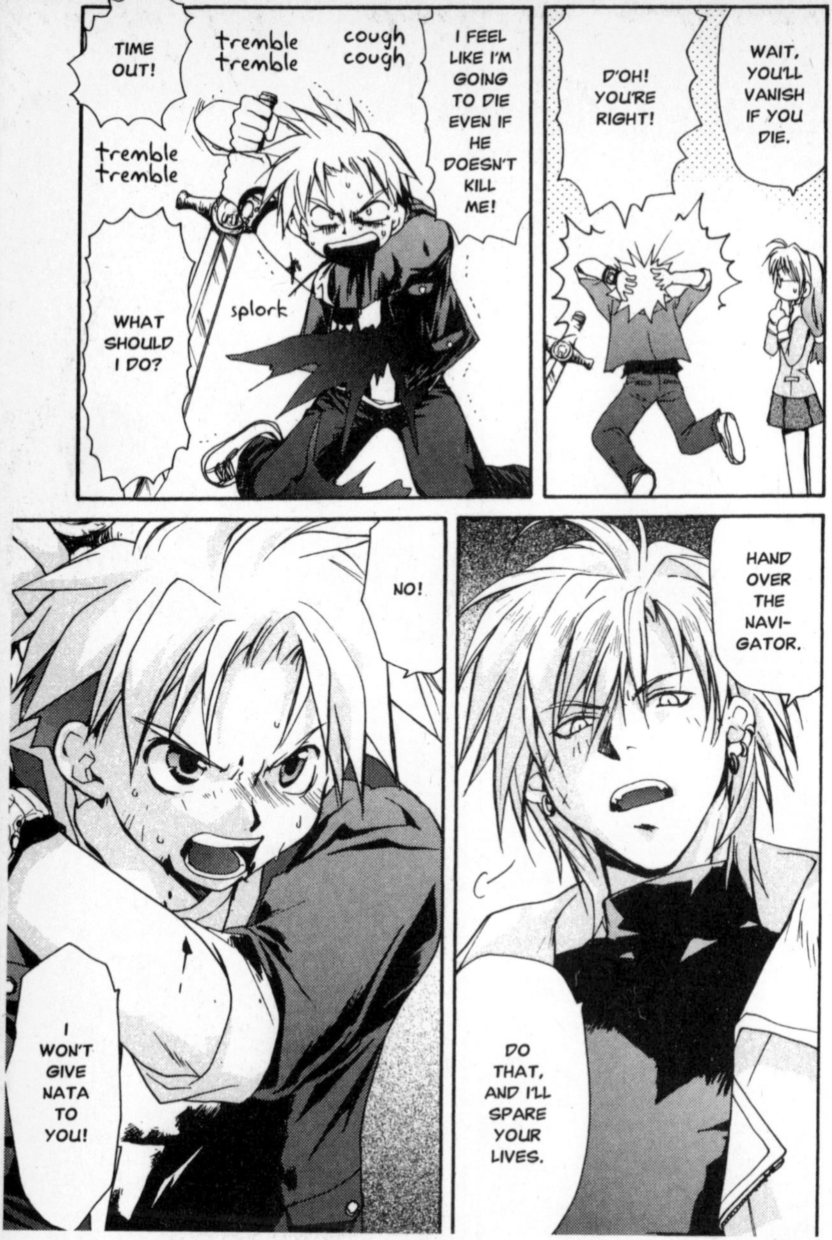
TIME OUT!
tremble tremble
cough cough
I FEEL LIKE I'M GOING TO DIE EVEN IF HE DOESN'T KILL ME!
tremble tremble
WHAT SHOULD I DO?
splork
WAIT, YOU'LL VANISH IF YOU DIE.
D'OH! YOU'RE RIGHT!
HAND OVER THE NAVI-GATOR.
DO THAT, AND I'LL SPARE YOUR LIVES.
NO!
I WON'T GIVE NATA TO YOU!

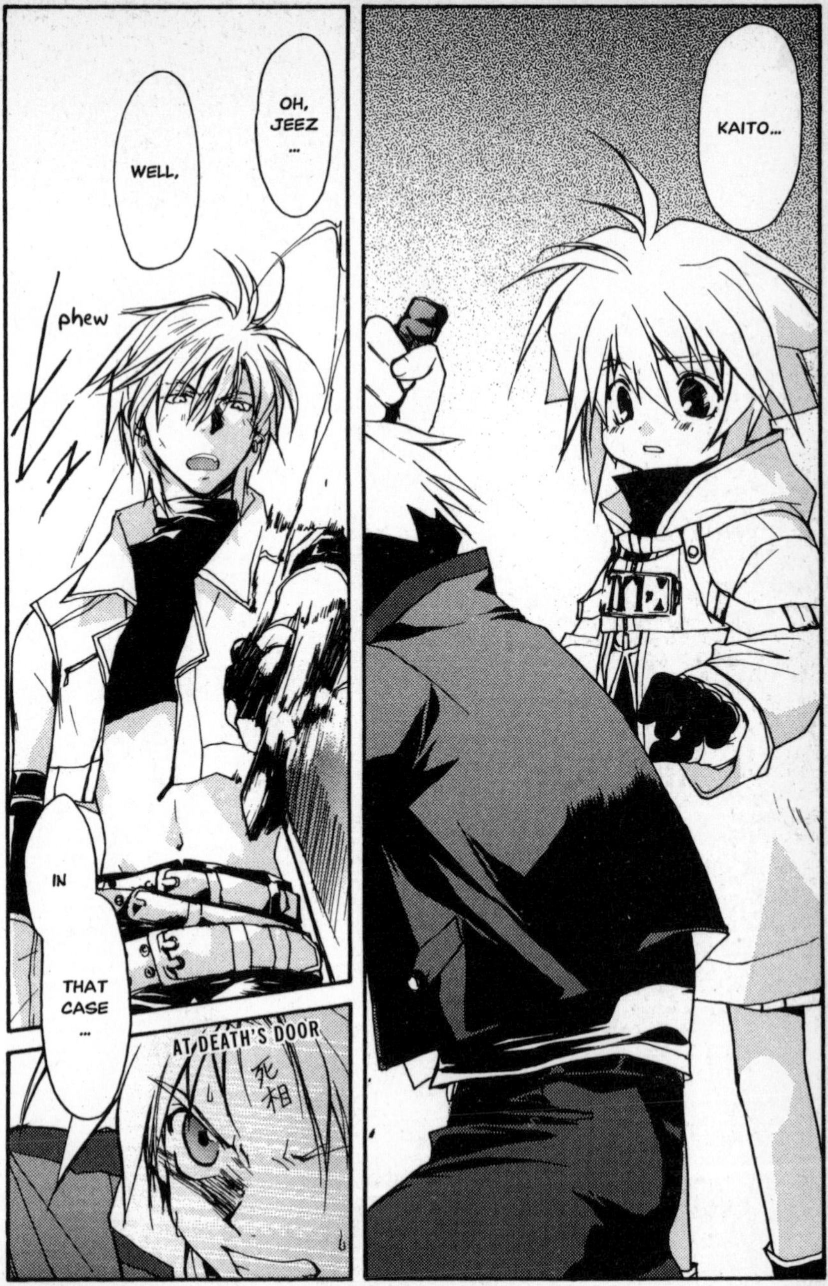
KAITO...
OH, JEEZ ...
WELL,
phew
IN THAT CASE ...
AT DEATH'S DOOR
死相

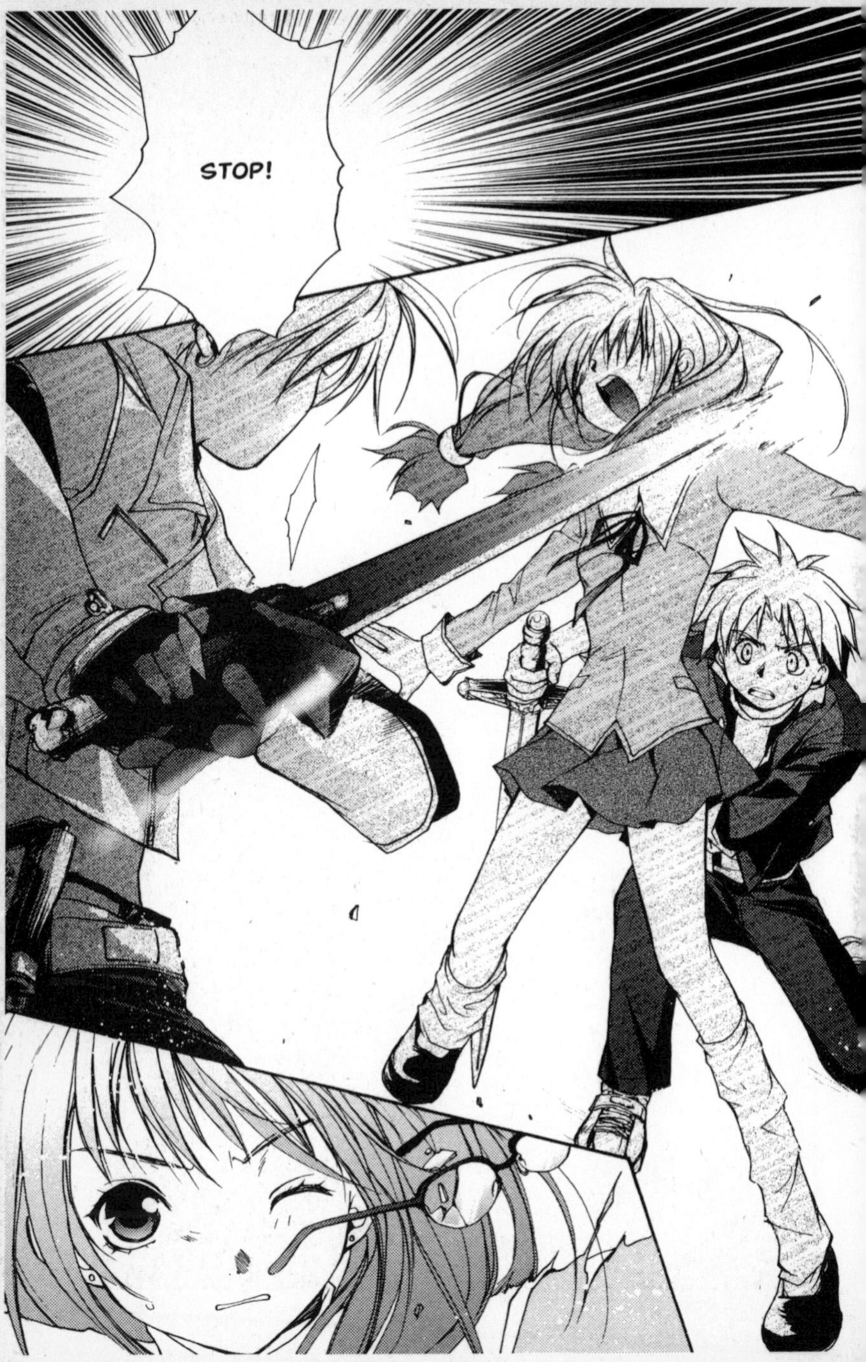
STOP!

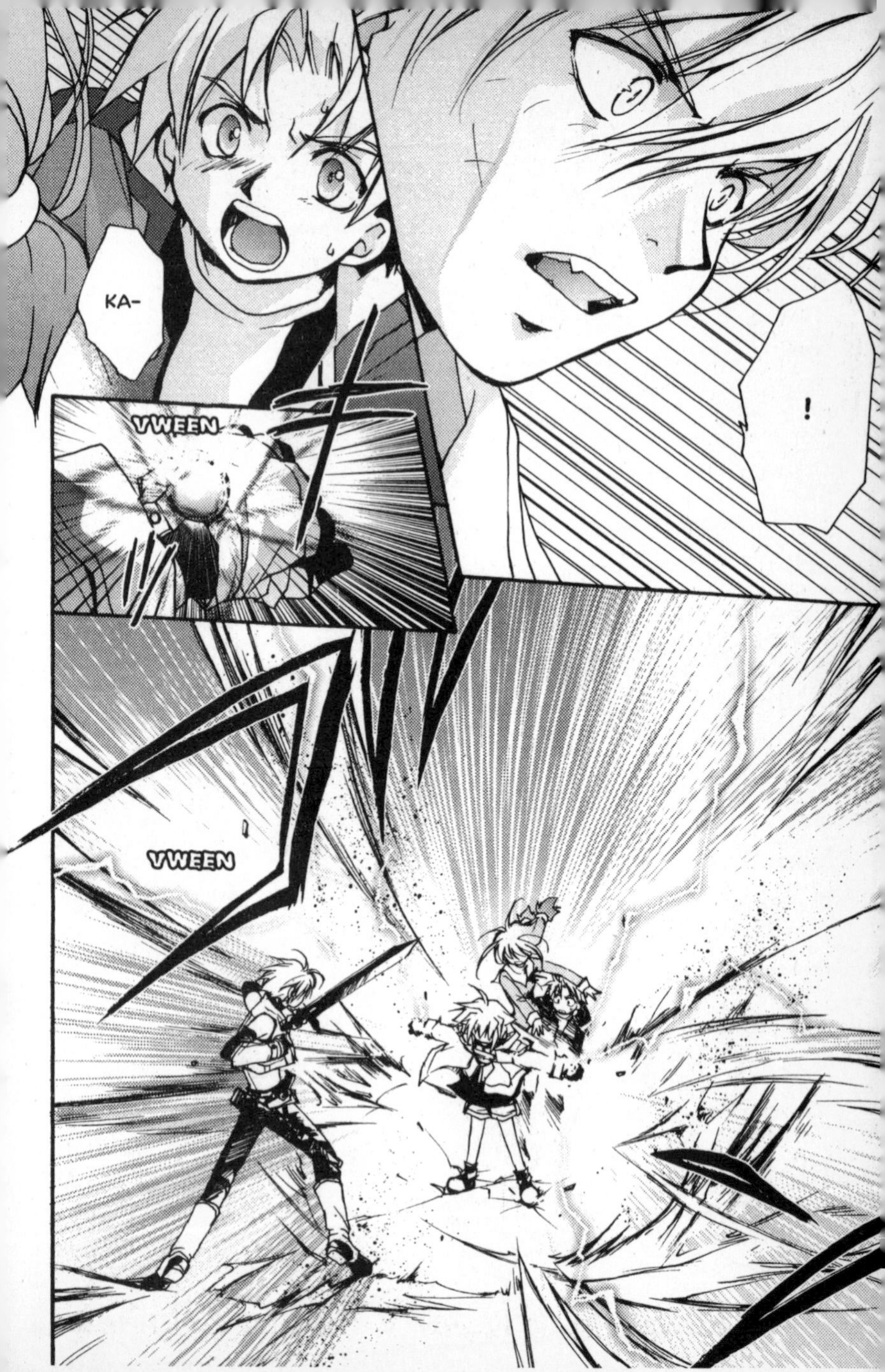
!
KA-
VWEEN
VWEEN

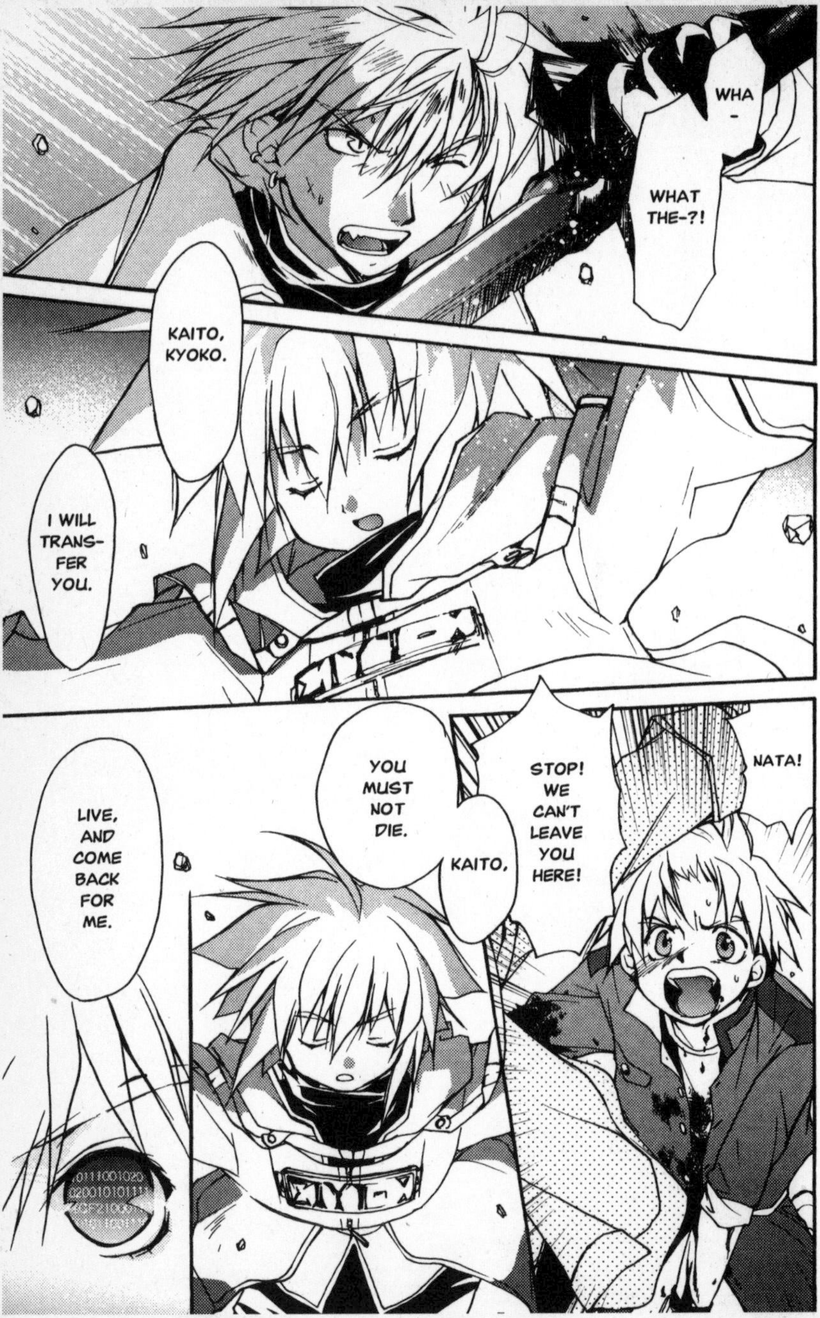
WHA-
WHAT THE-?!
KAITO, KYOKO.
I WILL TRANSFER YOU.
NATA!
STOP! WE CAN'T LEAVE YOU HERE!
KAITO,
YOU MUST NOT DIE.
LIVE, AND COME BACK FOR ME.

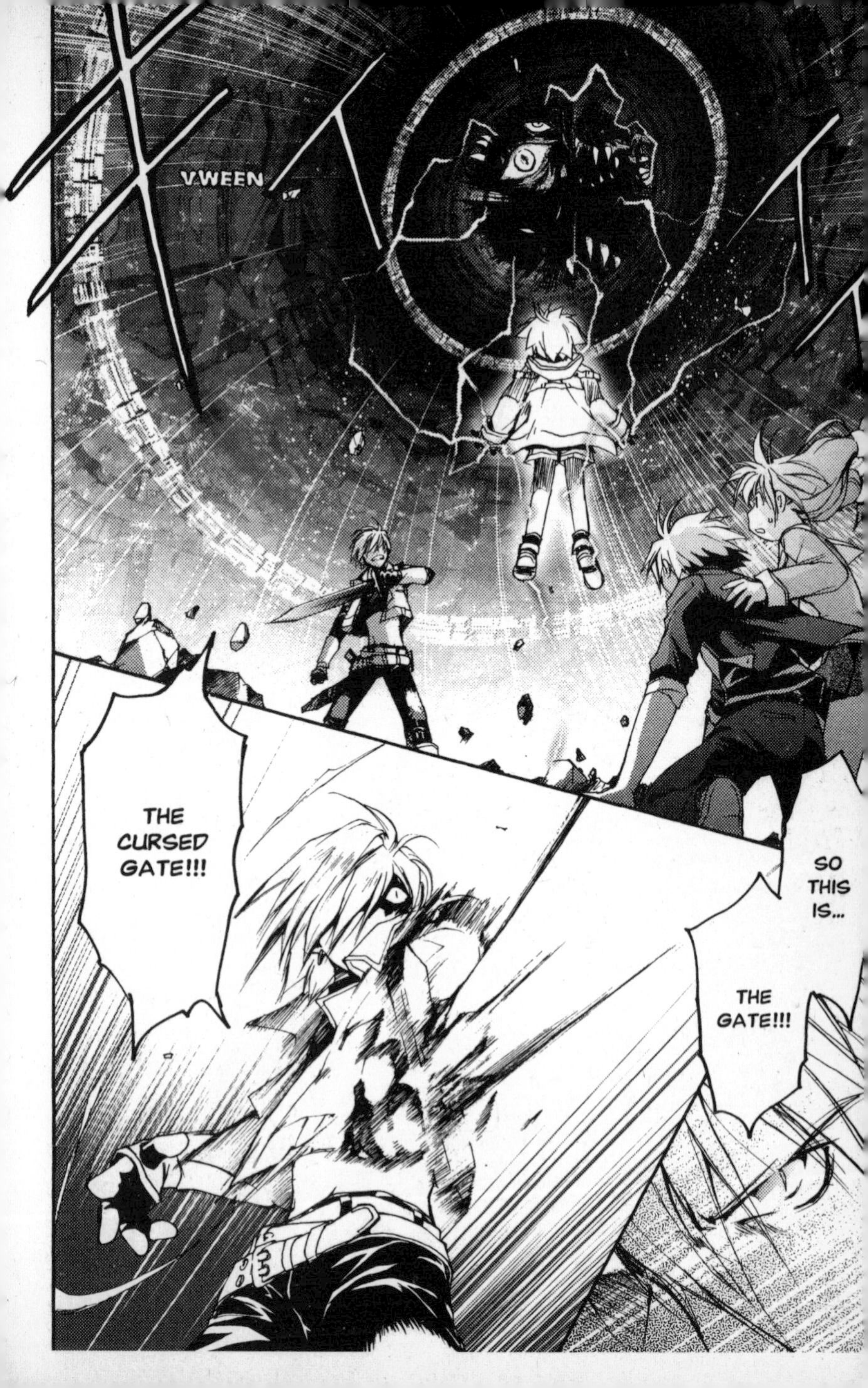
V-WEEN
SO THIS IS...
THE GATE!!!
THE CURSED GATE!!!

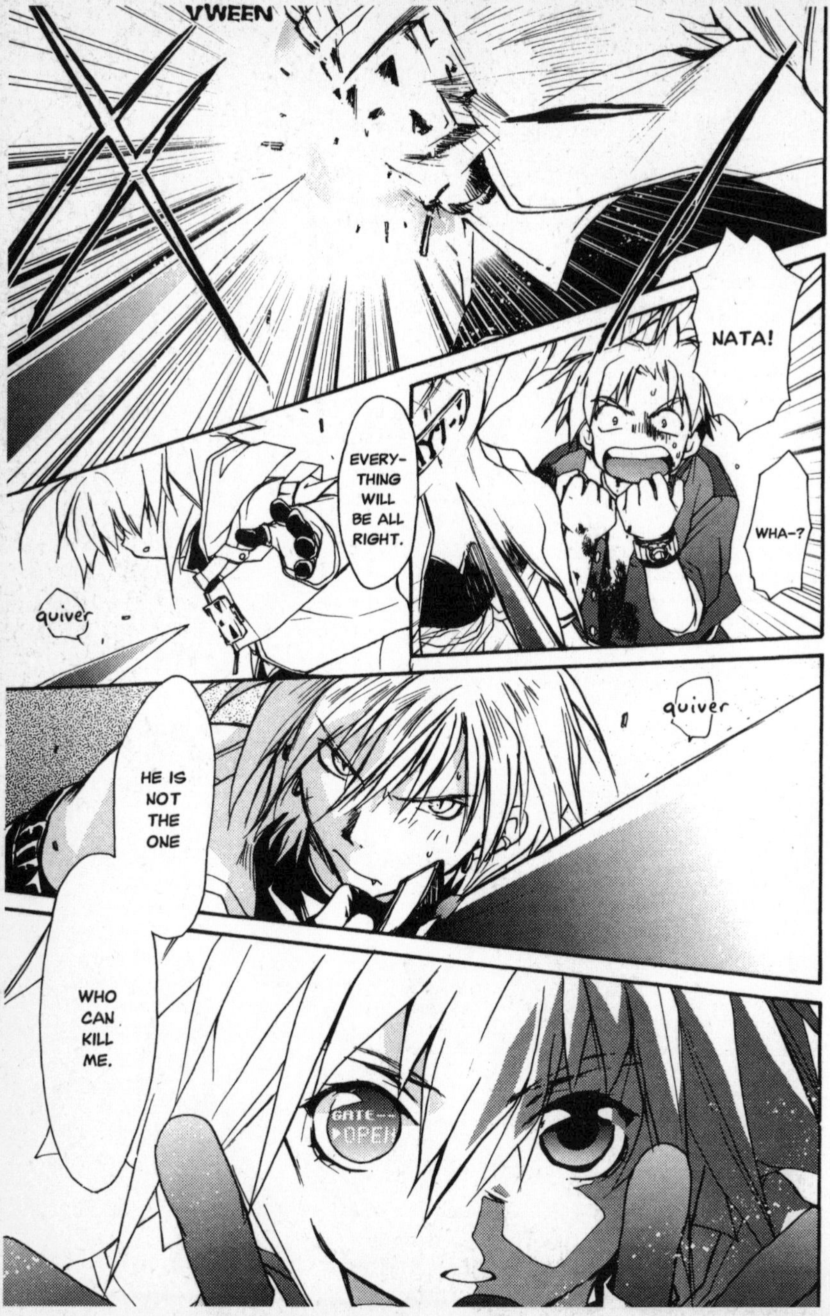
VWEEN
NATA!
EVERYTHING WILL BE ALL RIGHT.
WHA-?
quiver
quiver
HE IS NOT THE ONE
WHO CAN KILL ME.
GATE--
▶OPEN

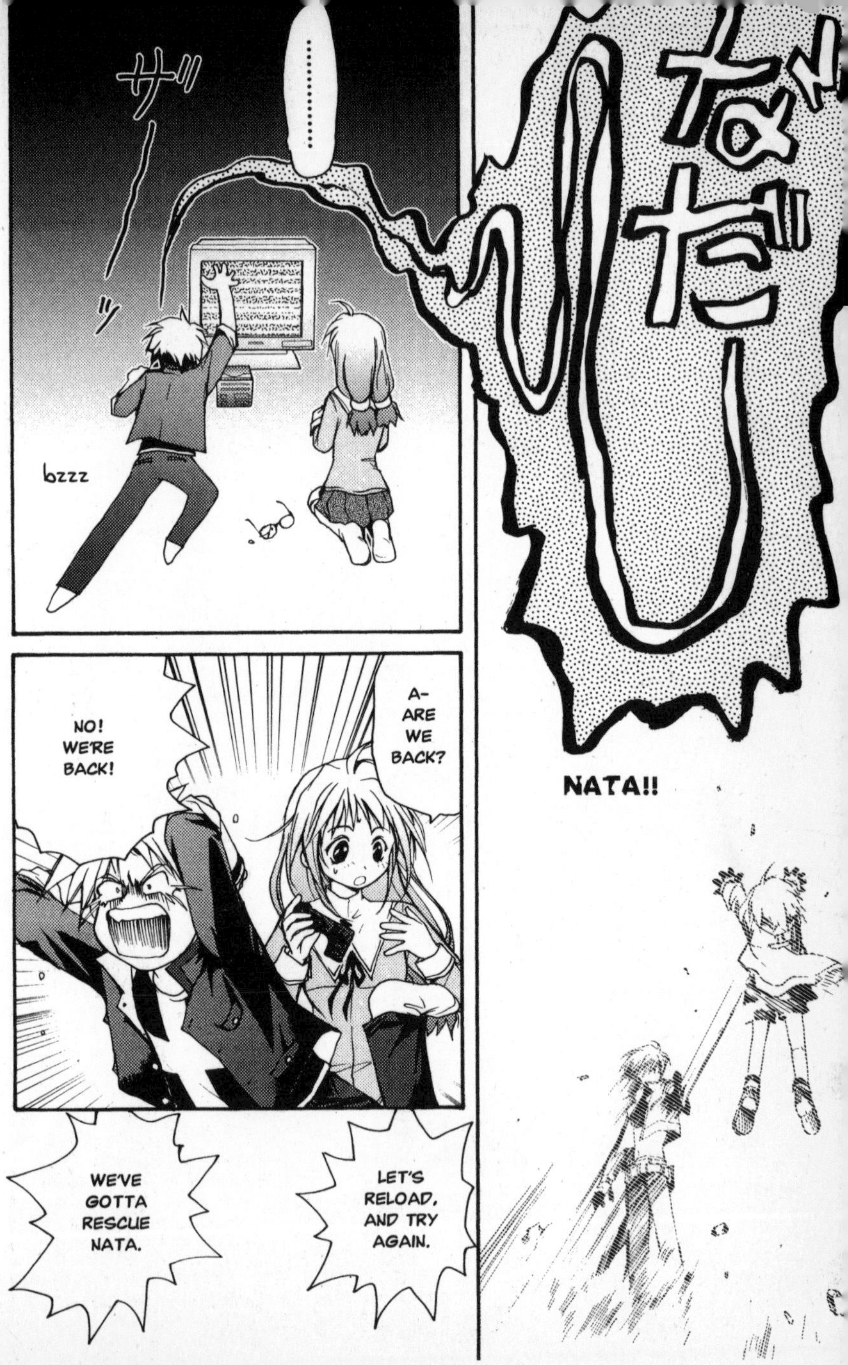
……
bzzz
なだ
NATA!!
A- ARE WE BACK?
NO! WE'RE BACK!
LET'S RELOAD, AND TRY AGAIN.
WE'VE GOTTA RESCUE NATA.

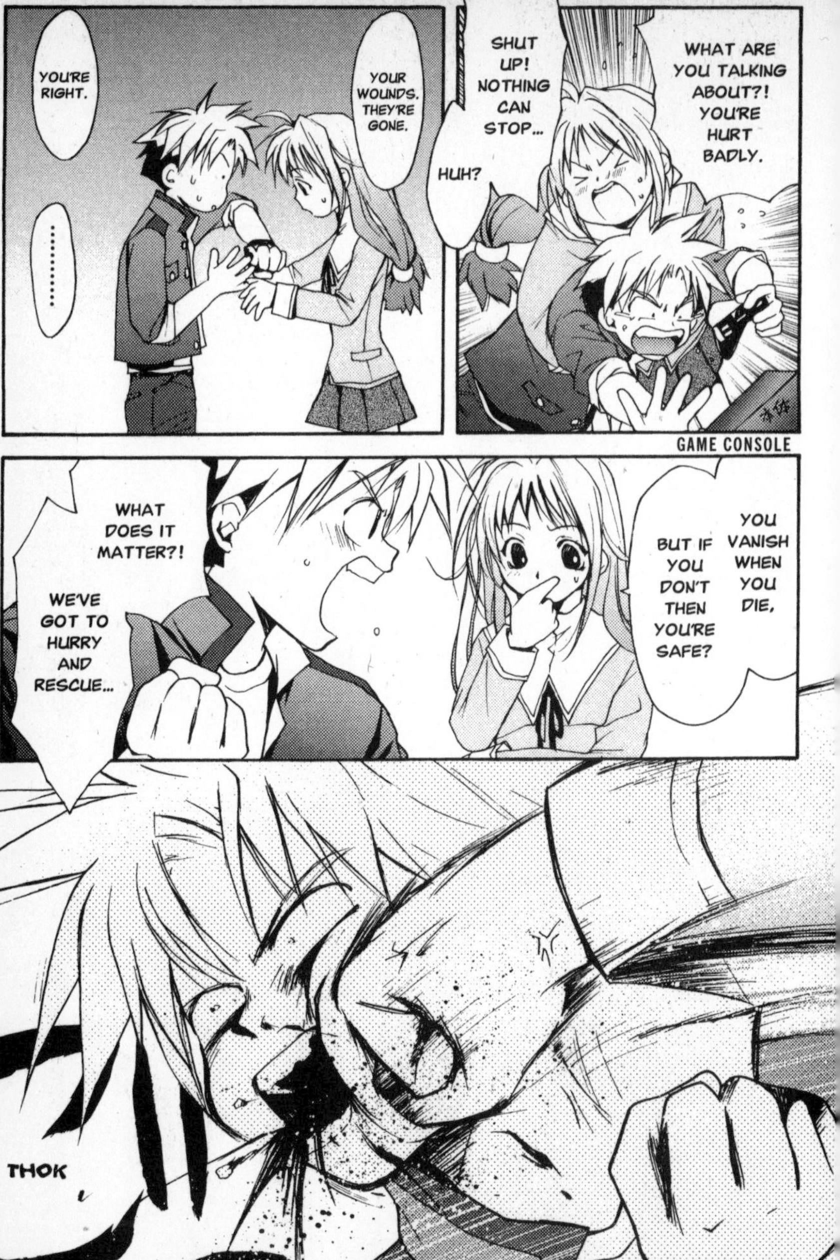
WHAT ARE YOU TALKING ABOUT?! YOU'RE HURT BADLY.
SHUT UP! NOTHING CAN STOP...
HUH?
YOUR WOUNDS. THEY'RE GONE.
YOU'RE RIGHT.
....
GAME CONSOLE
YOU VANISH WHEN YOU DIE,
BUT IF YOU DON'T THEN YOU'RE SAFE?
WHAT DOES IT MATTER?!
WE'VE GOT TO HURRY AND RESCUE...
THOK

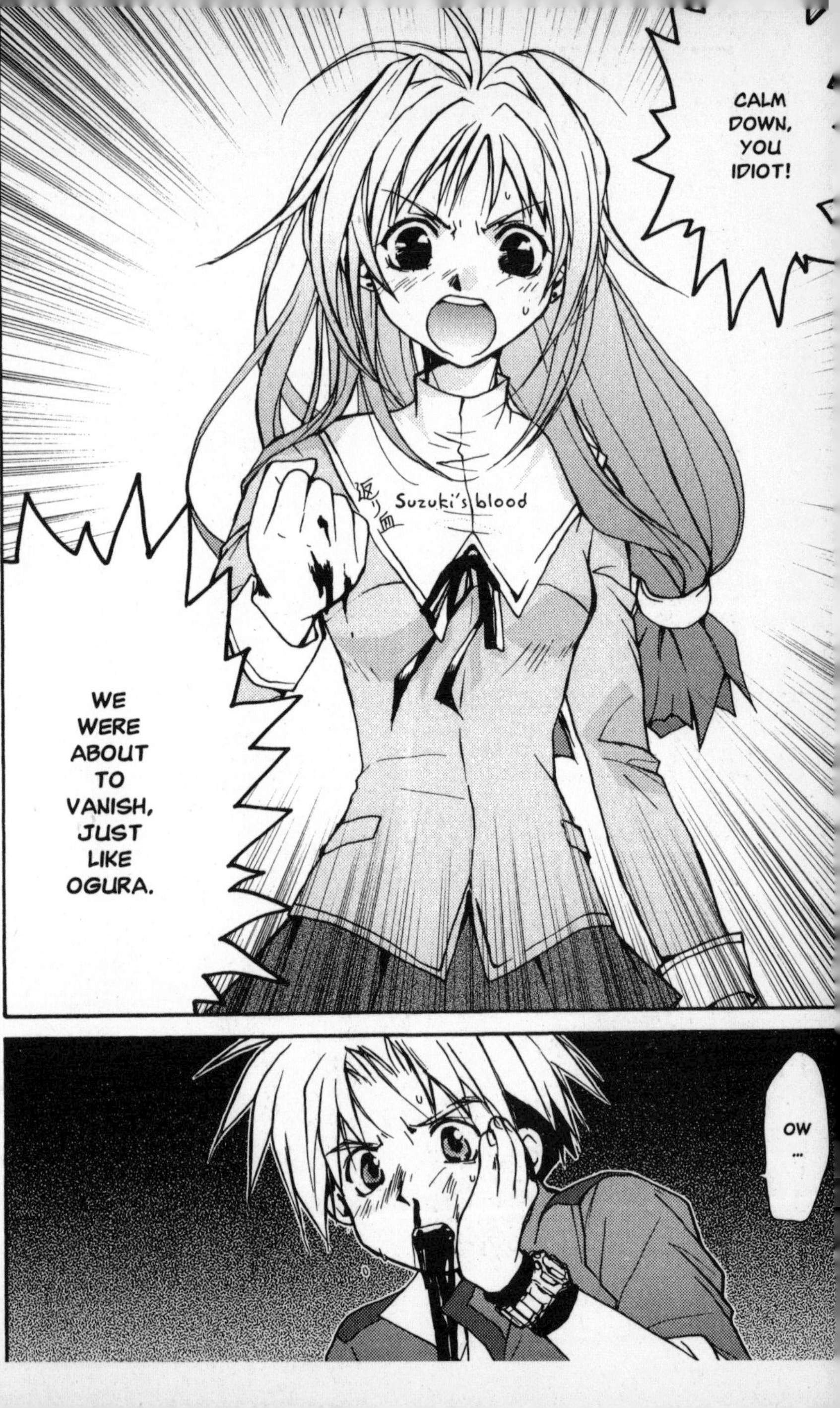
CALM DOWN, YOU IDIOT!
Suzuki's blood
WE WERE ABOUT TO VANISH, JUST LIKE OGURA.
OW ...

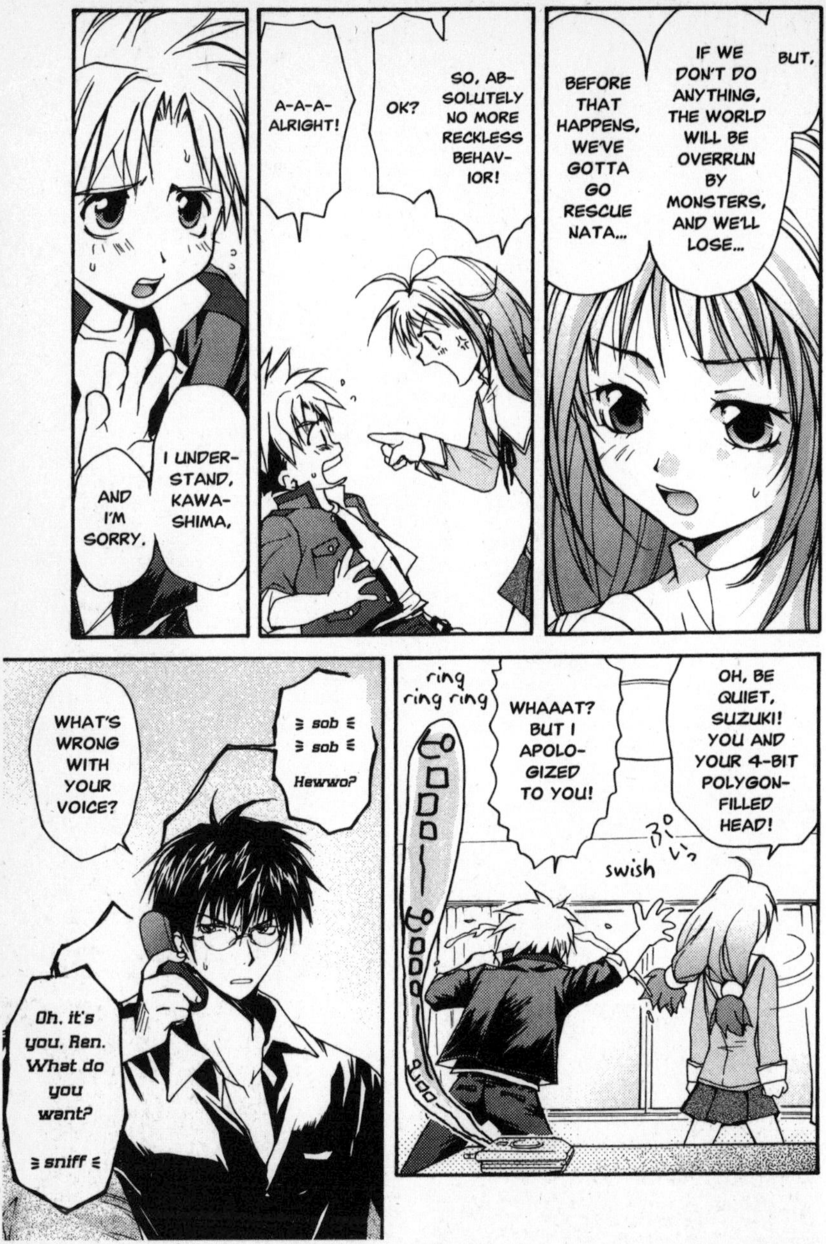
BUT,
IF WE DON'T DO ANYTHING, THE WORLD WILL BE OVERRUN BY MONSTERS, AND WE'LL LOSE...
BEFORE THAT HAPPENS, WE'VE GOTTA GO RESCUE NATA...
SO, AB-SOLUTELY NO MORE RECKLESS BEHAV-IOR!
OK?
A-A-A-ALRIGHT!
I UNDER-STAND, KAWA-SHIMA,
AND I'M SORRY.
OH, BE QUIET, SUZUKI! YOU AND YOUR 4-BIT POLYGON-FILLED HEAD!
WHAAAT? BUT I APOLO-GIZED TO YOU!
swish
ring ring ring
sob sob Hewwo?
WHAT'S WRONG WITH YOUR VOICE?
Oh, it's you, Ren. What do you want?
sniff

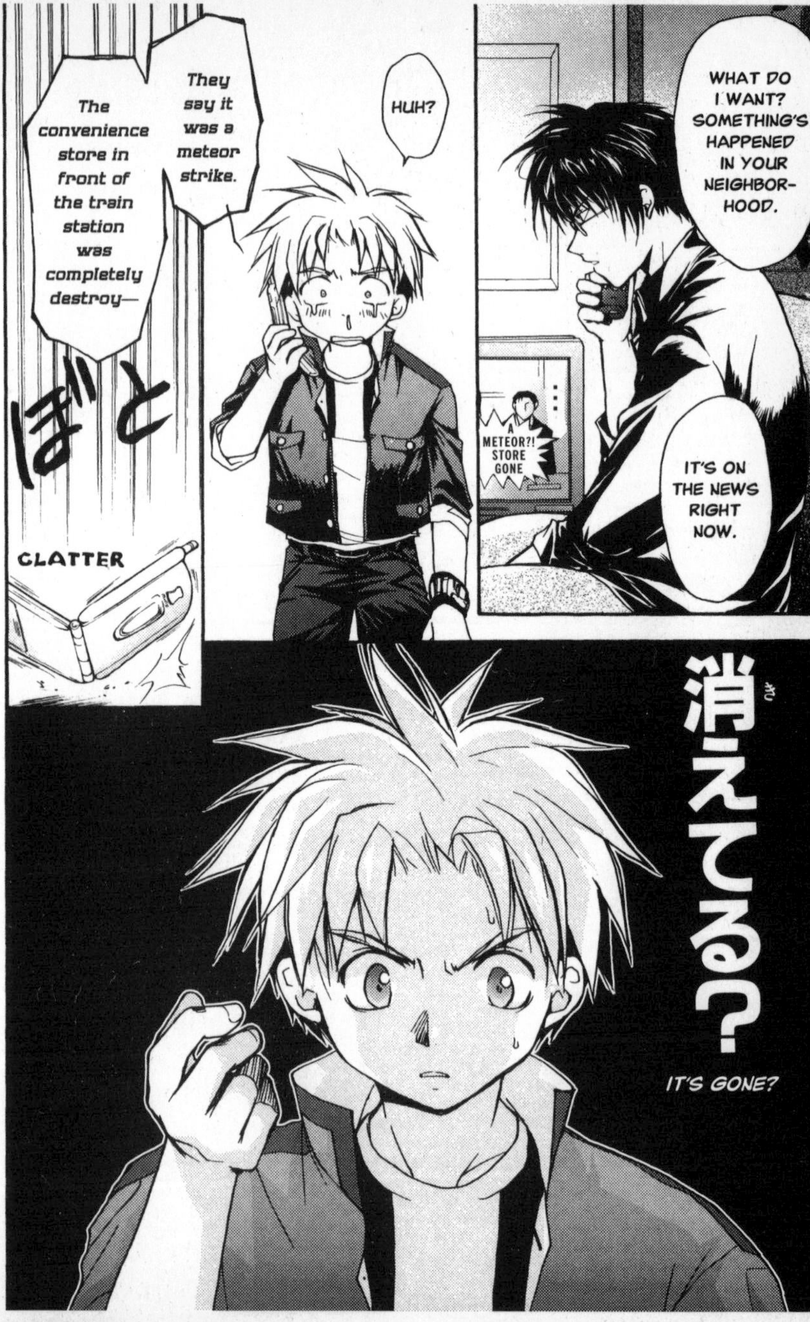

WHAT DO I WANT? SOMETHING'S HAPPENED IN YOUR NEIGHBOR-HOOD.
A METEOR?! STORE GONE
IT'S ON THE NEWS RIGHT NOW.
HUH?
They say it was a meteor strike.
The convenience store in front of the train station was completely destroy—
ぽと
CLATTER
消えてる?
IT'S GONE?

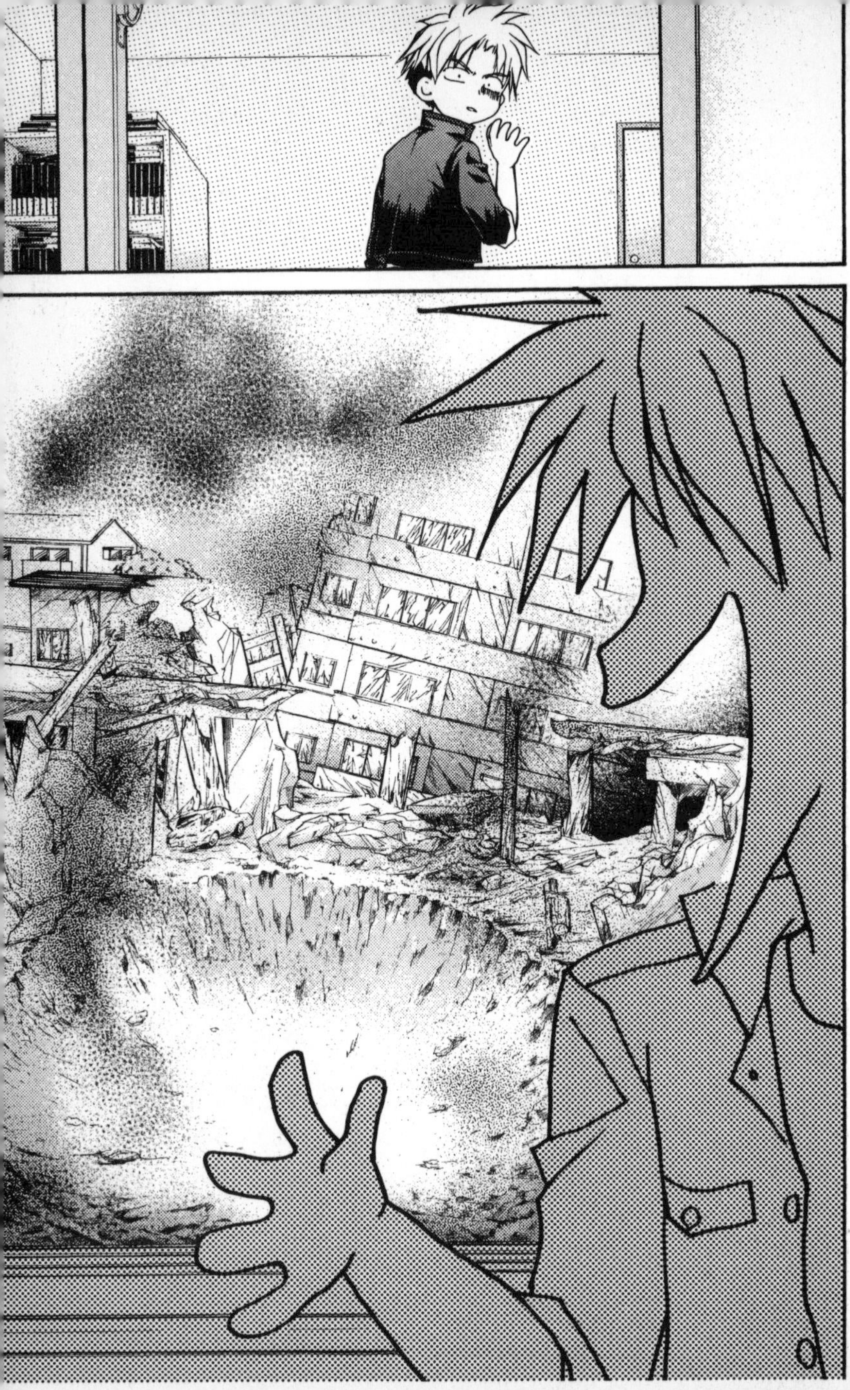

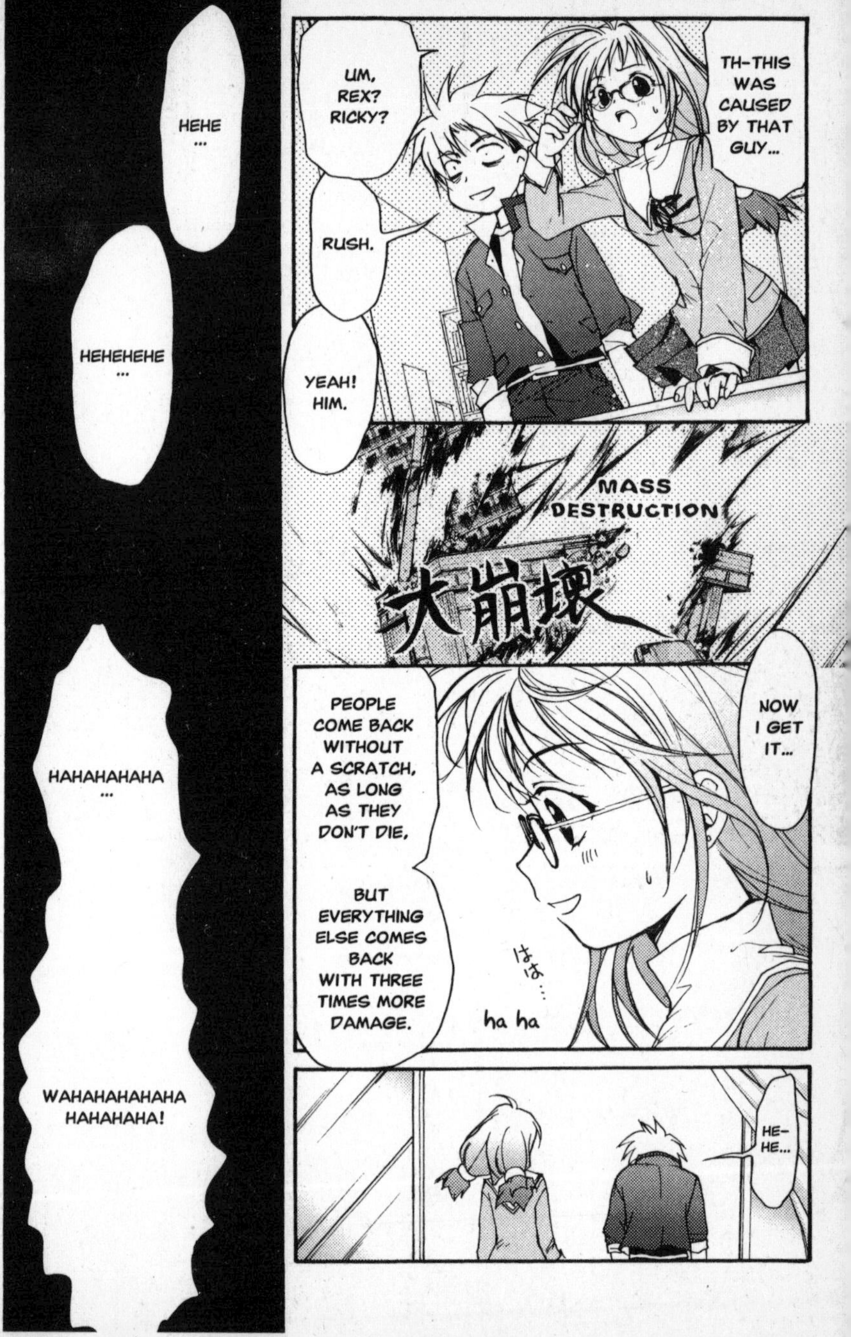
TH-THIS WAS CAUSED BY THAT GUY...
UM, REX? RICKY?
RUSH.
YEAH! HIM.
大崩壊
MASS DESTRUCTION
NOW I GET IT...
PEOPLE COME BACK WITHOUT A SCRATCH, AS LONG AS THEY DON'T DIE,
BUT EVERYTHING ELSE COMES BACK WITH THREE TIMES MORE DAMAGE.
はは…
ha ha
HE-HE...
HEHE...
HEHEHEHE...
HAHAHAHAHA...
WAHAHAHAHAHA HAHAHAHA!

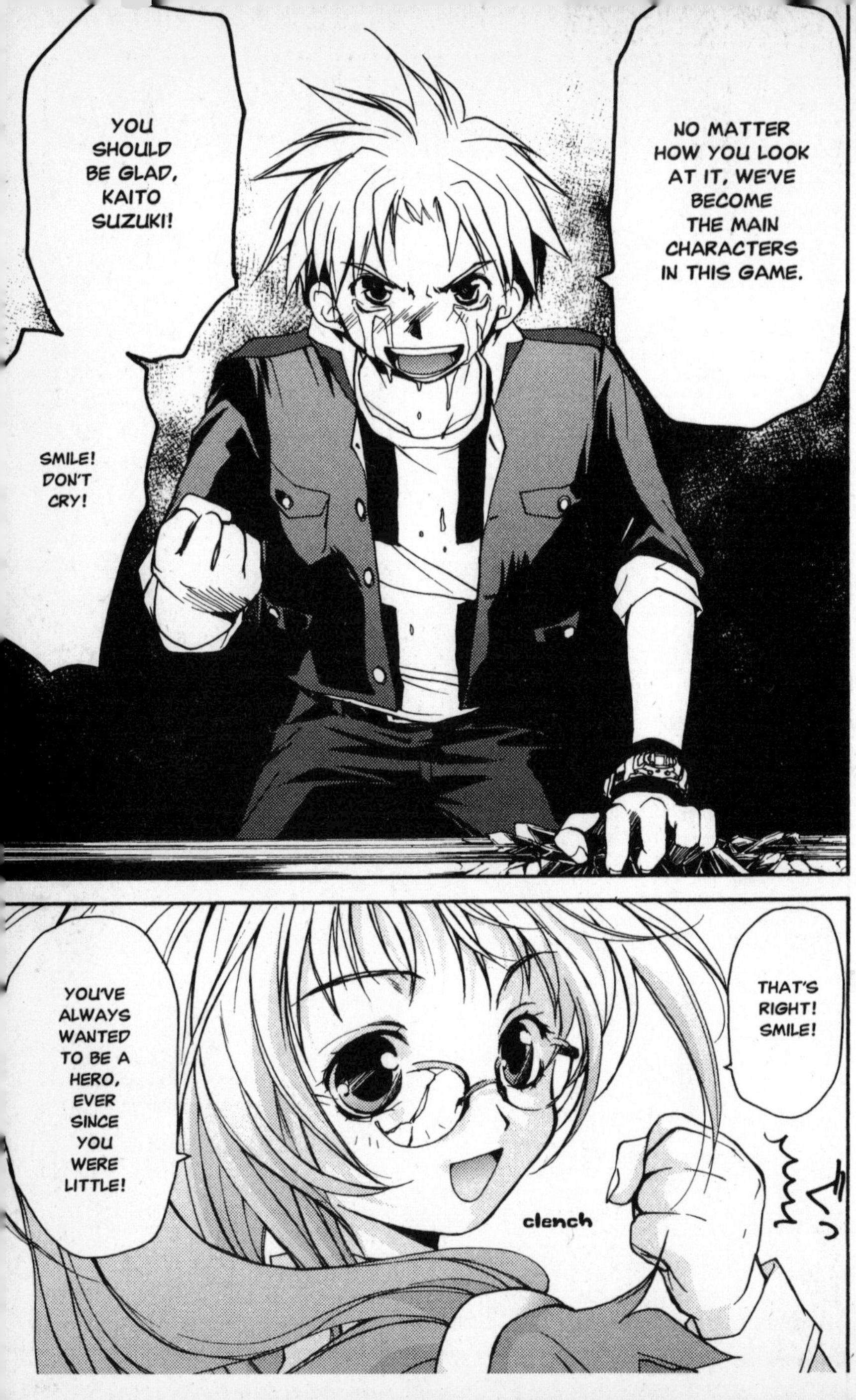
NO MATTER HOW YOU LOOK AT IT, WE'VE BECOME THE MAIN CHARACTERS IN THIS GAME.
YOU SHOULD BE GLAD, KAITO SUZUKI!
SMILE! DON'T CRY!
THAT'S RIGHT! SMILE!
YOU'VE ALWAYS WANTED TO BE A HERO, EVER SINCE YOU WERE LITTLE!
clench

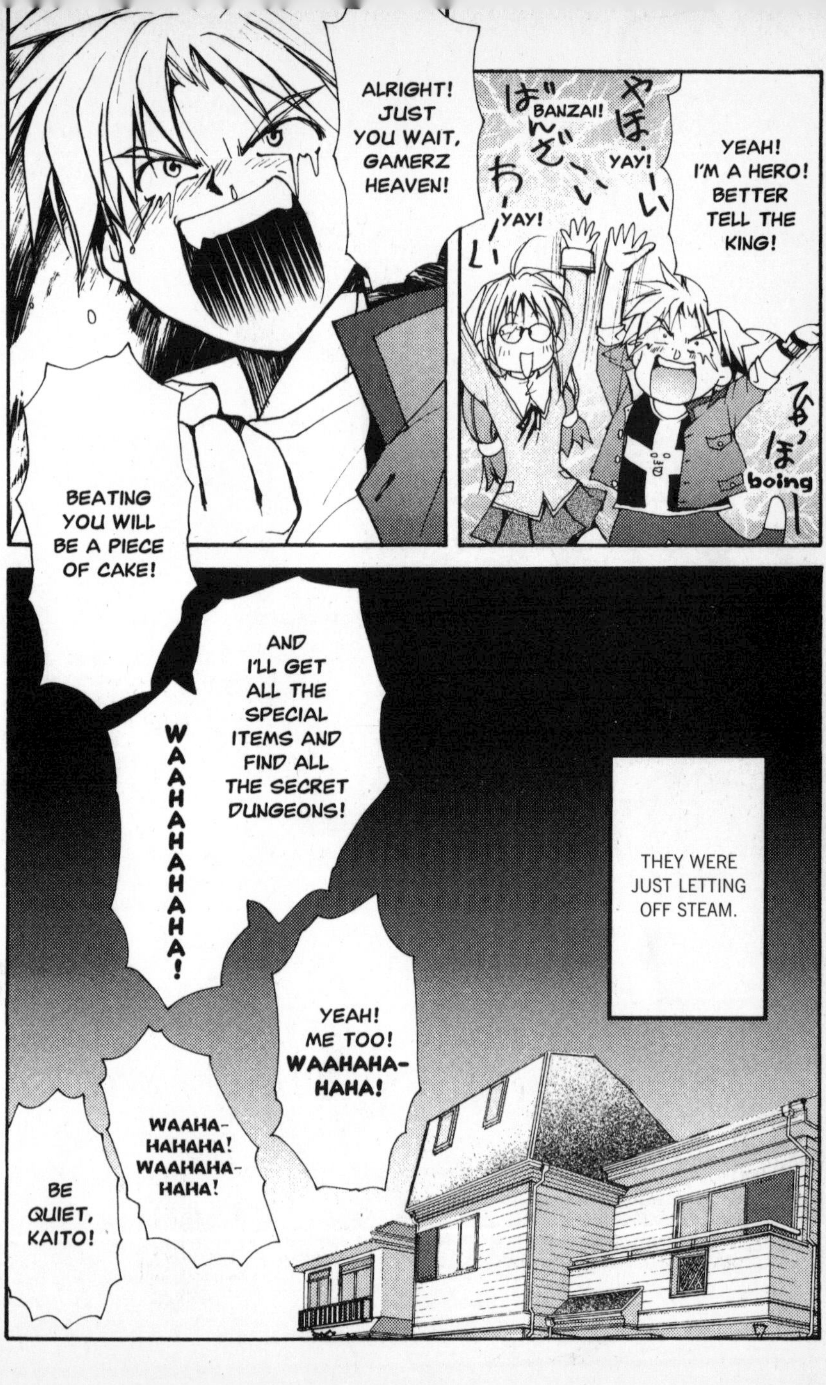
BANZAI!
YAY!
YAY!
YEAH! I'M A HERO! BETTER TELL THE KING!
boing
ALRIGHT! JUST YOU WAIT, GAMERZ HEAVEN!
BEATING YOU WILL BE A PIECE OF CAKE!
THEY WERE JUST LETTING OFF STEAM.
AND I'LL GET ALL THE SPECIAL ITEMS AND FIND ALL THE SECRET DUNGEONS!
WAAHAHAHAHAHA!
YEAH! ME TOO! WAAHAHA-HAHA!
WAAHA-HAHAHA! WAAHAHA-HAHA!
BE QUIET, KAITO!

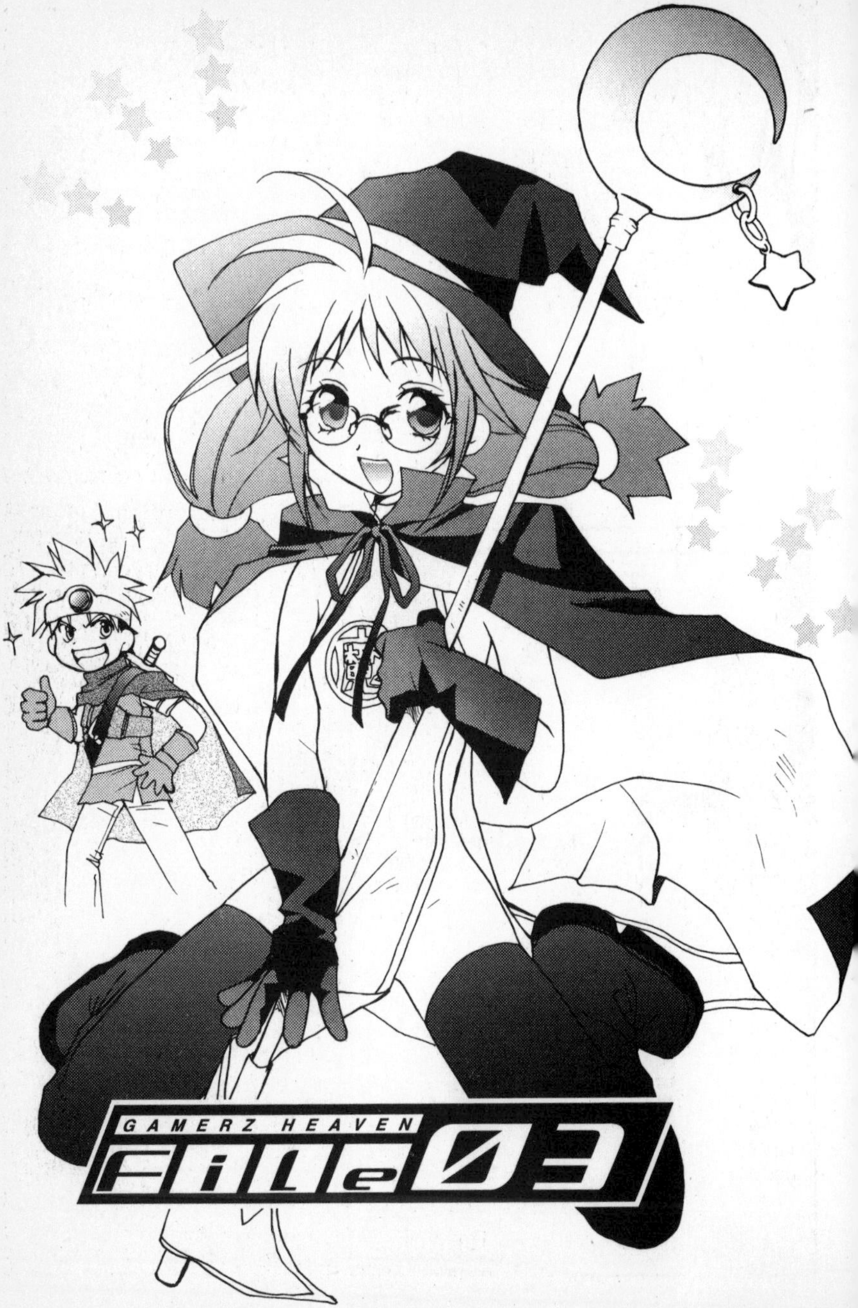
GAMERZ HEAVEN
FILe 03

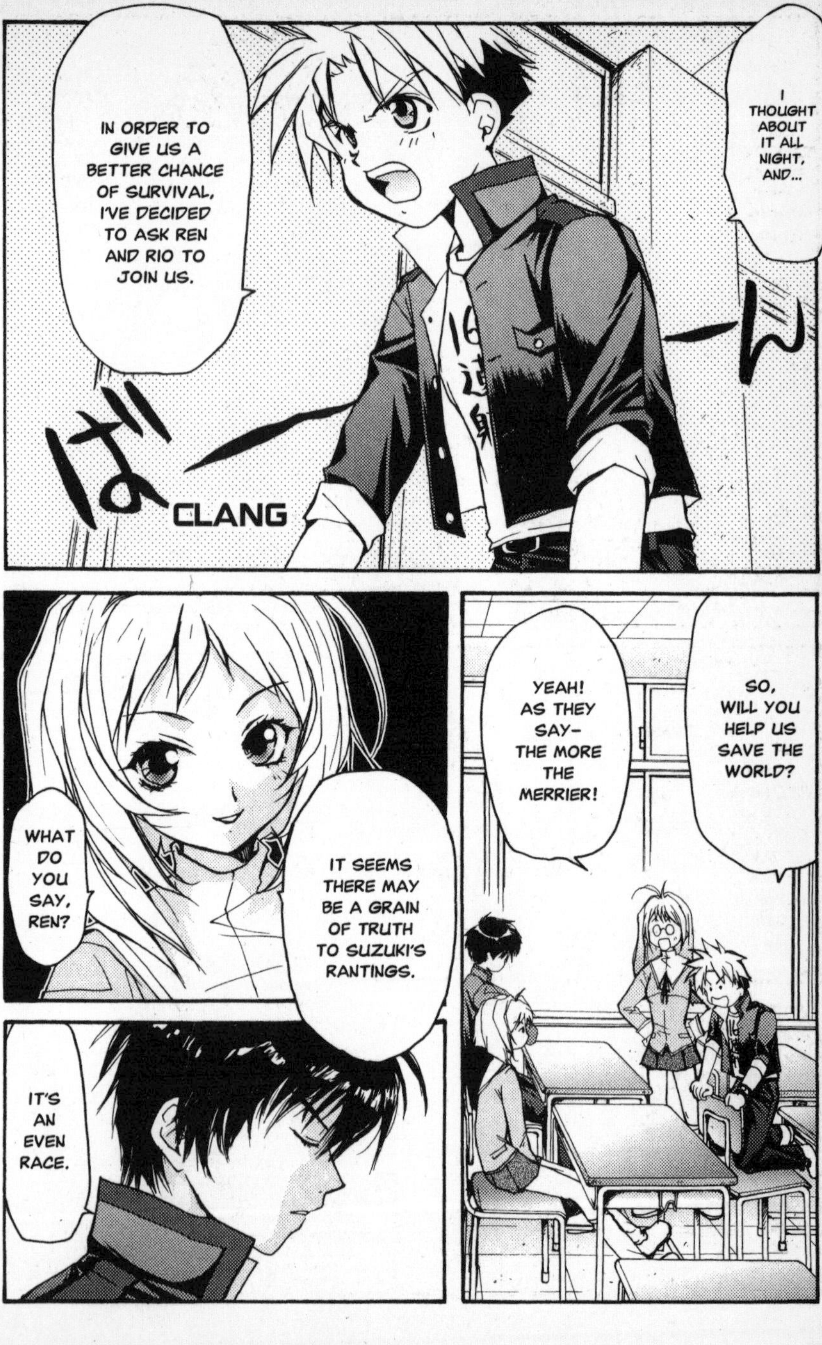

I THOUGHT ABOUT IT ALL NIGHT, AND...
IN ORDER TO GIVE US A BETTER CHANCE OF SURVIVAL, I'VE DECIDED TO ASK REN AND RIO TO JOIN US.
ば
ーん
CLANG
SO, WILL YOU HELP US SAVE THE WORLD?
YEAH! AS THEY SAY– THE MORE THE MERRIER!
IT SEEMS THERE MAY BE A GRAIN OF TRUTH TO SUZUKI'S RANTINGS.
WHAT DO YOU SAY, REN?
IT'S AN EVEN RACE.

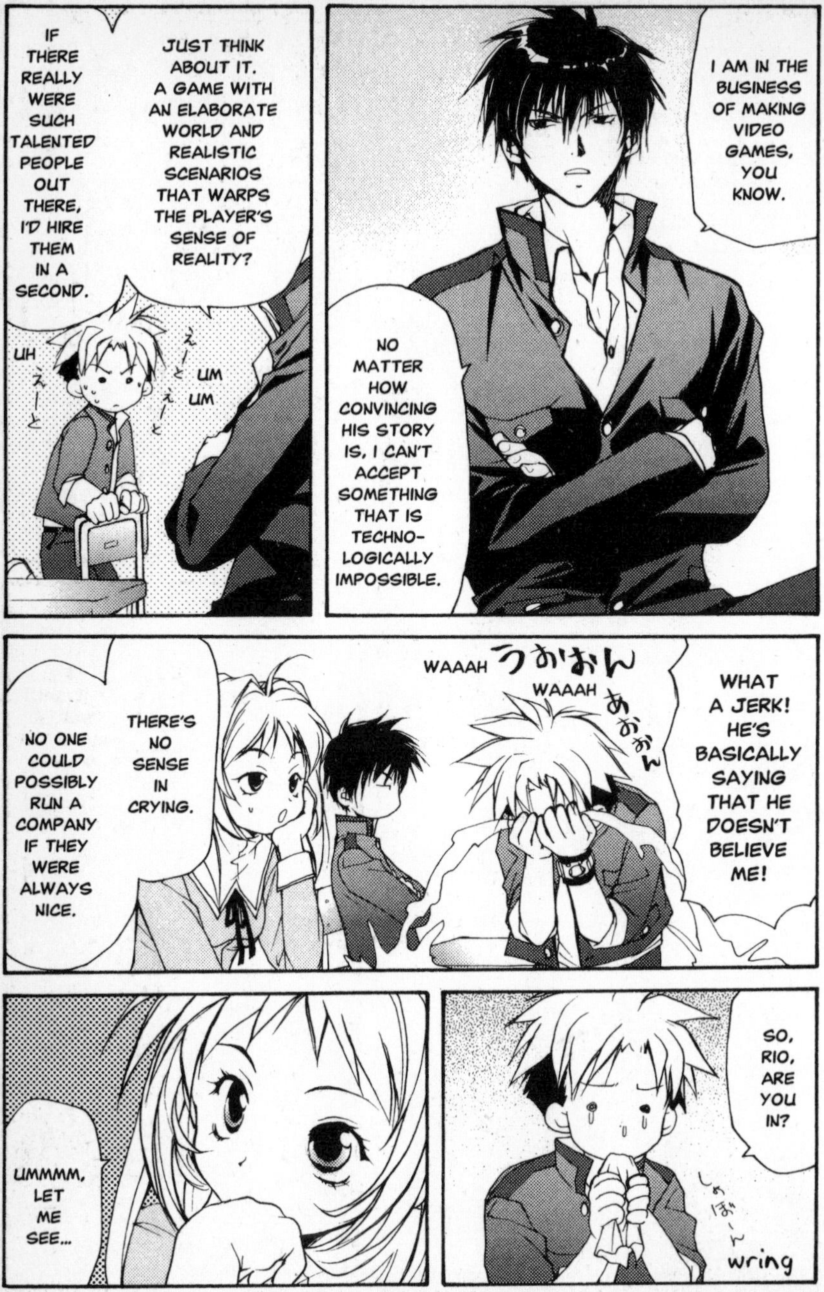
I AM IN THE BUSINESS OF MAKING VIDEO GAMES, YOU KNOW.
NO MATTER HOW CONVINCING HIS STORY IS, I CAN'T ACCEPT SOMETHING THAT IS TECHNO-LOGICALLY IMPOSSIBLE.
JUST THINK ABOUT IT. A GAME WITH AN ELABORATE WORLD AND REALISTIC SCENARIOS THAT WARPS THE PLAYER'S SENSE OF REALITY?
IF THERE REALLY WERE SUCH TALENTED PEOPLE OUT THERE, I'D HIRE THEM IN A SECOND.
UM UM えーと えーと
UH えーと
WAAAH うおおん
WAAAH あおおん
WHAT A JERK! HE'S BASICALLY SAYING THAT HE DOESN'T BELIEVE ME!
THERE'S NO SENSE IN CRYING.
NO ONE COULD POSSIBLY RUN A COMPANY IF THEY WERE ALWAYS NICE.
SO, RIO, ARE YOU IN?
wring
UMMMM, LET ME SEE...

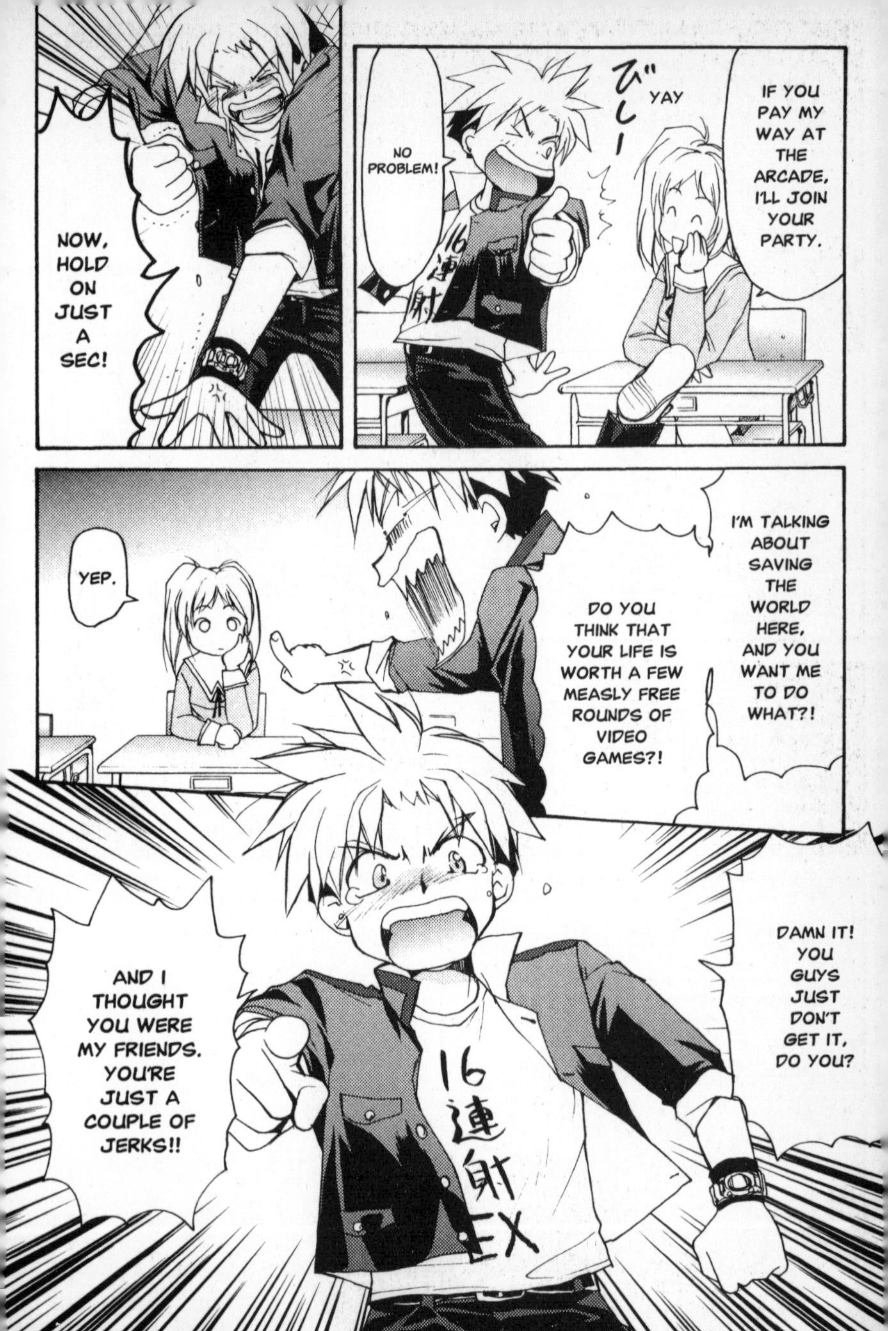
IF YOU PAY MY WAY AT THE ARCADE, I'LL JOIN YOUR PARTY.
YAY
びしー
NO PROBLEM!
NOW, HOLD ON JUST A SEC!
I'M TALKING ABOUT SAVING THE WORLD HERE, AND YOU WANT ME TO DO WHAT?!
DO YOU THINK THAT YOUR LIFE IS WORTH A FEW MEASLY FREE ROUNDS OF VIDEO GAMES?!
YEP.
DAMN IT! YOU GUYS JUST DON'T GET IT, DO YOU?
AND I THOUGHT YOU WERE MY FRIENDS. YOU'RE JUST A COUPLE OF JERKS!!
16連射EX

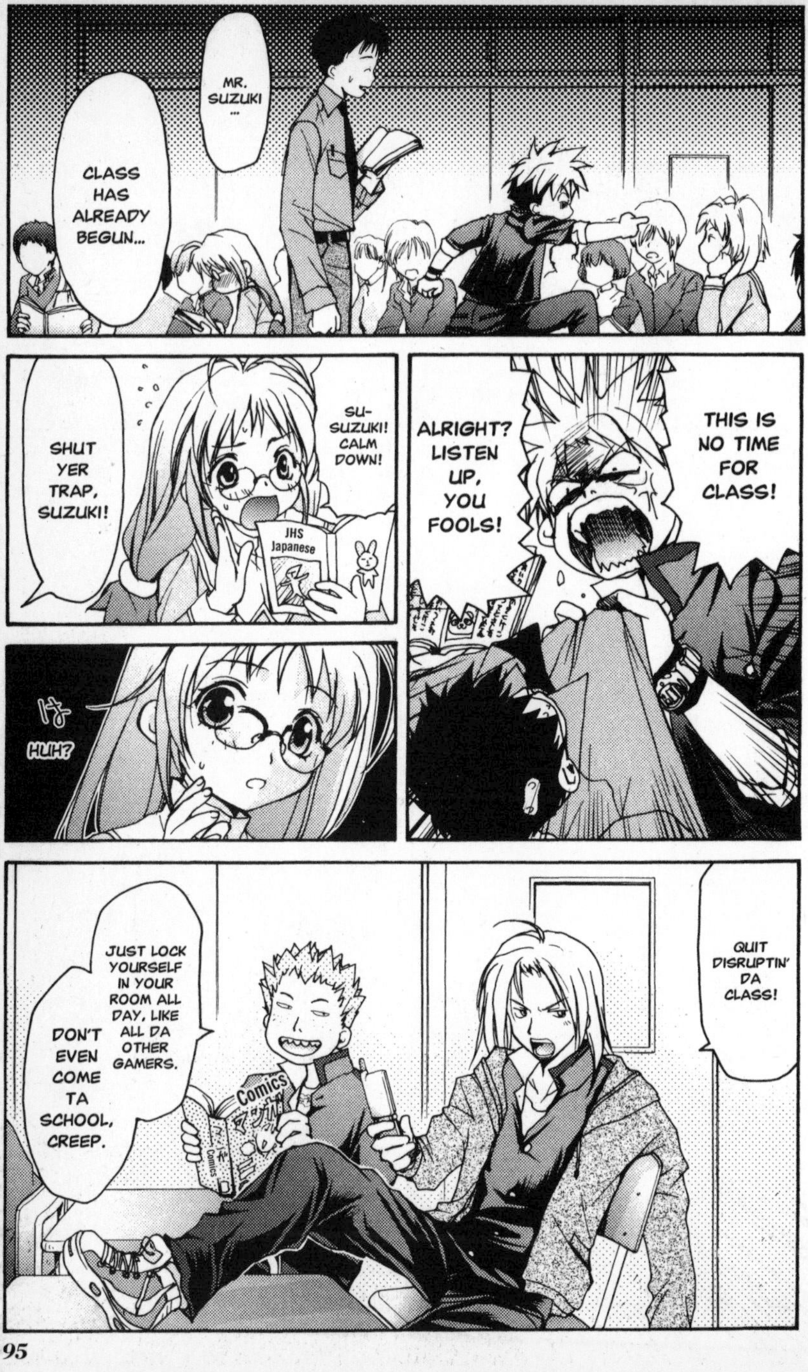
MR. SUZUKI...
CLASS HAS ALREADY BEGUN...
THIS IS NO TIME FOR CLASS!
ALRIGHT? LISTEN UP, YOU FOOLS!
SU-SUZUKI! CALM DOWN!
JHS Japanese
SHUT YER TRAP, SUZUKI!
は
HUH?
QUIT DISRUPTIN' DA CLASS!
JUST LOCK YOURSELF IN YOUR ROOM ALL DAY, LIKE ALL DA OTHER GAMERS.
DON'T EVEN COME TA SCHOOL, CREEP.
Comics
Comics

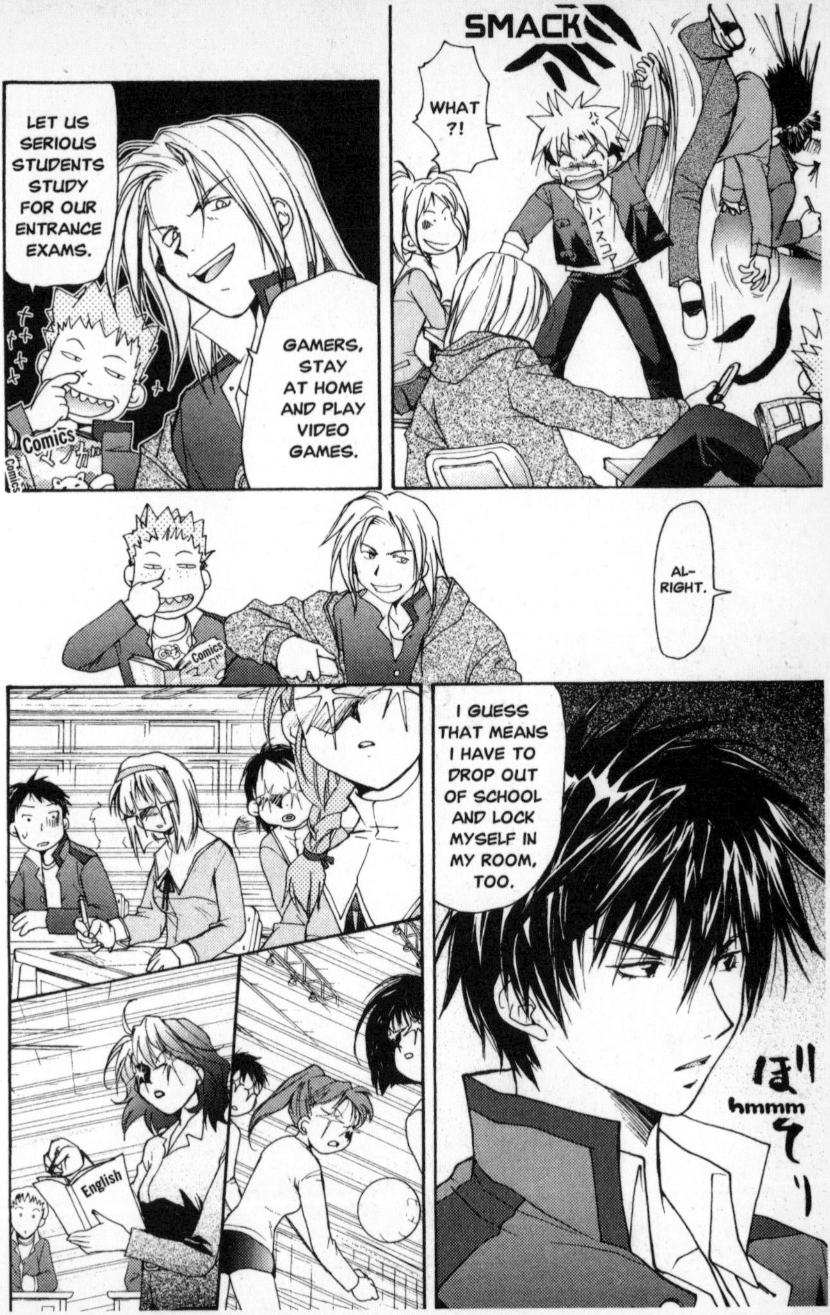
SMACK
WHAT ?!
LET US SERIOUS STUDENTS STUDY FOR OUR ENTRANCE EXAMS.
GAMERS, STAY AT HOME AND PLAY VIDEO GAMES.
Comics
AL-RIGHT.
I GUESS THAT MEANS I HAVE TO DROP OUT OF SCHOOL AND LOCK MYSELF IN MY ROOM, TOO.
ぽりぽり
hmmm
English

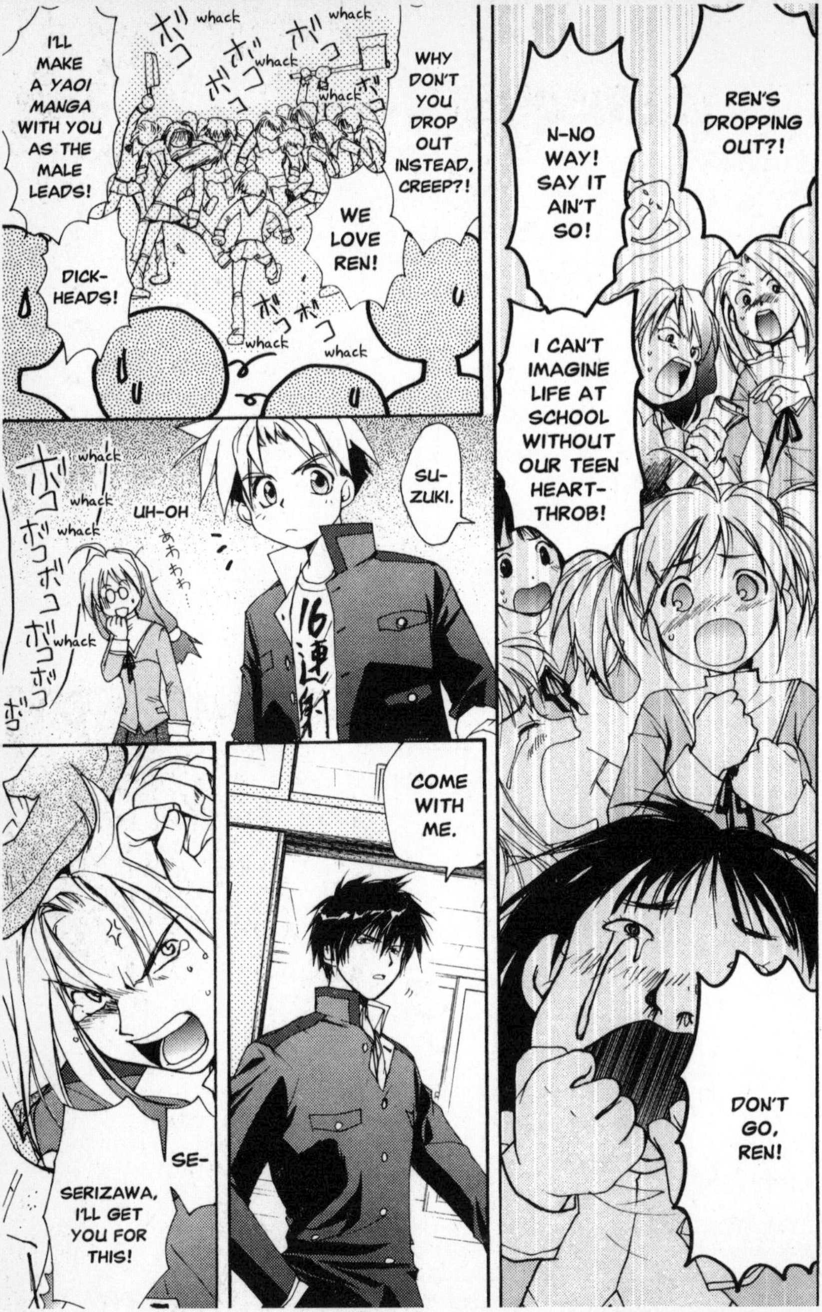
REN'S DROPPING OUT?!
N-NO WAY! SAY IT AIN'T SO!
I CAN'T IMAGINE LIFE AT SCHOOL WITHOUT OUR TEEN HEART-THROB!
DON'T GO, REN!
whack
whack
whack
whack
WHY DON'T YOU DROP OUT INSTEAD, CREEP?!
WE LOVE REN!
I'LL MAKE A YAOI MANGA WITH YOU AS THE MALE LEADS!
DICK-HEADS!
whack
whack
SU-ZUKI.
UH-OH
whack
whack
whack
whack
COME WITH ME.
SE-
SERIZAWA, I'LL GET YOU FOR THIS!

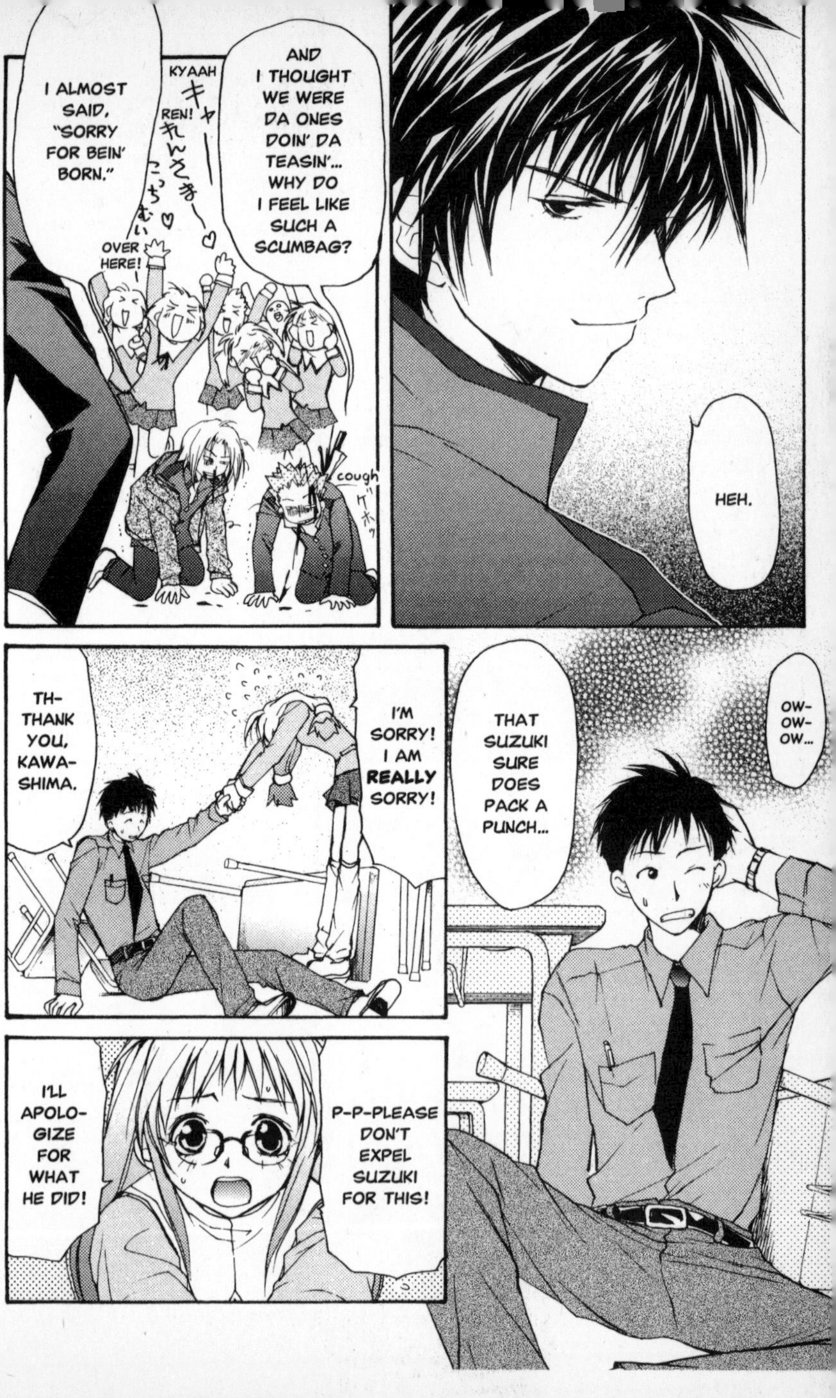
HEH.
AND I THOUGHT WE WERE DA ONES DOIN' DA TEASIN'... WHY DO I FEEL LIKE SUCH A SCUMBAG?
KYAAH
REN!
OVER HERE!
I ALMOST SAID, "SORRY FOR BEIN' BORN."
cough
OW-OW-OW...
THAT SUZUKI SURE DOES PACK A PUNCH...
I'M SORRY! I AM **REALLY** SORRY!
TH-THANK YOU, KAWA-SHIMA.
P-P-PLEASE DON'T EXPEL SUZUKI FOR THIS!
I'LL APOLO-GIZE FOR WHAT HE DID!

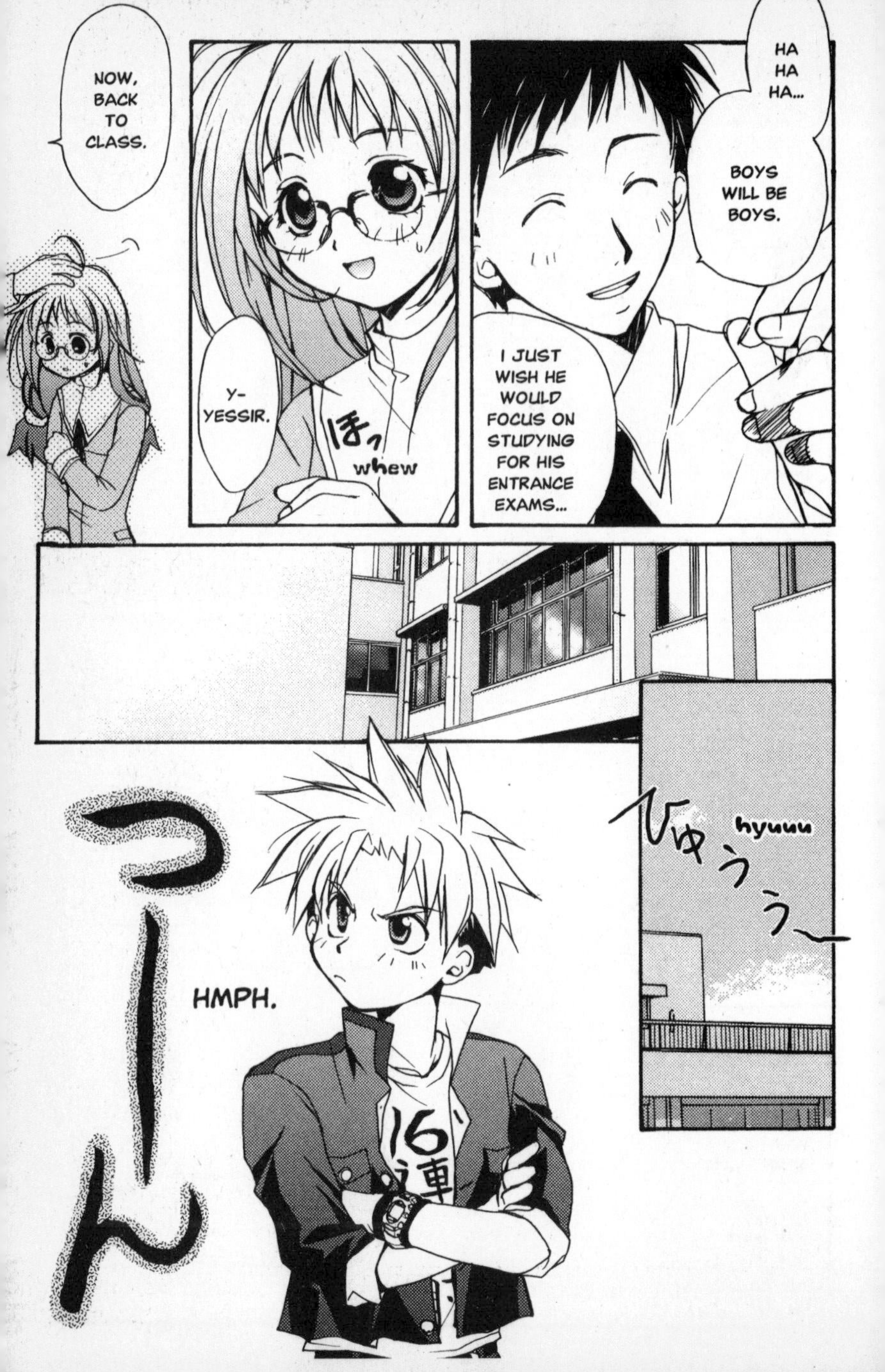
HA HA HA...
BOYS WILL BE BOYS.
I JUST WISH HE WOULD FOCUS ON STUDYING FOR HIS ENTRANCE EXAMS...
Y-YESSIR.
ほっ
whew
NOW, BACK TO CLASS.
ひゅううう~
hyuuu
HMPH.

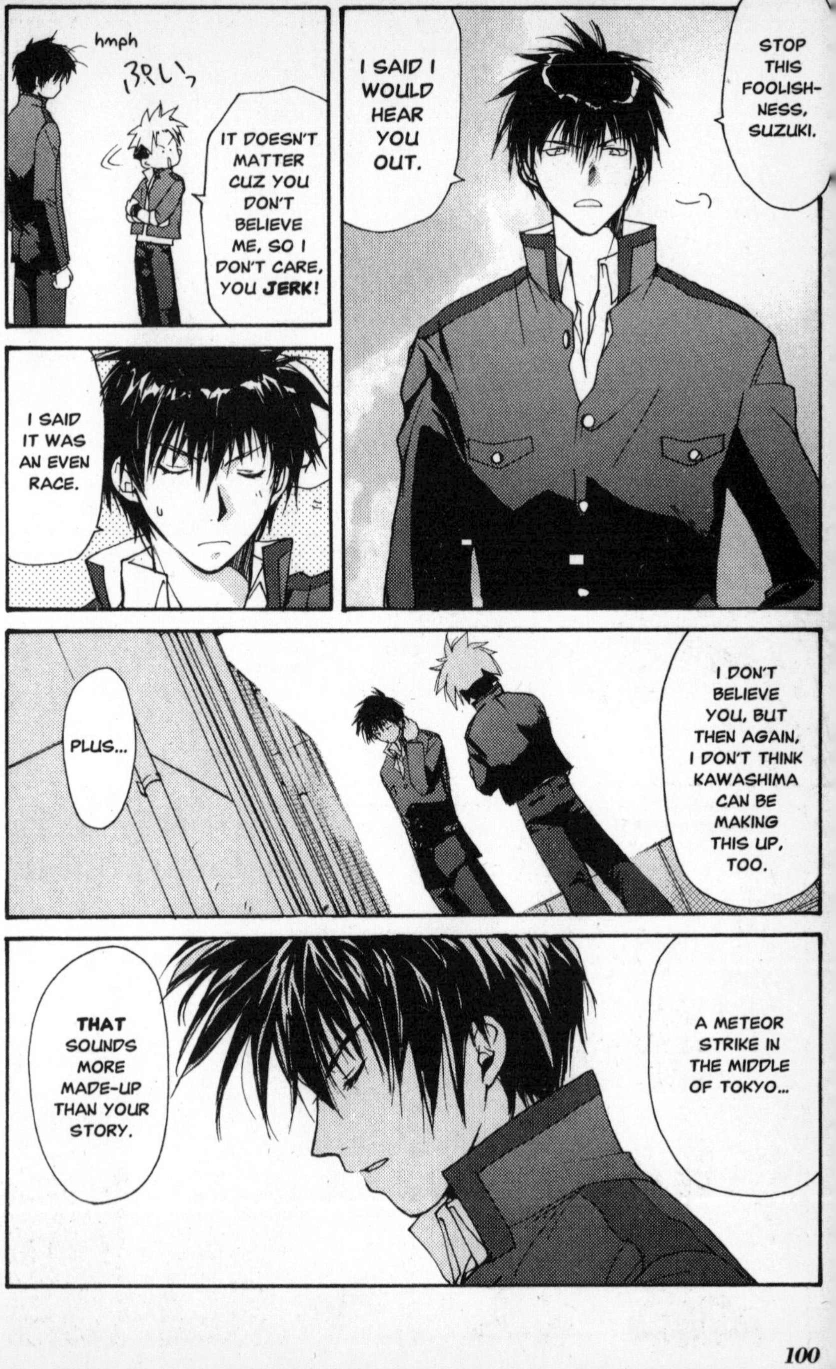
STOP THIS FOOLISHNESS, SUZUKI.
I SAID I WOULD HEAR YOU OUT.
hmph
ぷいっ
IT DOESN'T MATTER CUZ YOU DON'T BELIEVE ME, SO I DON'T CARE, YOU **JERK**!
I SAID IT WAS AN EVEN RACE.
I DON'T BELIEVE YOU, BUT THEN AGAIN, I DON'T THINK KAWASHIMA CAN BE MAKING THIS UP, TOO.
PLUS...
A METEOR STRIKE IN THE MIDDLE OF TOKYO...
THAT SOUNDS MORE MADE-UP THAN YOUR STORY.

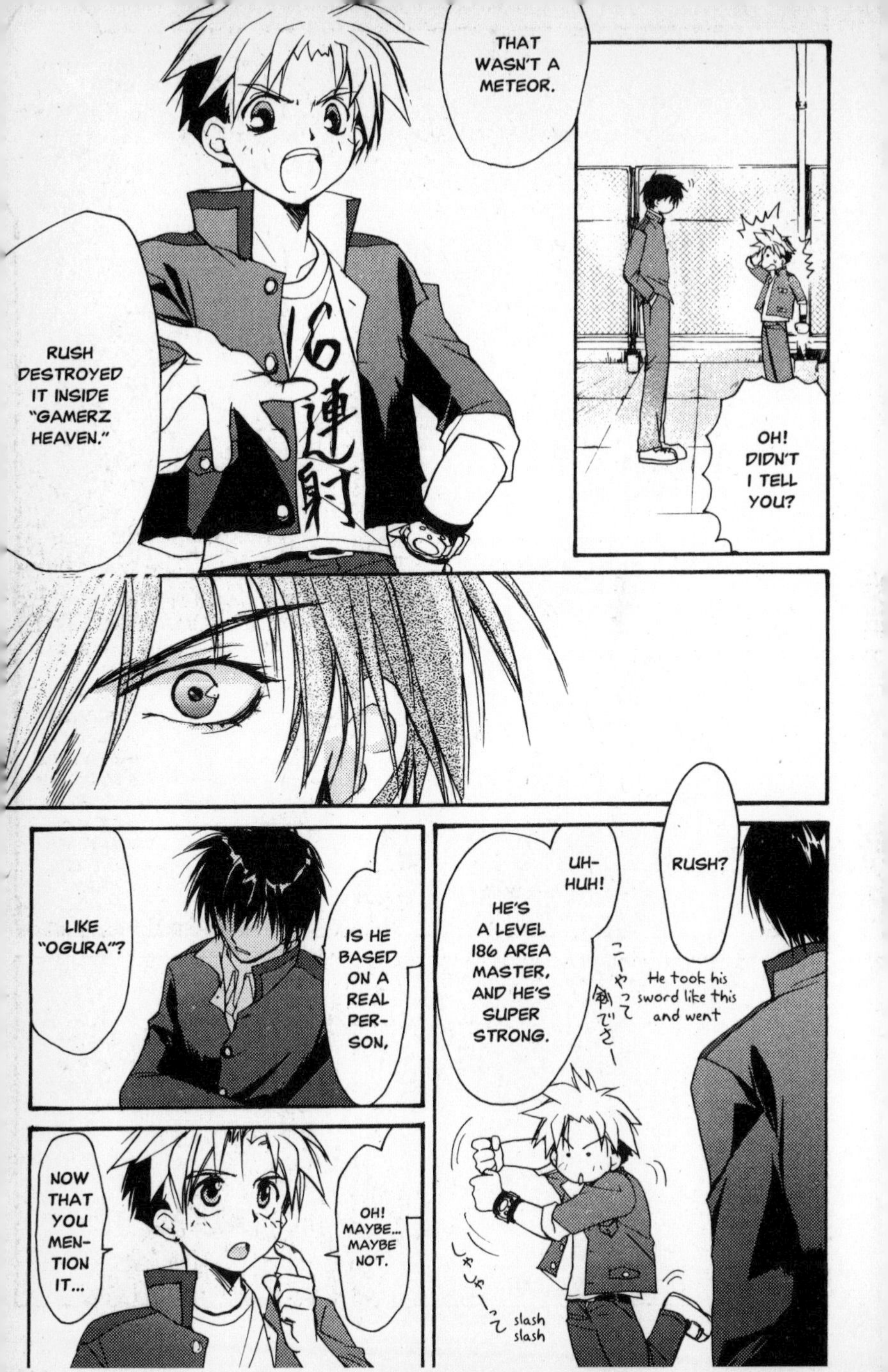

OH! DIDN'T I TELL YOU?
THAT WASN'T A METEOR.
RUSH DESTROYED IT INSIDE "GAMERZ HEAVEN."
16連射
RUSH?
UH-HUH!
HE'S A LEVEL 186 AREA MASTER, AND HE'S SUPER STRONG.
こーやって剣でさー
He took his sword like this and went
しゃしゃーって
slash slash
IS HE BASED ON A REAL PERSON,
LIKE "OGURA"?
OH! MAYBE... MAYBE NOT.
NOW THAT YOU MENTION IT...

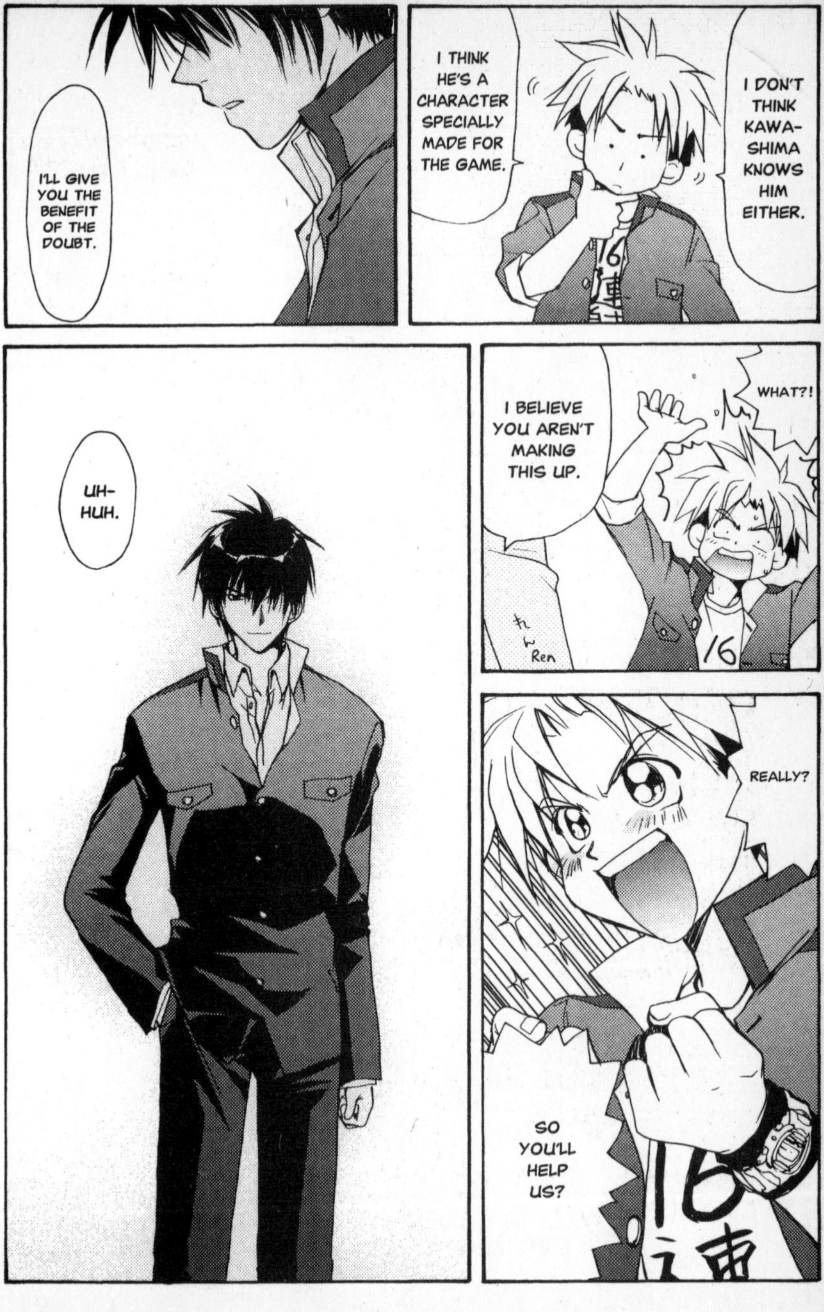
I DON'T THINK KAWA-SHIMA KNOWS HIM EITHER.
I THINK HE'S A CHARACTER SPECIALLY MADE FOR THE GAME.
I'LL GIVE YOU THE BENEFIT OF THE DOUBT.
I BELIEVE YOU AREN'T MAKING THIS UP.
WHAT?!
Ren
REALLY?
SO YOU'LL HELP US?
UH-HUH.

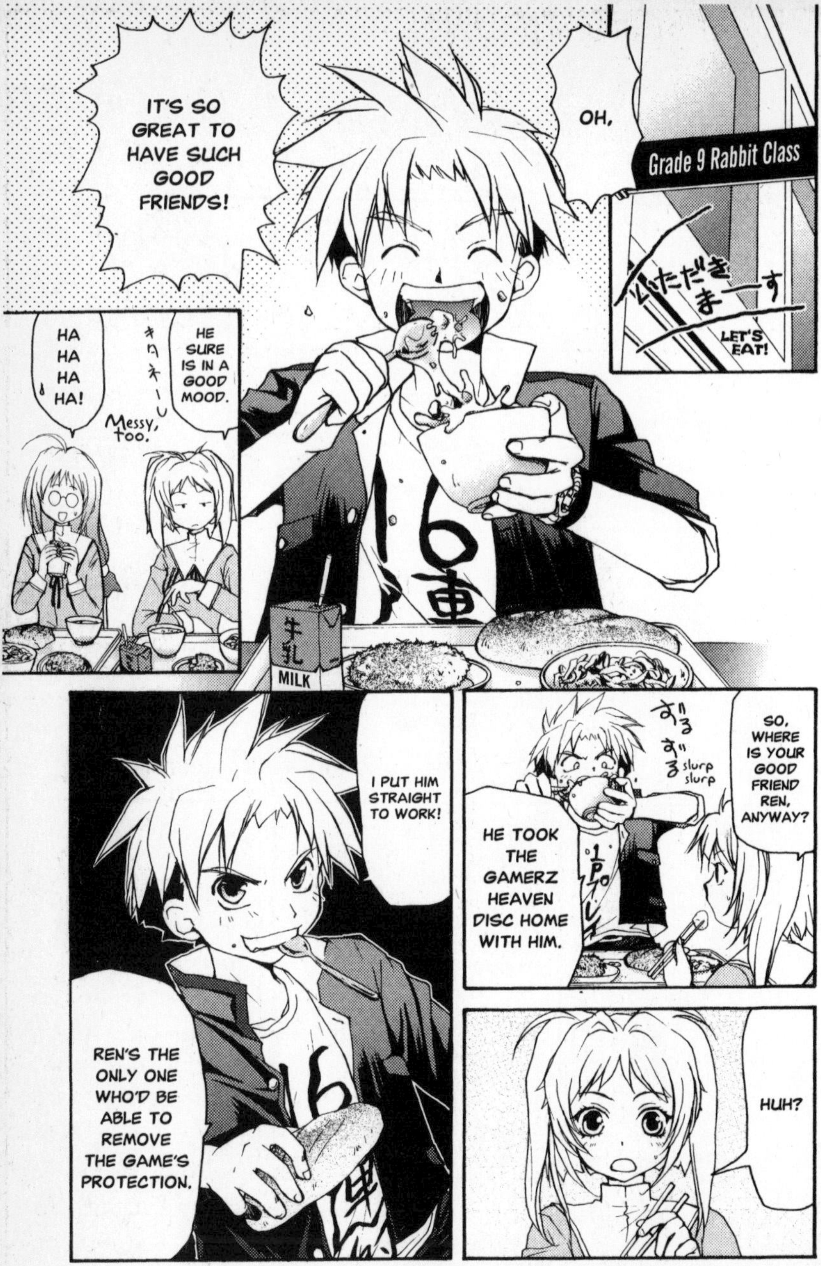

Grade 9 Rabbit Class
いただきまーす
LET'S EAT!
OH,
IT'S SO GREAT TO HAVE SUCH GOOD FRIENDS!
HE SURE IS IN A GOOD MOOD.
Messy, too.
HA HA HA HA!
牛乳
MILK
SO, WHERE IS YOUR GOOD FRIEND REN, ANYWAY?
ずるずる
slurp slurp
HE TOOK THE GAMERZ HEAVEN DISC HOME WITH HIM.
I PUT HIM STRAIGHT TO WORK!
REN'S THE ONLY ONE WHO'D BE ABLE TO REMOVE THE GAME'S PROTECTION.
HUH?

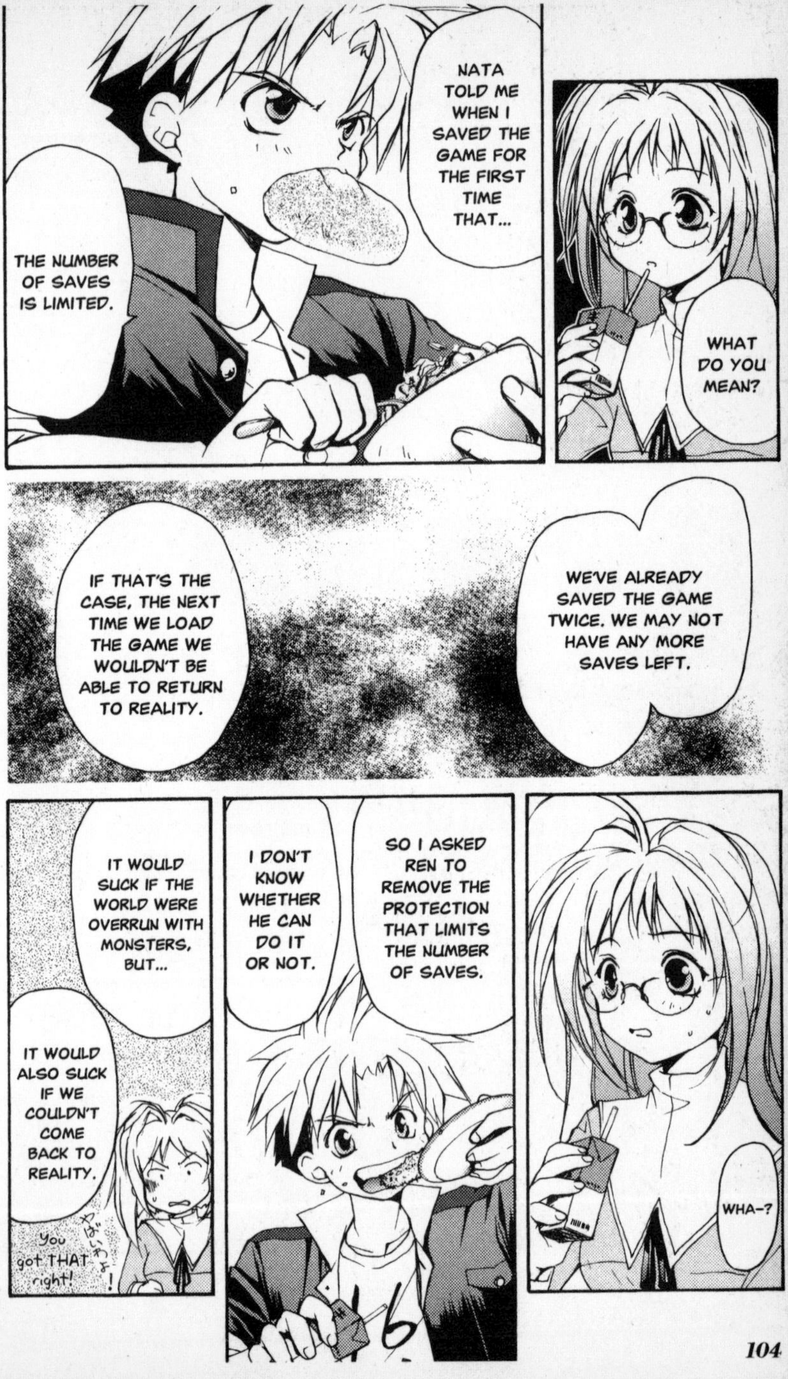
NATA TOLD ME WHEN I SAVED THE GAME FOR THE FIRST TIME THAT...
THE NUMBER OF SAVES IS LIMITED.
WHAT DO YOU MEAN?
WE'VE ALREADY SAVED THE GAME TWICE. WE MAY NOT HAVE ANY MORE SAVES LEFT.
IF THAT'S THE CASE, THE NEXT TIME WE LOAD THE GAME WE WOULDN'T BE ABLE TO RETURN TO REALITY.
WHA-?
SO I ASKED REN TO REMOVE THE PROTECTION THAT LIMITS THE NUMBER OF SAVES.
I DON'T KNOW WHETHER HE CAN DO IT OR NOT.
IT WOULD SUCK IF THE WORLD WERE OVERRUN WITH MONSTERS, BUT...
IT WOULD ALSO SUCK IF WE COULDN'T COME BACK TO REALITY.
やばいわよ!
You got THAT right!

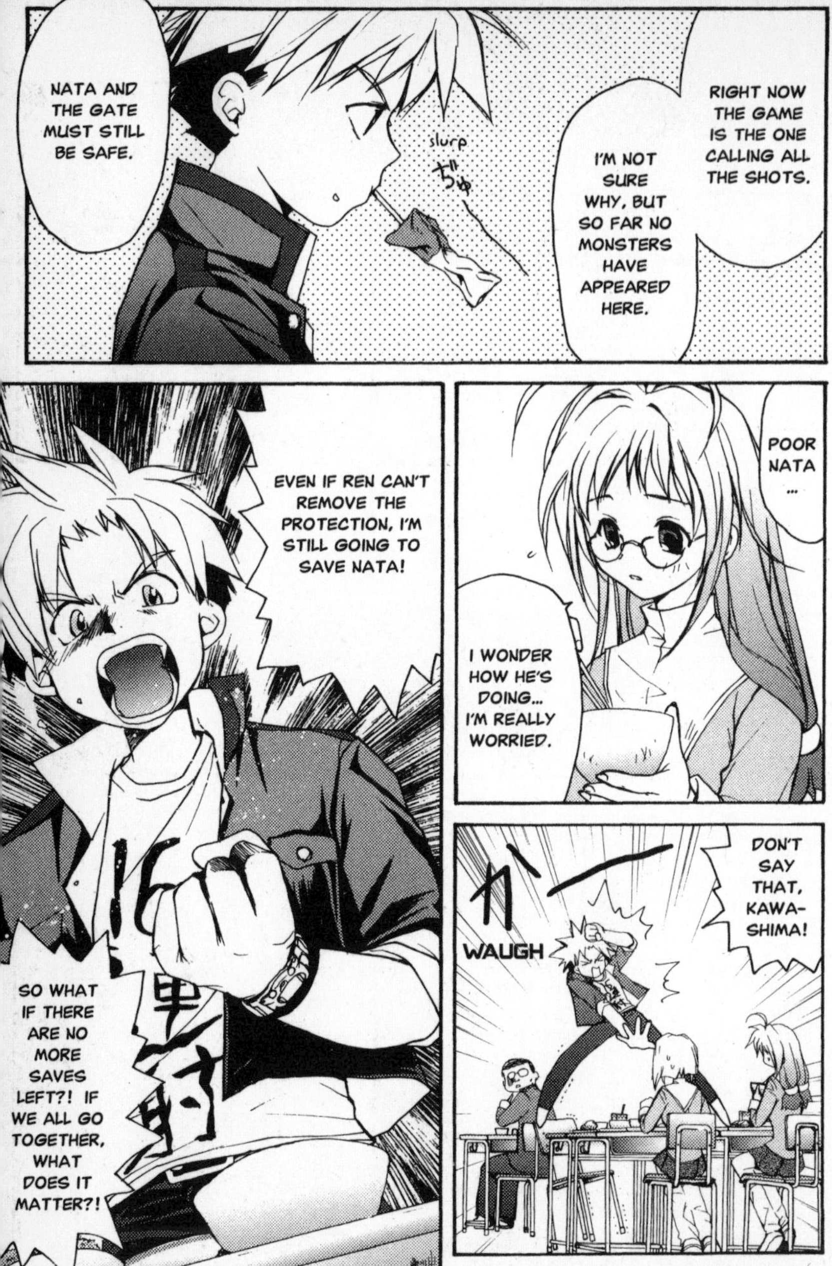

RIGHT NOW THE GAME IS THE ONE CALLING ALL THE SHOTS.
I'M NOT SURE WHY, BUT SO FAR NO MONSTERS HAVE APPEARED HERE.
NATA AND THE GATE MUST STILL BE SAFE.
slurp
POOR NATA...
I WONDER HOW HE'S DOING... I'M REALLY WORRIED.
DON'T SAY THAT, KAWA-SHIMA!
WAUGH
EVEN IF REN CAN'T REMOVE THE PROTECTION, I'M STILL GOING TO SAVE NATA!
SO WHAT IF THERE ARE NO MORE SAVES LEFT?! IF WE ALL GO TOGETHER, WHAT DOES IT MATTER?!

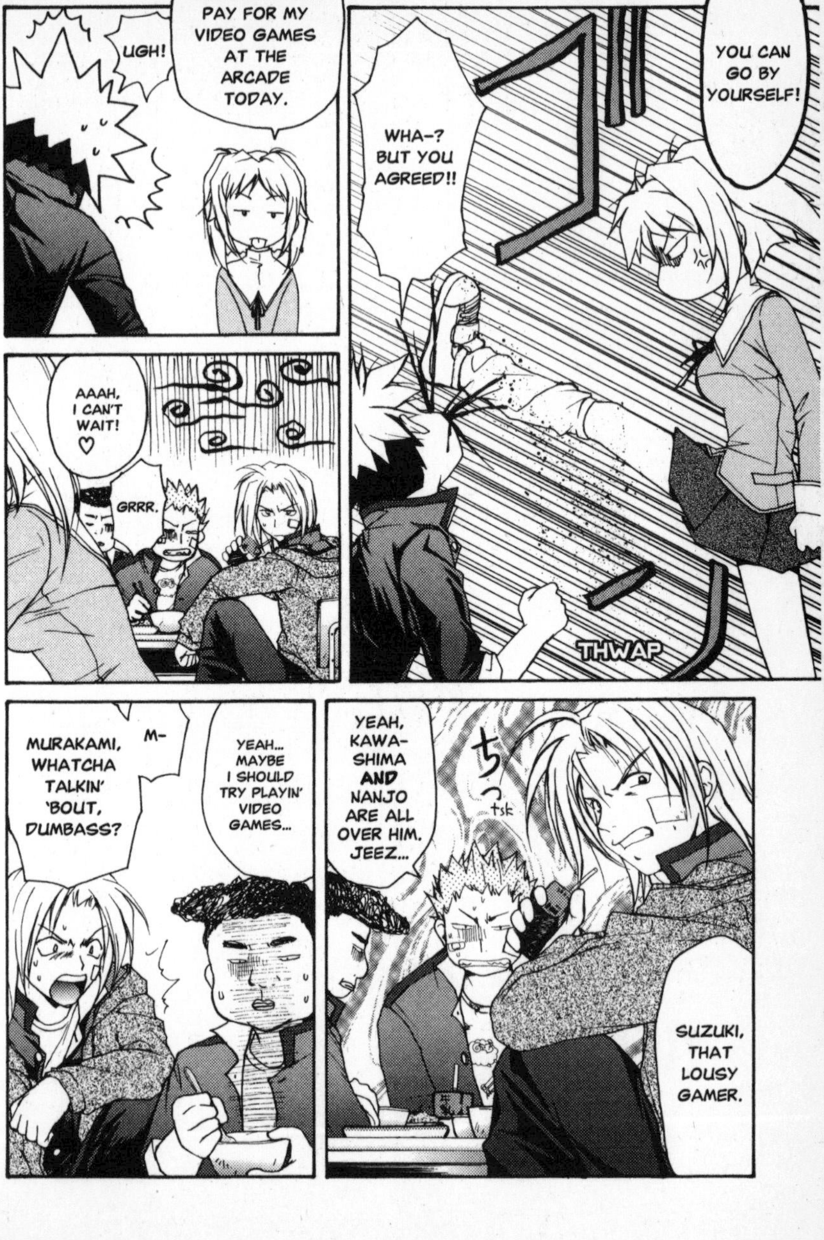
YOU CAN GO BY YOURSELF!
WHA-? BUT YOU AGREED!!
THWAP
I AGREED AS LONG AS YOU PAY FOR MY VIDEO GAMES AT THE ARCADE TODAY.
UGH!
AAAH, I CAN'T WAIT! ♡
GRRR.
SUZUKI, THAT LOUSY GAMER.
ちっ tsk
YEAH, KAWA-SHIMA AND NANJO ARE ALL OVER HIM. JEEZ...
YEAH... MAYBE I SHOULD TRY PLAYIN' VIDEO GAMES...
M-
MURAKAMI, WHATCHA TALKIN' 'BOUT, DUMBASS?

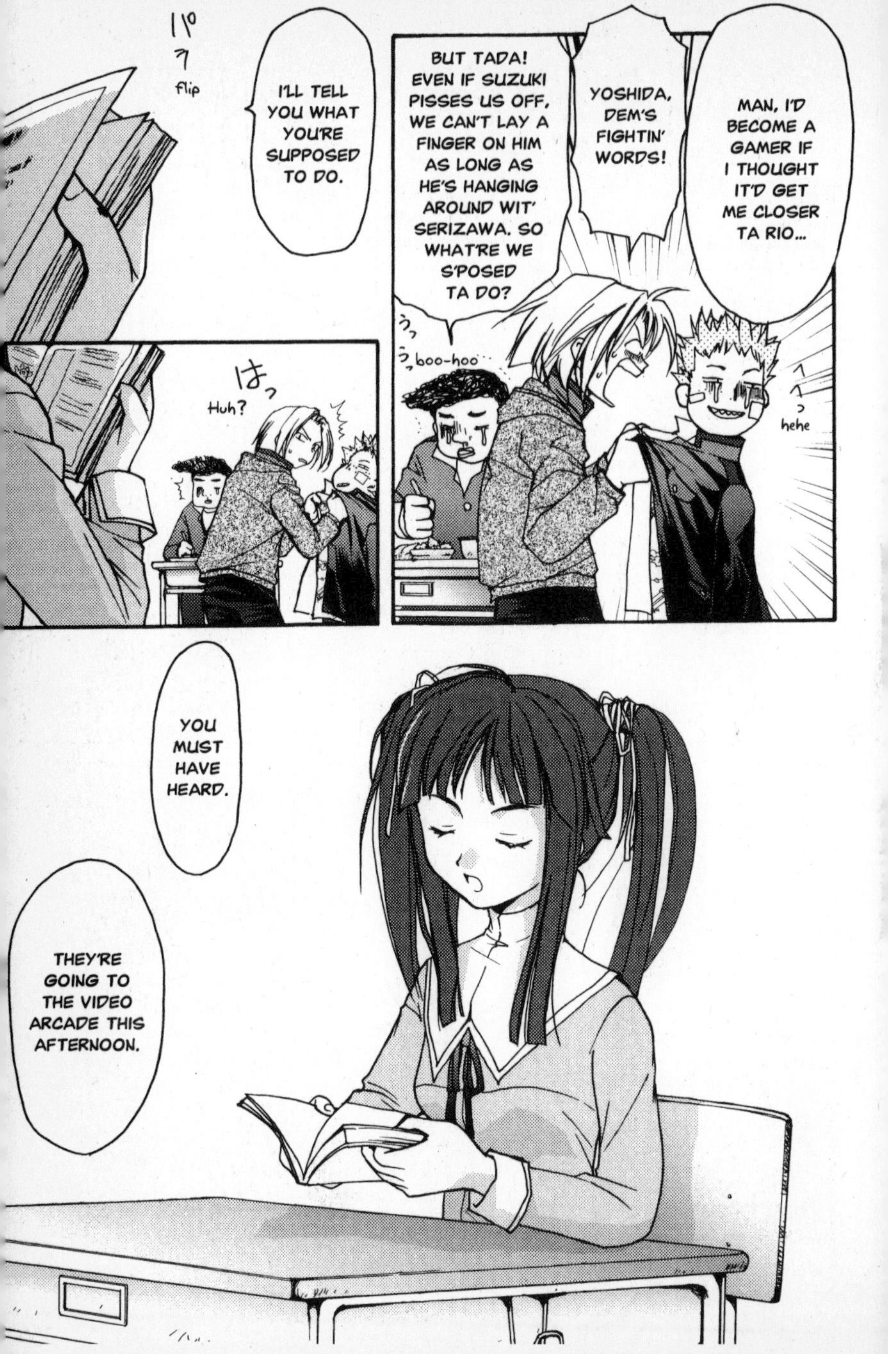

MAN, I'D BECOME A GAMER IF I THOUGHT IT'D GET ME CLOSER TA RIO...
へへっ
hehe
YOSHIDA, DEM'S FIGHTIN' WORDS!
BUT TADA! EVEN IF SUZUKI PISSES US OFF, WE CAN'T LAY A FINGER ON HIM AS LONG AS HE'S HANGING AROUND WIT' SERIZAWA. SO WHAT'RE WE S'POSED TA DO?
うっうっ
boo-hoo
パッ
flip
I'LL TELL YOU WHAT YOU'RE SUPPOSED TO DO.
はっ
Huh?
YOU MUST HAVE HEARD.
THEY'RE GOING TO THE VIDEO ARCADE THIS AFTERNOON.

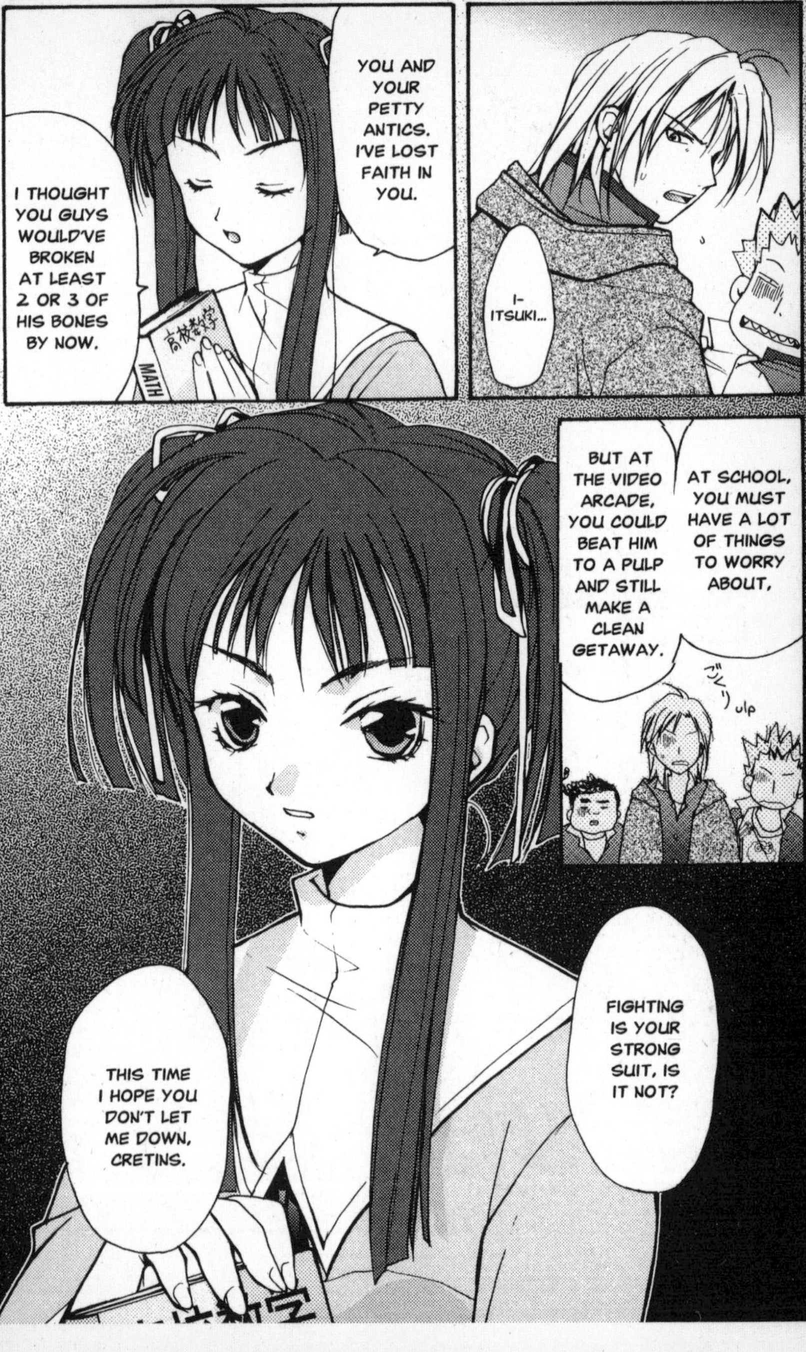
I- ITSUKI...
YOU AND YOUR PETTY ANTICS. I'VE LOST FAITH IN YOU.
I THOUGHT YOU GUYS WOULD'VE BROKEN AT LEAST 2 OR 3 OF HIS BONES BY NOW.
高校数学
MATH
AT SCHOOL, YOU MUST HAVE A LOT OF THINGS TO WORRY ABOUT,
BUT AT THE VIDEO ARCADE, YOU COULD BEAT HIM TO A PULP AND STILL MAKE A CLEAN GETAWAY.
ごくり
ulp
FIGHTING IS YOUR STRONG SUIT, IS IT NOT?
THIS TIME I HOPE YOU DON'T LET ME DOWN, CRETINS.

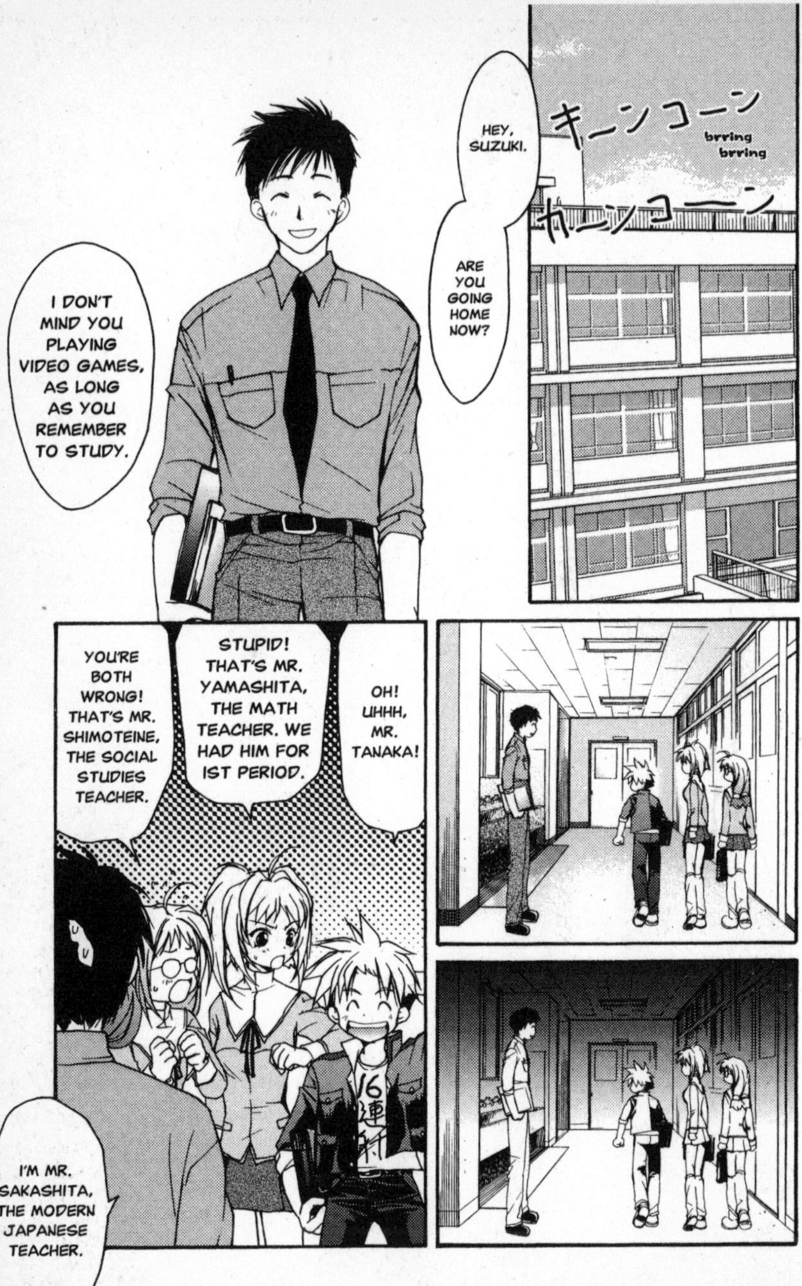

キーンコーン
brring brring
カーンコーン
HEY, SUZUKI.
ARE YOU GOING HOME NOW?
I DON'T MIND YOU PLAYING VIDEO GAMES, AS LONG AS YOU REMEMBER TO STUDY.
OH! UHHH, MR. TANAKA!
STUPID! THAT'S MR. YAMASHITA, THE MATH TEACHER. WE HAD HIM FOR 1ST PERIOD.
YOU'RE BOTH WRONG! THAT'S MR. SHIMOTEINE, THE SOCIAL STUDIES TEACHER.
I'M MR. SAKASHITA, THE MODERN JAPANESE TEACHER.

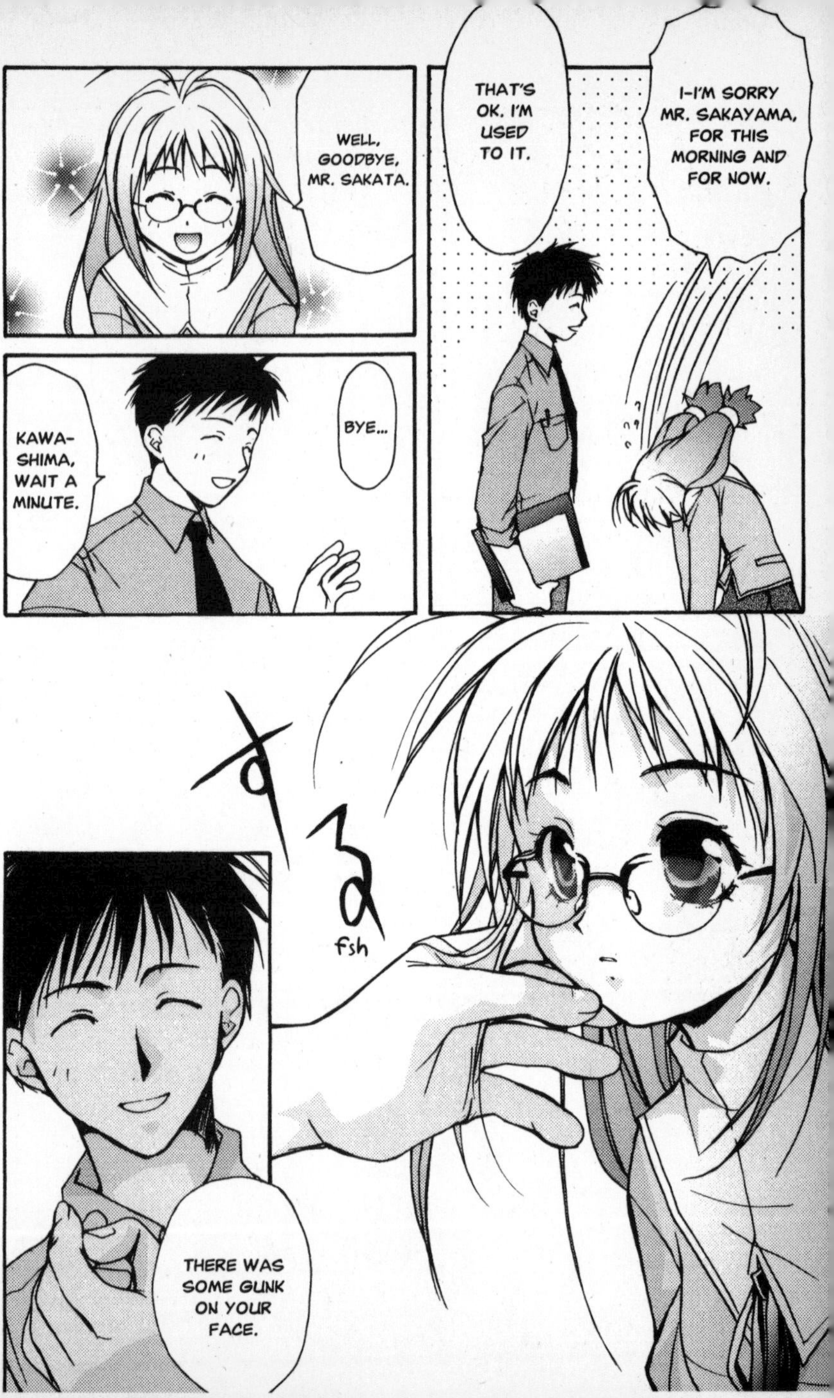
I-I'M SORRY MR. SAKAYAMA, FOR THIS MORNING AND FOR NOW.
THAT'S OK. I'M USED TO IT.
WELL, GOODBYE, MR. SAKATA.
BYE...
KAWA-SHIMA, WAIT A MINUTE.
fsh
THERE WAS SOME GUNK ON YOUR FACE.

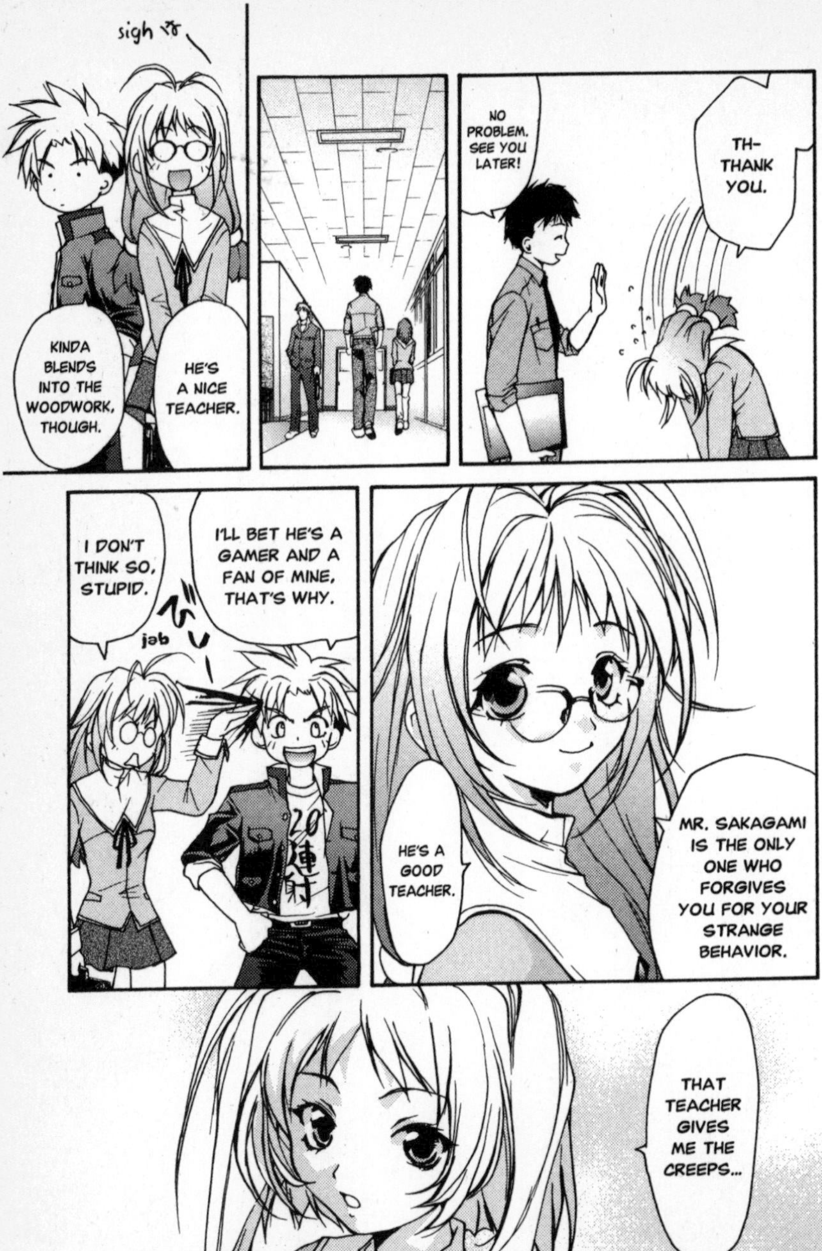

TH- THANK YOU.
NO PROBLEM. SEE YOU LATER!
sigh
HE'S A NICE TEACHER.
KINDA BLENDS INTO THE WOODWORK, THOUGH.
MR. SAKAGAMI IS THE ONLY ONE WHO FORGIVES YOU FOR YOUR STRANGE BEHAVIOR.
HE'S A GOOD TEACHER.
I'LL BET HE'S A GAMER AND A FAN OF MINE, THAT'S WHY.
I DON'T THINK SO, STUPID.
jab
THAT TEACHER GIVES ME THE CREEPS...

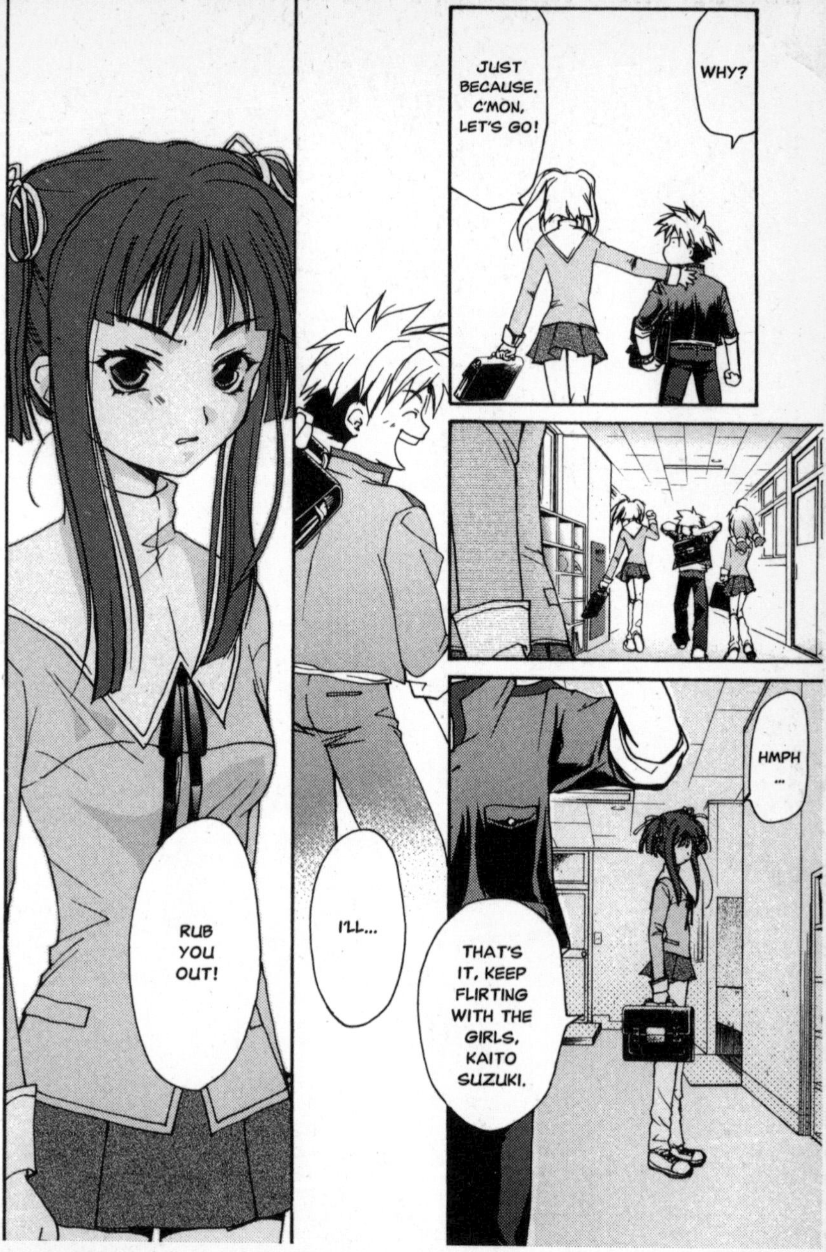
WHY?
JUST BECAUSE. C'MON, LET'S GO!
HMPH ...
THAT'S IT, KEEP FLIRTING WITH THE GIRLS, KAITO SUZUKI.
I'LL...
RUB YOU OUT!

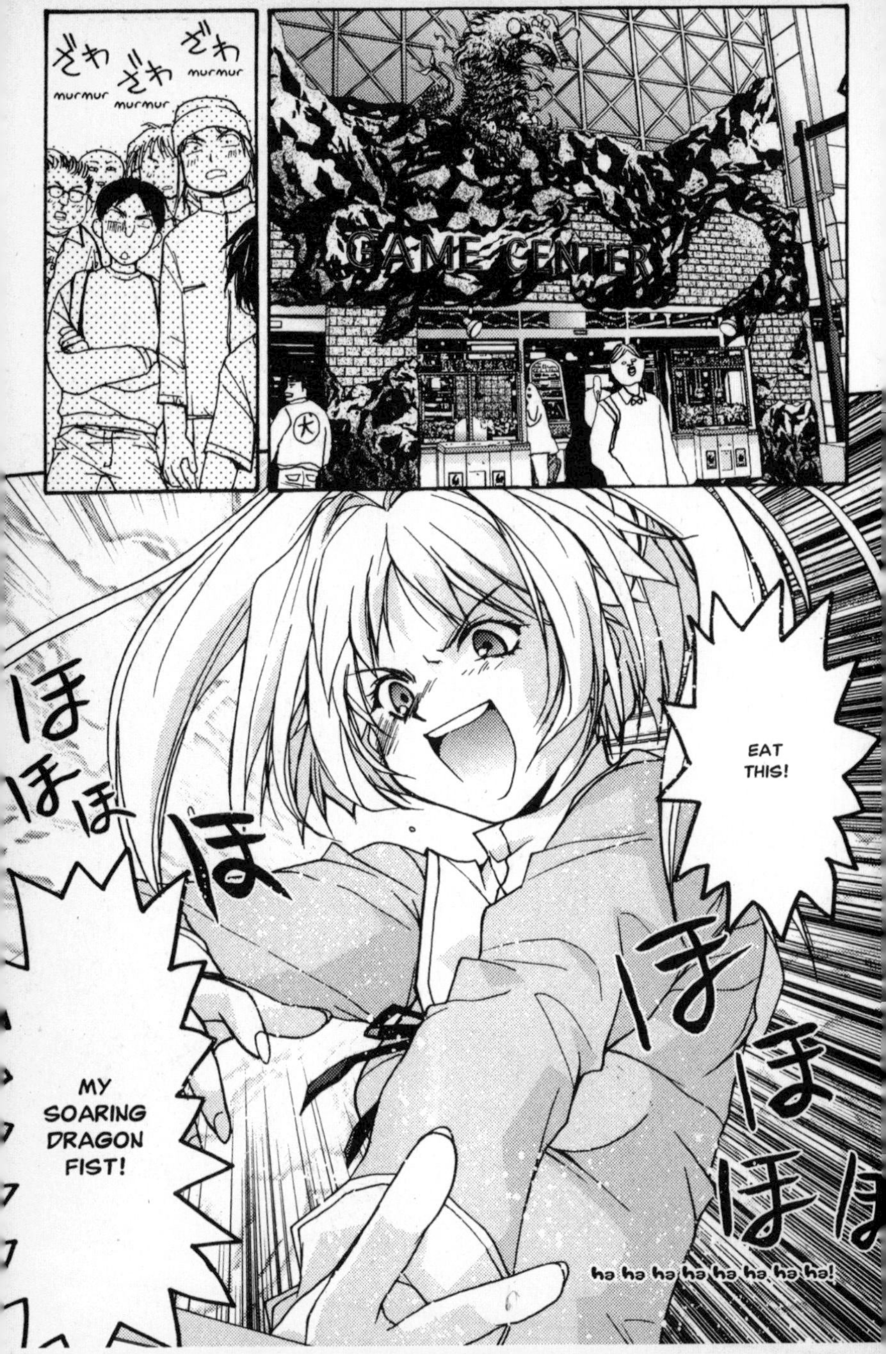
ざわ ざわ ざわ
murmur murmur murmur
GAME CENTER
EAT THIS!
MY SOARING DRAGON FIST!
ほほほほ
ほほほほ
ha ha ha ha ha ha ha ha!

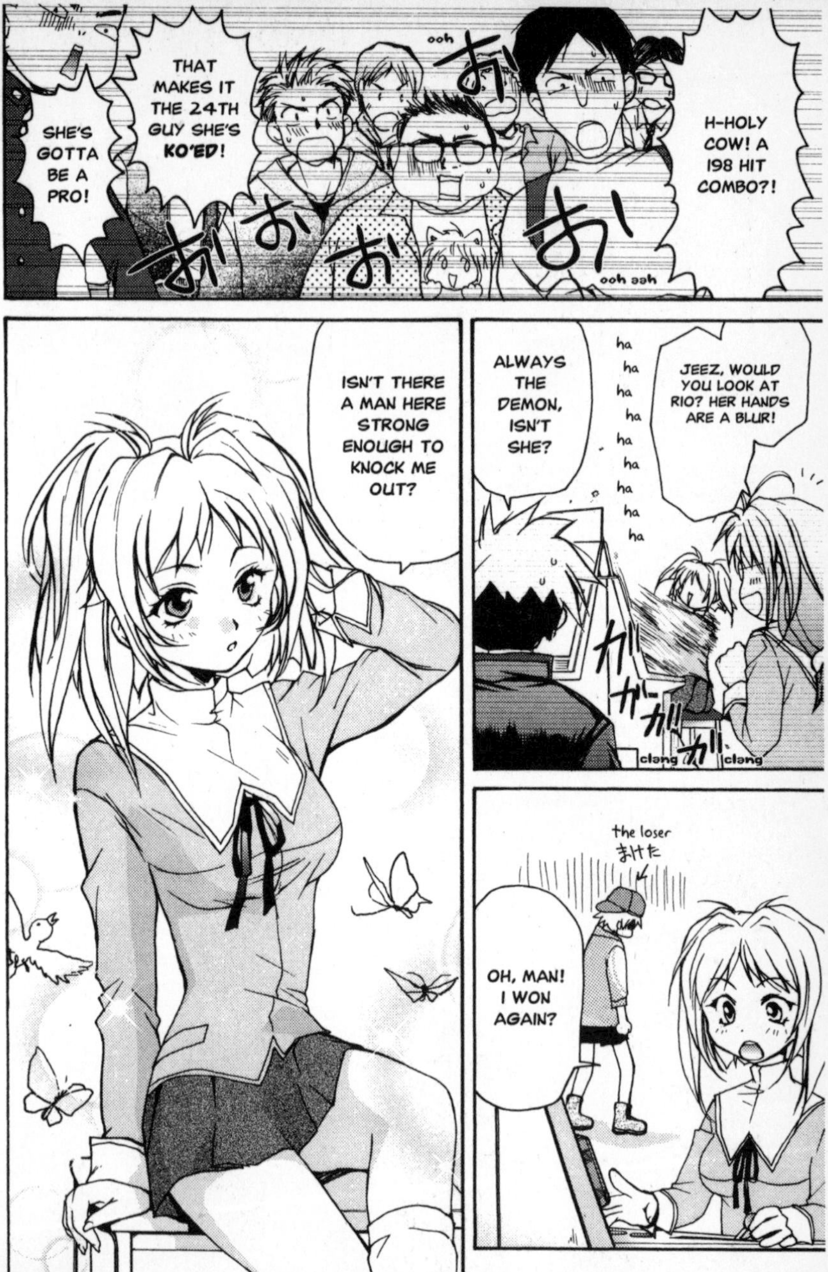
H-HOLY COW! A 198 HIT COMBO?!
ooh
あ
あ
ooh aah
お
お
あ
THAT MAKES IT THE 24TH GUY SHE'S KO'ED!
SHE'S GOTTA BE A PRO!
JEEZ, WOULD YOU LOOK AT RIO? HER HANDS ARE A BLUR!
ha ha ha ha ha ha ha ha ha
ALWAYS THE DEMON, ISN'T SHE?
clang
clang
ISN'T THERE A MAN HERE STRONG ENOUGH TO KNOCK ME OUT?
the loser
まけた
OH, MAN! I WON AGAIN?

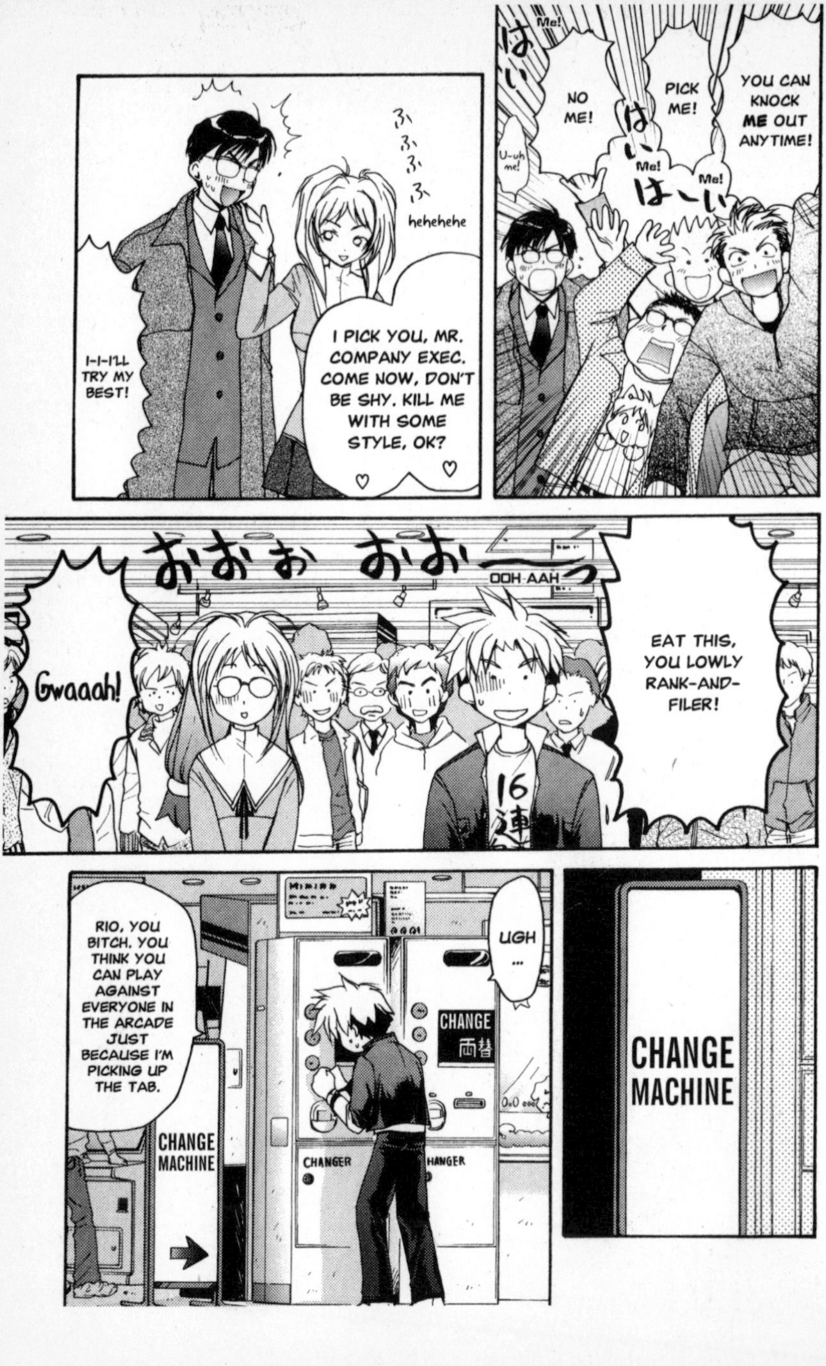
はい
Me!
YOU CAN KNOCK ME OUT ANYTIME!
PICK ME!
NO ME!
はい
Me!
U-uh me!
はーい
Me!
ふふふふ
hehehehe
I PICK YOU, MR. COMPANY EXEC. COME NOW, DON'T BE SHY. KILL ME WITH SOME STYLE, OK?
I-I-I'LL TRY MY BEST!
EAT THIS, YOU LOWLY RANK-AND-FILER!
おおぉ おおーっ
OOH-AAH
Gwaaah!
16 連
CHANGE MACHINE
UGH ...
CHANGE 両替
RIO, YOU BITCH. YOU THINK YOU CAN PLAY AGAINST EVERYONE IN THE ARCADE JUST BECAUSE I'M PICKING UP THE TAB.
CHANGE MACHINE
CHANGER
HANGER

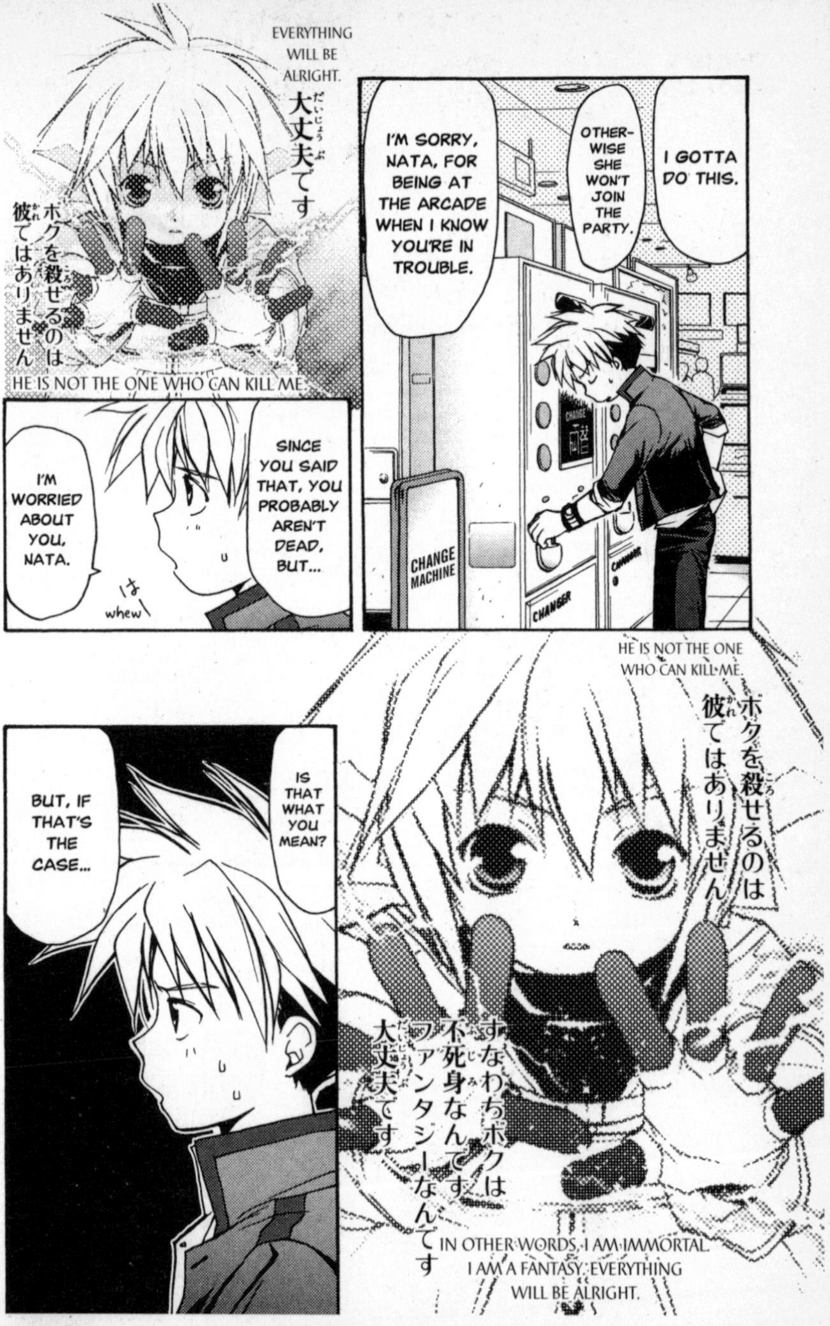
I GOTTA DO THIS.
OTHER-WISE SHE WON'T JOIN THE PARTY.
I'M SORRY, NATA, FOR BEING AT THE ARCADE WHEN I KNOW YOU'RE IN TROUBLE.
CHANGE MACHINE
CHANGER
CHANGER
EVERYTHING WILL BE ALRIGHT.
大丈夫です
ボクを殺せるのは彼ではありません
HE IS NOT THE ONE WHO CAN KILL ME.
SINCE YOU SAID THAT, YOU PROBABLY AREN'T DEAD, BUT...
I'M WORRIED ABOUT YOU, NATA.
は
whew
HE IS NOT THE ONE WHO CAN KILL ME.
ボクを殺せるのは彼ではありません
すなわちボクは不死身なんです
ファンタジーなんです
大丈夫です
IN OTHER WORDS, I AM IMMORTAL. I AM A FANTASY. EVERYTHING WILL BE ALRIGHT.
IS THAT WHAT YOU MEAN?
BUT, IF THAT'S THE CASE...

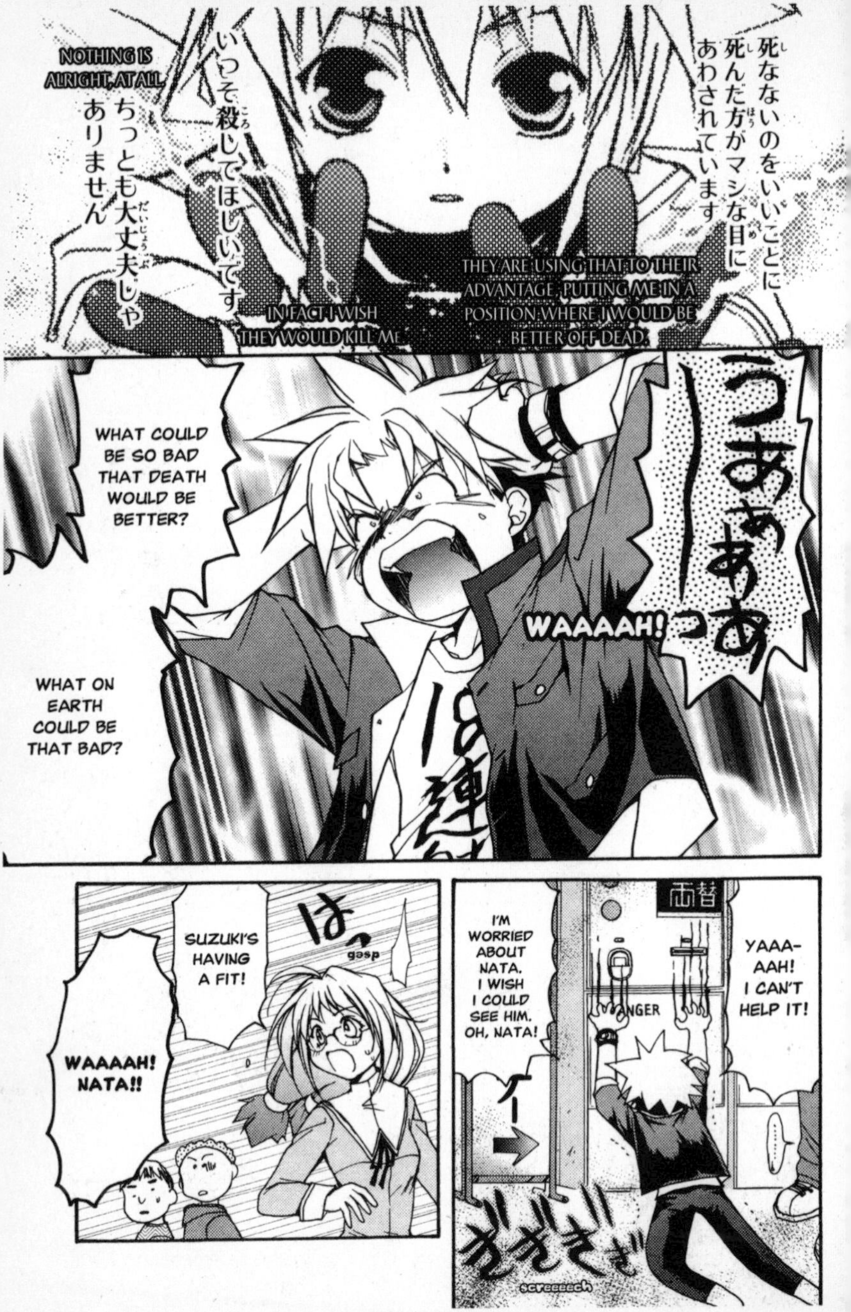
死なないのをいいことに死んだ方がマシな目にあわされています
THEY ARE USING THAT TO THEIR ADVANTAGE, PUTTING ME IN A POSITION WHERE I WOULD BE BETTER OFF DEAD.
いっそ殺してほしいです
IN FACT I WISH THEY WOULD KILL ME
ちっとも大丈夫じゃありません
NOTHING IS ALRIGHT, AT ALL
うあああああーーっ
WAAAAH!
WHAT COULD BE SO BAD THAT DEATH WOULD BE BETTER?
WHAT ON EARTH COULD BE THAT BAD?
YAAA-AAH! I CAN'T HELP IT!
I'M WORRIED ABOUT NATA. I WISH I COULD SEE HIM. OH, NATA!
ぎぎぎぎ
screeeech
は
gasp
SUZUKI'S HAVING A FIT!
WAAAAH! NATA!!

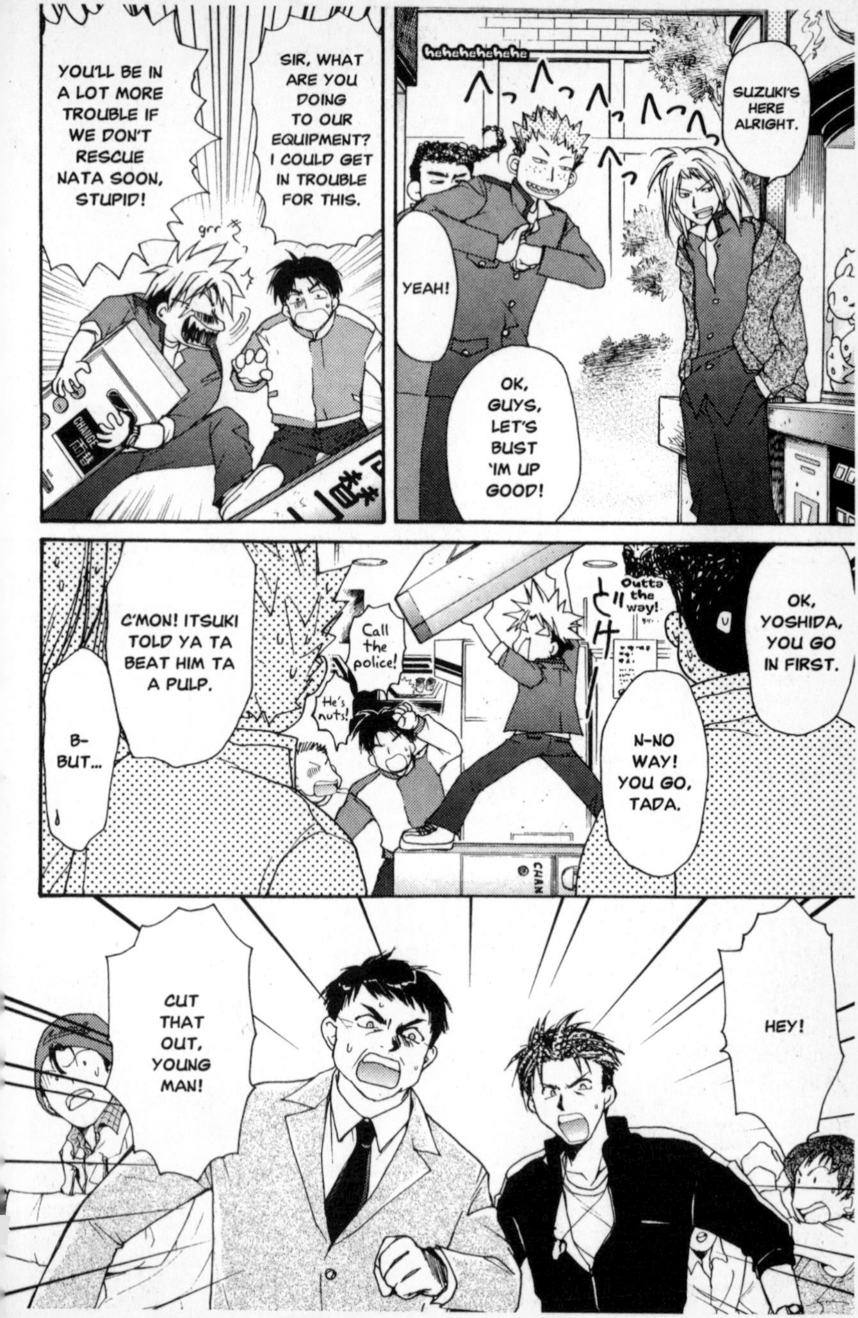
hehehehehehe
SUZUKI'S HERE ALRIGHT.
YEAH!
OK, GUYS, LET'S BUST 'IM UP GOOD!
SIR, WHAT ARE YOU DOING TO OUR EQUIPMENT? I COULD GET IN TROUBLE FOR THIS.
YOU'LL BE IN A LOT MORE TROUBLE IF WE DON'T RESCUE NATA SOON, STUPID!
grr
CHANGE
OK, YOSHIDA, YOU GO IN FIRST.
N-NO WAY! YOU GO, TADA.
Outta the way!
Call the police!
He's nuts!
C'MON! ITSUKI TOLD YA TA BEAT HIM TA A PULP.
B-BUT...
HEY!
CUT THAT OUT, YOUNG MAN!

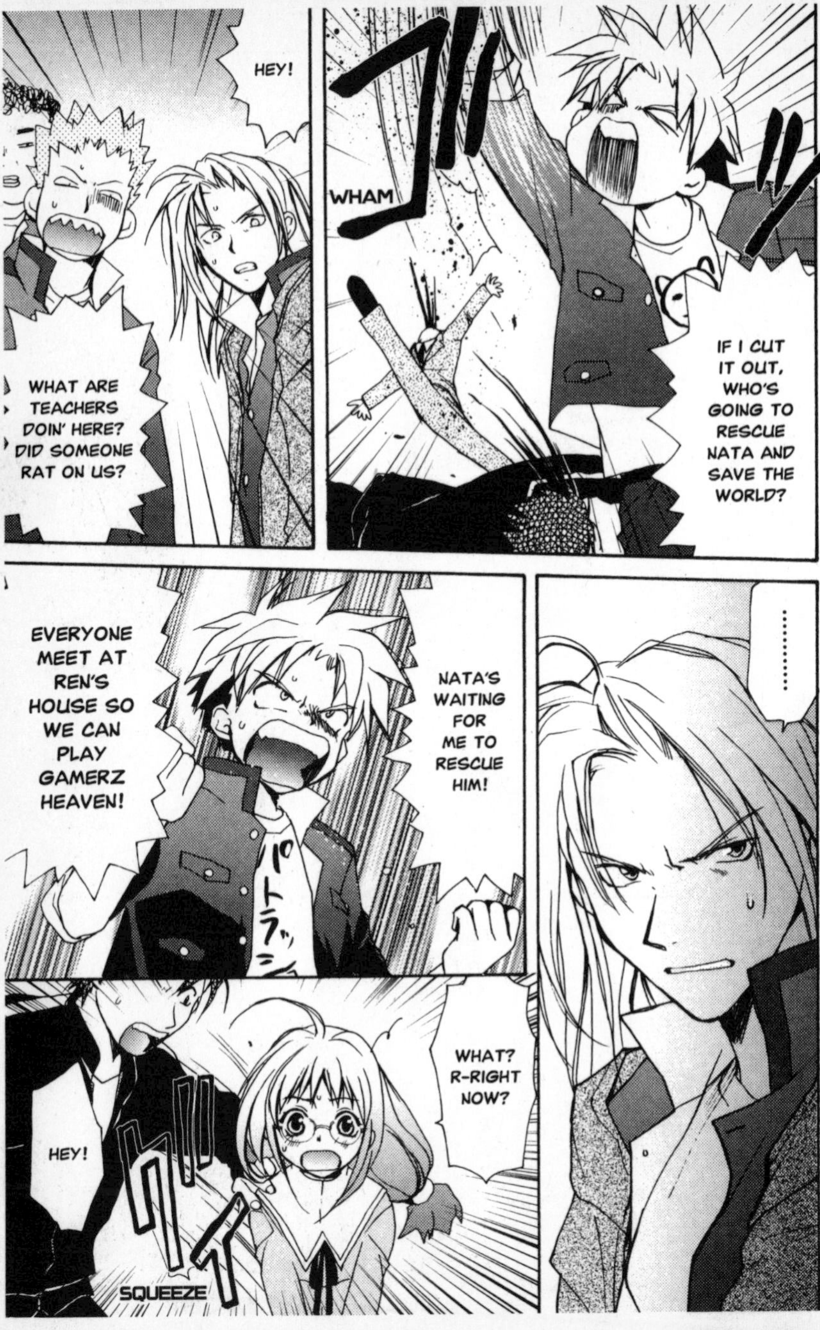
WHAM
IF I CUT IT OUT, WHO'S GOING TO RESCUE NATA AND SAVE THE WORLD?
HEY!
WHAT ARE TEACHERS DOIN' HERE? DID SOMEONE RAT ON US?
......
NATA'S WAITING FOR ME TO RESCUE HIM!
EVERYONE MEET AT REN'S HOUSE SO WE CAN PLAY GAMERZ HEAVEN!
パトラッシュ
WHAT? R-RIGHT NOW?
HEY!
SQUEEZE

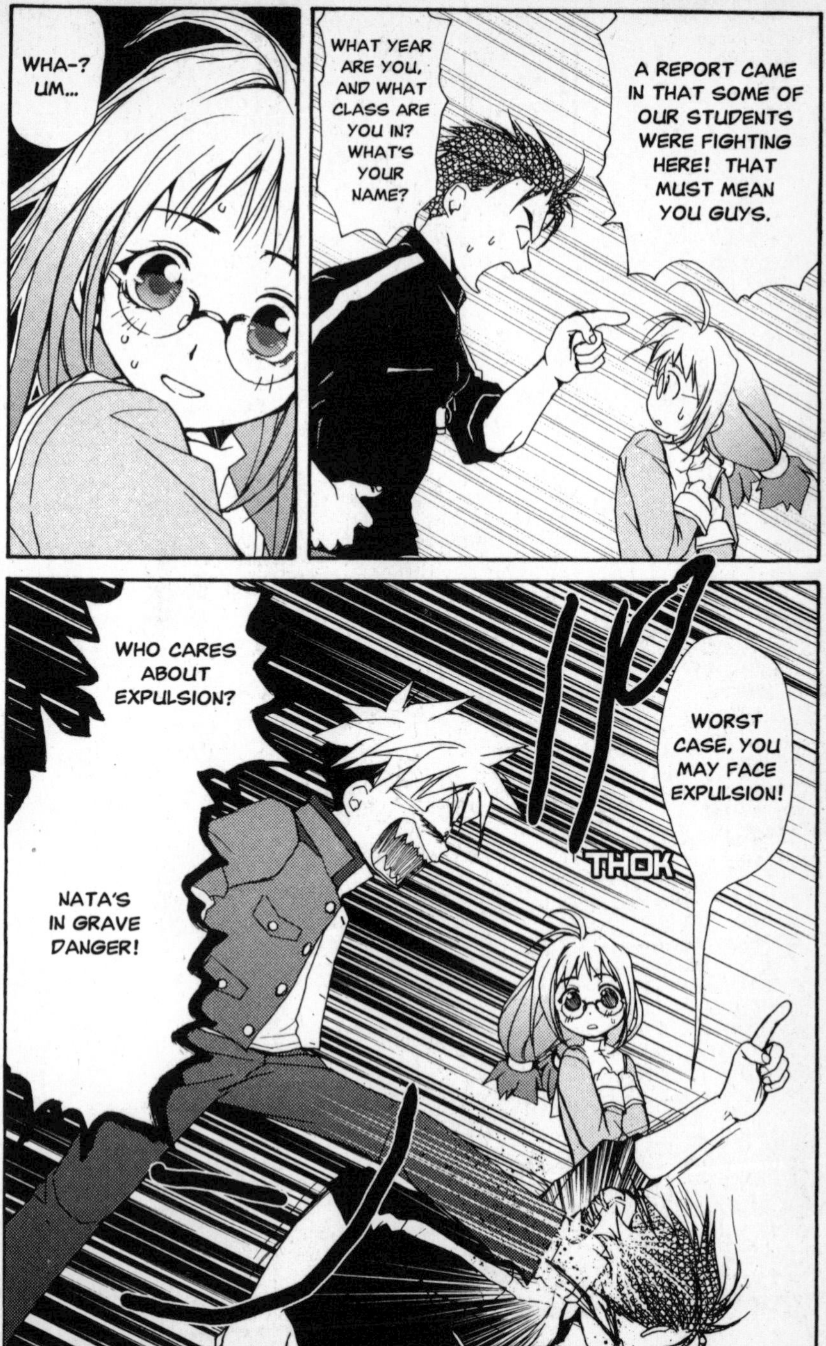
A REPORT CAME IN THAT SOME OF OUR STUDENTS WERE FIGHTING HERE! THAT MUST MEAN YOU GUYS.
WHAT YEAR ARE YOU, AND WHAT CLASS ARE YOU IN? WHAT'S YOUR NAME?
WHA-? UM...
WORST CASE, YOU MAY FACE EXPULSION!
THOK
WHO CARES ABOUT EXPULSION?
NATA'S IN GRAVE DANGER!

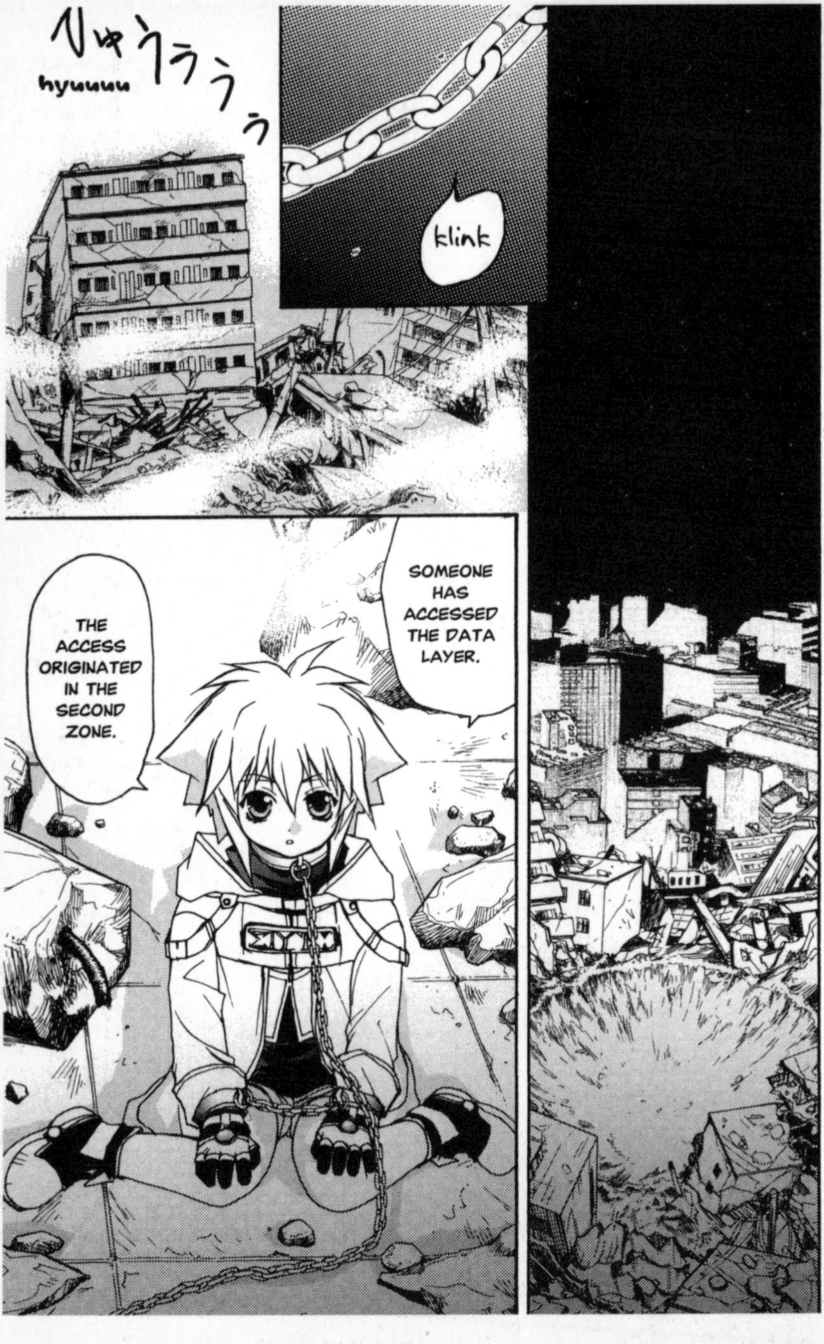
klink
hyuuuu
SOMEONE HAS ACCESSED THE DATA LAYER.
THE ACCESS ORIGINATED IN THE SECOND ZONE.

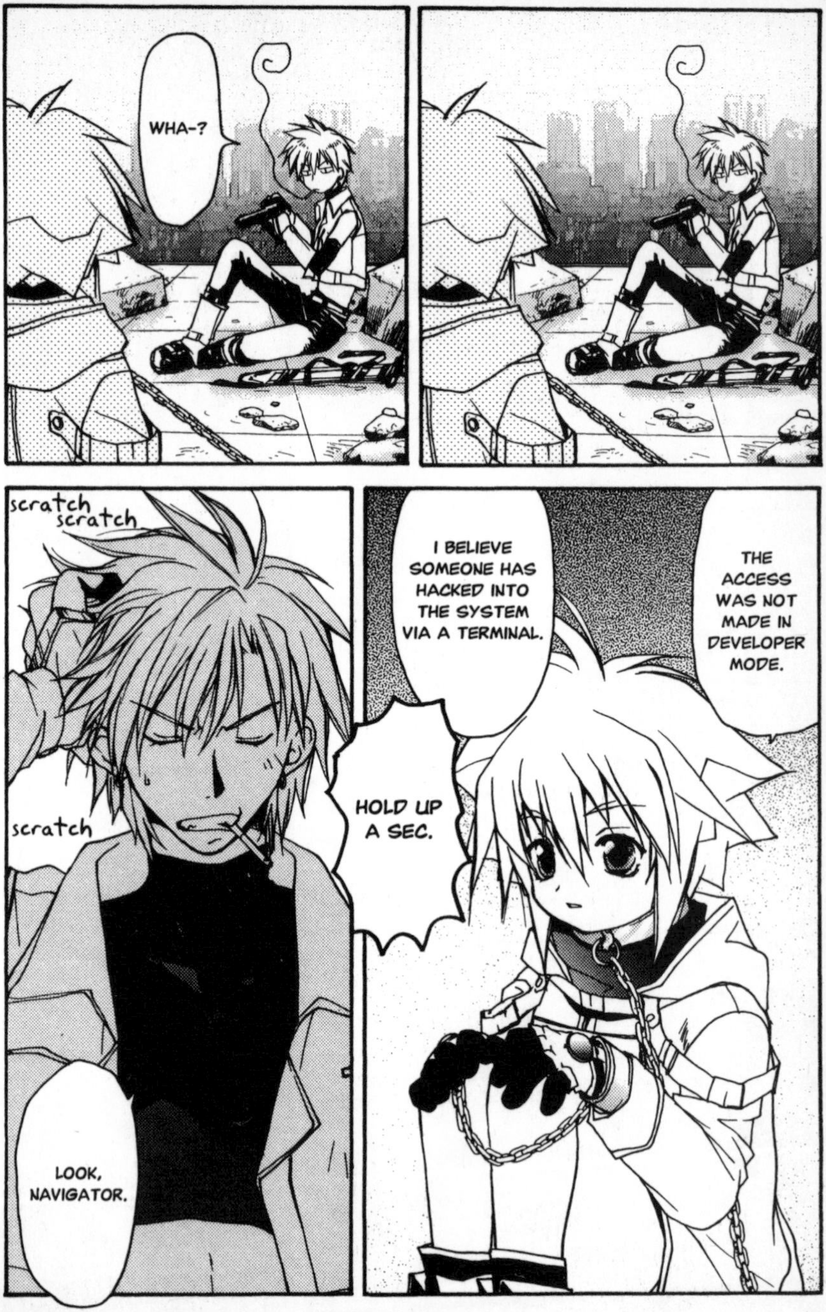
WHA-?
THE ACCESS WAS NOT MADE IN DEVELOPER MODE.
I BELIEVE SOMEONE HAS HACKED INTO THE SYSTEM VIA A TERMINAL.
HOLD UP A SEC.
scratch scratch
scratch
LOOK, NAVIGATOR.

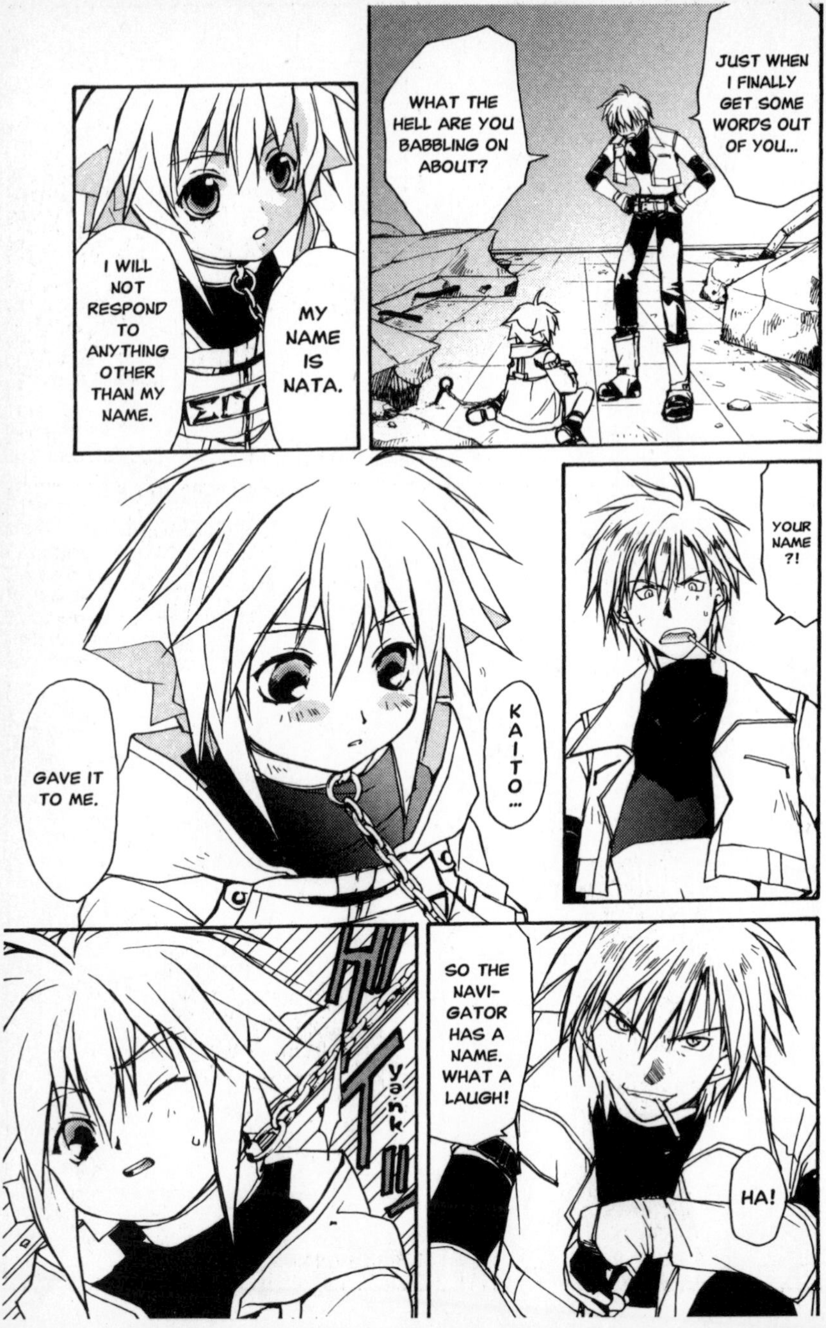
JUST WHEN I FINALLY GET SOME WORDS OUT OF YOU...
WHAT THE HELL ARE YOU BABBLING ON ABOUT?
MY NAME IS NATA.
I WILL NOT RESPOND TO ANYTHING OTHER THAN MY NAME.
YOUR NAME?!
KAITO...
GAVE IT TO ME.
SO THE NAVI-GATOR HAS A NAME. WHAT A LAUGH!
HA!
yank

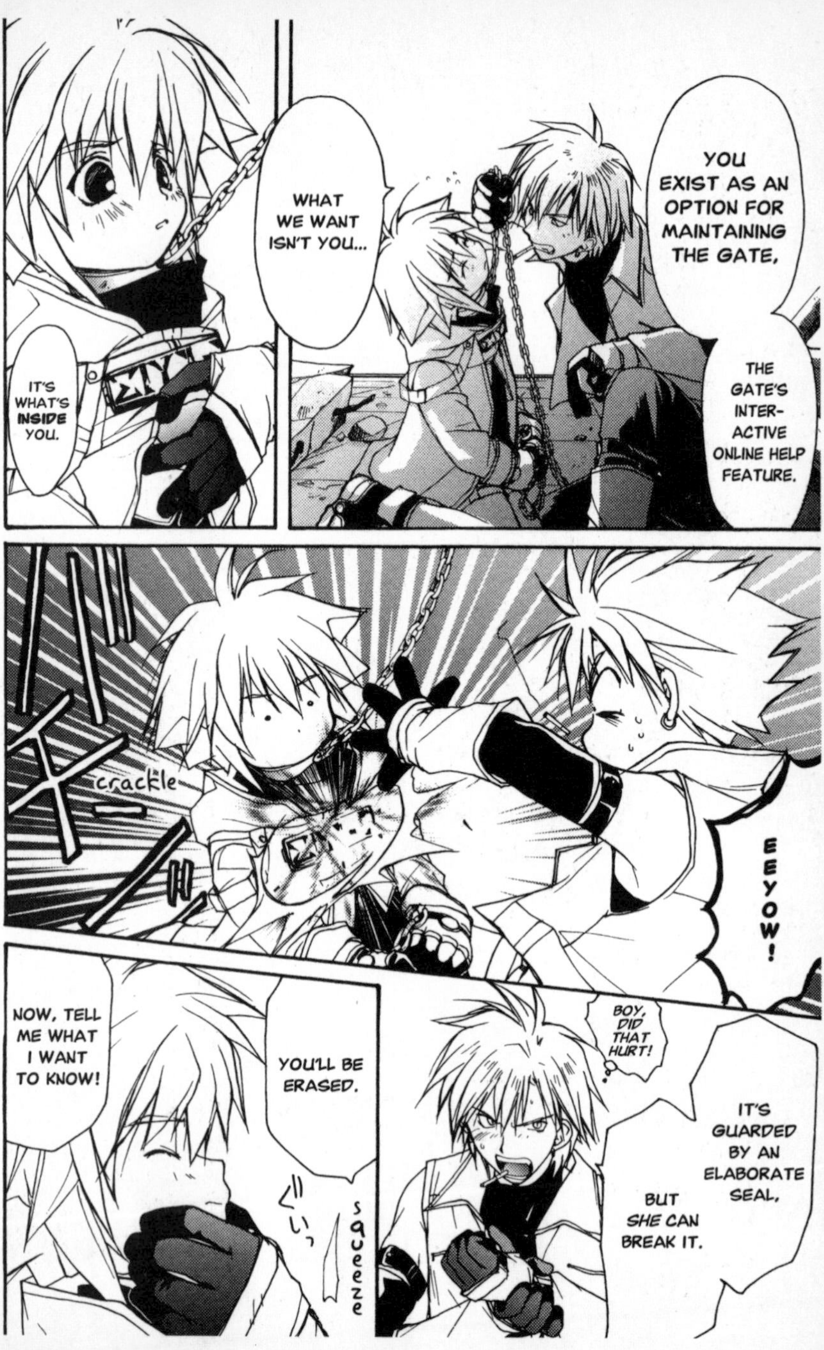
YOU EXIST AS AN OPTION FOR MAINTAINING THE GATE,
THE GATE'S INTER-ACTIVE ONLINE HELP FEATURE.
WHAT WE WANT ISN'T YOU...
IT'S WHAT'S **INSIDE** YOU.
EEYOW!
crackle
BOY, DID THAT HURT!
IT'S GUARDED BY AN ELABORATE SEAL,
BUT SHE CAN BREAK IT.
YOU'LL BE ERASED.
ぐいっ
squeeze
NOW, TELL ME WHAT I WANT TO KNOW!

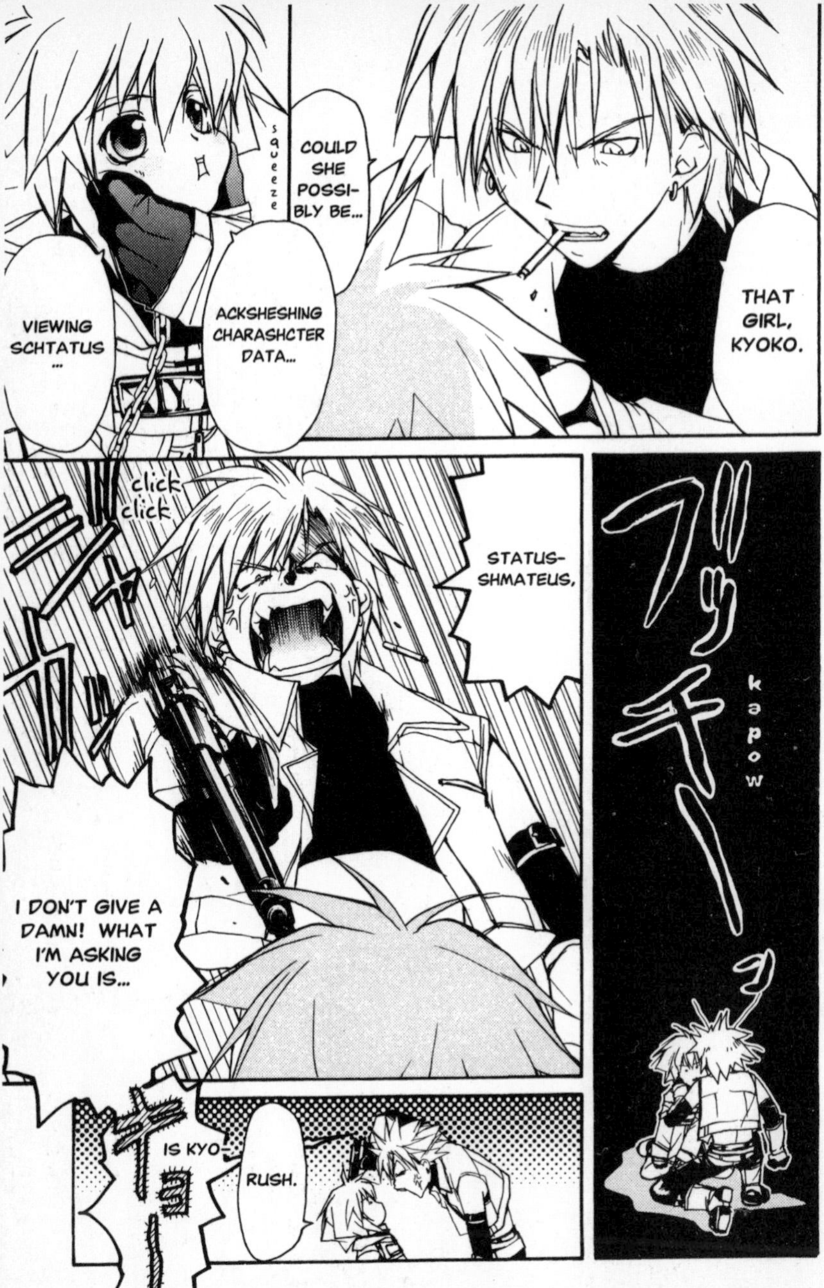

THAT GIRL, KYOKO.
COULD SHE POSSIBLY BE...
squeeze
ACKSHESHING CHARASHCTER DATA...
VIEWING SCHTATUS ...
ブッチーッ
kapow
STATUS-SHMATEUS,
click click
I DON'T GIVE A DAMN! WHAT I'M ASKING YOU IS...
IS KYO-
RUSH.

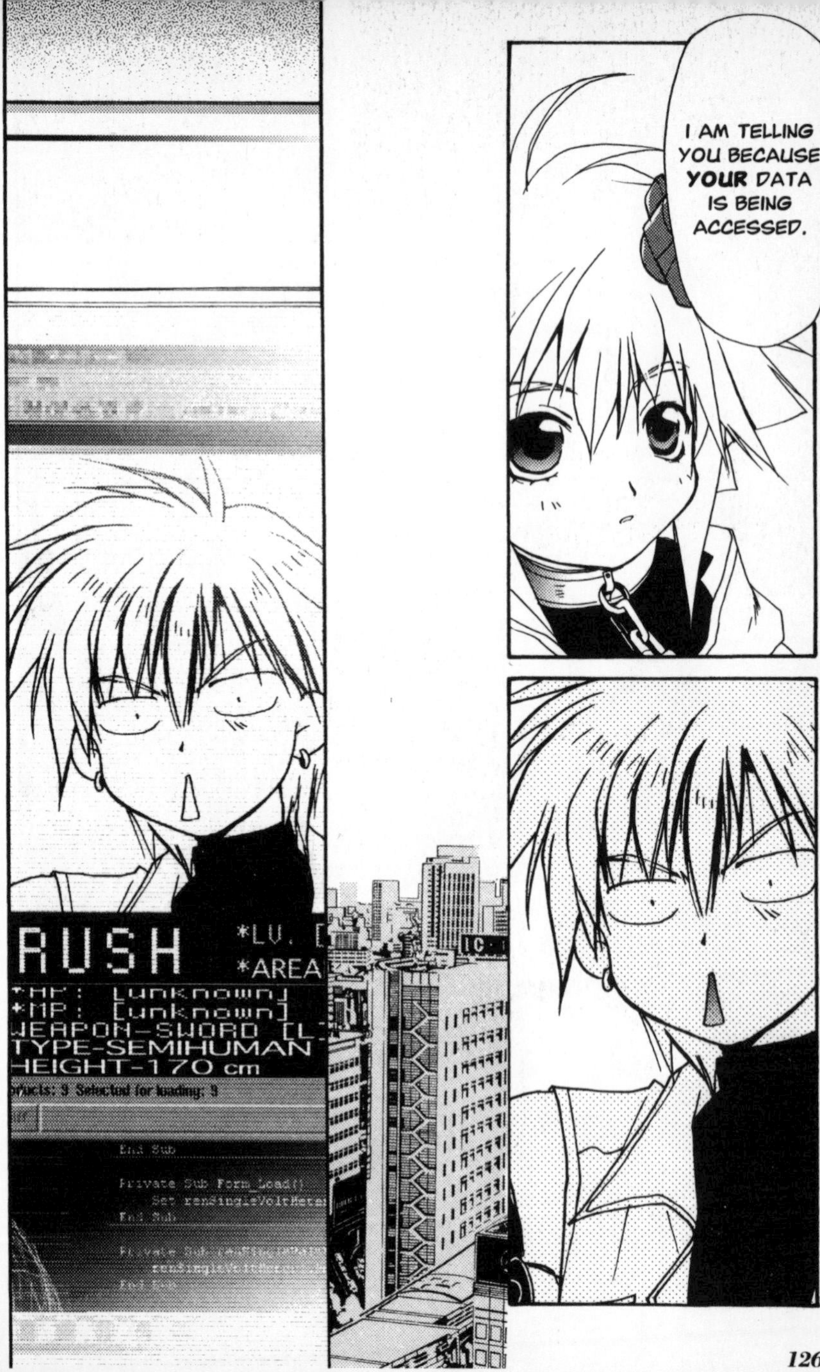
I AM TELLING YOU BECAUSE YOUR DATA IS BEING ACCESSED.
RUSH
*AREA
*HP: [unknown]
*MP: [unknown]
TYPE-SEMIHUMAN
HEIGHT-170 cm

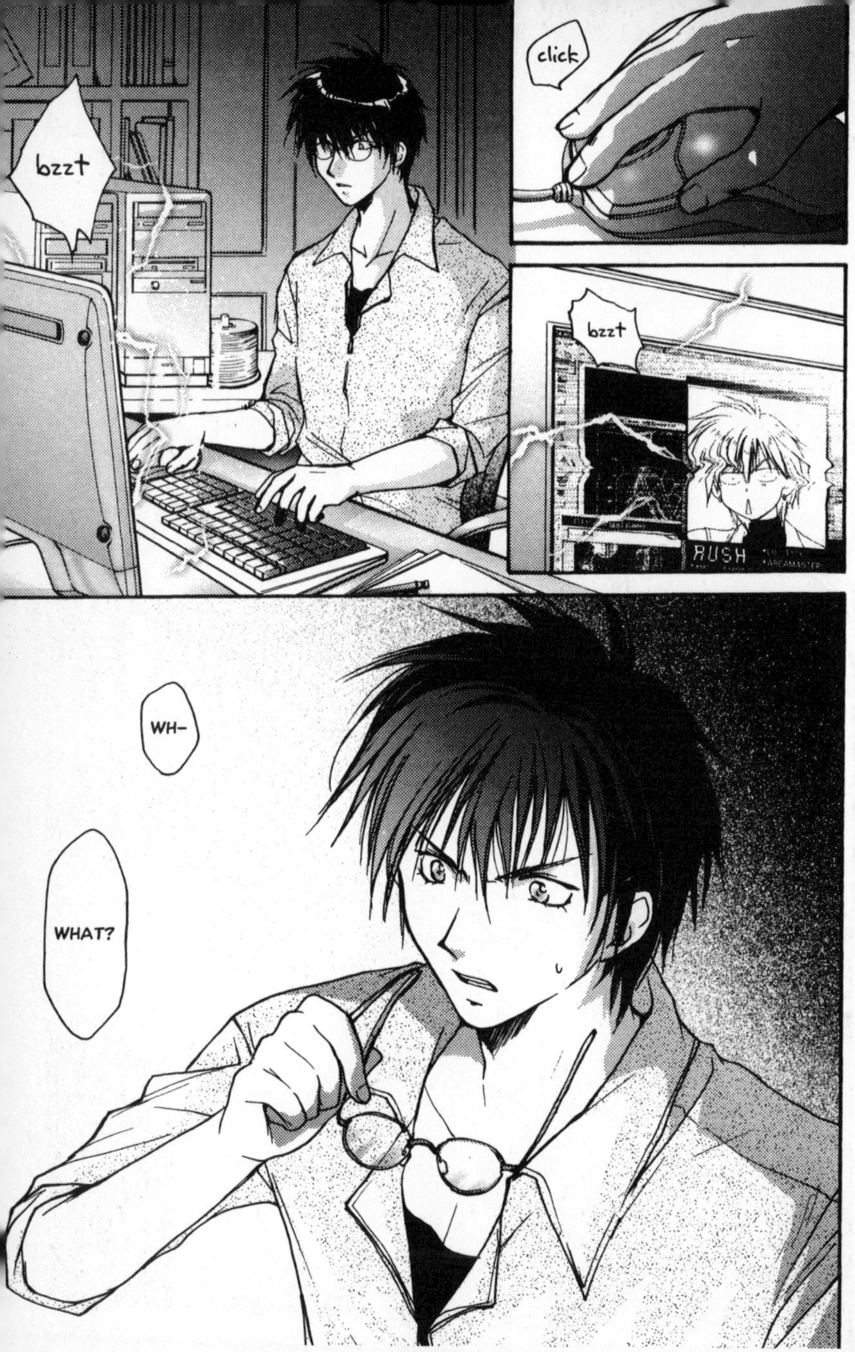
click
bzzt
RUSH
bzzt
WH-
WHAT?

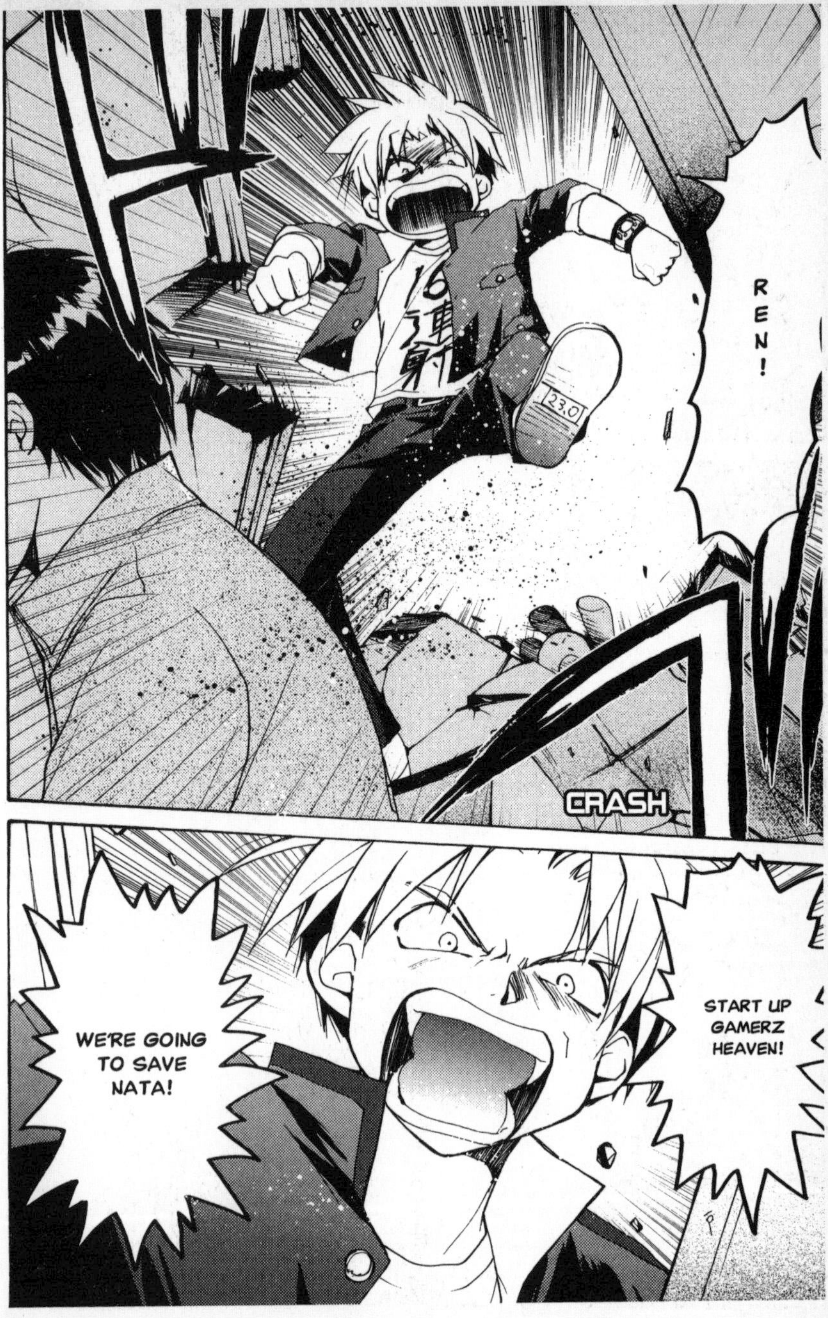
REN!
CRASH
START UP GAMERZ HEAVEN!
WE'RE GOING TO SAVE NATA!

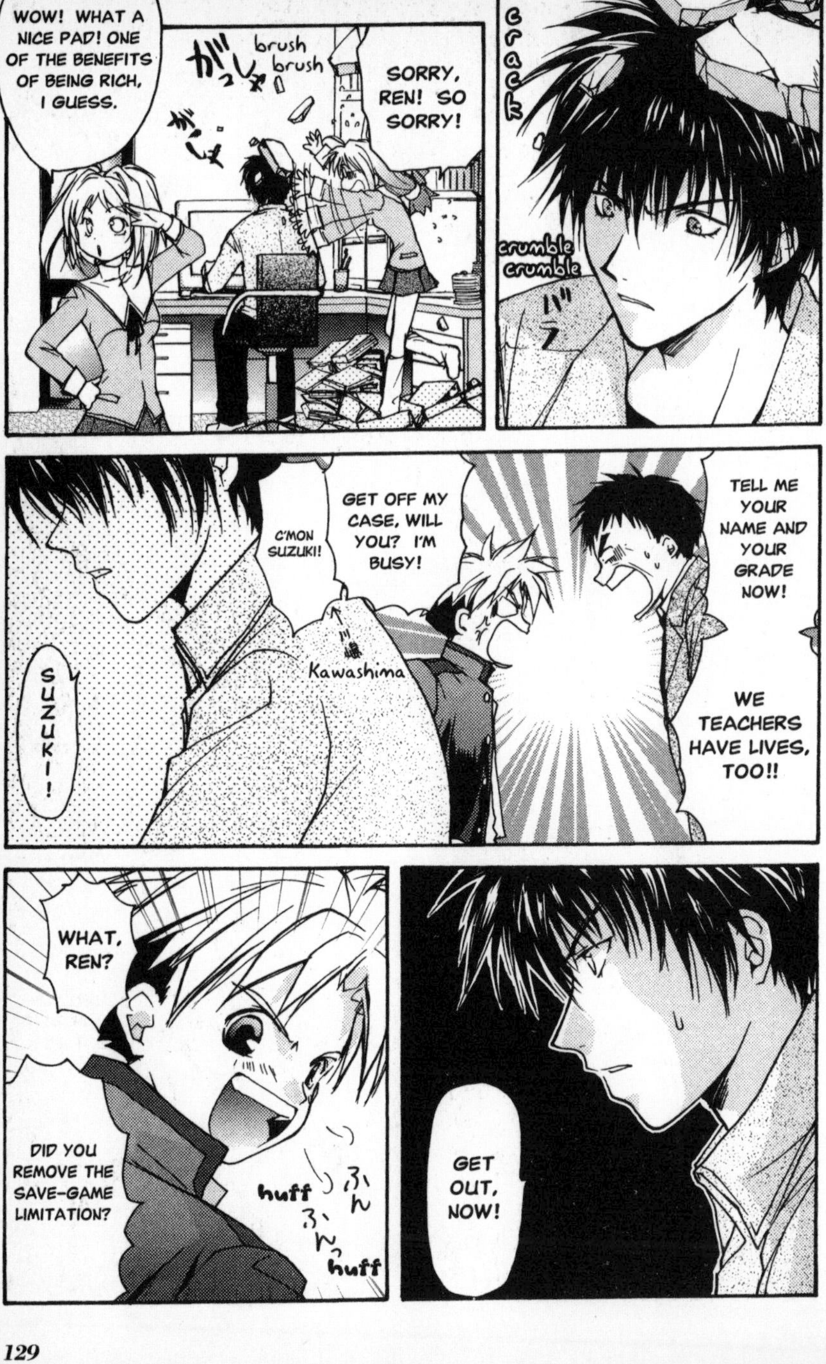
crack
crumble crumble
SORRY, REN! SO SORRY!
brush brush
WOW! WHAT A NICE PAD! ONE OF THE BENEFITS OF BEING RICH, I GUESS.
TELL ME YOUR NAME AND YOUR GRADE NOW!
WE TEACHERS HAVE LIVES, TOO!!
GET OFF MY CASE, WILL YOU? I'M BUSY!
C'MON SUZUKI!
Kawashima
SUZUKI!
GET OUT, NOW!
WHAT, REN?
DID YOU REMOVE THE SAVE-GAME LIMITATION?
huff huff

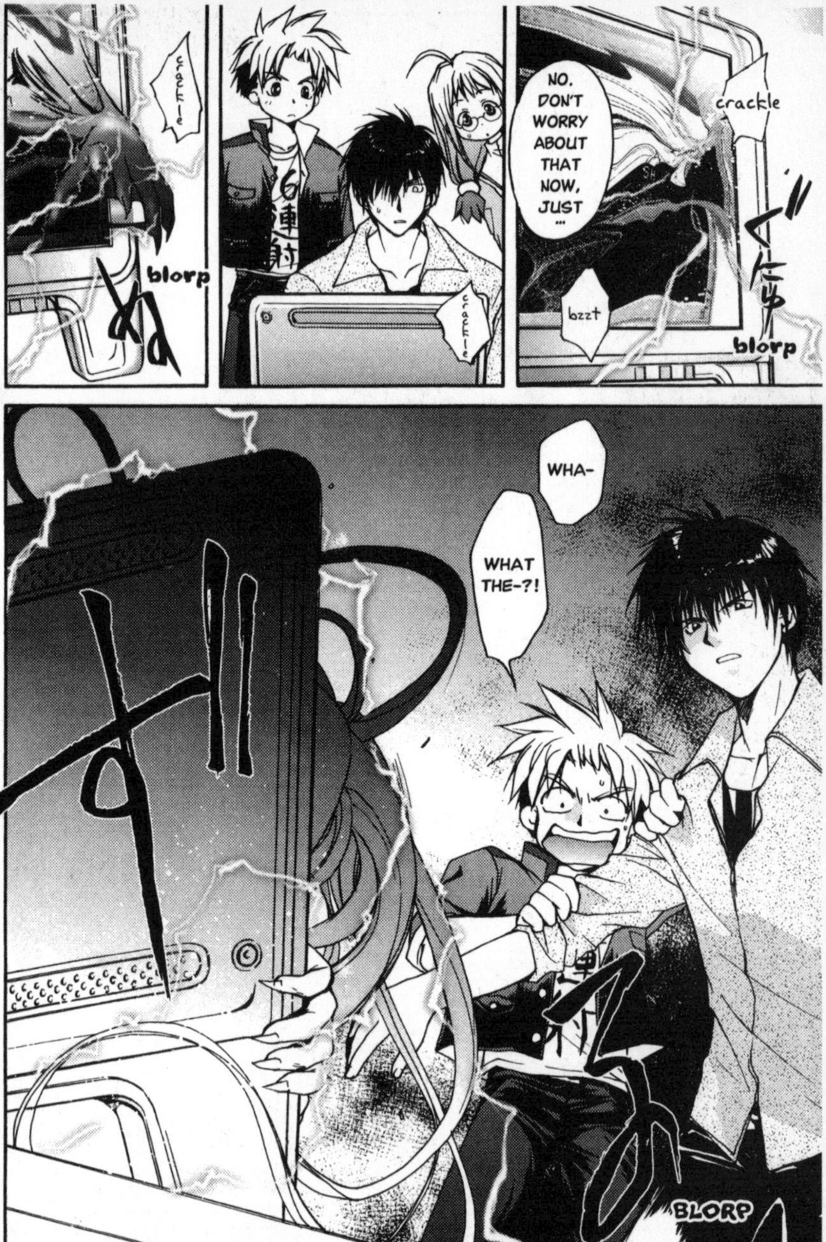

crackle
NO. DON'T WORRY ABOUT THAT NOW, JUST ...
bzzt
blorp
crackle
crackle
blorp
WHA-
WHAT THE-?!
BLORP

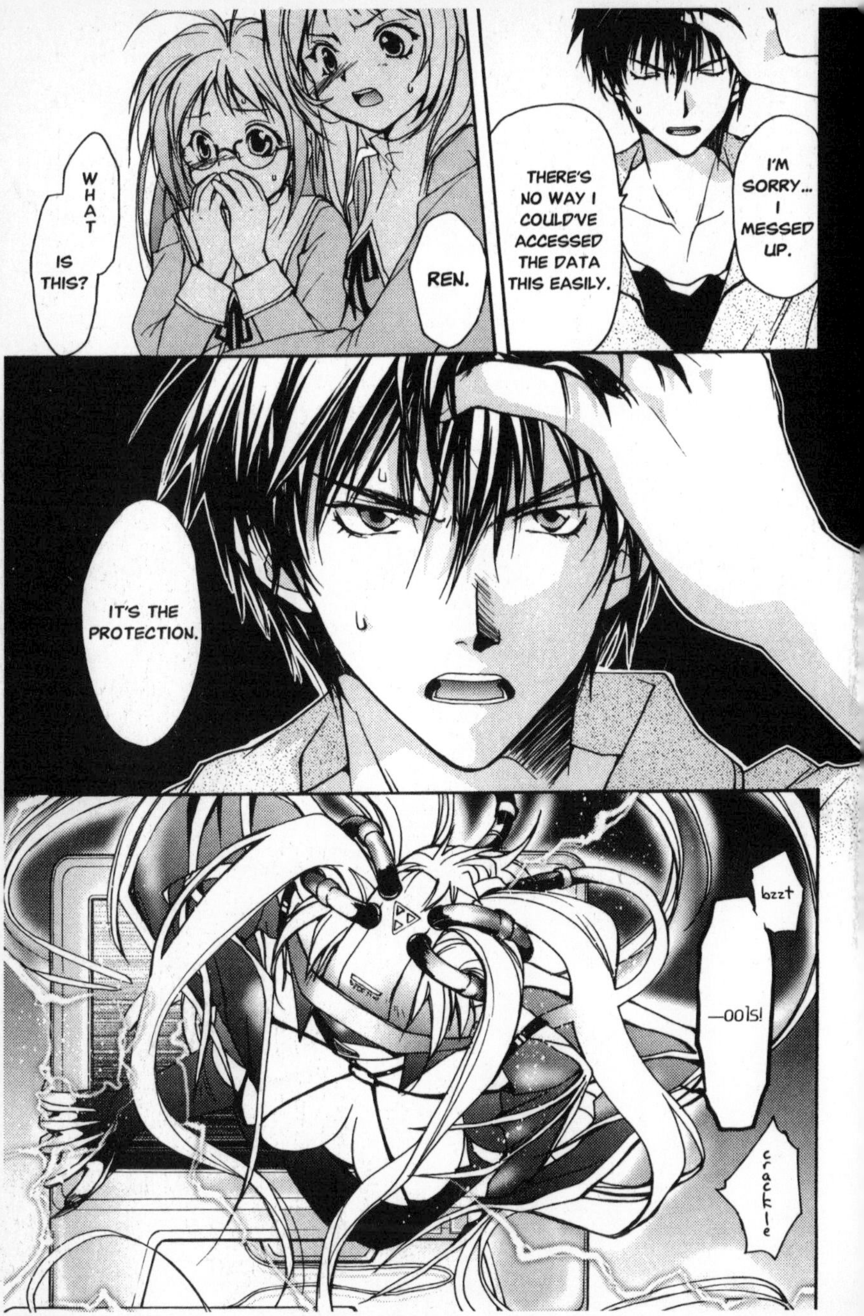
I'M SORRY... I MESSED UP.
THERE'S NO WAY I COULD'VE ACCESSED THE DATA THIS EASILY.
REN.
WHAT IS THIS?
IT'S THE PROTECTION.
bzzt
—OOLS!
crackle

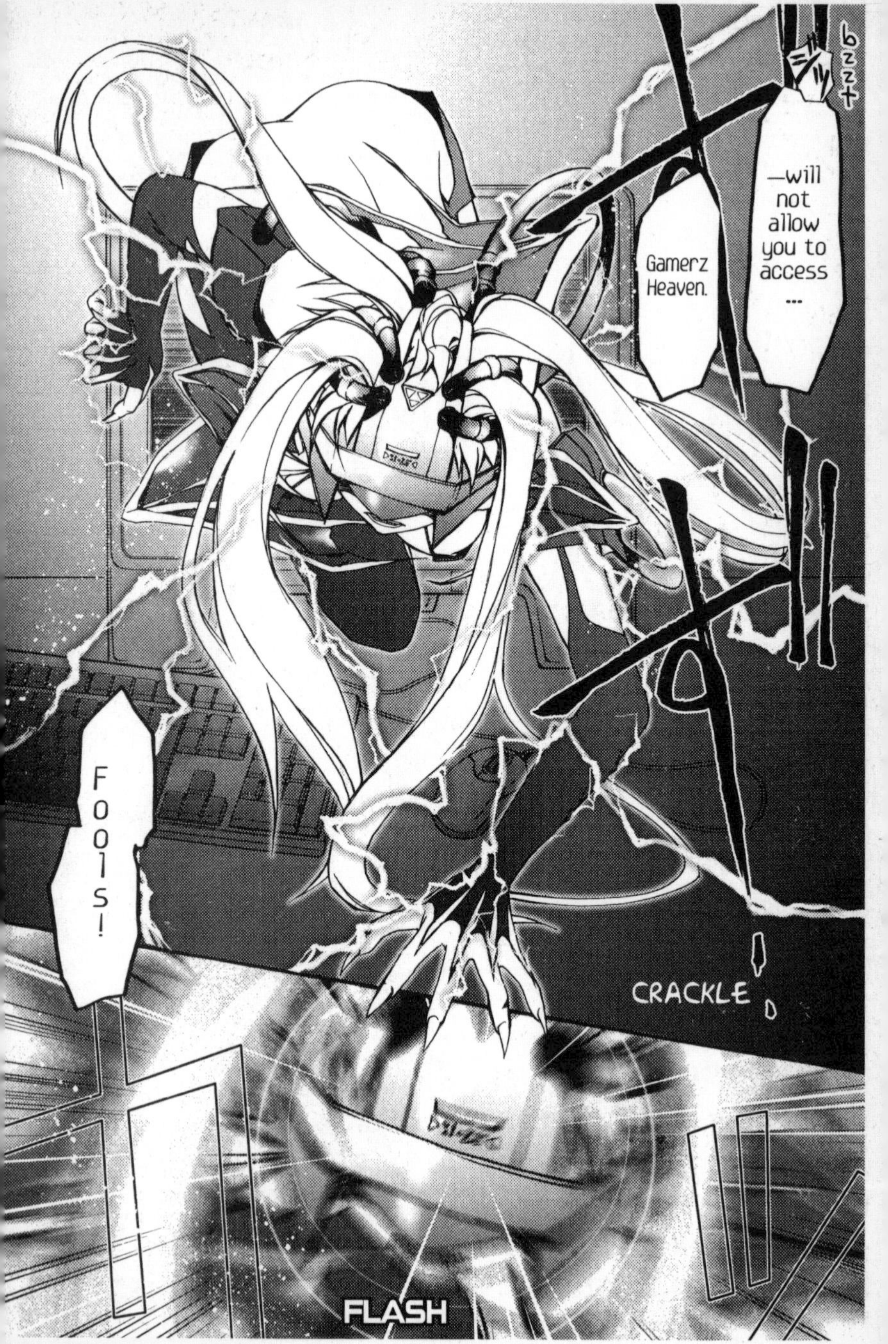
bzzt
—will not allow you to access ...
Gamerz Heaven.
Fools!
CRACKLE
FLASH

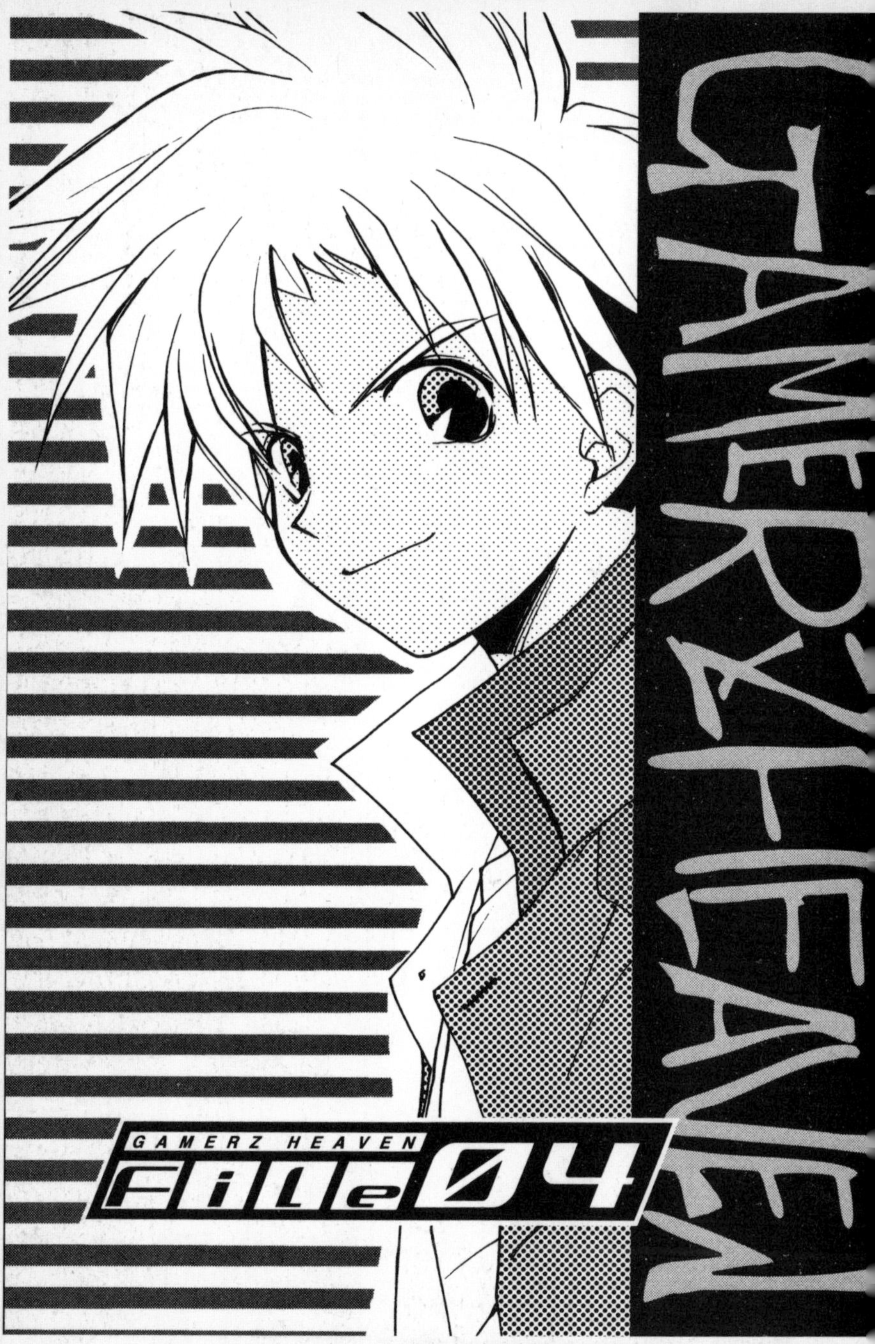
GAMERZ HEAVEN
GAMERZ HEAVEN
FiLe 04

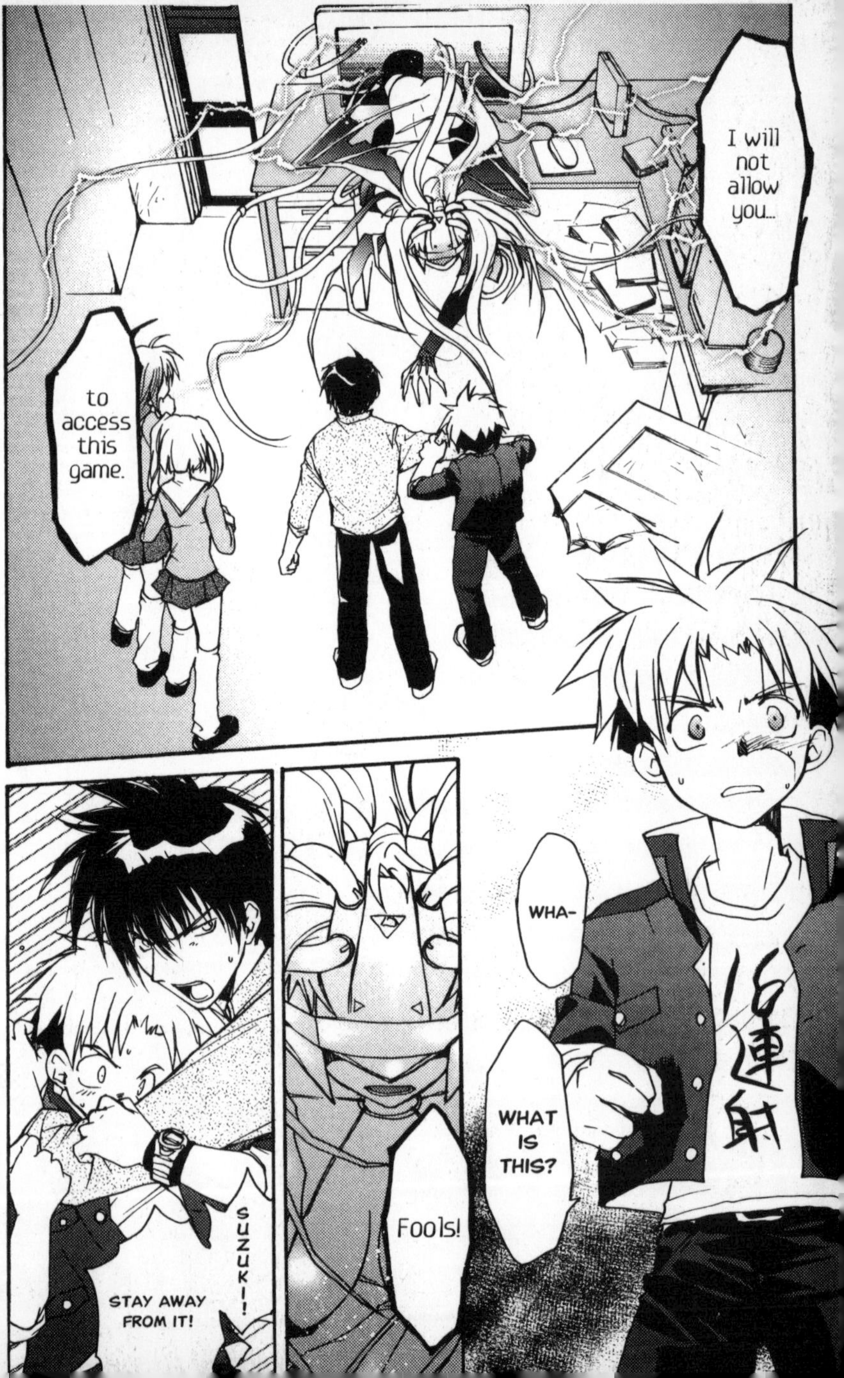
I will not allow you...
to access this game.
WHA-
WHAT IS THIS?
連射
Fools!
SUZUKI!!
STAY AWAY FROM IT!

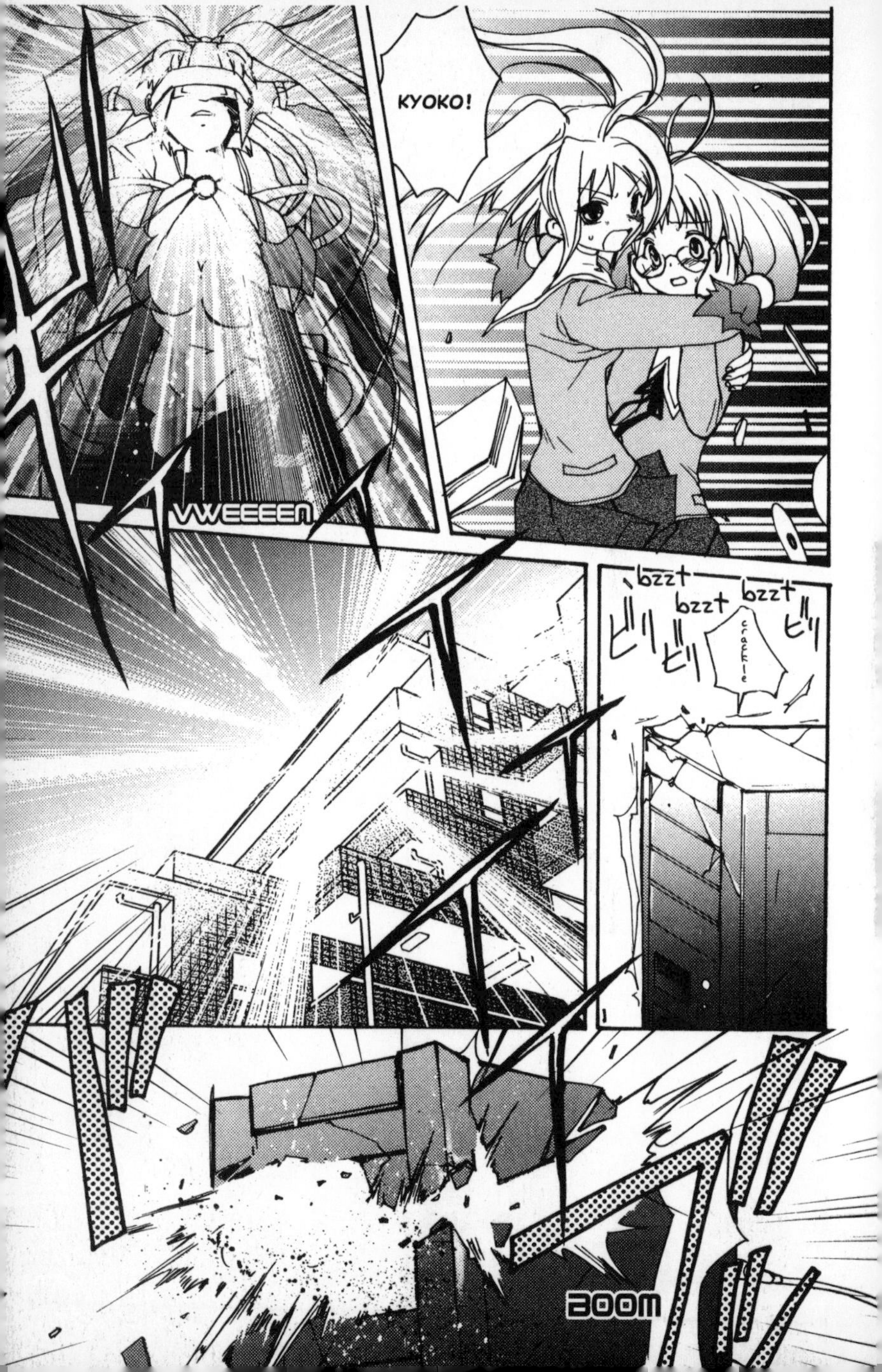

KYOKO!
VWEEEEN
bzzt
bzzt
bzzt
crackle
BOOM

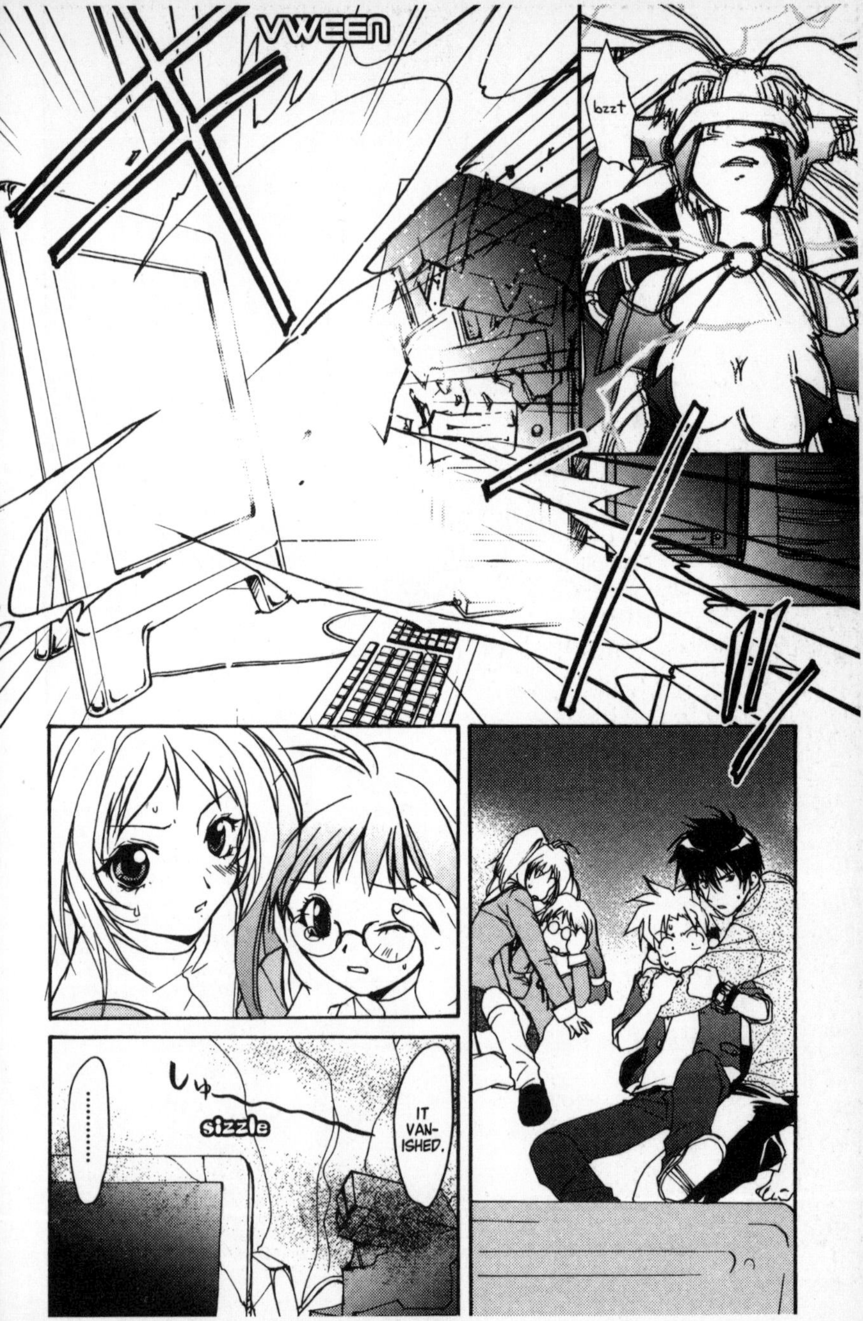
VWEEN
bzzt
しゅ
sizzle
IT VAN- ISHED.
....

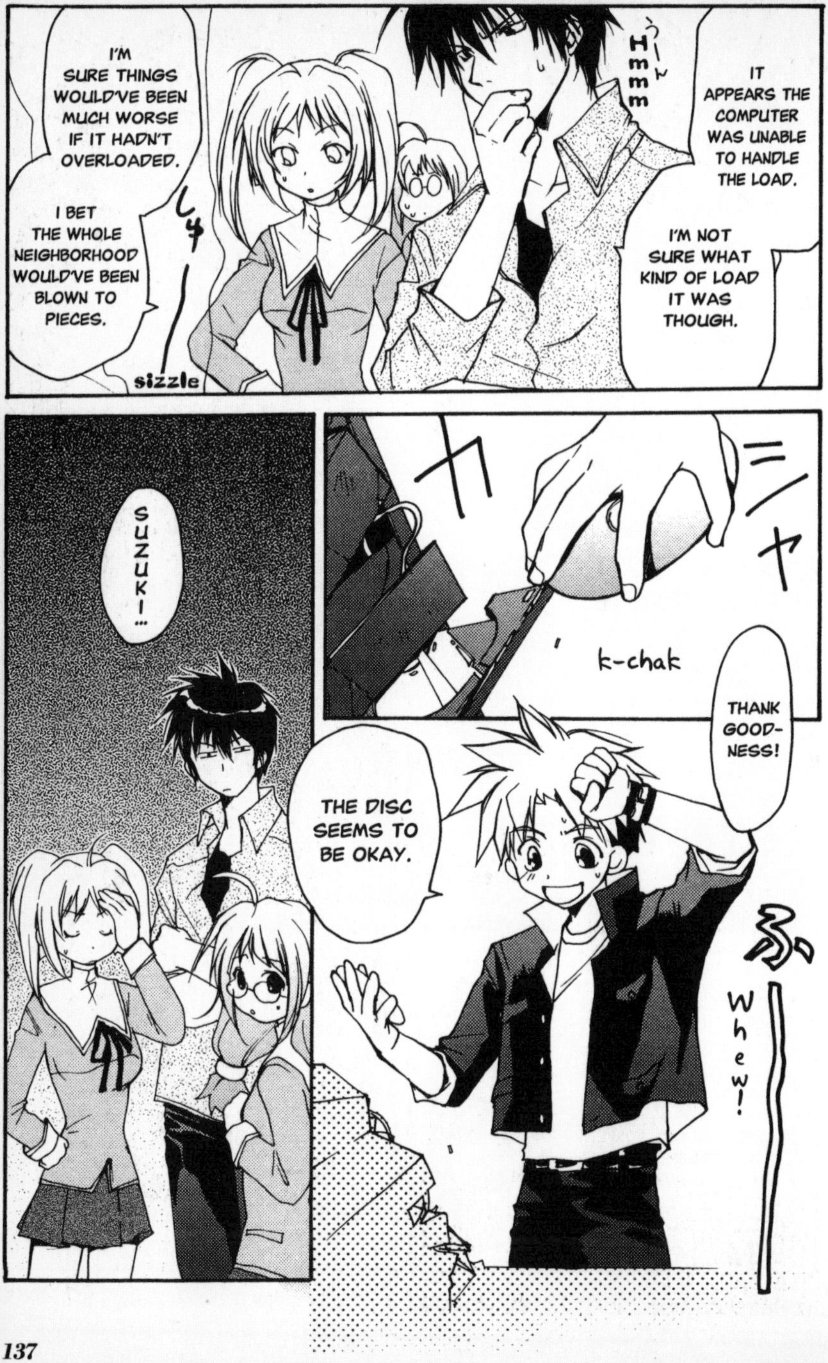
Hmmm
IT APPEARS THE COMPUTER WAS UNABLE TO HANDLE THE LOAD.
I'M NOT SURE WHAT KIND OF LOAD IT WAS THOUGH.
I'M SURE THINGS WOULD'VE BEEN MUCH WORSE IF IT HADN'T OVERLOADED.
I BET THE WHOLE NEIGHBORHOOD WOULD'VE BEEN BLOWN TO PIECES.
sizzle
k-chak
THANK GOODNESS!
THE DISC SEEMS TO BE OKAY.
Whew!
SUZUKI!...

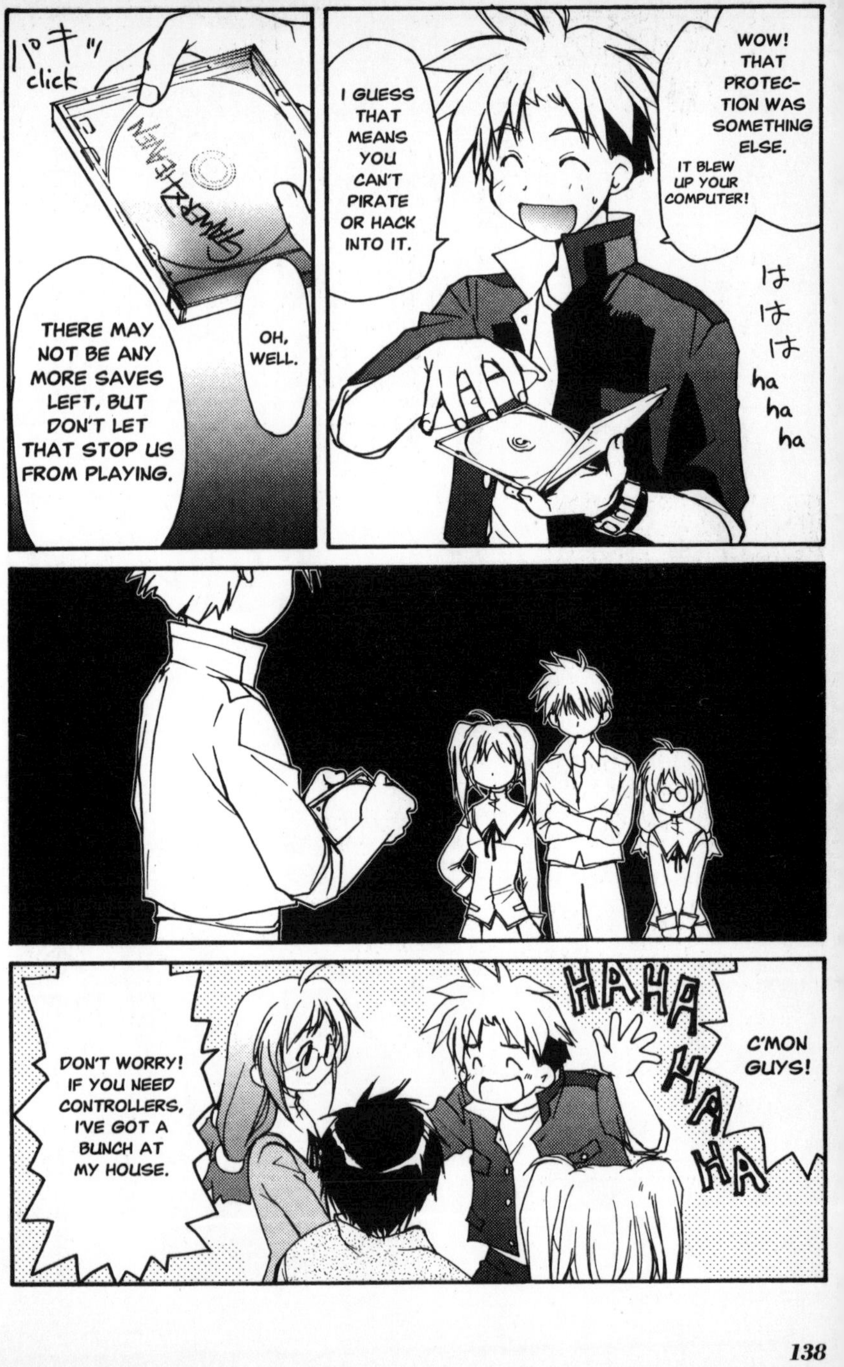

WOW! THAT PROTECTION WAS SOMETHING ELSE.
IT BLEW UP YOUR COMPUTER!
ははは
ha ha ha
I GUESS THAT MEANS YOU CAN'T PIRATE OR HACK INTO IT.
パキッ
click
OH, WELL.
THERE MAY NOT BE ANY MORE SAVES LEFT, BUT DON'T LET THAT STOP US FROM PLAYING.
C'MON GUYS!
HAHAHAHA
DON'T WORRY! IF YOU NEED CONTROLLERS, I'VE GOT A BUNCH AT MY HOUSE.

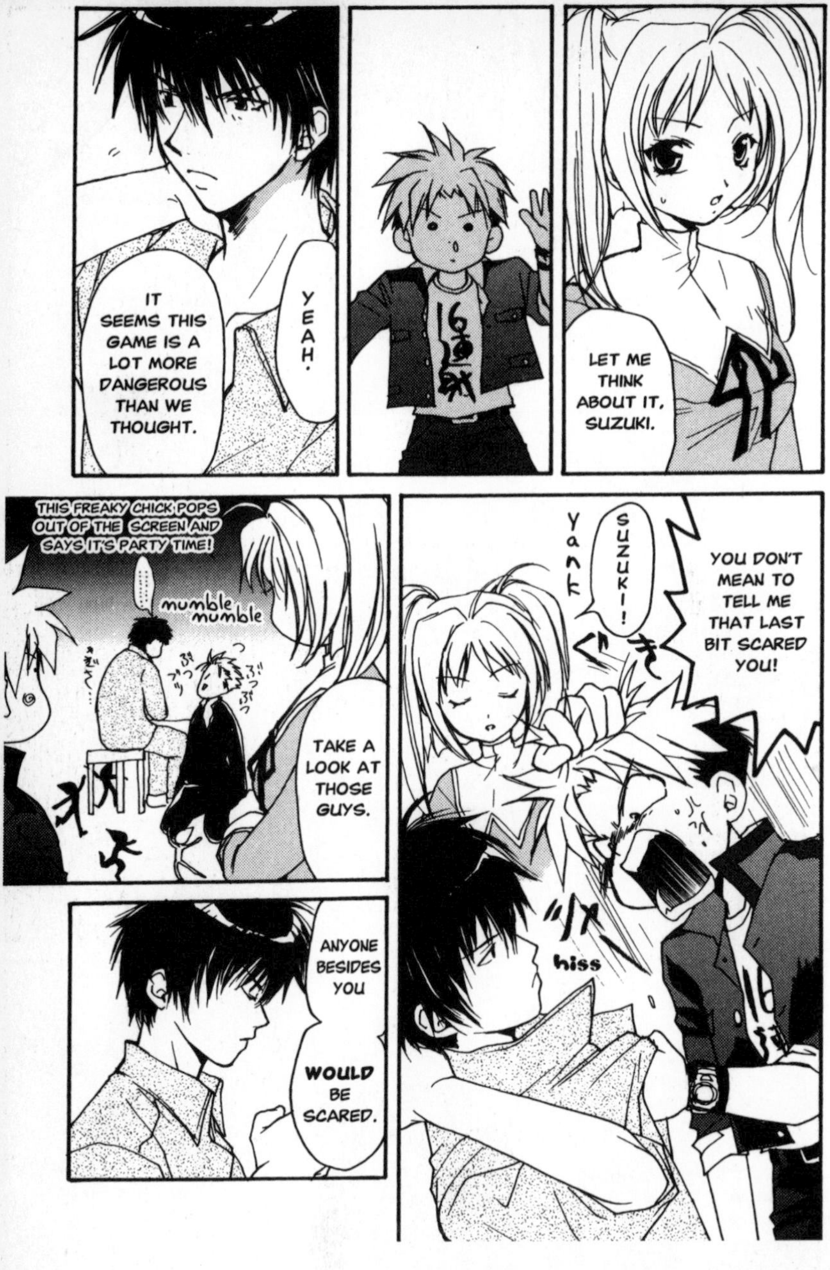
LET ME THINK ABOUT IT, SUZUKI.
IT SEEMS THIS GAME IS A LOT MORE DANGEROUS THAN WE THOUGHT.
YEAH.
YOU DON'T MEAN TO TELL ME THAT LAST BIT SCARED YOU!
SUZUKI!
Yank
TAKE A LOOK AT THOSE GUYS.
THIS FREAKY CHICK POPS OUT OF THE SCREEN AND SAYS IT'S PARTY TIME!
mumble mumble
ANYONE BESIDES YOU WOULD BE SCARED.
hiss

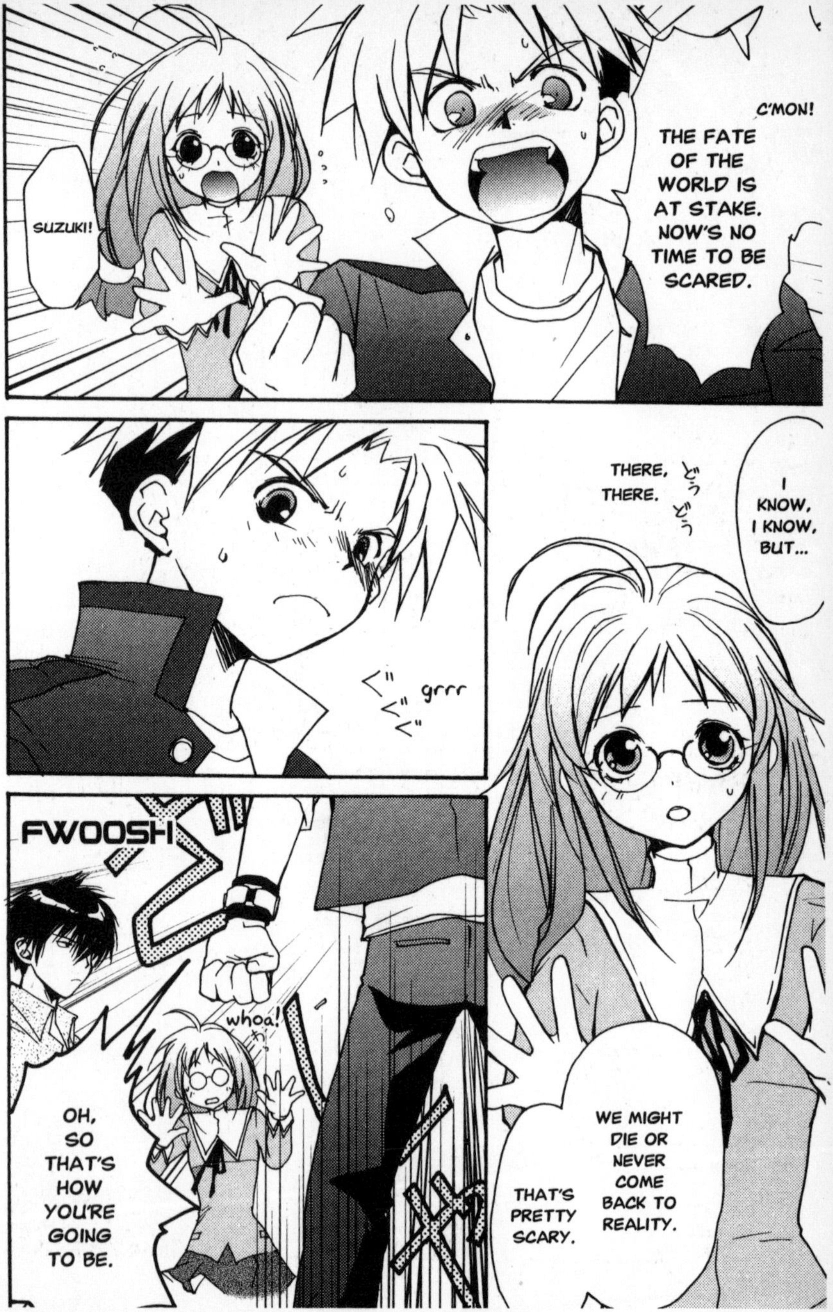
C'MON!
THE FATE OF THE WORLD IS AT STAKE. NOW'S NO TIME TO BE SCARED.
SUZUKI!
I KNOW, I KNOW, BUT...
THERE, THERE.
どう どう
ぐ ぐ ぐ
grrr
WE MIGHT DIE OR NEVER COME BACK TO REALITY.
THAT'S PRETTY SCARY.
FWOOSH
whoa!
OH, SO THAT'S HOW YOU'RE GOING TO BE.

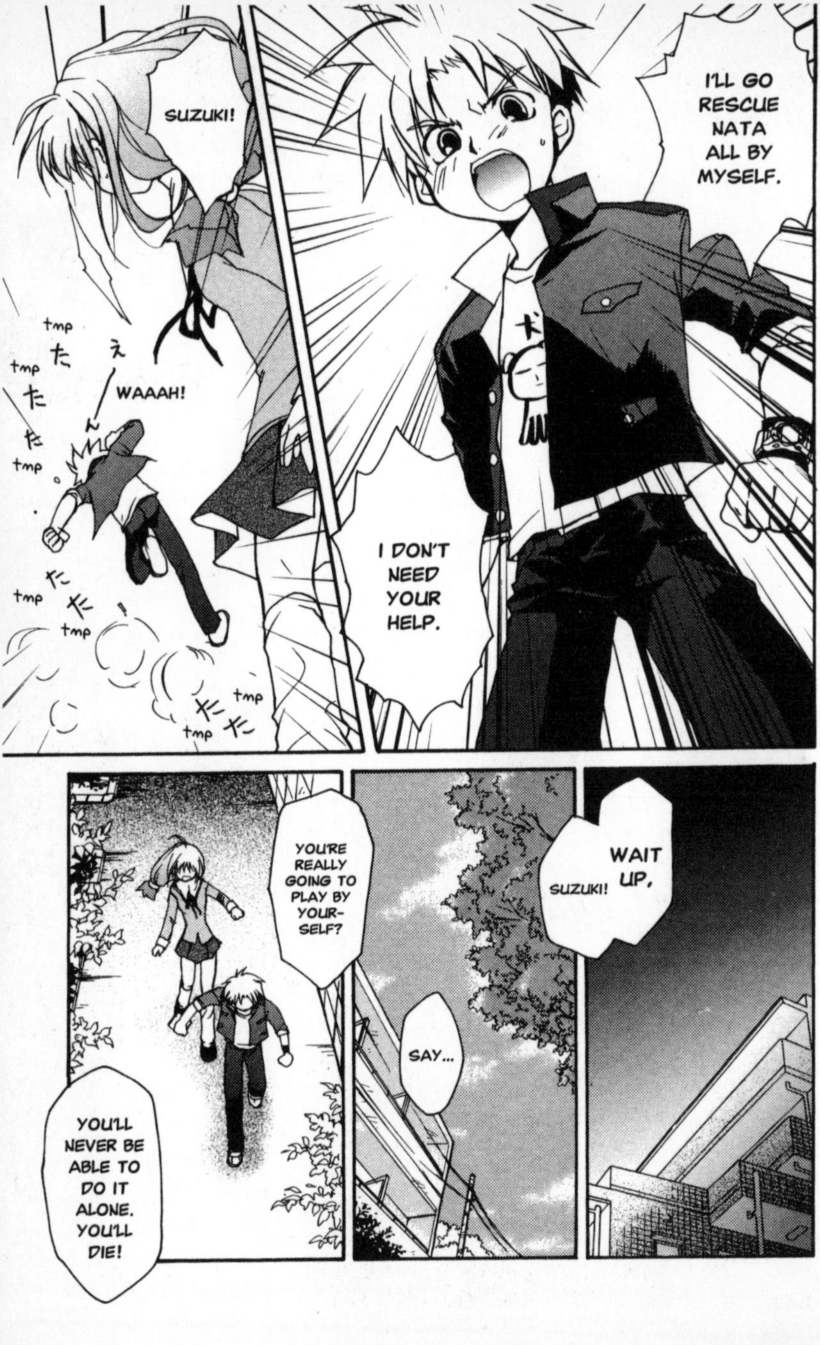
I'LL GO RESCUE NATA ALL BY MYSELF.
I DON'T NEED YOUR HELP.
SUZUKI!
WAAAH!
えーん
tmp
た
tmp
た
た
tmp
た
tmp
だ
tmp
だ
tmp
だ
tmp
だ
WAIT UP, SUZUKI!
SAY...
YOU'RE REALLY GOING TO PLAY BY YOUR-SELF?
YOU'LL NEVER BE ABLE TO DO IT ALONE. YOU'LL DIE!

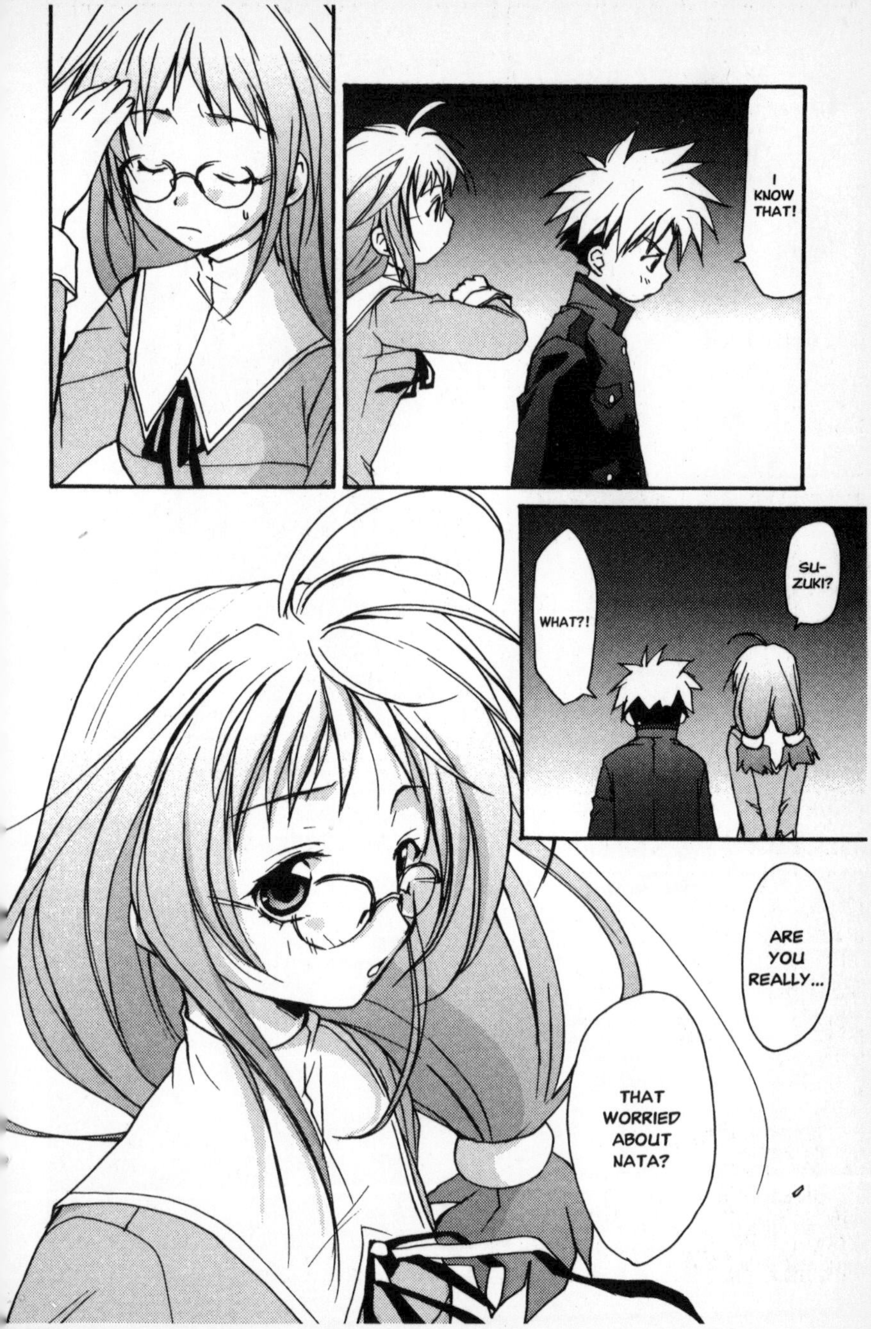
I KNOW THAT!
SU-ZUKI?
WHAT?!
ARE YOU REALLY...
THAT WORRIED ABOUT NATA?

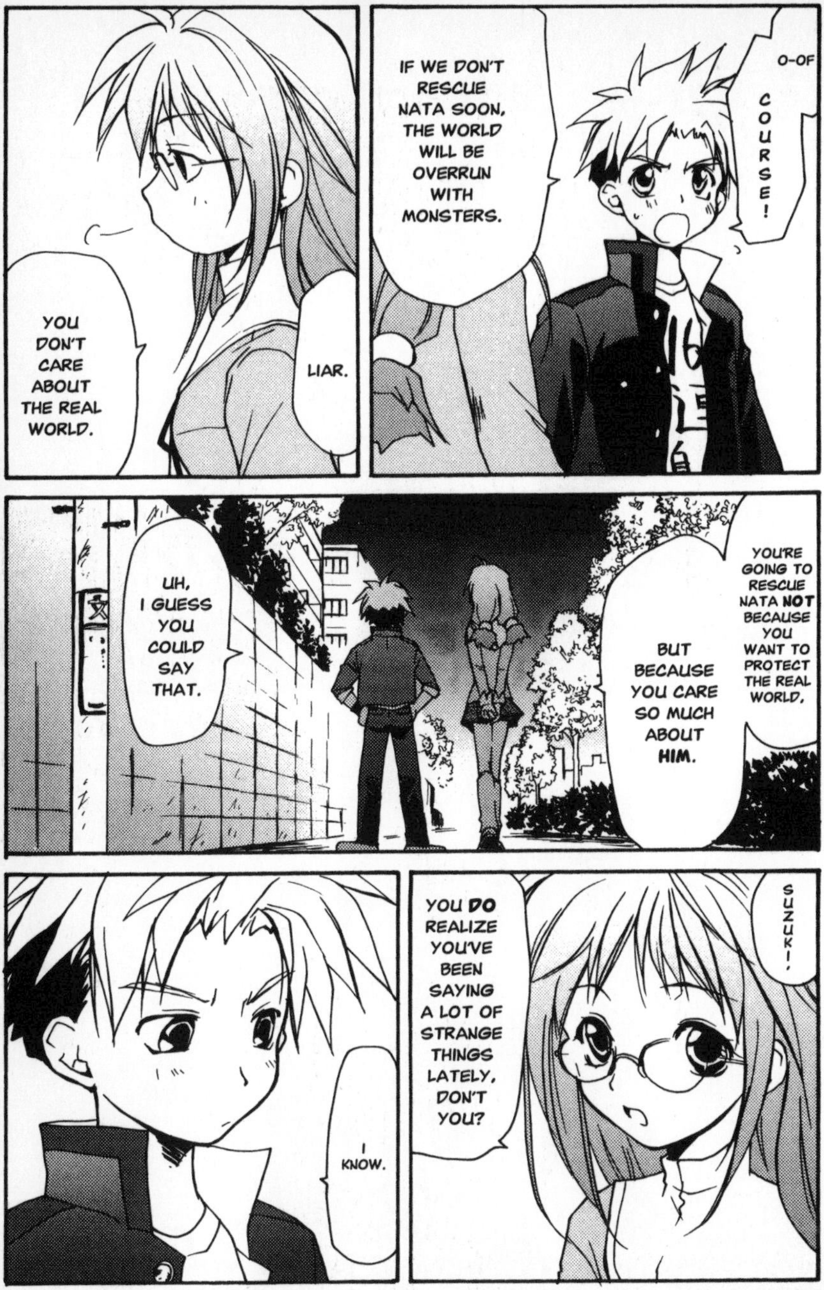
O-OF COURSE!
IF WE DON'T RESCUE NATA SOON, THE WORLD WILL BE OVERRUN WITH MONSTERS.
LIAR.
YOU DON'T CARE ABOUT THE REAL WORLD.
YOU'RE GOING TO RESCUE NATA **NOT** BECAUSE YOU WANT TO PROTECT THE REAL WORLD,
BUT BECAUSE YOU CARE SO MUCH ABOUT **HIM**.
UH, I GUESS YOU COULD SAY THAT.
SUZUKI!
YOU **DO** REALIZE YOU'VE BEEN SAYING A LOT OF STRANGE THINGS LATELY, DON'T YOU?
I KNOW.

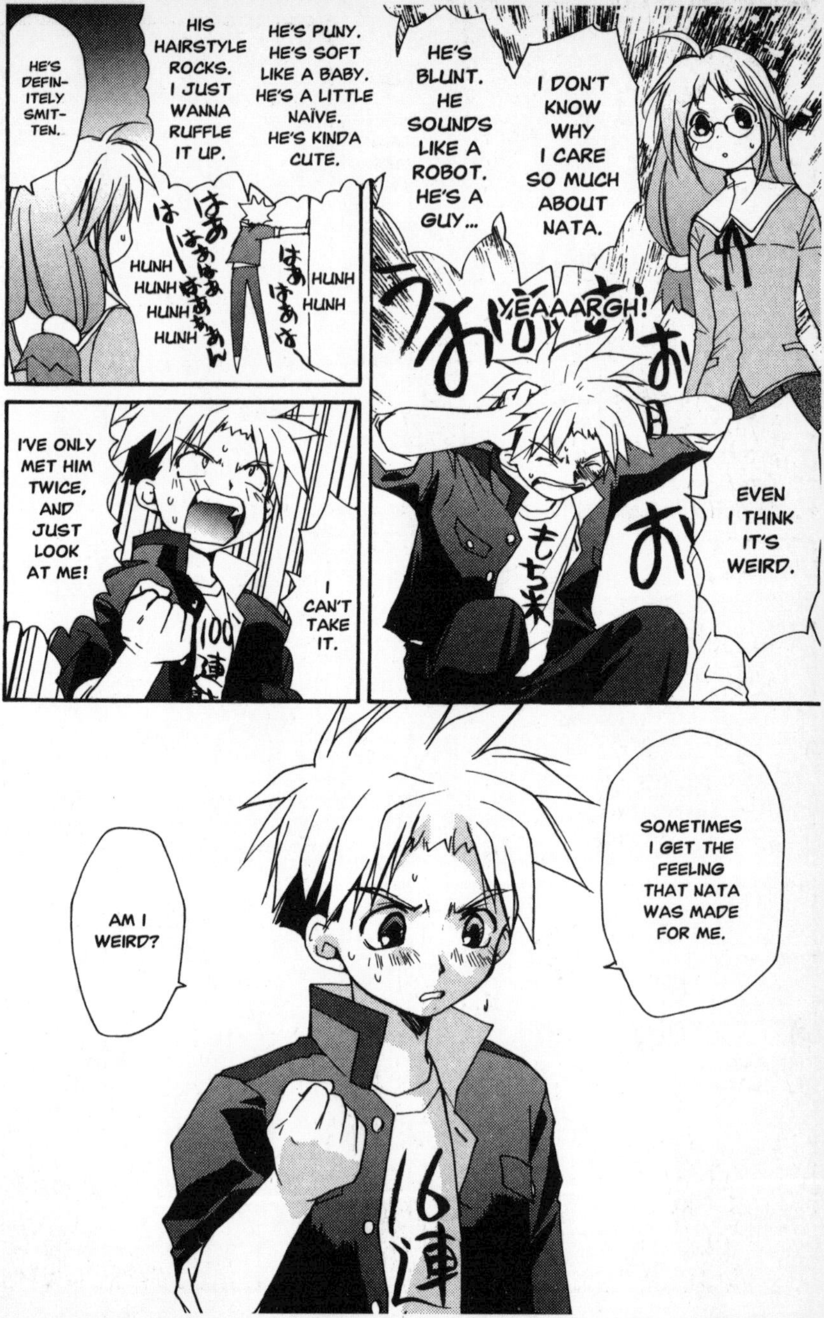

I DON'T KNOW WHY I CARE SO MUCH ABOUT NATA.
HE'S BLUNT. HE SOUNDS LIKE A ROBOT. HE'S A GUY...
HE'S PUNY. HE'S SOFT LIKE A BABY. HE'S A LITTLE NAÏVE. HE'S KINDA CUTE.
HIS HAIRSTYLE ROCKS. I JUST WANNA RUFFLE IT UP.
HUNH HUNH
HUNH HUNH HUNH HUNH
HE'S DEFIN-ITELY SMIT-TEN.
YEAAARGH!
EVEN I THINK IT'S WEIRD.
I CAN'T TAKE IT.
I'VE ONLY MET HIM TWICE, AND JUST LOOK AT ME!
SOMETIMES I GET THE FEELING THAT NATA WAS MADE FOR ME.
AM I WEIRD?

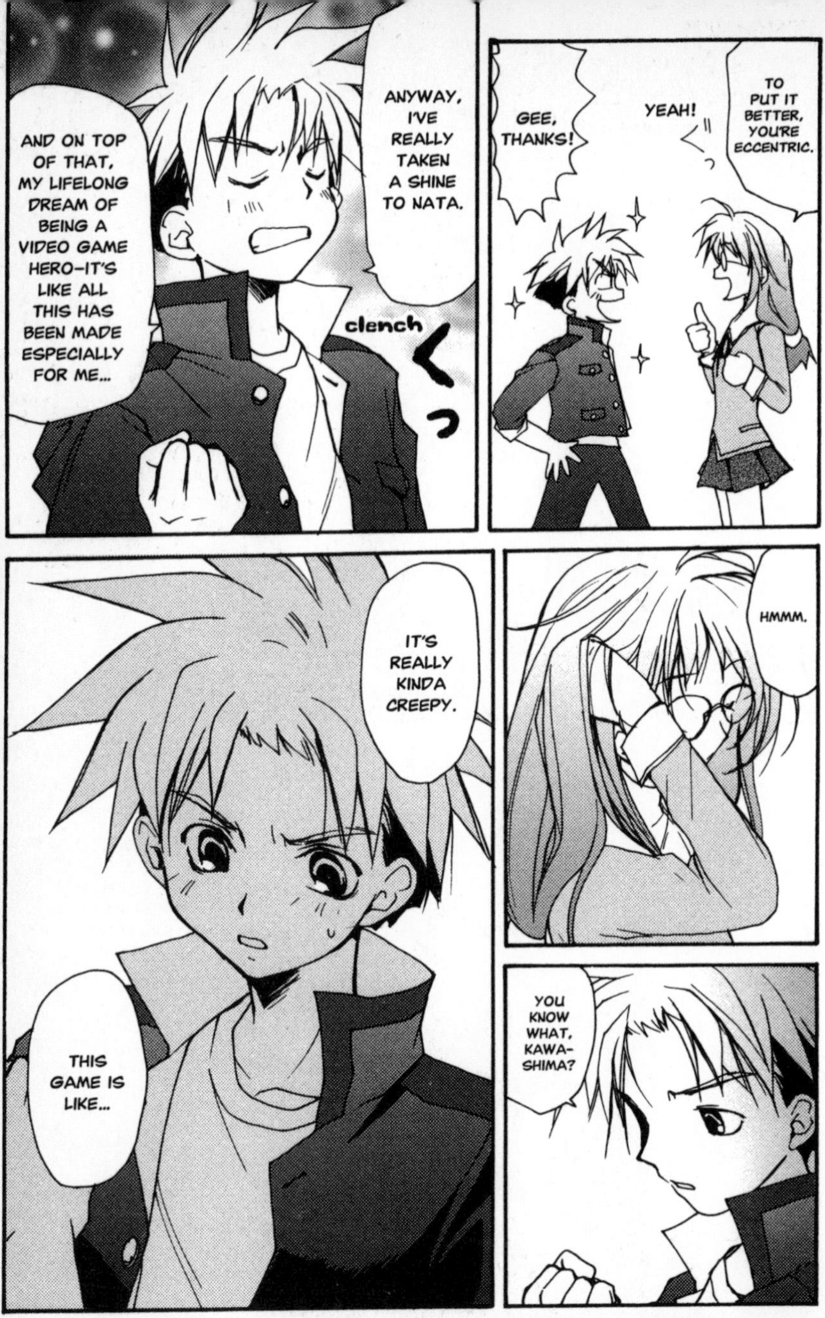
TO PUT IT BETTER, YOU'RE ECCENTRIC.
YEAH!
GEE, THANKS!
ANYWAY, I'VE REALLY TAKEN A SHINE TO NATA.
AND ON TOP OF THAT, MY LIFELONG DREAM OF BEING A VIDEO GAME HERO—IT'S LIKE ALL THIS HAS BEEN MADE ESPECIALLY FOR ME...
clench
くっ
HMMM.
YOU KNOW WHAT, KAWA-SHIMA?
IT'S REALLY KINDA CREEPY.
THIS GAME IS LIKE...

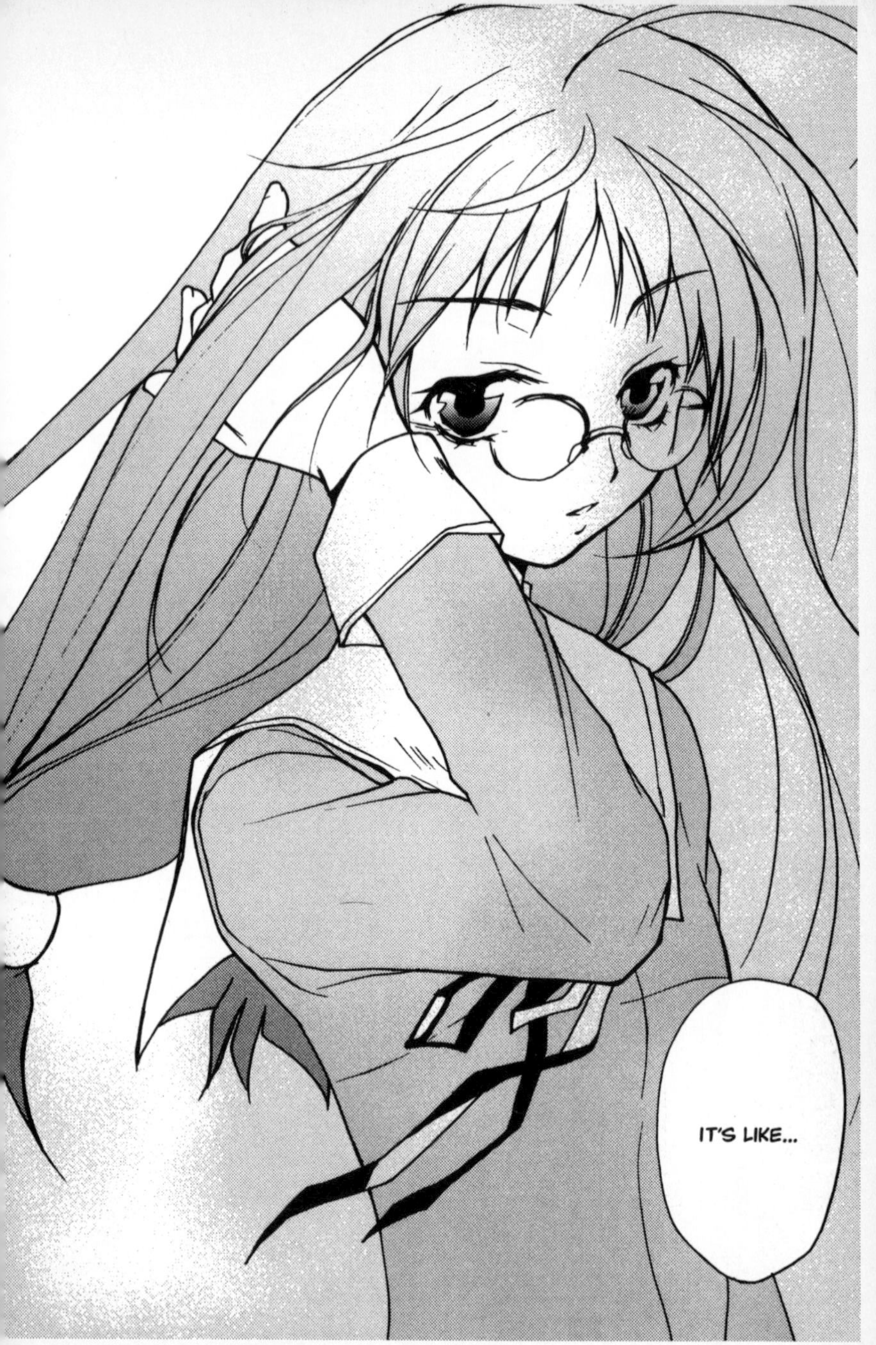

IT'S LIKE...

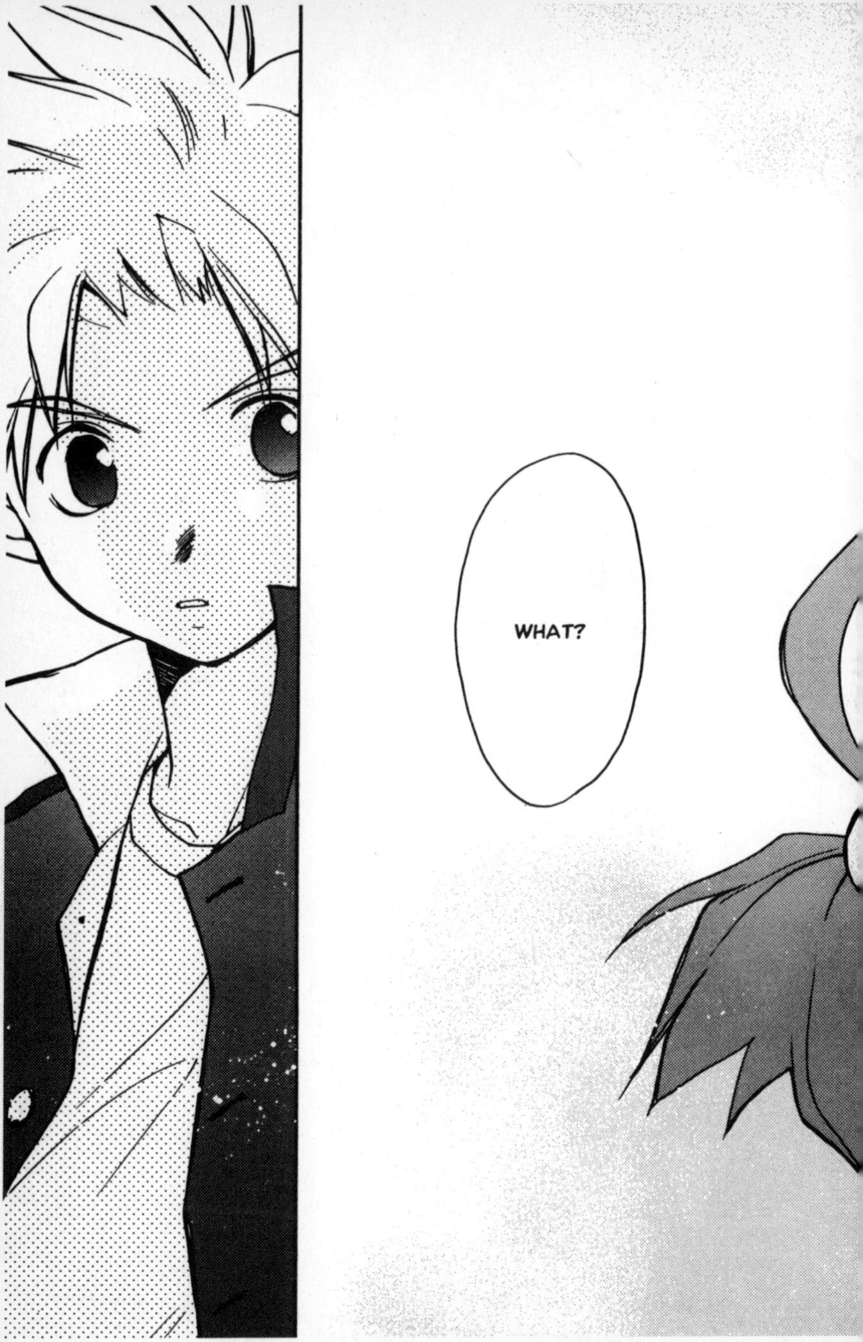
WHAT?

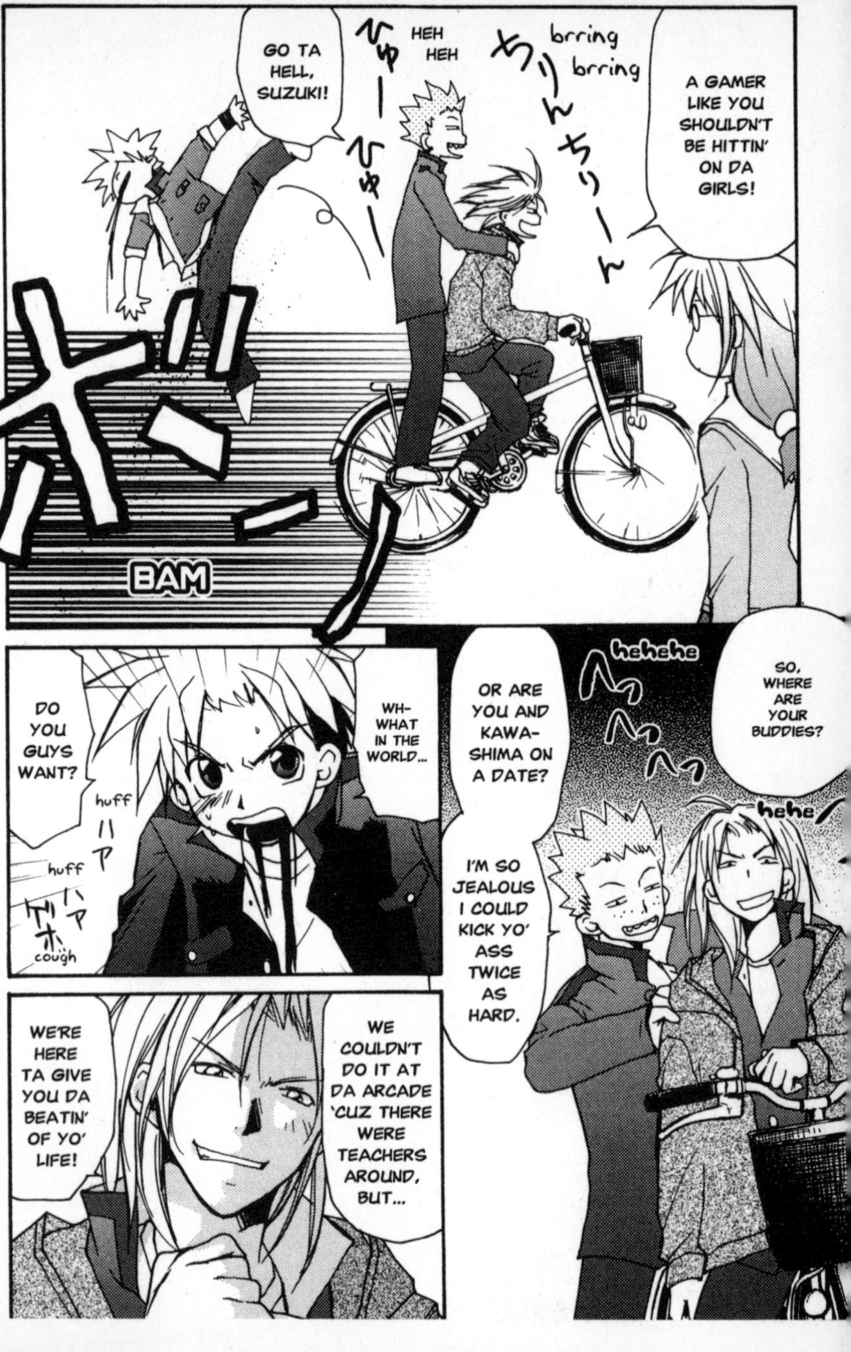
A GAMER LIKE YOU SHOULDN'T BE HITTIN' ON DA GIRLS!
ちりん ちりーん
brring brring
HEH HEH
ひゅー ひゅー
GO TA HELL, SUZUKI!
BAM
SO, WHERE ARE YOUR BUDDIES?
hehehe
hehe
OR ARE YOU AND KAWA-SHIMA ON A DATE?
I'M SO JEALOUS I COULD KICK YO' ASS TWICE AS HARD.
WH- WHAT IN THE WORLD...
DO YOU GUYS WANT?
huff
ハァ
huff
ハァ
ゲホ
cough
WE COULDN'T DO IT AT DA ARCADE 'CUZ THERE WERE TEACHERS AROUND, BUT...
WE'RE HERE TA GIVE YOU DA BEATIN' OF YO' LIFE!

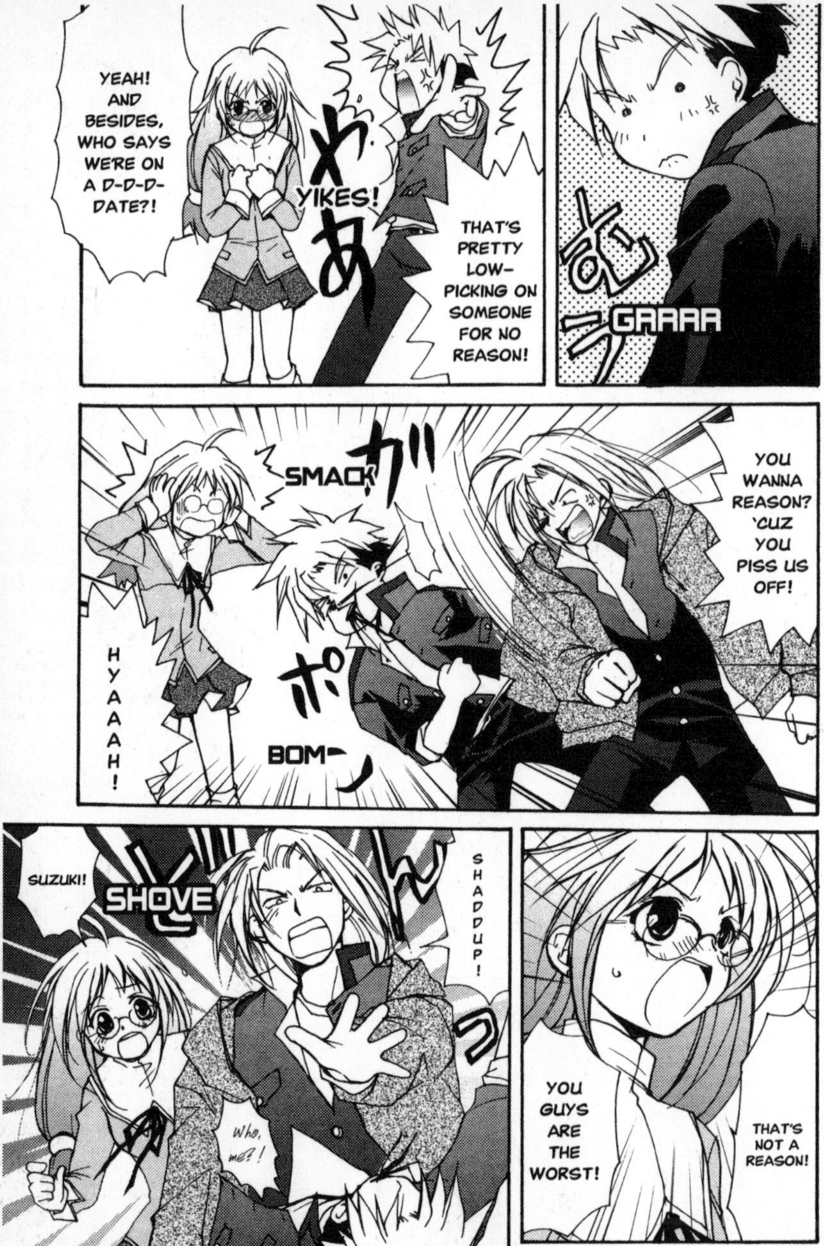

GRAAAR
THAT'S PRETTY LOW— PICKING ON SOMEONE FOR NO REASON!
YIKES!
YEAH! AND BESIDES, WHO SAYS WE'RE ON A D-D-D-DATE?!
YOU WANNA REASON? 'CUZ YOU PISS US OFF!
SMACK
BOM
HYAAAAH!
THAT'S NOT A REASON!
YOU GUYS ARE THE WORST!
SHADDUP!
SHOVE
SUZUKI!
Who, me?!

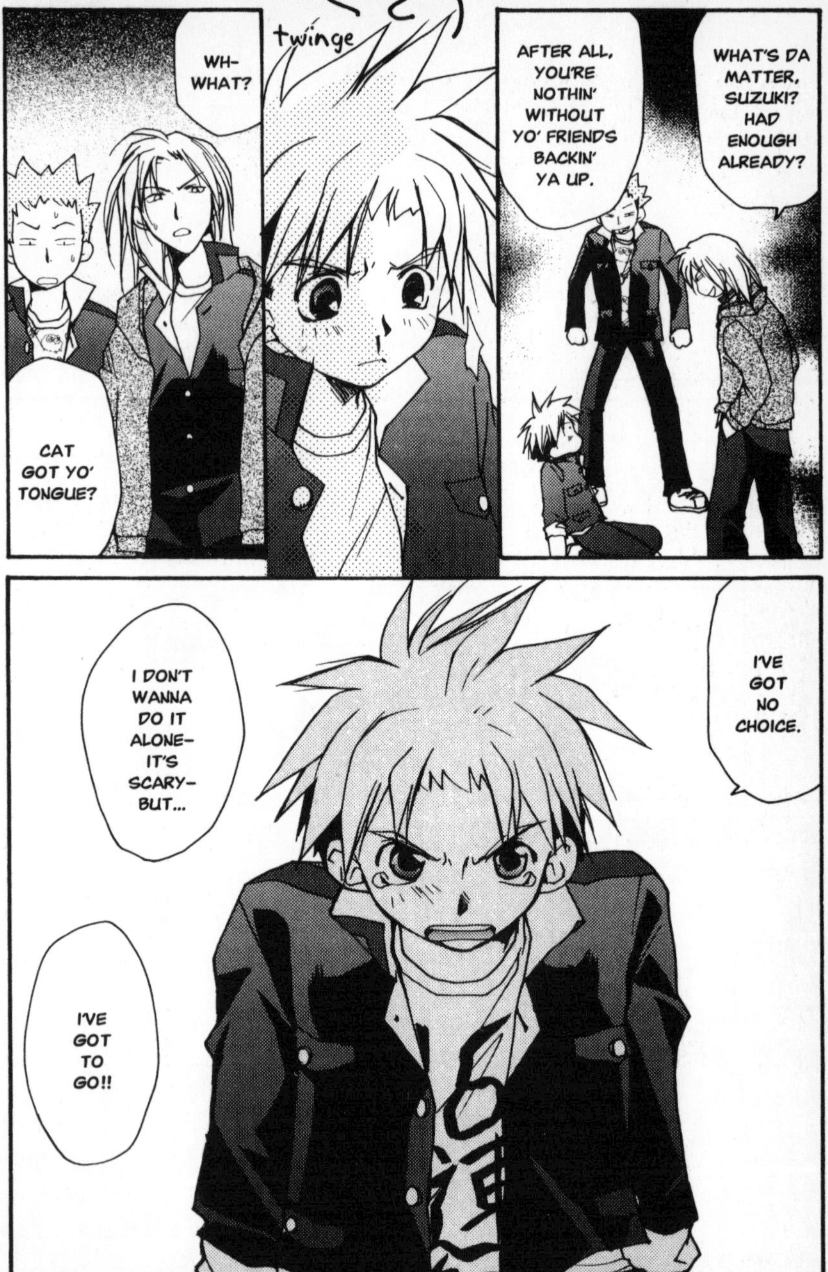
WHAT'S DA MATTER, SUZUKI? HAD ENOUGH ALREADY?
AFTER ALL, YOU'RE NOTHIN' WITHOUT YO' FRIENDS BACKIN' YA UP.
ぐさり
twinge
WH- WHAT?
CAT GOT YO' TONGUE?
I'VE GOT NO CHOICE.
I DON'T WANNA DO IT ALONE- IT'S SCARY- BUT...
I'VE GOT TO GO!!

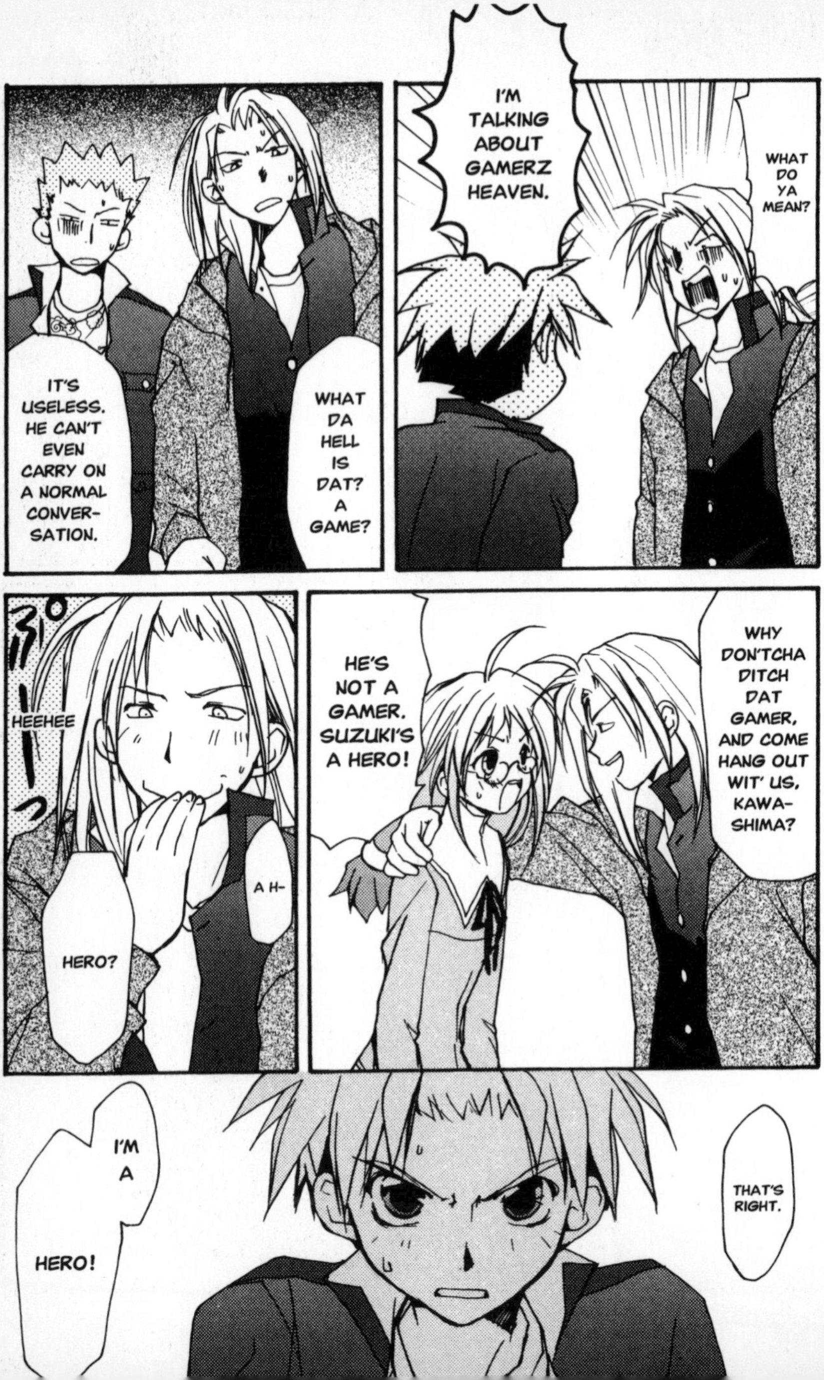
WHAT DO YA MEAN?
I'M TALKING ABOUT GAMERZ HEAVEN.
WHAT DA HELL IS DAT? A GAME?
IT'S USELESS. HE CAN'T EVEN CARRY ON A NORMAL CONVER-SATION.
WHY DON'TCHA DITCH DAT GAMER, AND COME HANG OUT WIT' US, KAWA-SHIMA?
HE'S NOT A GAMER. SUZUKI'S A HERO!
A H-
HERO?
HEEHEE
THAT'S RIGHT.
I'M A HERO!

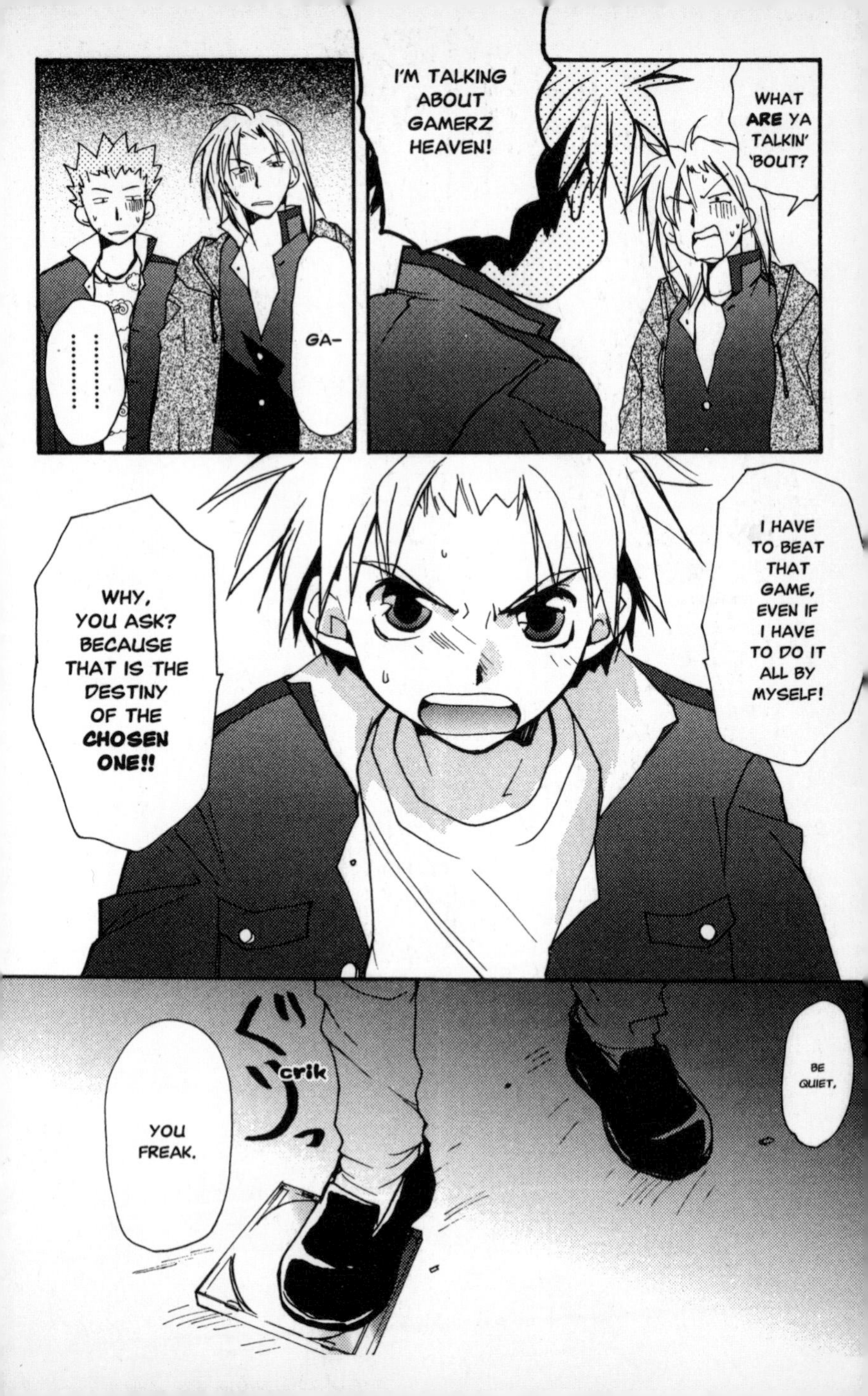
WHAT ARE YA TALKIN' 'BOUT?
I'M TALKING ABOUT GAMERZ HEAVEN!
GA-
......
I HAVE TO BEAT THAT GAME, EVEN IF I HAVE TO DO IT ALL BY MYSELF!
WHY, YOU ASK? BECAUSE THAT IS THE DESTINY OF THE CHOSEN ONE!!
BE QUIET,
crik
YOU FREAK.

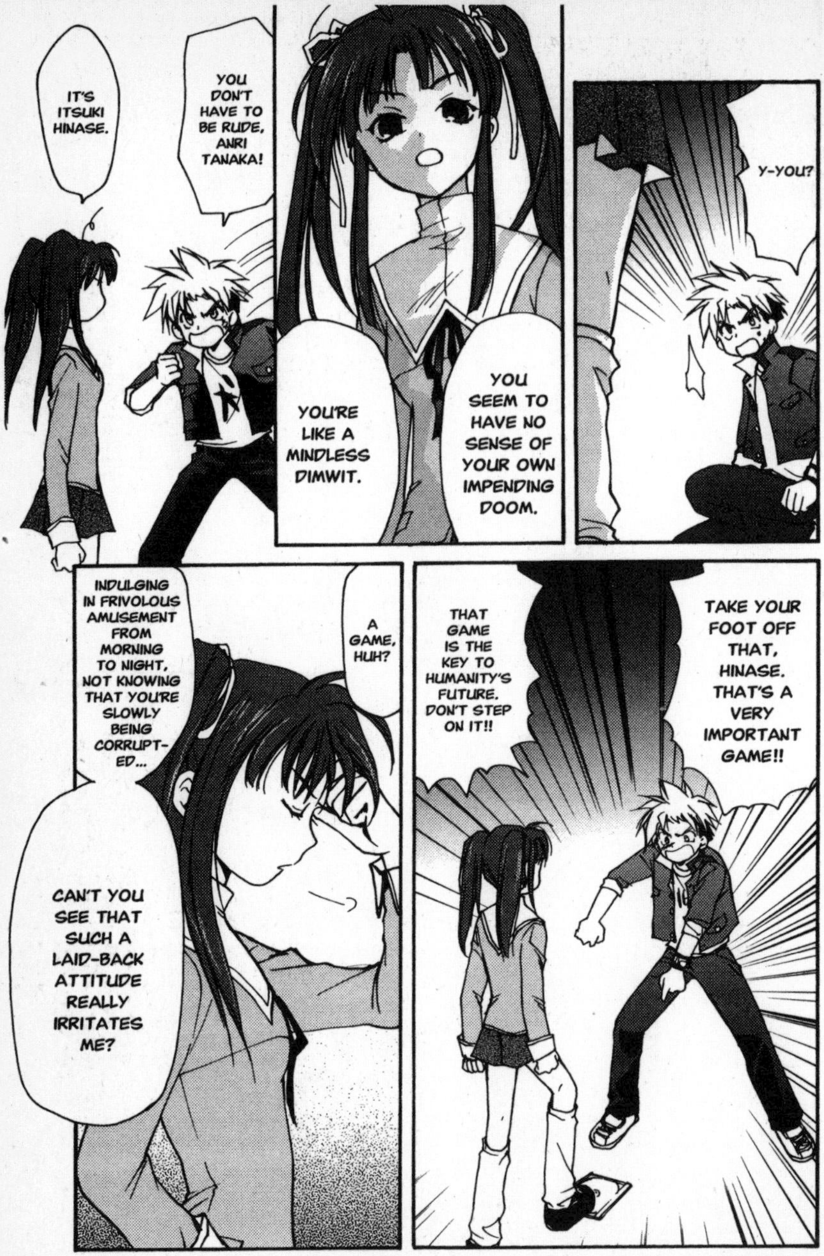
Y-YOU?
YOU SEEM TO HAVE NO SENSE OF YOUR OWN IMPENDING DOOM.
YOU'RE LIKE A MINDLESS DIMWIT.
YOU DON'T HAVE TO BE RUDE, ANRI TANAKA!
IT'S ITSUKI HINASE.
TAKE YOUR FOOT OFF THAT, HINASE. THAT'S A VERY IMPORTANT GAME!!
THAT GAME IS THE KEY TO HUMANITY'S FUTURE. DON'T STEP ON IT!!
A GAME, HUH?
INDULGING IN FRIVOLOUS AMUSEMENT FROM MORNING TO NIGHT, NOT KNOWING THAT YOU'RE SLOWLY BEING CORRUPTED...
CAN'T YOU SEE THAT SUCH A LAID-BACK ATTITUDE REALLY IRRITATES ME?

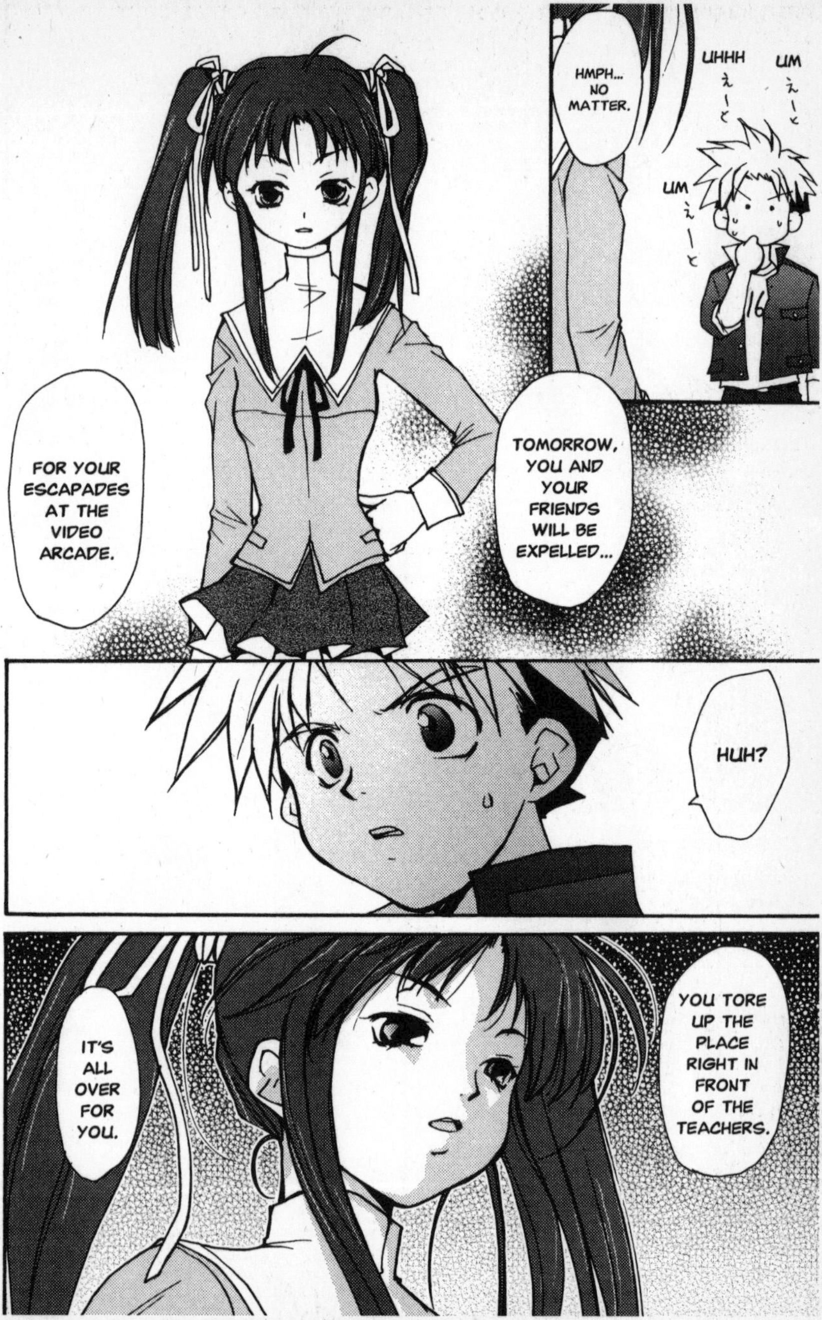
HMPH... NO MATTER.
UHHH えーと
UM えーと
UM えーと
TOMORROW, YOU AND YOUR FRIENDS WILL BE EXPELLED...
FOR YOUR ESCAPADES AT THE VIDEO ARCADE.
HUH?
YOU TORE UP THE PLACE RIGHT IN FRONT OF THE TEACHERS.
IT'S ALL OVER FOR YOU.

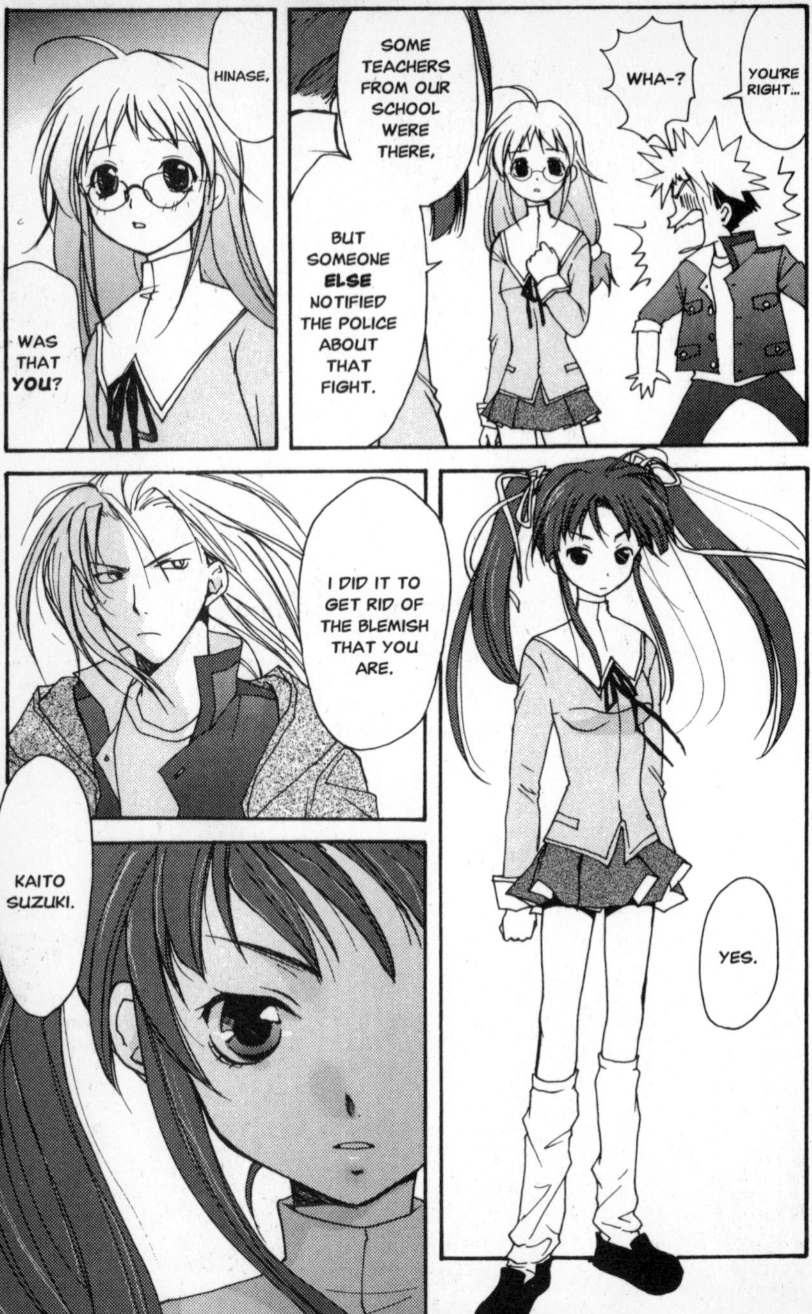
YOU'RE RIGHT...
WHA-?
SOME TEACHERS FROM OUR SCHOOL WERE THERE,
BUT SOMEONE ELSE NOTIFIED THE POLICE ABOUT THAT FIGHT.
HINASE,
WAS THAT YOU?
YES.
I DID IT TO GET RID OF THE BLEMISH THAT YOU ARE.
KAITO SUZUKI.

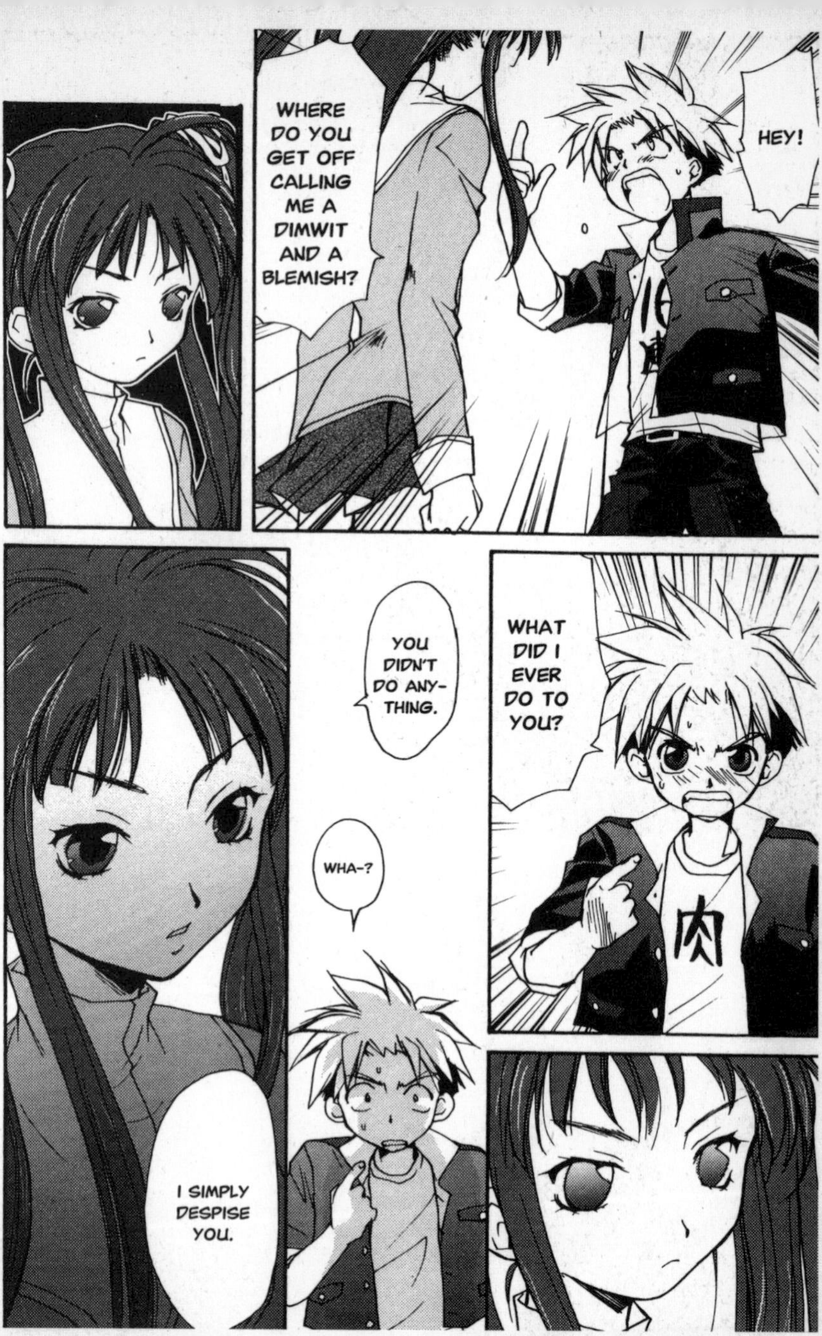
HEY!
WHERE DO YOU GET OFF CALLING ME A DIMWIT AND A BLEMISH?
WHAT DID I EVER DO TO YOU?
YOU DIDN'T DO ANY-THING.
WHA-?
I SIMPLY DESPISE YOU.

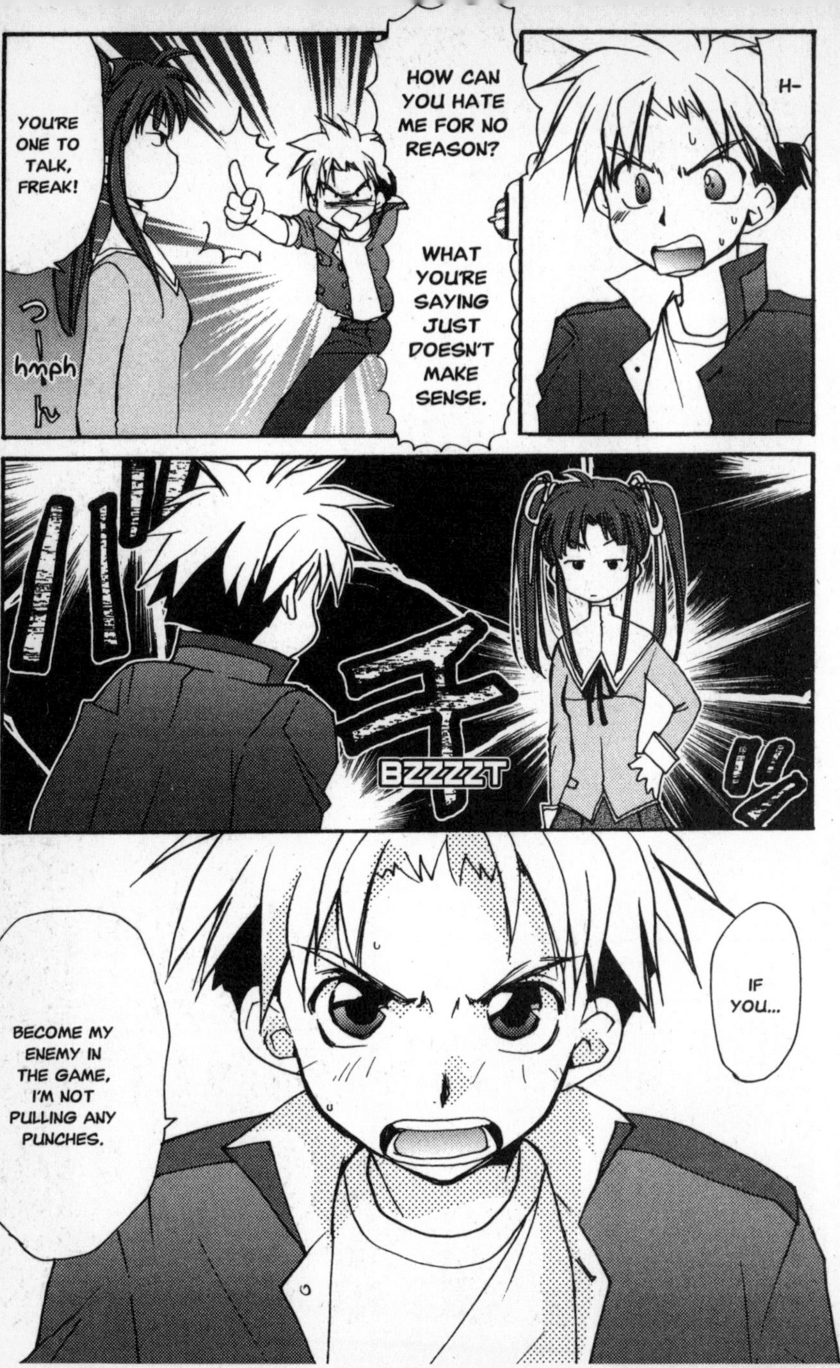
H-
HOW CAN YOU HATE ME FOR NO REASON?
WHAT YOU'RE SAYING JUST DOESN'T MAKE SENSE.
YOU'RE ONE TO TALK, FREAK!
hmph
BZZZZT
IF YOU...
BECOME MY ENEMY IN THE GAME, I'M NOT PULLING ANY PUNCHES.

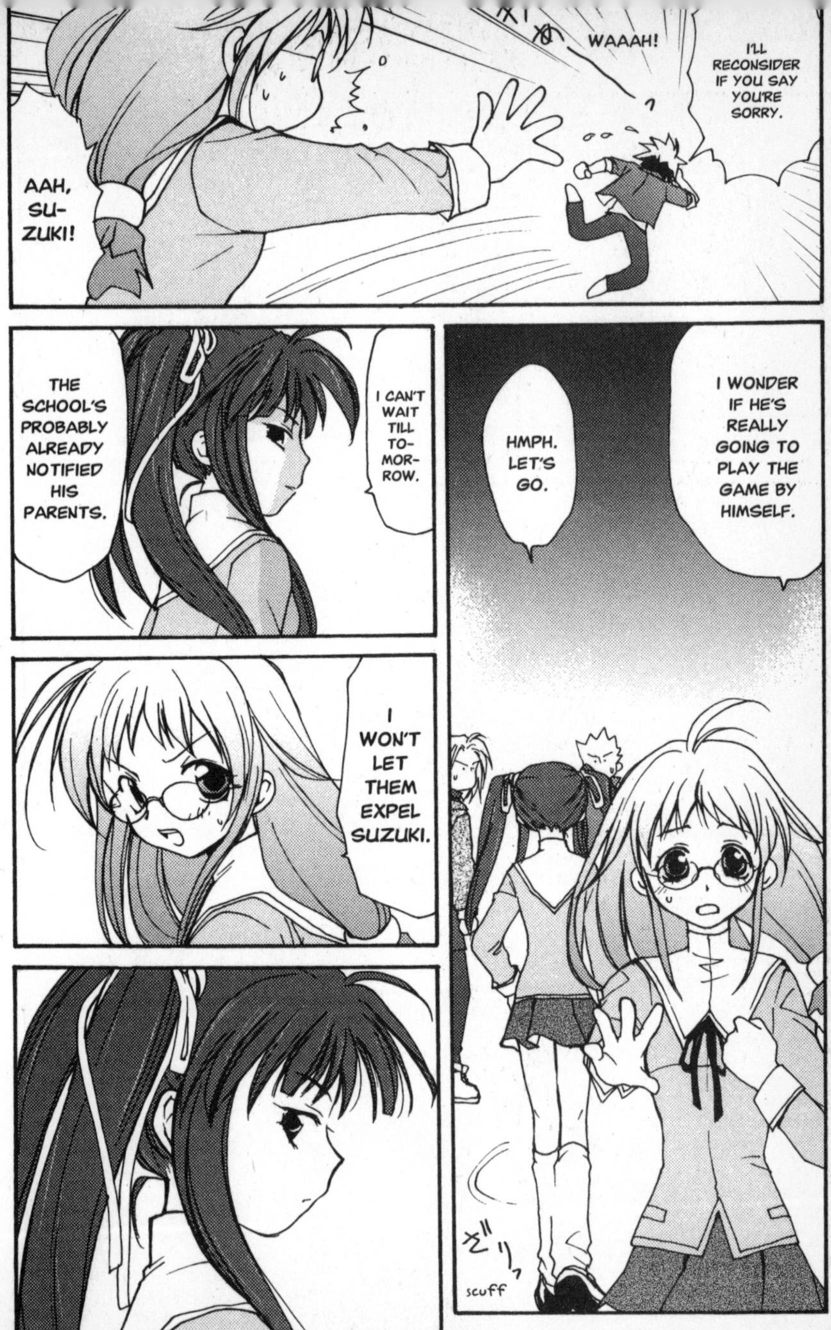
WAAAH!
I'LL RECONSIDER IF YOU SAY YOU'RE SORRY.
AAH, SU-ZUKI!
THE SCHOOL'S PROBABLY ALREADY NOTIFIED HIS PARENTS.
I CAN'T WAIT TILL TO-MOR-ROW.
HMPH. LET'S GO.
I WONDER IF HE'S REALLY GOING TO PLAY THE GAME BY HIMSELF.
I WON'T LET THEM EXPEL SUZUKI.
scuff

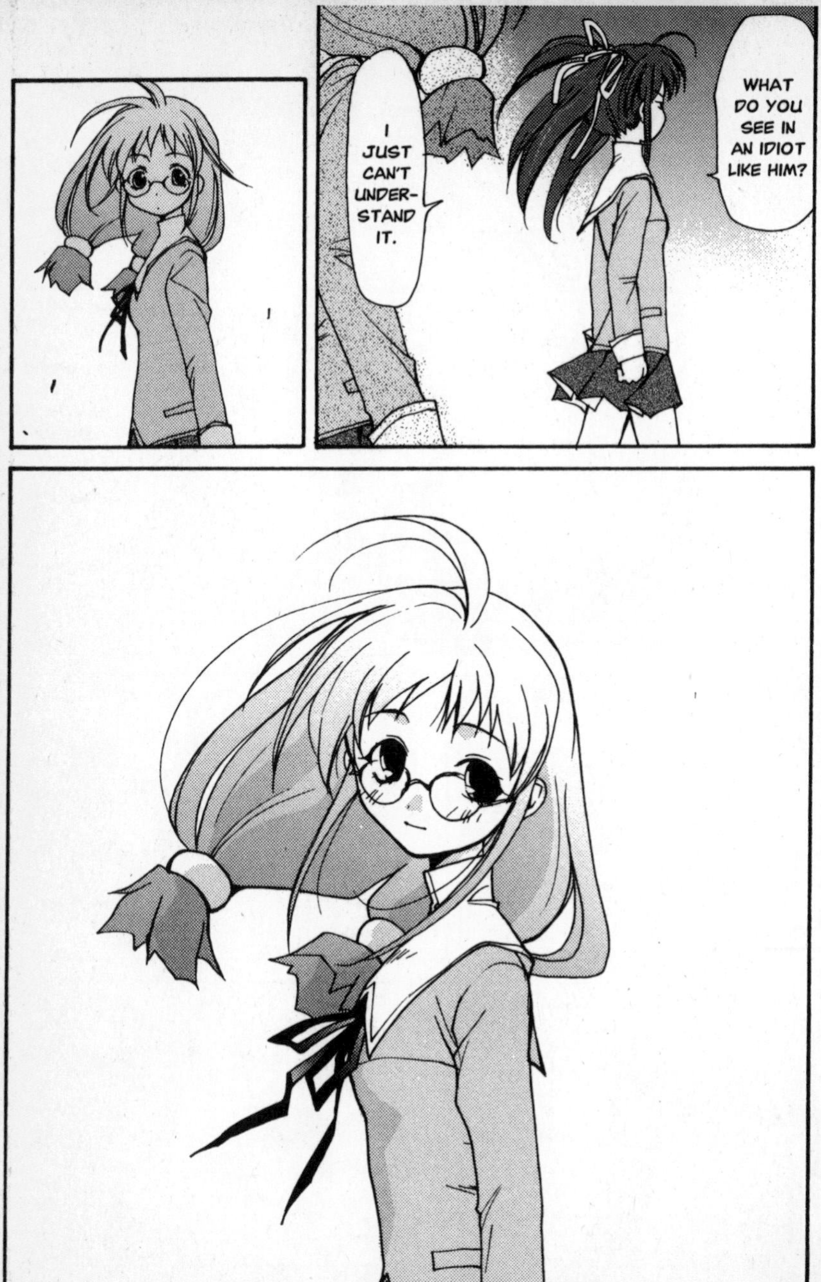
WHAT DO YOU SEE IN AN IDIOT LIKE HIM?
I JUST CAN'T UNDER-STAND IT.

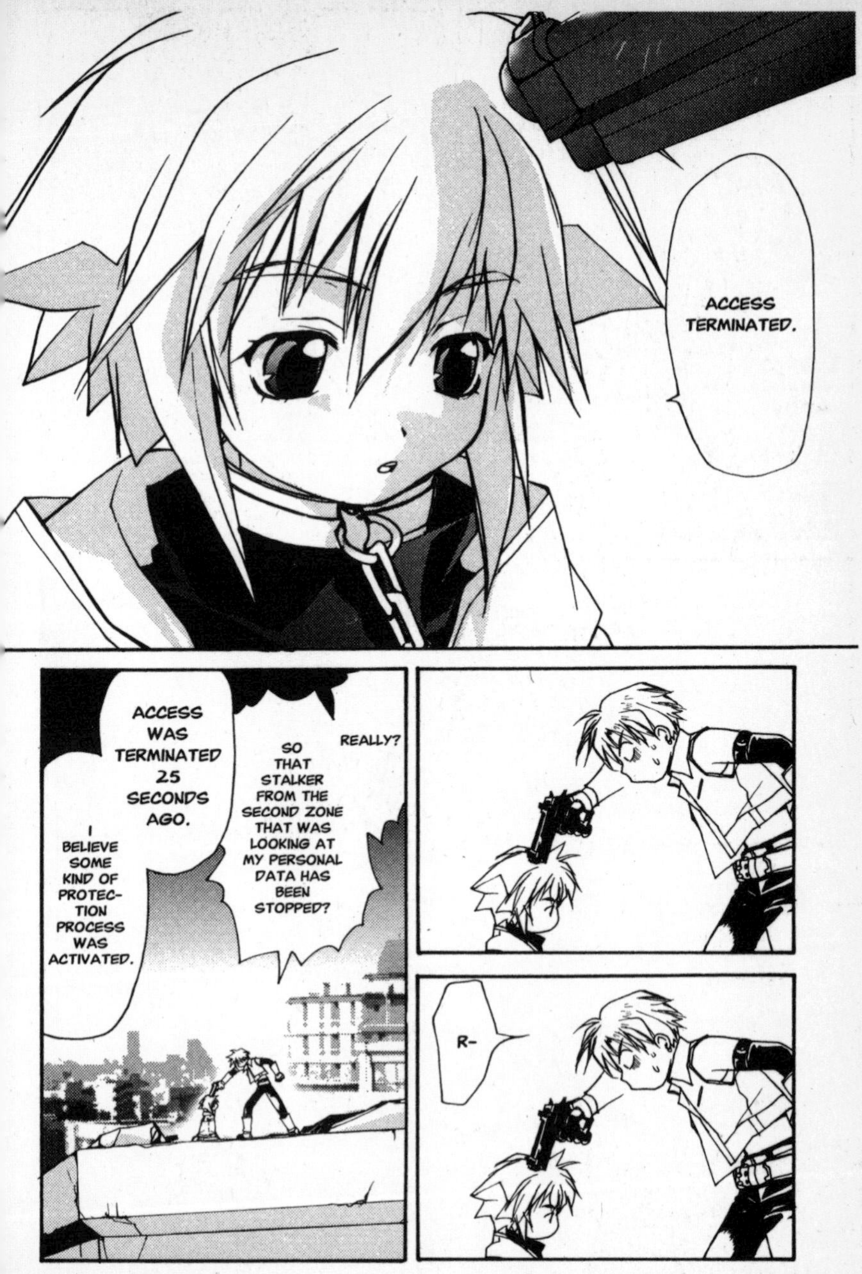
ACCESS TERMINATED.
SO THAT STALKER FROM THE SECOND ZONE THAT WAS LOOKING AT MY PERSONAL DATA HAS BEEN STOPPED?
REALLY?
ACCESS WAS TERMINATED 25 SECONDS AGO.
I BELIEVE SOME KIND OF PROTEC-TION PROCESS WAS ACTIVATED.
R-

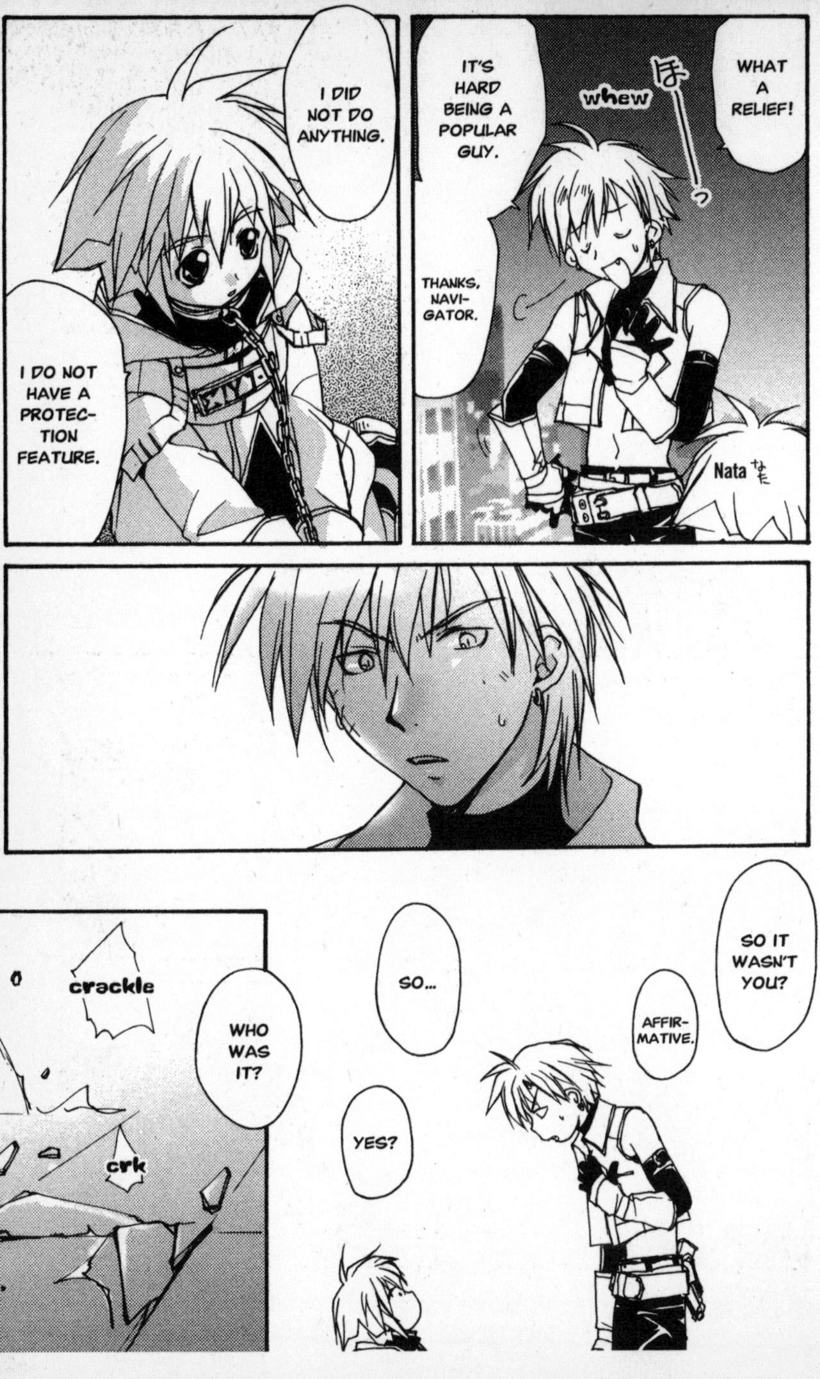
WHAT A RELIEF!
whew
ほ—っ
IT'S HARD BEING A POPULAR GUY.
THANKS, NAVIGATOR.
Nata なた
I DID NOT DO ANYTHING.
I DO NOT HAVE A PROTECTION FEATURE.
SO IT WASN'T YOU?
AFFIRMATIVE.
SO...
YES?
WHO WAS IT?
crackle
crk

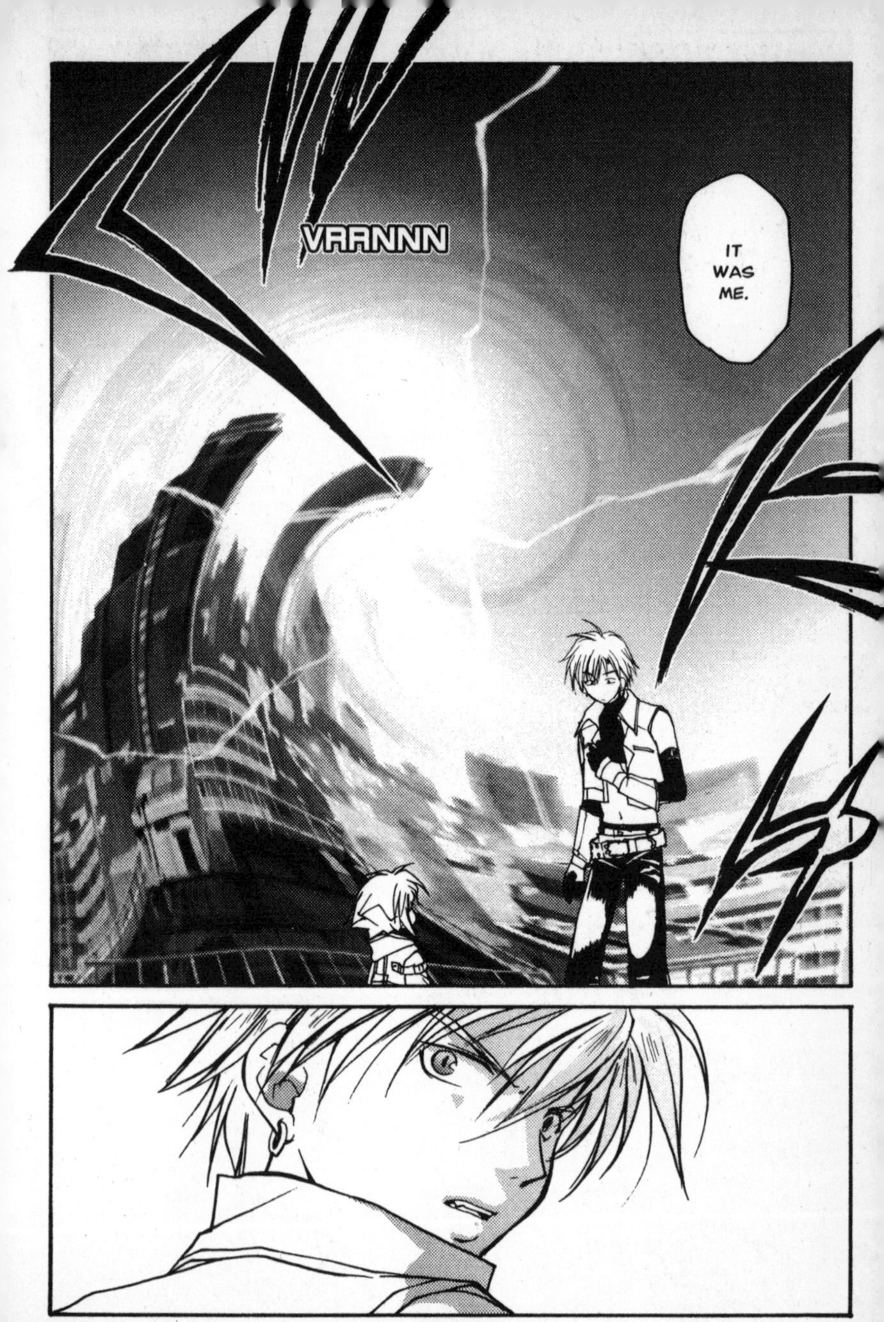
VRRNNN
IT WAS ME.

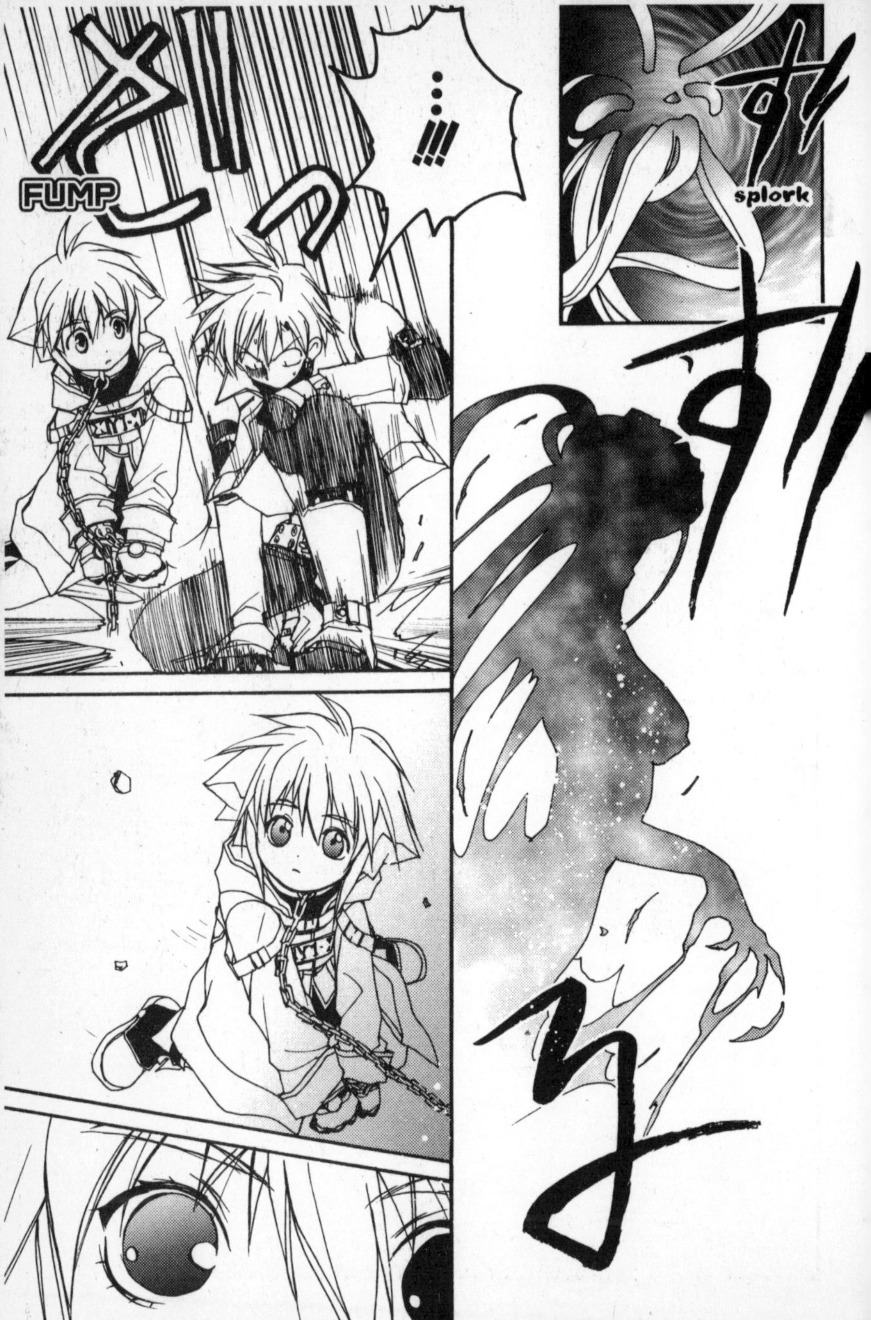
splork
...!!!
FUMP

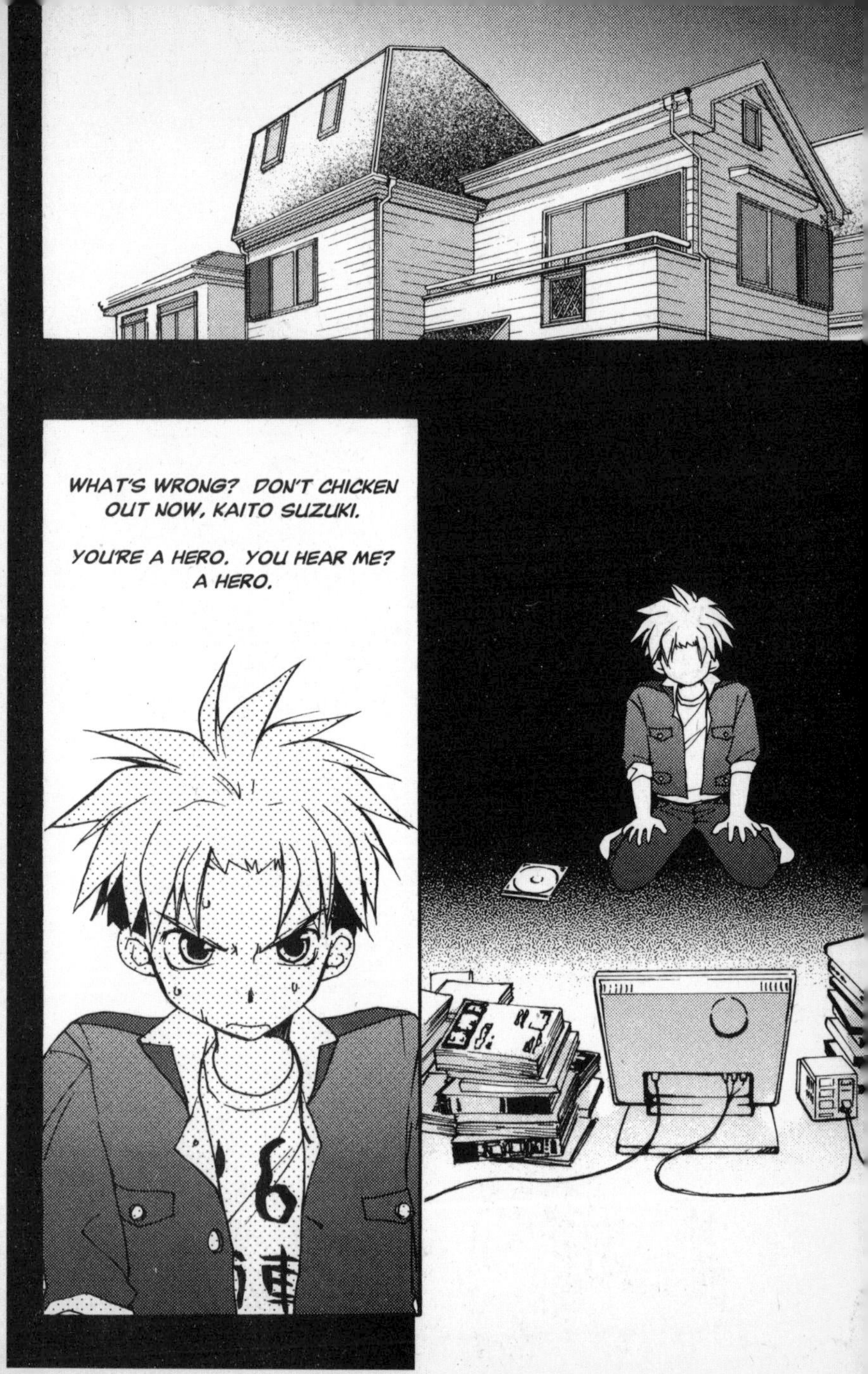
WHAT'S WRONG? DON'T CHICKEN OUT NOW, KAITO SUZUKI.
YOU'RE A HERO. YOU HEAR ME? A HERO.

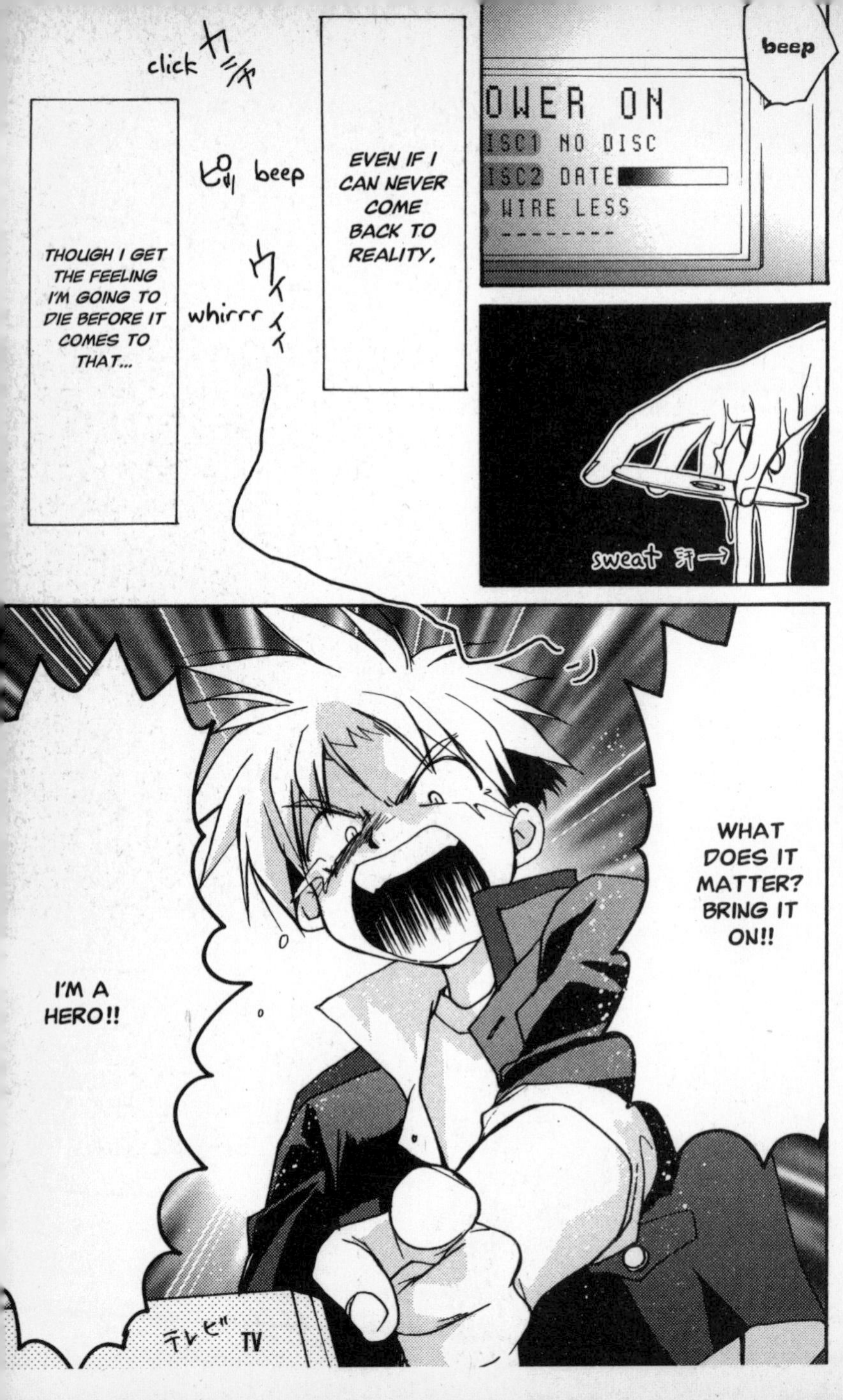
beep
OWER ON
ISC1 NO DISC
ISC2 DATE
WIRE LESS
sweat 汗ー
click カシャ
ピッ beep
ウイイイ whirrr
EVEN IF I CAN NEVER COME BACK TO REALITY,
THOUGH I GET THE FEELING I'M GOING TO DIE BEFORE IT COMES TO THAT...
WHAT DOES IT MATTER? BRING IT ON!!
I'M A HERO!!
テレビ TV

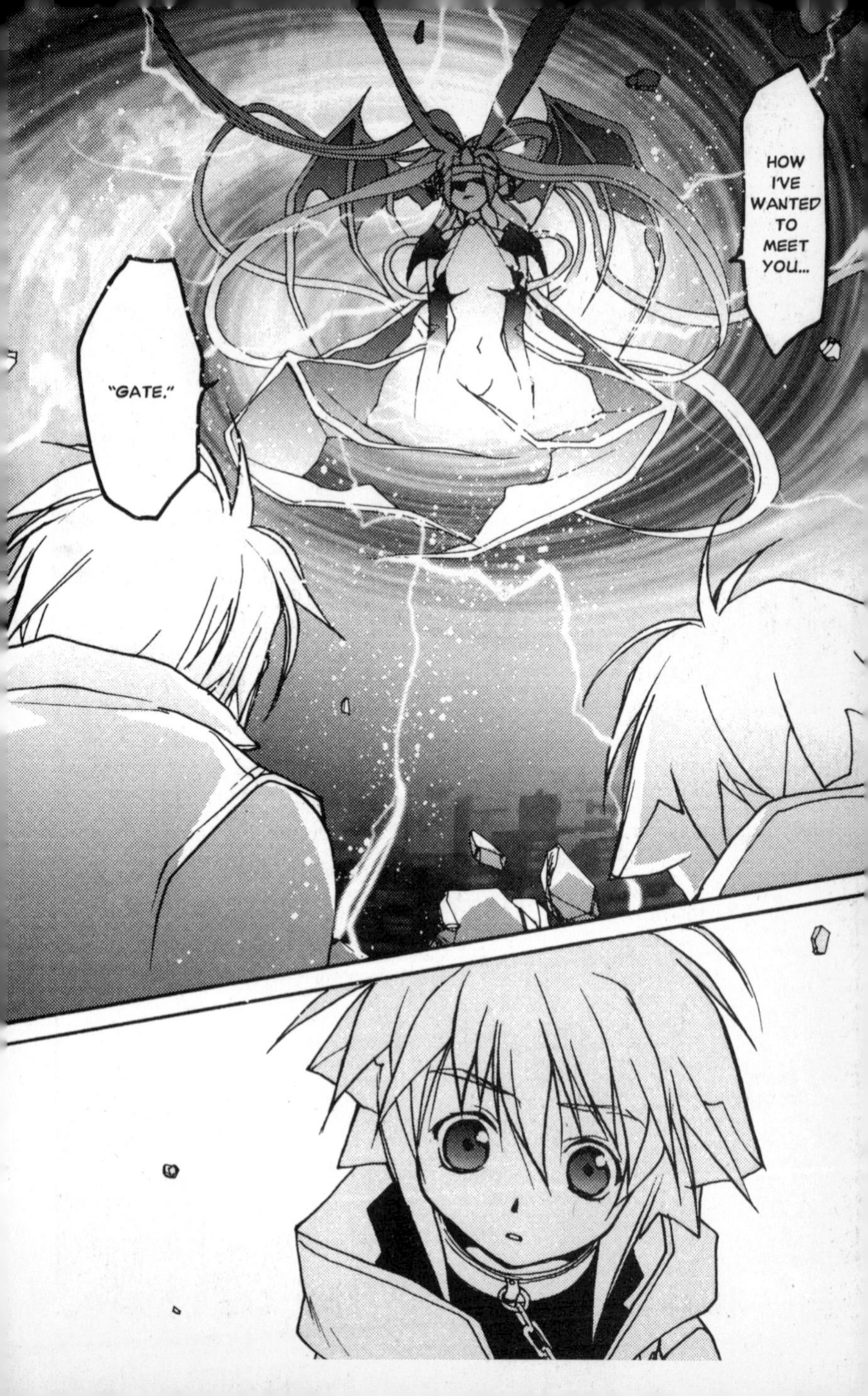
HOW I'VE WANTED TO MEET YOU...
"GATE."

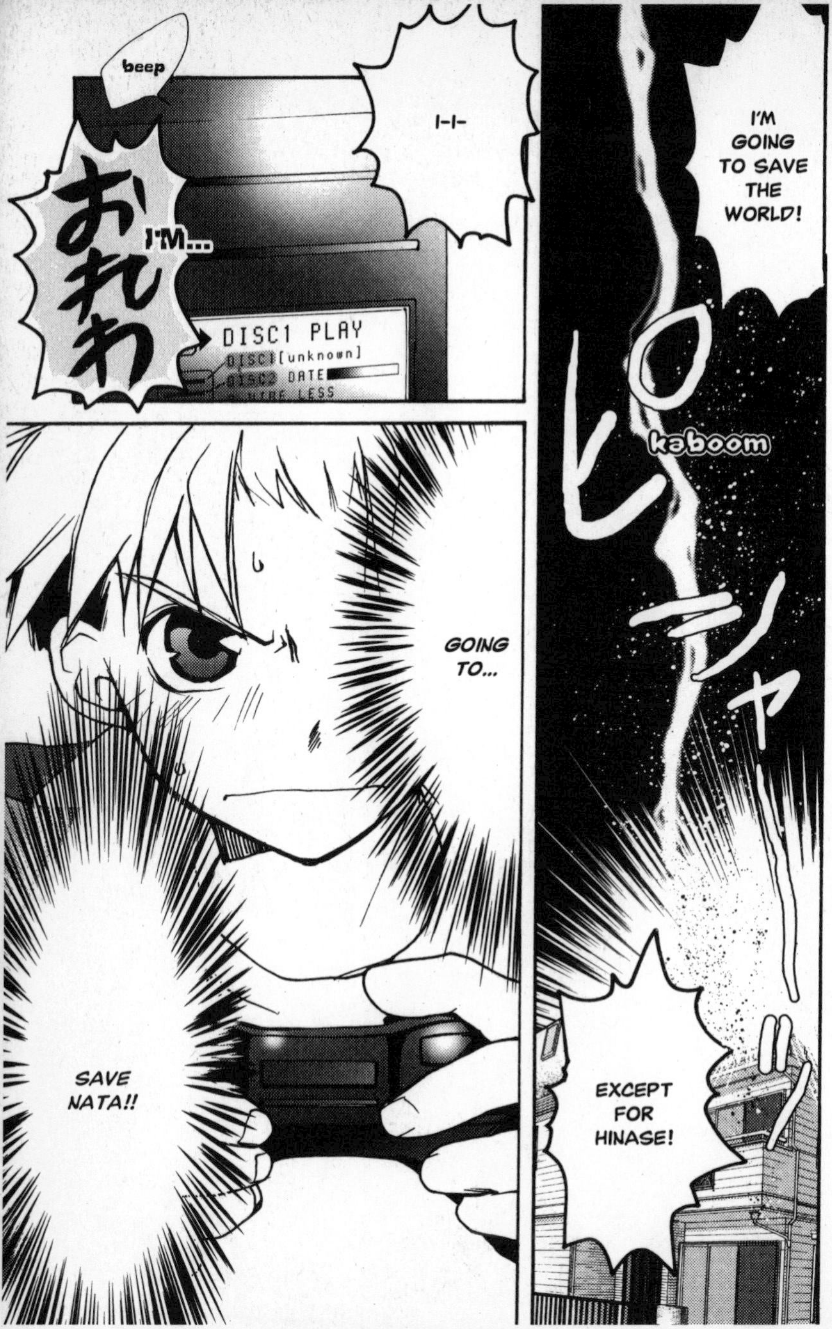
beep
I-I-
おれわ
I'M...
DISC1 PLAY
DISC1 [unknown]
DISC2 DATE
GOING TO...
SAVE NATA!!
I'M GOING TO SAVE THE WORLD!
kaboom
EXCEPT FOR HINASE!

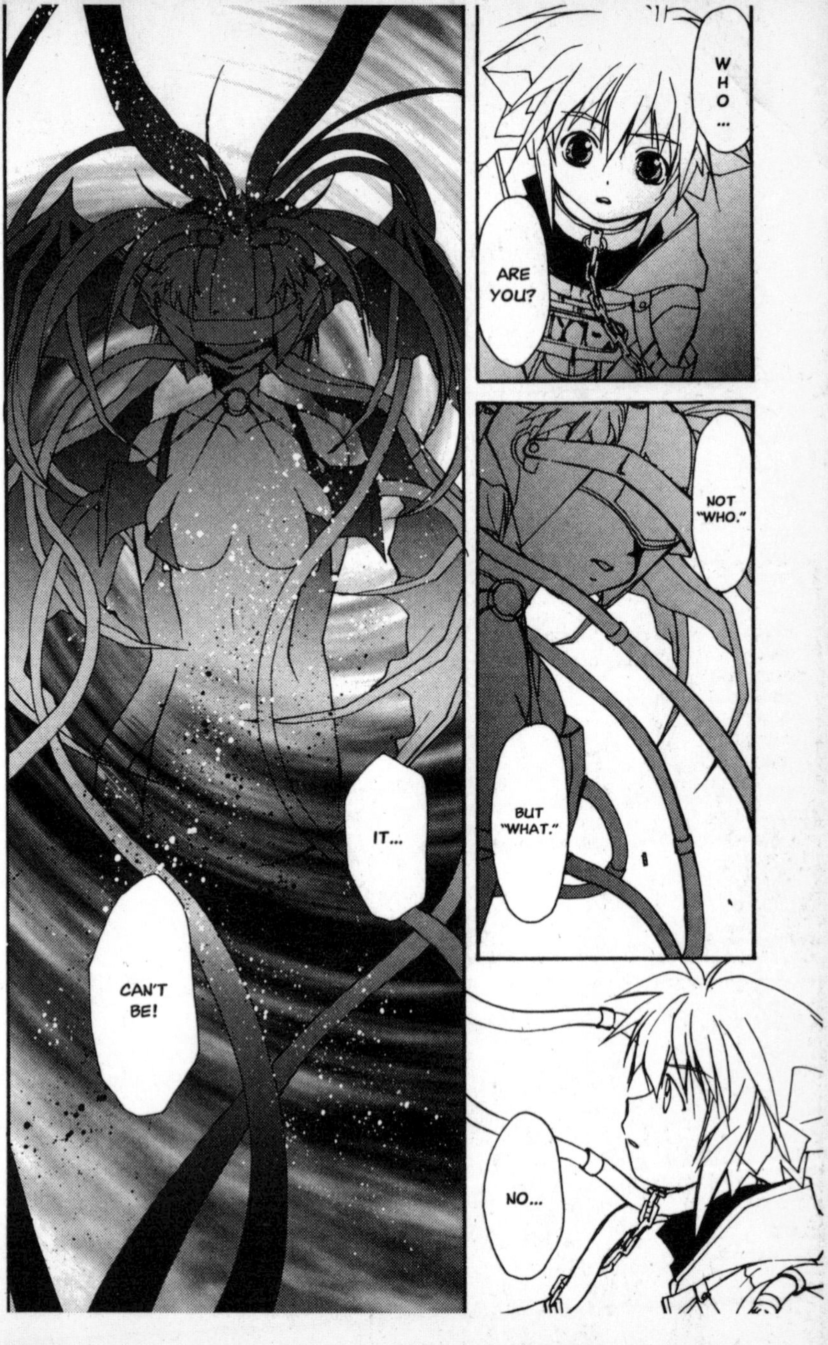
WHO ...
ARE YOU?
NOT "WHO."
BUT "WHAT."
IT...
CAN'T BE!
NO...

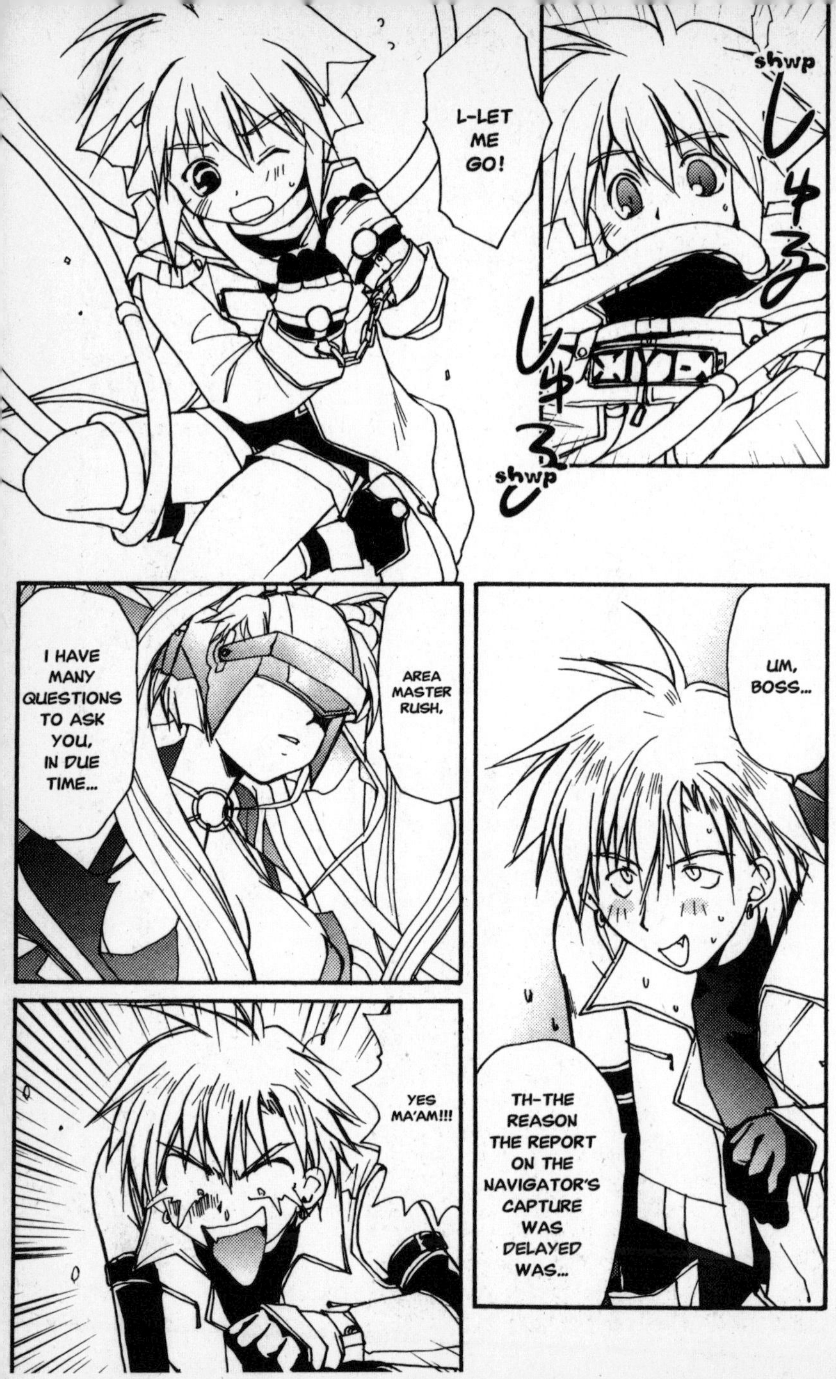
shwp
しゅる
しゅる
shwp
L-LET ME GO!
UM, BOSS...
TH-THE REASON THE REPORT ON THE NAVIGATOR'S CAPTURE WAS DELAYED WAS...
AREA MASTER RUSH,
I HAVE MANY QUESTIONS TO ASK YOU, IN DUE TIME...
YES MA'AM!!!

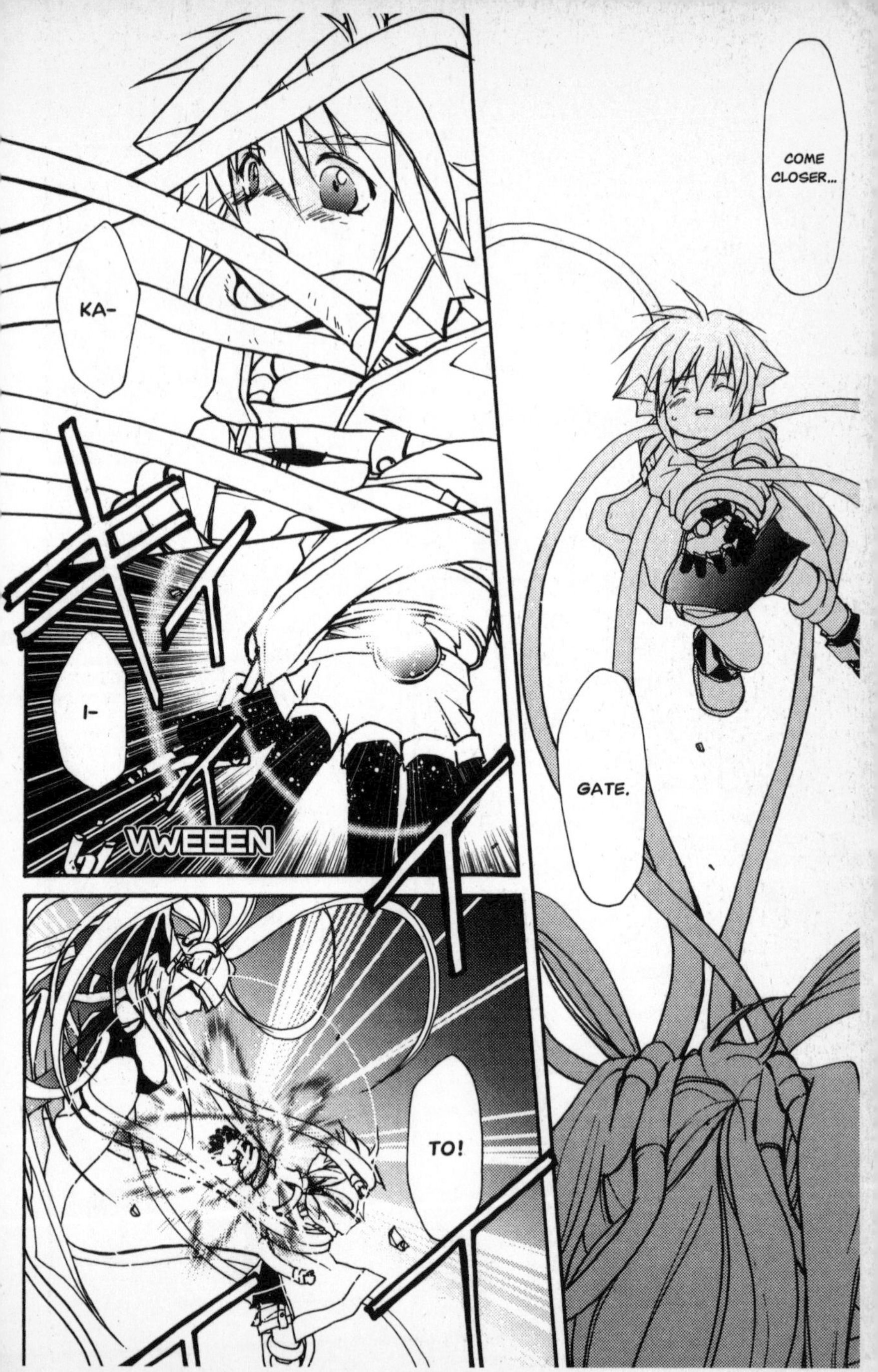
COME CLOSER...
GATE.
KA-
I-
VWEEEN
TO!

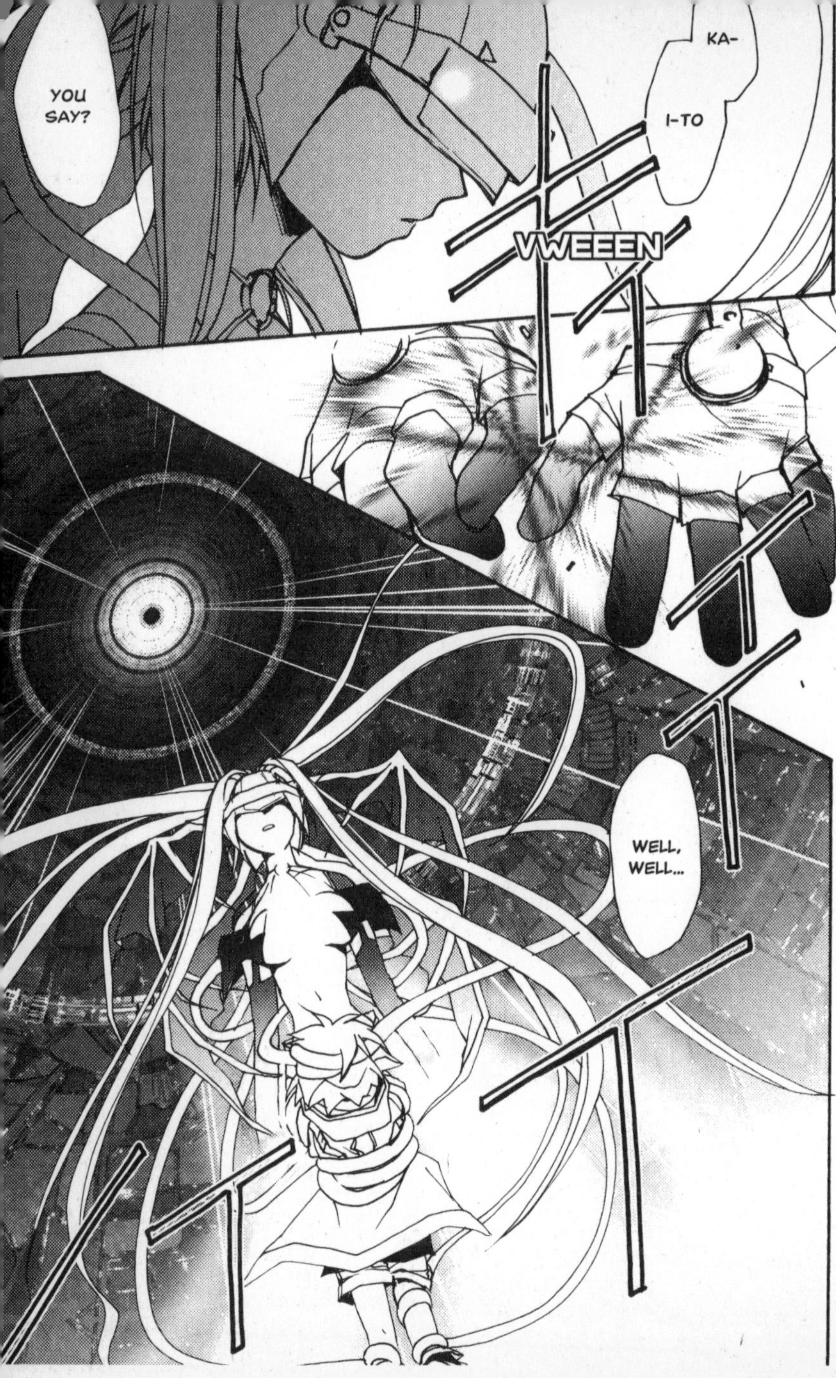
KA-
I-TO
YOU SAY?
VWEEEN
WELL, WELL...

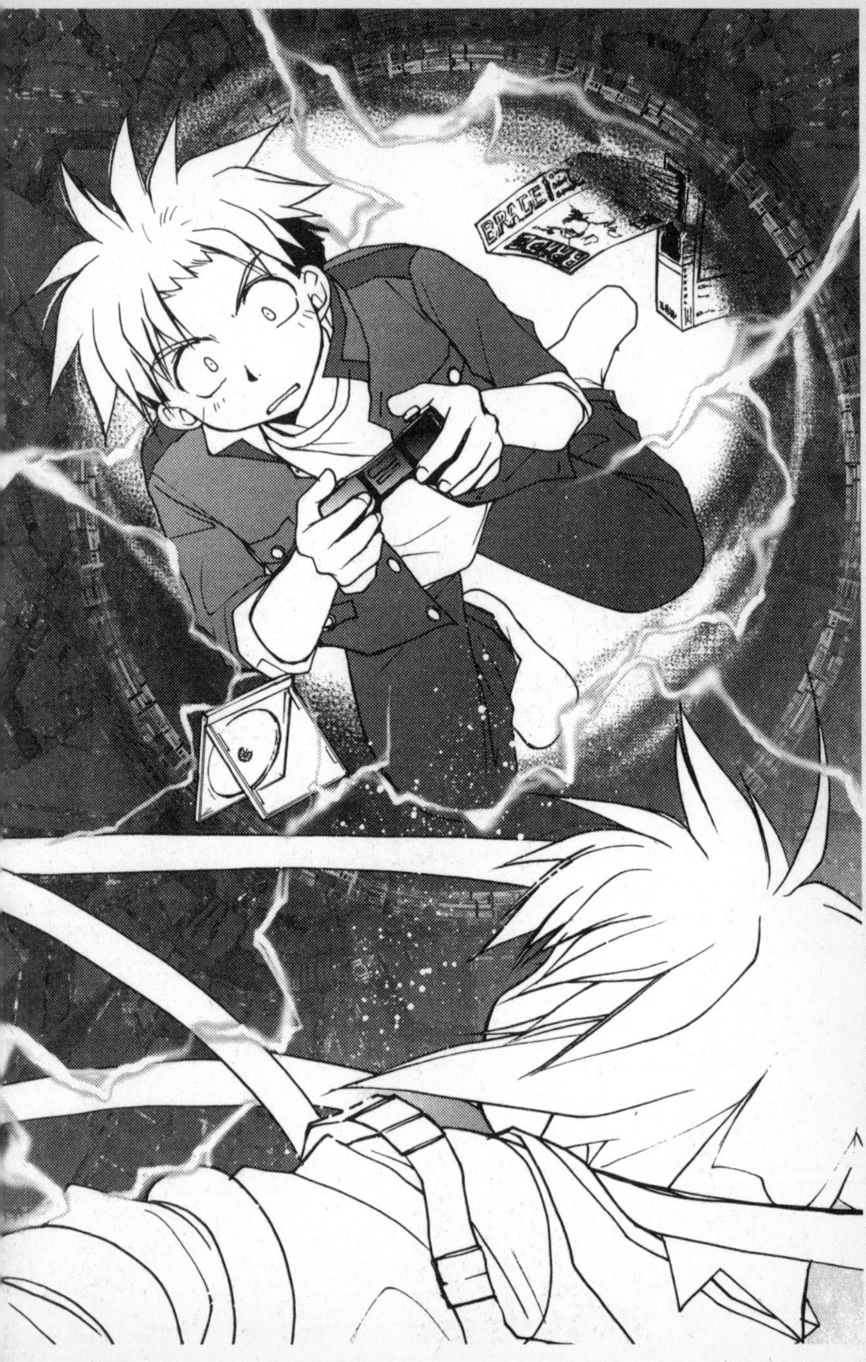

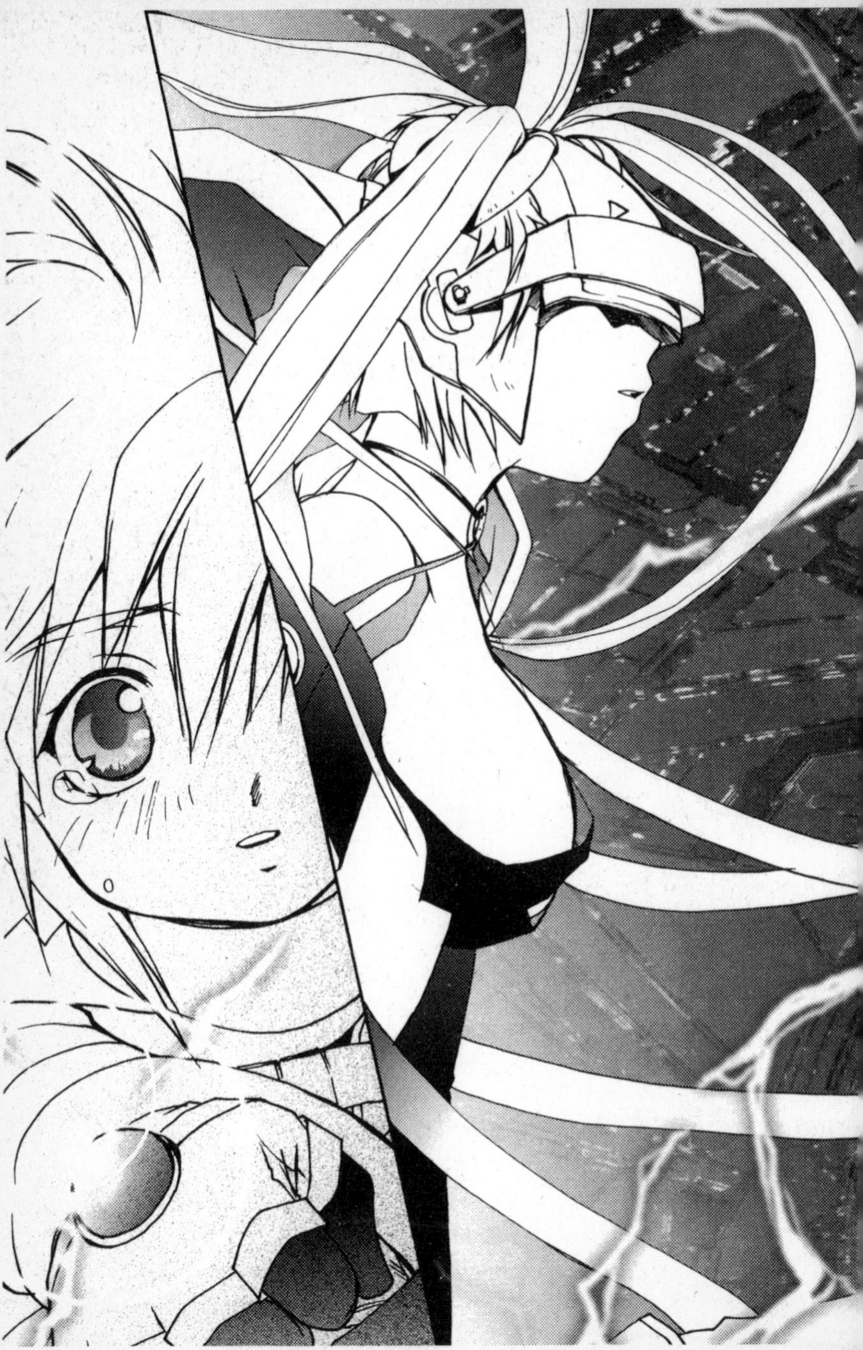

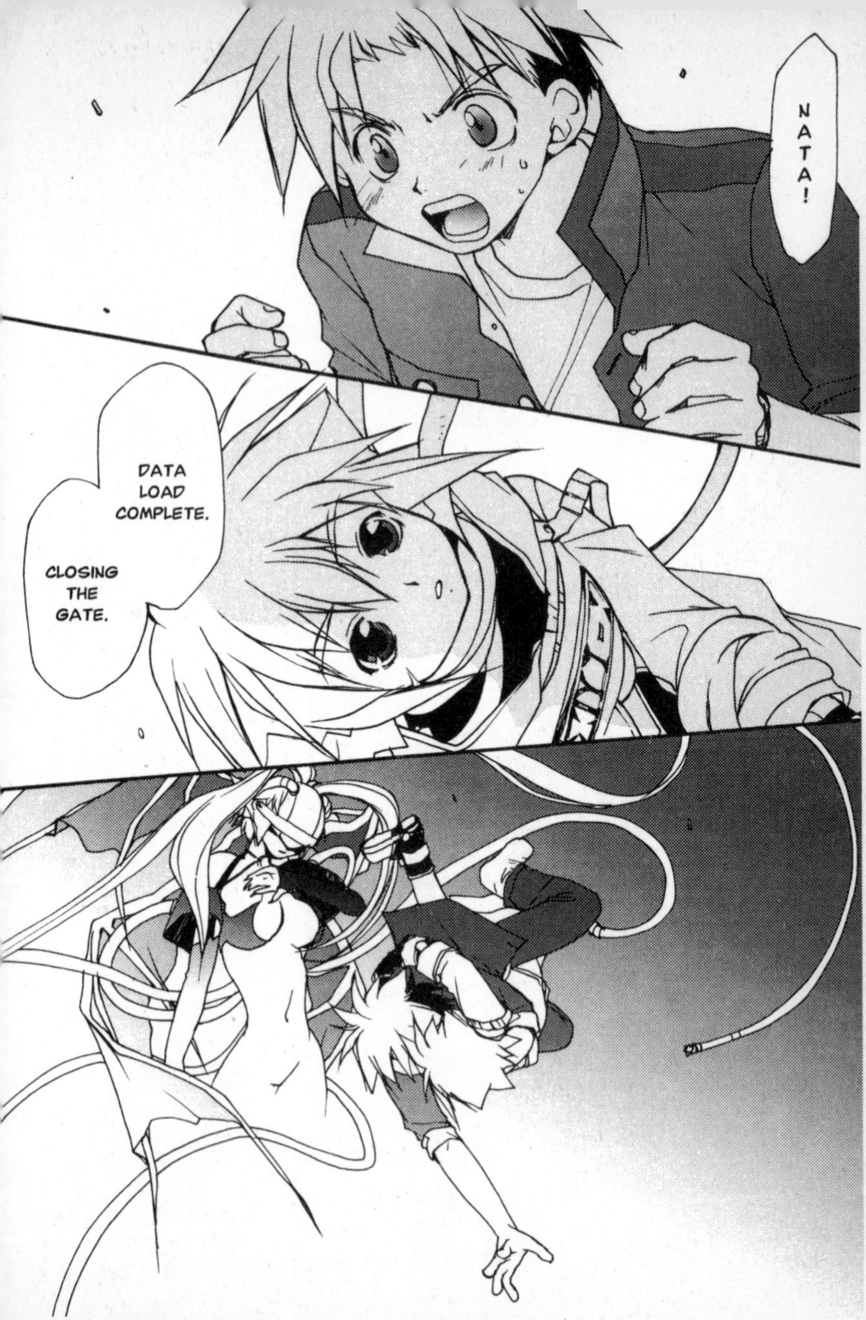
NATA!
DATA LOAD COMPLETE.
CLOSING THE GATE.

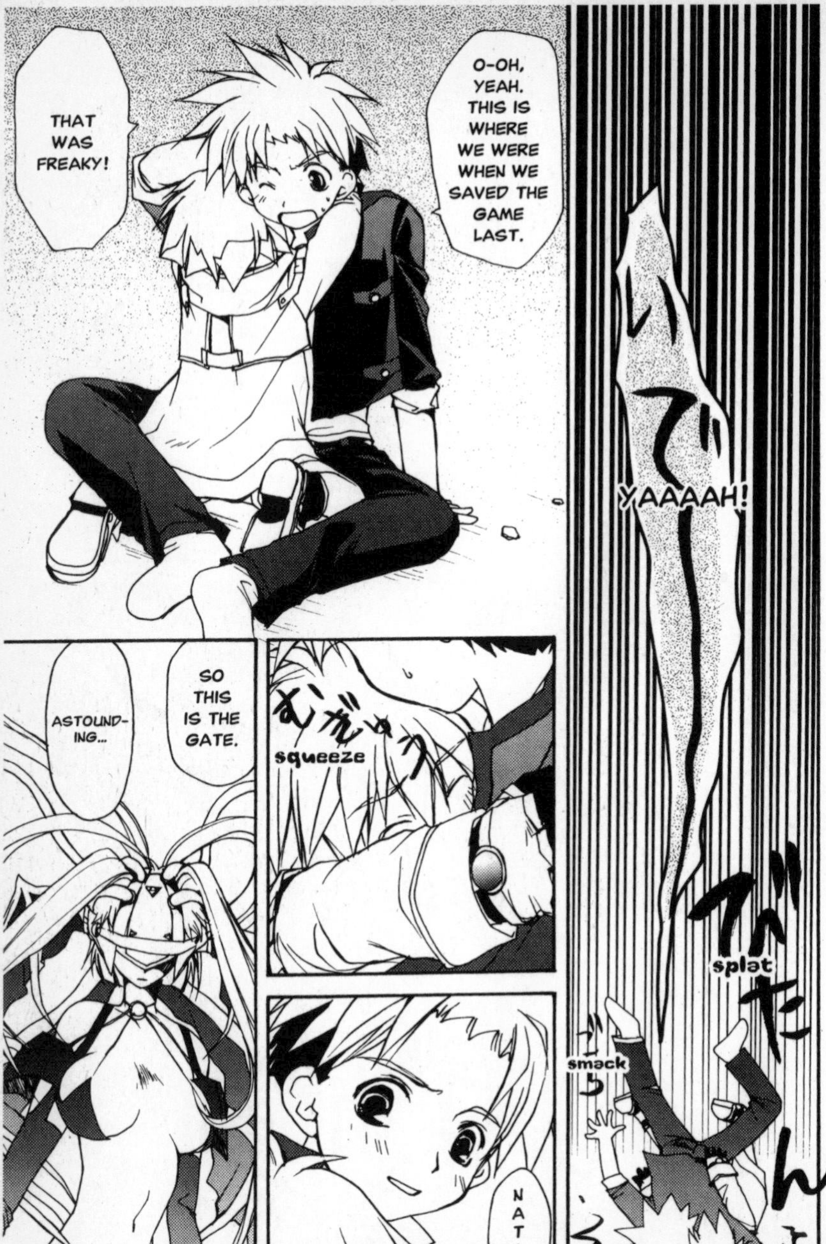
YAAAAH!
splat
smack
O-OH, YEAH. THIS IS WHERE WE WERE WHEN WE SAVED THE GAME LAST.
THAT WAS FREAKY!
squeeze
SO THIS IS THE GATE.
ASTOUNDING...
NATA...

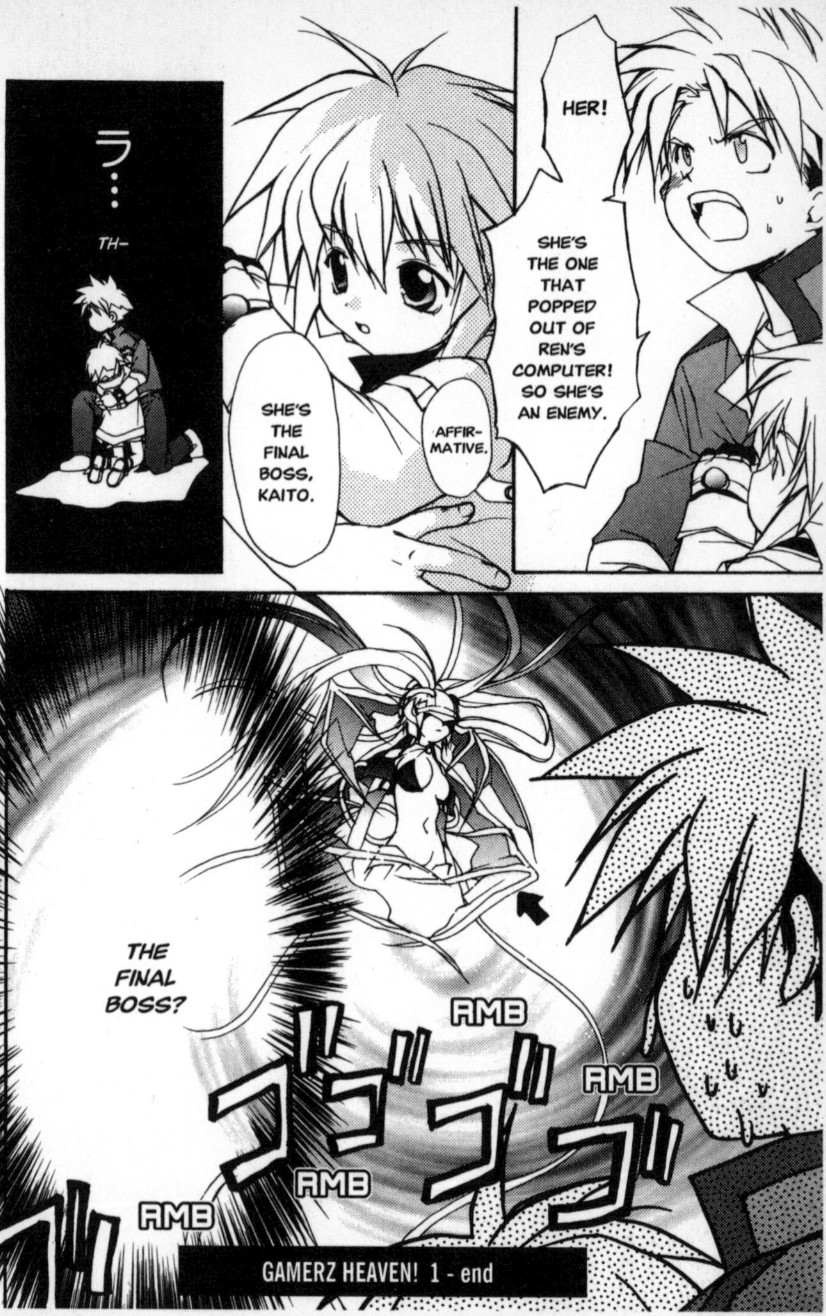
HER!
SHE'S THE ONE THAT POPPED OUT OF REN'S COMPUTER! SO SHE'S AN ENEMY.
AFFIR-MATIVE.
SHE'S THE FINAL BOSS, KAITO.
ラ…
TH-
THE FINAL BOSS?
RMB
RMB
RMB
RMB
GAMERZ HEAVEN! 1 - end

© Maki Murakami 2003
All rights reserved.
First published in 2003 by MAG Garden Corporation.
English translation rights arranged with MAG Garden Corporation.

Translator JOSH COLE
Lead Translator/Translation Supervisor JAVIER LOPEZ
ADV Manga Translation Staff KAY BERTRAND, AMY FORSYTH, BRENDAN FRAYNE,
HARUKA KANEKO-SMITH, EIKO McGREGOR AND MADOKA MOROE

Print Production/Art Studio Manager LISA PUCKETT
Pre-press Manager KLYS REEDYK
Art Production Manager RYAN MASON
Sr. Designer/Creative Manager JORGE ALVARADO
Graphic Designer/Group Leader SCOTT SAVAGE
Graphic Designer LISA RAPER
Graphic Artists CHY LING, NATALIA MORALES, CHRIS LAPP AND NANAKO TSUKIHASHI
Graphic Intern MARK MEZA

International Coordinator TORU IWAKAMI
International Coordinator ATSUSHI KANBAYASHI

Publishing Editor SUSAN ITIN
Assistant Editor MARGARET SCHAROLD
Editorial Assistant VARSHA BHUCHAR
Proofreaders SHERIDAN JACOBS AND STEVEN REED
Research/Traffic Coordinator MARSHA ARNOLD

Executive VP, CFO, COO KEVIN CORCORAN

President, CEO & Publisher JOHN LEDFORD

Email: editor@adv-manga.com
www.adv-manga.com
www.advfilms.com

For sales and distribution inquiries please call 1.800.282.7202

ADV MANGA™ is a division of A.D. Vision, Inc.
10114 W. Sam Houston Parkway, Suite 200, Houston, Texas 77099

English text © 2004 published by A.D. Vision, Inc. under exclusive license.
ADV MANGA is a trademark of A.D. Vision, Inc.

ISBN: 1-4139-0202-2
First printing, November 2004
10 9 8 7 6 5 4 3 2 1
Printed in Canada

TRANSLATOR'S NOTES

Gamerz Heaven Vol. 01

PG. 66

Mild Sevens
Mild Sevens are a popular brand of cigarettes in Japan. For the years 2002-2003, the three top-selling cigarette brands were all in the Mild Seven line, accounting for almost a quarter of the cigarettes sold in Japan.

Data from:
http://www.jti.co.jp/JTI/tobacco/data/data4.html

PG. 72

Ooka Echizen
Ooka Echizen is a long-running *jidai-geki* (historical drama) on Japanese TV. Set in the Tokugawa period (1603-1867), Echizen is a judge for the shogunate. He sports a cherry blossom tattoo. Normally, the only Japanese at this time who would have tattoos were the Yakuza (Japanese mafia) and other criminal types. Echizen uses this to his advantage, going undercover and showing his tattoo to sneak into criminal hideouts and gather evidence. In court, the criminals would protest their innocence, but in a typically melodramatic scene, Echizen would reveal his tattoo, and the bad guys would confess to their crimes.

PG. 92

16 Bursts/Sec
Written on Suzuki's shirt, this refers to the number of times you can continuously press a button on a game controller. In Japan, there is a man, Toshiyuki Takahashi, who is said to be able to press a button 16 times per second.

There is a website hosted by Hudson Soft, where you can test your button pressing skills against "Master" Takahashi.

http://www.hudson.co.jp/hde/vol006/omake/tr16/

PG. 94

16 Bursts/Sec EX
The logo on Suzuki's shirt changed.

PG. 96

High Score
The logo on Suzuki's shirt changed again.

PG. 97

yaoi
Yaoi are male-on-male homoerotic comics for women.

PG. 102

1 Player Game
The logo on Suzuki's shirt changed again.

PG. 111

20 Bursts/Sec
The logo on Suzuki's shirt changed again.

PG. 119

Patrache
The logo on Suzuki's shirt changed again.

PG. 141

Dog
The logo on Suzuki's shirt changed again.

Patrache is the name of the dog in "A Dog of Flanders," originally a book by the Flemish author Oui'da which was popularized by an animated series in Japan.

PG. 144

mochi gome
Mochi gome is glutinous rice used to make *o-mochi* (rice cakes).

PG. 144

100 Bursts/Sec
The logo on Suzuki's shirt changed again. Twice in one page!

PG. 153

Dog
The logo on Suzuki's shirt changed again.

PG. 156

Meat
The logo on Suzuki's shirt changed again.

GAMERZ HEAVEN

VIDEO GAME MAYHEM HAS NEVER GONE THIS FAR!
KAITO NOW MUST COMPETE TO SAVE HIS VIRTUAL
FRIEND NATA FROM THE CLUTCHES OF AREA MASTER
RUSH AND THE FINAL BOSS. THROWING CAUTION TO
THE WIND, KAITO FINDS HIMSELF IN THE HEAT OF
THE BATTLE, BUT DOES HE HAVE THE MOVES TO
SAVE THE GAME? MEANWHILE, NATA SUFFERS
UNCERTAINTY IN HIS STRANGE WORLD AS THE
DANGERS BECOME EVEN MORE REAL FOR HIS REAL
WORLD SAVIORS. AND LATER, WHEN KAITO
RECOGNIZES THE AREA BOSS, WILL HE BE ABLE
TO SAVE THE GAME AND MOVE ON TO THE
NEXT LEVEL? THE LIVES ARE RUNNING OUT
IN THE NEXT EXCITING ROUND OF

GAMERZ HEAVEN, VOLUME 2!

COMING 2005!

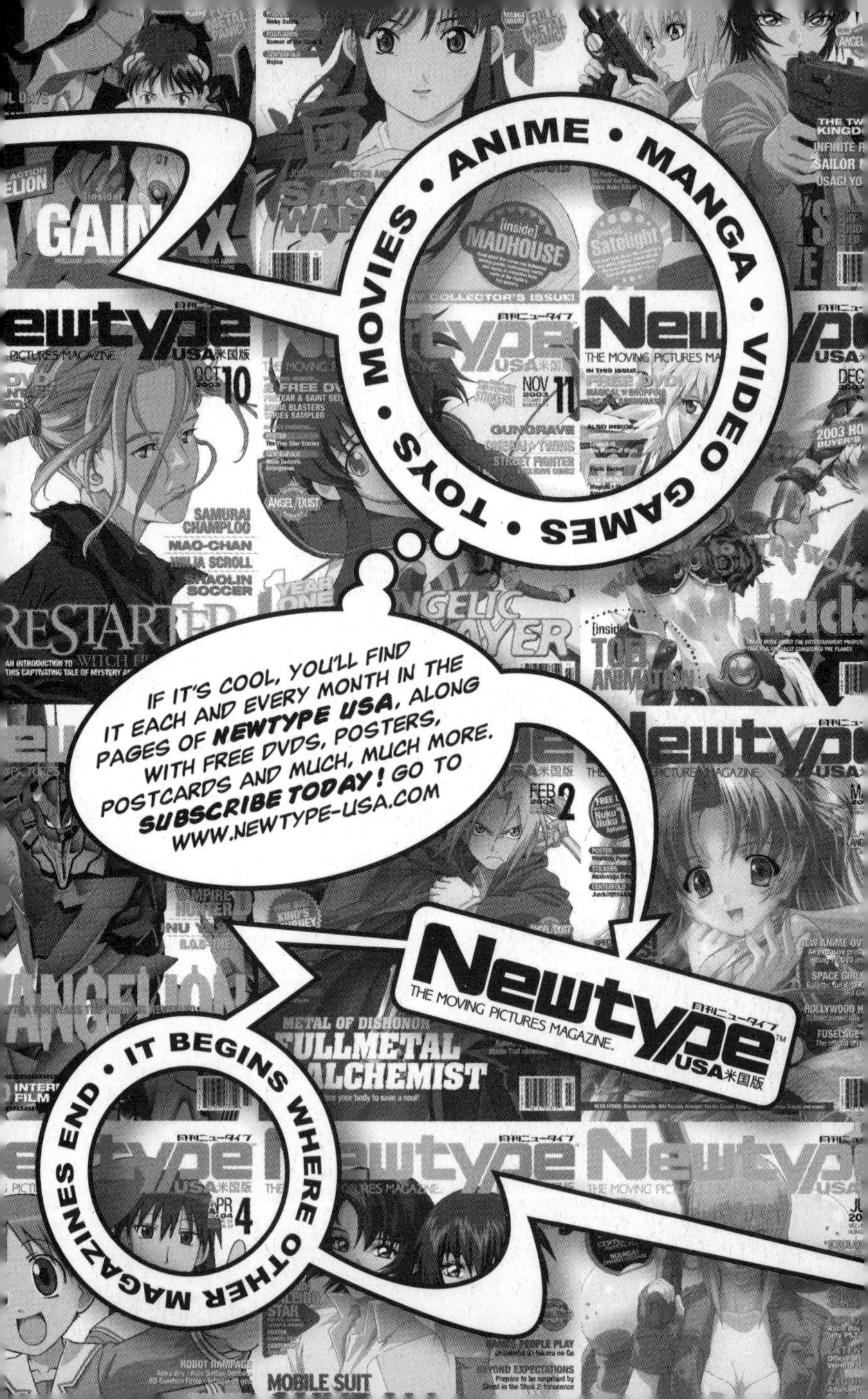

ANIME • MANGA • VIDEO GAMES • TOYS • MOVIES •
IF IT'S COOL, YOU'LL FIND IT EACH AND EVERY MONTH IN THE PAGES OF NEWTYPE USA, ALONG WITH FREE DVDS, POSTERS, POSTCARDS AND MUCH, MUCH MORE. SUBSCRIBE TODAY! GO TO WWW.NEWTYPE-USA.COM
Newtype
THE MOVING PICTURES MAGAZINE.
月刊ニュータイプ
USA 米国版
IT BEGINS WHERE OTHER MAGAZINES END •

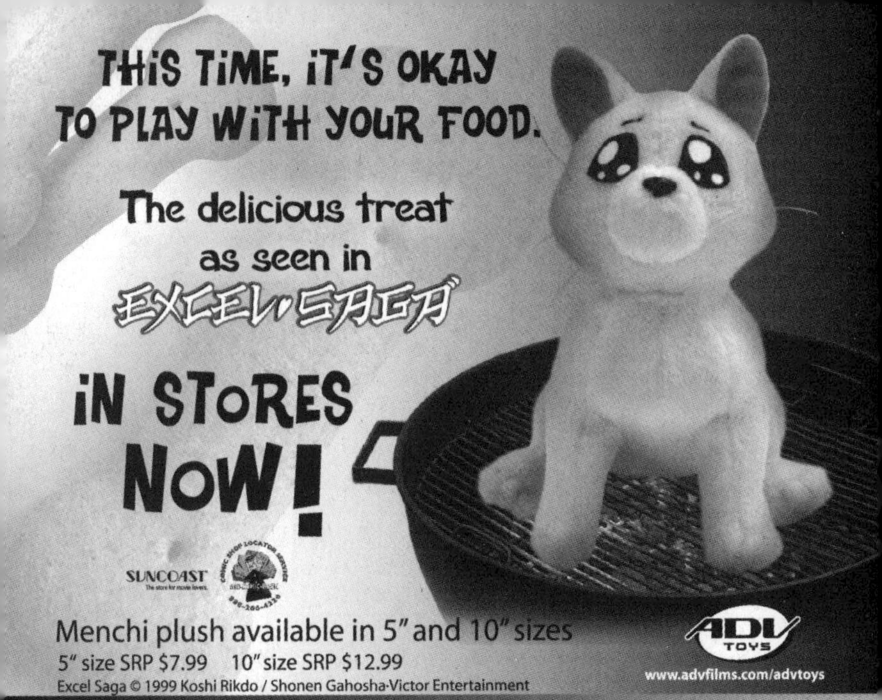
THIS TIME, IT'S OKAY
TO PLAY WITH YOUR FOOD.
The delicious treat
as seen in
EXCEL SAGA
IN STORES
NOW!
SUNCOAST
Menchi plush available in 5″ and 10″ sizes
5″ size SRP $7.99 10″ size SRP $12.99
Excel Saga © 1999 Koshi Rikdo / Shonen Gahosha-Victor Entertainment
ADV TOYS
www.advfilms.com/advtoys

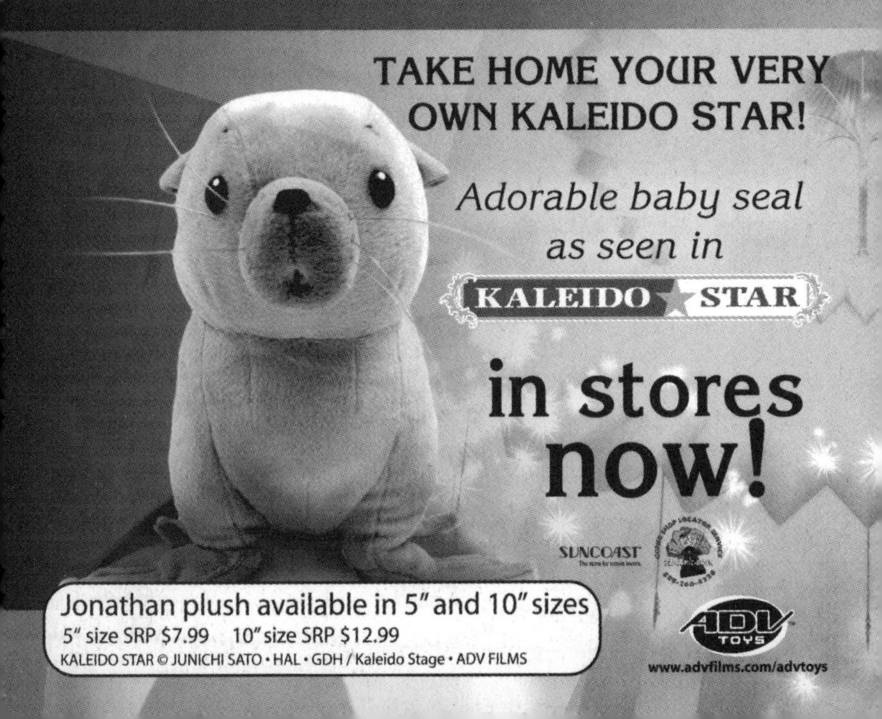
TAKE HOME YOUR VERY
OWN KALEIDO STAR!
Adorable baby seal
as seen in
KALEIDO STAR
in stores
now!
SUNCOAST
Jonathan plush available in 5″ and 10″ sizes
5″ size SRP $7.99 10″ size SRP $12.99
KALEIDO STAR © JUNICHI SATO • HAL • GDH / Kaleido Stage • ADV FILMS
ADV TOYS
www.advfilms.com/advtoys

PEACEMAKER KUROGANE VOL. 1

the end of an era, as the last samurai battle to protect kyoto...

Japan is in the midst of a revolution as old ways crumble and new ways triumph. The Shinsengumi is an elite group of swordsmen formed to protect the city of Kyoto. One of the newest members is a young boy named Tetsunosuke Ichimura, who is serving as a page to the Vice-Commander, Hijikata. A six-gun wielding swordsman with the moniker Ryoma Sakamoto tries to contact Tetsunosuke and his brother, because he recognizes them as the sons of someone he refers to only as the "Peacemaker." But, who was the Peacemaker?

WRITTEN AND ILLUSTRATED BY NANAE CHRONO

available october 2004

...AND DON'T MISS PEACEMAKER— THE NEW HIT ANIME FROM ADV FILMS.

www.adv-manga.com